A Thousand Thirsty Beaches

A

Smuggling Alcohol

THOUSAND

from Cuba to the South

THIRSTY

during Prohibition

BEACHES

{ LISA LINDQUIST DORR }

THE UNIVERSITY OF NORTH CAROLINA PRESS

CHAPEL HILL

This book was published with the assistance of
the Fred W. Morrison Fund of the University of
North Carolina Press.

Designed by April Leidig
Set in Minion by Copperline Book Services, Inc.

The University of North Carolina Press has been a
member of the Green Press Initiative since 2003.

Portions of Chapter 4 appeared previously in Lisa Lindquist Dorr, "Bootlegging Aliens:
Unsanctioned Immigration and the Underground Economy of Smuggling from Cuba
during Prohibition," *Florida Historical Quarterly* 93, no. 1 (Summer 2014): 44–73. Reprinted
with permission.

Portions of Chapters 5 and 6 appeared previously in Lisa Lindquist Dorr, "A Place for
Themselves in the Modern World: Southern Women and Alcohol in the Age of Prohibition,
1912–1933," in *Signposts: New Directions in Southern Legal History*, ed. Sally E. Hadden and
Patricia Hagler Minter (Athens: University of Georgia Press, 2013), 319, 320, 323–26, 327,
332–33, 335. © 2013 by the University of Georgia Press. Reprinted with permission.

Portions of Chapter 6 appeared previously in Lisa Lindquist Dorr, "Fifty Percent Moonshine
and Fifty Percent Moonshine: Social Life and College Youth Culture in Alabama, 1913–1933,"
in *Manners and Southern History*, ed. Ted Ownby (Jackson: University Press of Mississippi,
2007), 58–62. Reprinted with permission.

Cover illustrations: Map of Mexico, Cuba, Central America, and West Indies (courtesy
of the David Rumsey Map Collection, www.davidrumsey.com); tourists at photo booth
(courtesy of the State Archives of Florida); motorboat *My Fagela* (National Archives and
Records Administration); truck with seized liquor (McCall Rare Book and Manuscript
Library, University of South Alabama)

Library of Congress Cataloging-in-Publication Data
Names: Dorr, Lisa Lindquist, author.
Title: A thousand thirsty beaches : smuggling alcohol from Cuba to the South during
    Prohibition / by Lisa Lindquist Dorr.
Description: Chapel Hill : University of North Carolina Press, [2018] | Includes
    bibliographical references and index.
Identifiers: LCCN 2018005191 | ISBN 9781469643274 (cloth : alk. paper) | ISBN 9781469663968
    (pbk. : alk. paper) | ISBN 9781469643281 (ebook)
Subjects: LCSH: Prohibition—Southern States—History—20th century. | Smuggling—
    Gulf Coast (U.S.)—History—20th century. | Smuggling—Cuba—History—20th century. |
    United States—Foreign relations—Cuba. | Cuba—Foreign relations—United States. |
    United States. Coast Guard—History—20th century.
Classification: LCC HV5089 .D645 2018 | DDC 364.1/3361097509042—dc23
    LC record available at https://lccn.loc.gov/2018005191

Contents

Illustrations

Acknowledgments

MENTION TO ALMOST ANY SOUTHERNER that you are writing a book on Prohibition, and you are likely to hear a story about where their great-granddaddy hid his hooch. Ask southern students to find out how their family survived the Great Depression, and many will come back amazed to learn that a family member was the local bootlegger. As those anecdotes suggest, stories of alcohol and drinking often lurk below the surface of the southern past, politely allowing steadfast temperance to enjoy the limelight. Such subterfuge, however, may not be unique to the South. Raised by hardworking midwestern and immigrant stock, I never saw alcohol at family events and can even remember fancy parties with upward of fifty guests where the only beverage was coffee. Only after I began research for this book did I learn that my upright grandmother's ne'er-do-well uncle met his wife at a blind tiger in Detroit that she operated with her mother in the 1920s. Little matter that he already had a wife and child in the old country. It may be the norm rather than the exception to bury memories of an intemperate, disreputable past.

This book, which explores the hidden rivers of booze that supplied Americans with drink, began simply enough as a study of Prohibition in the South. Its trajectory, however, shifted in 2006 when I traveled to Havana, Cuba, as part of the University of Alabama's Cuba Initiative, which promoted academic exchange and collaboration between faculty at the University of Alabama and the Universidad de la Habana. While at a reception one evening, I entered a conversation with the elderly and esteemed historian of the Universidad de la Habana, Dr. Alberto Prieto. I spoke no Spanish and he spoke little English, but despite our language barrier, I described my new research project on Prohibition in the South. As I recall, he proceeded to take the cocktail napkin out of my hand and draw me a map of the northern coast of Cuba. With a few arrows pointing to the southern coast of the United States, he introduced me to what would be my project for the next many years: much of the liquor that entered the United States during Prohibition was smuggled through Cuba. While subsequent trips to Cuba were more useful for academic exchange than for research, archives in the United States contained boxes and boxes of documents that provided the bones of this book.

No book, however, is the sum total of documents and stories. Books are collaborative efforts even if they have only a single author, and my debts are significant. Archivists at the National Archives and Records Administration in Washington, D.C.; College Park, Maryland; Morrow, Georgia; and Fort Worth, Texas, were unfailingly helpful, as were those at the State Archives of Florida and the Alabama Department of Archives and History. I received a Littleton Griswold grant from the American Historical Association and a Global South fellowship from Tulane University, which allowed me to make my initial visits to archives. A three-year research stipend as a College of Arts and Sciences Leadership Board Faculty Fellow helped me finish most of my research. As I told the Leadership Board, historians, unlike faculty in the hard sciences, are cheap — or at least those that conduct their research in the southern United States are. Their support was invaluable. My ability to turn that research into a manuscript owes thanks to Dr. Robert F. Olin, Dean of the College of Arts and Sciences at the University of Alabama. As I was about to begin the writing process, I was encouraged to accept a position as an associate dean. Dean Olin's insistence that I should carve out time from my workday to write made progress on the book possible. It also, incidentally, made me much more efficient in how I allocated my time. For many reasons beyond just those, I am forever grateful for his support.

I also owe heavy thanks to colleagues and friends who offered me their help. Merrily Harris, who has deciphered aspects of the Deep South for me since we met, opened her home when I was conducting research in Washington, D.C. She deserves much more than thanks for lodging. Kari Frederickson, my dear friend since I moved to Tuscaloosa, offered encouragement as well as a steady stream of useful advice on everything from breakfast eateries to structuring my introduction. In many ways, I owe her so much. Anthony Stanonis offered to read the entire manuscript just as I began to despair that I would ever finish the project. His packages from Belfast helped solidify the story I wanted to tell. Ted Ownby, who nurtured my first publication on drinking and the South as part of the Porter Fortune Symposium, gave me advice at the very end of the writing process that removed considerable chaff from the wheat of the manuscript. I also benefited from numerous conference co-panelists, commentators, and audience members who humorously confirmed not only the entertainment value but also the historical significance of rum-running and drinking in the South. Their comments, suggestions, and asides helped polish the scholarship that has emerged from this research project. Portions of this book were previously published by the University Press of Mississippi, the University of Georgia Press, and the *Florida Historical Quarterly*. I appreciate their permission to reprint them here.

My acknowledgments would not be complete without noting the indescribably large debt of gratitude I owe my parents, who told me stories of their families and their childhoods for as long as I can remember. Even though they are a nurse and an engineer by training, I fervently believe my love for the past came from them. They have always encouraged me in this profession, letting me know that they think being a professor — or an associate dean — is about the coolest job anyone could have. Most days, I agree. And finally, this is for Fiona and Sophie, who have been hearing for years that I want to finish my book. They have always confirmed for me the truth of my father's long-ago statement that raising kids was the most fun he ever had.

A Thousand Thirsty Beaches

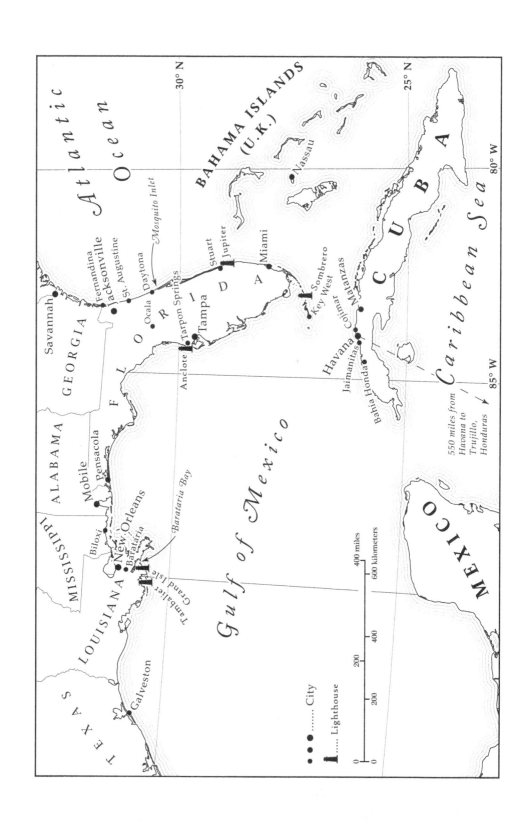

Introduction

B
Y THE TIME HE WROTE to the attorney general in Washington, D.C., Aubrey Boyles, the U.S. Attorney for the district court in Mobile, Alabama, was clearly frustrated. On the front lines of the Rum War in the South since 1920, he well knew the persistence and ingenuity of smugglers trying to import liquor illegally into the United States. In early 1926, the *Jose Luis* had been spotted by the Coast Guard cutter *Tallapoosa* anchored fifteen miles from shore in Barataria Bay off the Louisiana coast. When the *Tallapoosa* approached, the schooner's captain claimed that the *Jose Luis* was in distress, having lost two masts and its rudder in foul weather off the coast of Cuba, but he insisted the boat needed no assistance. The captain of the *Tallapoosa*, however, was suspicious. The *Jose Luis*'s cargo manifest indicated that the boat had cleared from the port of Havana for Trujillo, Honduras, with over 3,000 cases of assorted liquors on board. Only 700 cases of liquor remained in the hold, however, and several smaller boats had been captured nearby with liquor matching the *Jose Luis*'s cargo. More importantly, weather reports indicated that there was simply no way, with the prevailing winds, that the *Jose Luis* could have drifted to where the Coast Guard found it. All evidence indicated that the *Jose Luis* was a rum runner. The captain ordered the seizure of the *Jose Luis* and its crew and towed them to Mobile, Alabama. Summing up the case, Boyles shared his worry with his superiors that the *Jose Luis* represented a new tactic by rum runners. He feared smugglers might anchor disabled vessels off the American coast to sell their illegal cargo to boats traveling out from shore. A vessel in distress would be able to avoid the navigation laws that mandated ships travel directly to their stated destinations.

Opposite. Map of Cuba and the Southern Coast of the United States
(Amy Catherine Anderson and Alex Fries, University
of Alabama Cartographic Research Lab)

Calling the tactic "the newest and I think the shrewdest ruse the rum runners have yet used in their illicit trade," he pleaded for the United States to enact rum treaties with Caribbean nations to engage their help in enforcing Prohibition. Without those treaties, Boyles lamented, Coast Guard efforts were likely to end as did the case involving the *Jose Luis*. The charges against the *Jose Luis*'s crew were dismissed in court, their vessel was returned to them with its remaining cargo, and they were free to continue their illegal trade.[1] Little wonder Boyles was frustrated.

By 1926, when Boyles penned his letter, liquor smuggled into the United States along its 18,000 miles of border and coastline had become one of the three primary sources of illegal alcohol across the nation, the others being diverted industrial liquor and moonshine. Despite Boyles's fears, using disabled ships as floating liquor emporiums did not become a favored strategy among rum runners, though the United States would indeed enact a treaty with Cuba within a year. His letter, however, conveyed the challenges towns like Mobile, located along the southern coast, faced during Prohibition. While moonshiners in Appalachia and elsewhere provided their illicitly distilled spirits and bootleggers transformed denatured industrial alcohol into potentially lethal brews, the largest source of illegal alcohol was the smuggled variety, much of which landed on the shores of the southern coast of the United States.[2] The South's proximity to liquor-laden isles in the Caribbean, coastal geography, and long-standing appreciation of liquor-fueled good times beckoned potential smugglers. While Boyles was intent on stopping the traffic, many of his fellow southerners preferred instead to chase the easy profit smuggling promised. The battle between smugglers and officials like Boyles did more than merely demonstrate the difficulty of prohibiting alcohol; it drew the South to the center of debates about federal power, social change, and modern life. Smugglers with ships like the *Jose Luis*, encouraged by the quest for profit, global migration and commerce, and ongoing demand for alcohol, turned the southern coast into a distribution hub for illegal liquor. Alcohol traveled from liquor-exporting islands in the Caribbean to serve local markets in the South or passed through the southern coast on its way to markets farther north. This wide-reaching, well-organized, and immensely profitable traffic in liquor eventually expanded to include other contraband cargoes — undocumented immigrants and narcotics — once federal laws restricting immigration and controlling drugs made smuggling them profitable. Throughout the era, smuggling in the South corrupted officials and thrilled the drinking public even as the southern coast hosted some of the most concentrated efforts to enforce federal law. Those efforts reached not only into southern communities like Mobile but into foreign capitals like Havana as well, where American officials insisted the Cuban government help enforce American laws. In the process, the battle over alcohol accelerated the South's embrace of national trends in business, consumer culture, sociability, and personal pleasure that characterized the period. As *A Thousand Thirsty Beaches* will show, Prohibition, while failing to rid the nation of liquor, nonetheless left an enduring legacy. It expanded federal power in unprecedented ways, simultaneously tied the South more tightly both to its American neighbors to the north and to foreign neighbors "south of the South," and accelerated southern trends toward modernization.

Smuggling liquor by sea was not only a primary source of illicit liquor during Prohibition; it also created one of the most enduring images of the Prohibition Era: the rum runner. More than other sources of bootleg booze, rum-running had—and perhaps still has—what one writer in the *Saturday Evening Post* called "a romantic tinge." "The booze that comes from Rum Row," he noted in 1926, "still looms largest in the public mind."[3] It was not long after Prohibition went into effect on January 16, 1920, that the makings of this extensive, organized, and profitable smuggling trade developed. Indeed, Gertrude Lythgoe, a wholesaling agent for a British liquor concern who eventually became known as the Bootleg Queen of the Bahamas, recalled that almost as soon as the Eighteenth Amendment was ratified, she was transferred from London to Nassau. Her employer anticipated the need for a wholesale agent to serve the expected stream of smugglers seeking to purchase liquor in the Caribbean to take to American shores. By March 1920, the *New York Times* reported that bottles of illegal spirits were arriving in New York aboard steamers from Cuba. By October, the *Times* noted the increase in trade aboard rum-running ships. By December, signs outside saloons in New York City advertised "Why go to Cuba?" slyly suggesting one need not travel to find the liquor that increasingly drew tourists to Havana. While most of the initial media attention on Prohibition enforcement focused on cities like New York, northern urban areas by no means cornered the market on the illegal importation of intoxicating beverages. By the end of 1921, well before "Rum Row" became common shorthand for the floating marketplaces of booze along the eastern seaboard, government officials across the country were wringing their hands at their inability to stop liquor from coming into the country by sea. Navy and Coast Guard fleets were small and outdated, and their efforts were overwhelmed by the sheer volume of the traffic in liquor. As the *New York Times* noted at the end of that year, "For every rum-running schooner overhauled and captured, a dozen had escaped to land their cargoes on a thousand thirsty beaches from Cape Breton to the sunny shores of Florida."[4]

That smugglers would ply their trade in the South, using profit-driven networks that extended from Cuba and across the country, ultimately made perfect sense. Southern beaches had historically lured smugglers as far back as the Spanish conquest. Prohibition was merely a new iteration of illicit commerce that had characterized much of the nation's economic history.[5] The South itself was particularly suited to liquor smuggling. The region's long, sparsely populated coastline with its numerous inlets, waterways, and beaches appealed to profit-driven smugglers; its proximity to foreign isles teeming with booze made long sea voyages unnecessary. Southerners, moreover, still liked their liquor. Despite the image of an evangelical, abstemious South, not all southerners had embraced Prohibition. They made their views clear with their pocketbooks, with their willingness to continue to incorporate drinking into their leisure and entertainment, and with their eagerness to profit by bootlegging. The southern coastline thus became a crossroads where rum runners and their co-conspirators from the South, eager for high-end spirits, converged and together sought to evade the law to their mutual benefit. These enterprising smugglers and bootleggers leveraged the new roads and railroads that allowed tourists to travel south for booze and relaxation and also facilitated the travel of liquor northward. They did so in a region that was accelerating its embrace of consumer culture and its connection to the market as cafés, stores, hotels, and filling stations, many of which sold liquor, dotted the landscape. Opposing the traffic in liquor, the Coast Guard, the Customs Bureau, the Bureau of Immigration, the State Department, and what one government agent jokingly called "Uncle Sam's booze cops of the West Indies" raced to plug the leaks in the porous dyke of U.S. law enforcement. The waters off the southern coast hosted some of the most visible efforts by the Coast Guard to prevent smuggling. Southern towns and cities hosted Coast Guard bases, customs offices, and federal courts, all of which played a primary role in efforts to stop the traffic and punish its purveyors, even extending across the waters to enlist the help of islands like Cuba to enforce a decidedly American law. The South was a central player in this drama. Whether about commerce or consumption or law enforcement, the liquor traffic pulled the South toward a national vision of modern life while it simultaneously enabled northerners to share and participate in southern culture itself.

While the liquor traffic presents a picture of a more entrepreneurial, modern, and misbehaving South, it presents a different picture of Prohibition as well. Prohibition often evokes images of gangsters, urban speakeasies, or backwoods moonshine stills. The Purple Gang of Detroit or Al Capone's violent quest to corner the liquor market in Chicago are familiar touchstones of the era. While rum-running is generally remembered, how the trade worked, how federal officials sought to stop it, and why it might be significant beyond its "tinge" of romance are less familiar.[6] Shifting the story to rum-running and the South, however, recasts the story of Prohibition entirely. As a Coast Guard officer wrote in 1928, "The trade [in the South] is not syndicated. . . . Smuggling is carried on by a large number of small units, for the most part acting independently."[7] The small smuggling outfits that operated in the South lacked the notoriety of organized crime syndicates elsewhere but were no less successful moving alcohol. And they did so without the wholesale murder that characterized the trade in other areas. Instead, numerous small and not-so-small operators of all varieties took advantage of the ongoing demand for liquor to make money. Their enterprise shifts the focus from northeastern cities to the seas along the southern coast and to smaller towns, cities, and sparsely settled coastal areas along the southern Atlantic and the Gulf of Mexico. Though these locations may have appeared isolated, they were nonetheless well connected to global trade networks that traveled through Havana, across the Straits of Florida, and throughout the South. Described as "the northern rim of [the] Caribbean," the South shared colonial relationships, systems of slavery, monocrop agriculture, trade, and cultural exchange with the region since the fifteenth century.[8] Bootleggers merely took advantage of these long-standing networks to meet ongoing demands for liquor.

It did not take long for smuggling to move beyond alcohol. Smugglers also saw profit in illegal cargoes prohibited by other federal legislation. Immigrants barred from entering the United States by new quota laws sought travel on rum-running ships. They shared space with the growing traffic in illegal narcotics. Immigrants and drugs along with alcohol traversed the South, putting the region in the thick of debates about international migrations and trafficking laws. In fact, the enforcement mechanisms developed to counter the smuggling of alcohol would continue to target these other forms of contraband well beyond the repeal of Prohibition. Once liquor landed, smugglers and the black market in liquor exploited illicit economic connections and personal contacts, utilized modern forms of transportation, and accelerated the development of a consumer culture. The burgeoning commercial sector in the South, from cafés to filling stations, from hotels to restaurants to pleasure resorts, provided a retail network for alcohol that helped bootleggers profit from their illegal trade. Many southerners' continued appreciation for the pleasures of alcohol smoothed the trade at every level. Despite concerted efforts to the contrary and despite the South's dry reputation, liquor was a thriving business in the region. The South in this story is remarkably modern, a place connected to the social and cultural trends of the 1920s and to debates about immigration, the embrace of business, and the reach of the market.

As smugglers and law enforcement officers vied for the upper hand along the beaches, the seas, and even the international ports where liquor originated, the story also follows a different cast of characters, most of whom are little known beyond the government documents that recorded their exploits. The colorful characters like Izzy Einstein, the master prohibition agent from New York City, and mobster Al Capone that populate many stories of Prohibition make only cameo appearances. Instead, a liquor wholesaler in Havana, an intelligence officer in the Coast Guard, crooked officials on the take, rebellious young people, tourists, and innumerable small sellers across the South take center stage. Officials reported evidence of liquor all along the southern coast, from the high-end cocktails in New Orleans to the mysterious caches along southern beaches that brought "smiles" to Mobile, Pensacola, Gulfport, Palm Beach, and Key West, all evidence of the limits of federal power.[9] The U.S. government recognized the importance of enforcement on the high seas even if it could not muster the resources to control illegal trade effectively. As one newspaper sagely reported, "It would take all the navies in the world to successfully block" the importation of liquor.[10]

The sheer scope and tenacity of the smuggling problem became apparent less than a year into the Noble Experiment and remained throughout the era. Indeed, reports in the national press of antismuggling efforts appeared to be a continuing cycle of statements of resolve, insistence of progress, and sobering indications that smugglers and bootleggers continued to elude the government's grasp. Despite the early appearance of Cuban liquor in New York, by the summer of 1923, Prohibition Commissioner Roy Haynes confidently asserted that the end of rum-running was just around the corner. Having measured the problem, he insisted that the amount of liquor imported into the United States since Prohibition was but a small fraction of what had been brought into the country "during the regime of the open saloon." He loudly insisted, "Rum-running is doomed."[11] The primary obstacle, in his view, was not smuggling itself but public perception. The biggest danger that Prohibition faced, he suggested, was the public's belief that reports of smuggling indicated Prohibition was failing. Such reports, he argued, were nothing more than propaganda "to befool the nation into believing that prohibition enforcement is a hollow sham."[12] A year later, however, it seemed that smuggling, rather than being doomed, was thriving. By the spring of 1924, reports indicated that smuggling was actually increasing, and officials estimated that approximately 100,000 cases of liquor landed along the Atlantic and the Gulf of Mexico each month.[13] By midsummer, while no one was willing to estimate the amounts, it was clear that the flood of liquor to the nation's shores remained "substantial."[14] Despite an increase in appropriations for the Coast Guard for ships and manpower devoted to enforcement on the high seas, smugglers continued to land their contraband cargo with little interference.

Perhaps, the government surmised, a change in leadership was in order. In 1925, Haynes was replaced by General Lincoln C. Andrews, who soon announced that the federal government captured less than 5 percent of the liquor smuggled into the United States. Over the course of his tenure, Andrews made loud statements about employing well-qualified Prohibition agents and laid out a structure for cooperation among the various federal agencies and state and local law enforcement. In 1926, his forces predicted the "greatest enforcement campaign will soon be in full swing," with a patrol fleet of nearly 400 vessels, approximately 10,000 officers and more than $29 million in funds, with the overall goal of making the country "alcoholically dry."[15] By the spring of 1927, Andrews confidently asserted that rum-running had been brought under control.[16] At least initially he seemed correct, and he left office soon thereafter. Focus on the seas shifted from stopping the wholesale smuggling of thousands of cases at a time to detecting smaller cargoes of liquor hidden in shipments of other commodities. The attention to liquor smuggling, however, made the smuggling of other cargoes more attractive. What Haynes had earlier called the "twin sister" of liquor smuggling, the smuggling of immigrants who sought to evade the nation's newly imposed immigration restrictions, drew increasing amounts of attention. But even this seeming progress did not last. By 1929, two years after General Andrews had left his post, rum-running remained in the news, and officials likened chasing rum runners to a game of checkers. When one area of the nation's border seemed secure, rum runners merely moved their operations to another location. The game began the moment Prohibition went into effect and continued until repeal. When Coast Guard forces began to gain an edge on Rum Row off the coast of New York and New Jersey in the early 1920s, the trade merely shifted south. When the United States successfully negotiated a treaty to enlist the Cuban government's aid in preventing shipments destined for the United States, trade increased along the water borders of the Midwest. When efforts to interrupt smuggling concentrated along the Great Lakes, the islands once again resumed their trade.[17] Despite occasional moments of progress, the U.S. government could never fully end the illegal importation of liquor into the United States. Increased pressure to apprehend smugglers and their wares merely pushed the trade elsewhere, from the Northeast to the South to the Great Lakes and back to the South.

The persistence of smuggling and the continued demand for liquor was simply not what temperance advocates had anticipated when they pushed for a national amendment to outlaw intoxicating beverages. By the twentieth century, temperance was a seasoned reform movement. Most Americans were familiar with the depiction of alcohol as the consummate social evil, having been the target of reformers since the early nineteenth century. The rhetoric about the dangers of alcohol presented drinking as a catalyst for moral, economic, and spiritual demise. By the first decades of the twentieth century, temperance reformers focused less on sin and instead pointed to liquor consumption as the agent that destroyed otherwise moral, upstanding, increasingly middle-class families. Articles like "Alcohol: Its Use and Abuse" that appeared in popular media before the passage of the Eighteenth Amendment linked even moderate drinking to an astonishing number of physical maladies, from inflammation of the kidneys to infectious diseases.[18] Temperance advocates tied drinking to crime, and women quickly joined temperance efforts, recognizing the disastrous effect of men's drinking on children and families. According to reformers, alcohol debased moral character, destroyed domestic happiness, filled the prisons and the poorhouses, engendered an abnormal appetite that destroyed moral sensibility and physical power, and brought many millions to poverty, misery, and premature death.[19] Temperance advocates specifically decried saloons, the primary purveyor of liquor for poor and working-class Americans, and argued that closing saloons would invariably improve the lives of their customers and their communities.[20] By the twentieth century, temperance crusader Billy Sunday could assert that alcohol's "influence is degrading on the individual, the family, politics and business and upon everything that you touch in this old world," and he confidently insisted that "all are agreed" as to alcohol's "ill effects."[21] Such a dangerous substance, in temperance rhetoric, could not be safely imbibed in even the smallest of quantities. The only effective remedy, advocates believed, was to eliminate alcohol from the nation entirely.

Beginning at the state level, efforts expanded to prohibit alcohol through law. Women's groups like the Women's Christian Temperance Union not only forced the issue of alcohol onto the national political stage but used their efforts to enhance women's larger public influence and eventual direct political participation as a result.[22] Efforts to prohibit alcohol gained enormous traction with the limits on distilling and brewing enacted to aid the war effort during World War I. And with a worried eye toward the expected redistricting caused by the increasing numbers of immigrants recorded in the looming 1920 census who were assumed to prefer strong drink, dry advocates set a goal of enacting a national prohibition amendment to the U.S. Constitution before 1920. Even though the otherwise disorganized and fractured wet coalition managed to limit the time allowed for ratification, the Eighteenth Amendment was nonetheless ratified at surprising speed. Framers of the amendment set it to take effect one year after ratification, to allow time for the liquor industry to dispose of its existing liquor supplies and for state and federal government officials to develop a plan for enforcement, something that Prohibitionists insisted would be easily accomplished.[23] That Americans would continue to want to drink alcohol even without the organized efforts of the liquor industry to promote it took dry advocates entirely by surprise.

The South came to the temperance party a bit later than other areas of the country. Southerners, and southern white men in particular, had long relished drinking as part of both genteel sociability and raucous male leisure, though always tempered by concern for the effects of drinking among enslaved people and poor whites. By the late nineteenth century, however, southern evangelicals embraced what they believed to be the transformative power of temperance for their communities. Initially, southern communities focused on the control of liquor, through either costly licensing provisions, local options laws that allowed communities to vote to prohibit the liquor trade within their borders, or dispensary systems whereby state and county officials controlled the liquor traffic themselves. While southerners found licensing and dispensaries to be excellent sources of public revenue, they remained concerned about the large amounts of liquor their fellow residents continued to consume and the sheer scope of the market for liquor. Areas that prohibited liquor sales within their jurisdiction through local option laws were dismayed by the ease with which interested residents could nonetheless obtain alcohol across state or county lines. Many communities eventually came to the conclusion that alcohol control was impossible while domestic sources of alcohol remained available. National Prohibition, they hoped, would eliminate those sources, allowing the virtues of a dry population to blossom. They were, however, sadly mistaken. As under local option laws, demand for alcohol among southerners of all stripes continued unabated. And while they looked to national Prohibition to eliminate the domestic market for alcohol, they failed to anticipate how eager foreign sources would be to provide supplies of liquor for drinking. Ultimately, Prohibition made clear that the market in alcohol followed simple laws of supply and demand. As long as demand remained, which it did nationwide, Americans, including southerners, would find ways to supply it.[24]

There were, however, peculiarities to Prohibition sentiment in the South. Alcohol had long been a privilege of whiteness, and whites had found ways to limit access to alcohol for African Americans, especially enslaved African Americans, though many elite white southerners expressed equal concern about drinking by poor whites. After emancipation, many African Americans embraced temperance as a tool of racial uplift and supported campaigns to limit the availability of alcohol. Others, unsurprisingly, used their freedom to embrace the pleasures in drink. To many southern whites, however, drinking among blacks was one more indication that African Americans were reverting to savagery outside the supposedly civilizing institution of slavery. In the South, the push for Prohibition was tied to concerns about dangerous black men, and Prohibition became a potential tool to control the black population. Despite white intent, however, Prohibition did not work as planned. African Americans, like white southerners, saw Prohibition as an entrepreneurial opportunity. They profited from Prohibition by selling liquor and participated in bootlegging outfits run by whites. They too exploited continuing demand for liquor and used the proceeds to improve their own situations.[25]

While southerners both black and white had their own hopes and dreams for Prohibition, reformers nationwide saw it as needed progressive reform for the South as a whole. They hoped Prohibition would bring sober industrious- ness and prosperity, characteristics that would lessen the South's status as a national problem.[26] Ultimately, Prohibition brought a measure of prosperity, but it did so to industrious bootleggers and smugglers, as well as some fam- ilies, much to reformers' chagrin. And while it brought the cultural values of many southerners more in line with those in the north, those values now embraced drinking, dancing, dating, and vice. While reformers wanted to bring the South closer to the national fold, they did not envision smugglers using southern towns as distribution points for liquor headed to Chicago and New York as the vehicle of economic reform. And while they decried southerners' supposed cultural backwardness, they did not anticipate that the nation's social and cultural values would reunite at "blind tigers," dance halls, the beaches of Miami, or the bars in Havana. In other words, few imag- ined that hopes for a more modern South would be partially realized at the bottom of a liquor bottle.

Nevertheless, once the Eighteenth Amendment and the Volstead Act be- came the law of the land, the potential pitfalls of Prohibition became buried in the avalanche of glib assurances that the battle over demon rum had been won. Prohibition prohibited the manufacture, sale, transportation, impor- tation, and export of intoxicating liquors. The law did not ban the actual consumption of alcohol; drafters of the law hoped consumers would be more willing to testify against those who provided their illegal liquor if they were not facing charges themselves.[27] And it also did not ban the possession of alcoholic beverages in private homes or the manufacture of wine and hard cider for domestic consumption by homeowners, family members, and guests. This seeming contradiction neatly solved the problem of what to do with alcohol purchased legally before Prohibition went into effect, and Prohi- bitionists fully anticipated home consumption would disappear after existing supplies were consumed. Once alcohol was no longer available, they believed, Americans would lose their taste for it. Certainly many did, as consumption declined considerably and remained lower even after repeal, but not nearly to the extent temperance advocates expected.

Proponents so fervently believed Americans would accept and obey the law that they also insisted the resources needed to enforce Prohibition would be minimal and would diminish as demand for alcohol disappeared. Thus Congress allocated a paltry level of funding for enforcement, assuming that with the help of state Prohibition laws and local law enforcement, and a declining demand for alcohol, the task would be cheap and easy. Time soon proved their assumptions to be wildly off the mark. Nevertheless, Prohibition began with great optimism in many quarters, and Americans either eagerly or dejectedly anticipated a nation without liquor. As enforcement proved to be increasingly ineffective, however, that optimism began to shift. By the mid-1920s, as alcohol continued to flow largely unabated, Americans began to question the level of intrusion effective enforcement of Prohibition would require. Many were troubled by the deaths associated with Prohibition, bemoaning a law that not only killed sworn enforcement officers and their prey but also took the lives of civilians who drank alcohol rendered poisonous by the federal government. As the deaths mounted, Americans began to turn against the law with shudders of distaste. By the end of the 1920s, large segments of the population actively disdained the law and saw little point in attempting to enforce it at all.[28]

What the Prohibition amendment prohibited, ultimately, was the business end of alcohol — its supply side rather than its demand side — and it virtually guaranteed the growth of a vast black market in booze. Despite the promises of Prohibition's supporters, it quickly became apparent that the American people were unwilling to give up liquor entirely. Bootleggers across the country soon realized the potential profits in making it available. In this vacuum smugglers sought to meet demand by importing illicit beverages from surrounding countries where the trade in alcohol remained legal, places like Canada, Mexico, the Bahamas, and Cuba, all of which had plenty of reasons to want to encourage Americans to continue to drink despite the law. West Coast drinkers bought booze smuggled from Mexico to the south and British Columbia to the north. Hundreds of boats brought liquor across the Detroit River from Canada, where distilleries dotted the riverbank across from Detroit. The French ports of St. Pierre and Miquelon and Halifax in the Canadian Maritimes provided ready supplies of liquor shipped from Europe for transport to the northeastern coast of the United States. And to the south, the islands of the Caribbean hosted numerous ships supplying alcohol to the southern coast from Galveston to Key West and north along the southern Atlantic coast. European makers of cognac, whiskey, scotch, gin, vodka, wine, and champagne, unwilling to lose their American market entirely, shipped thousands of cases of liquor to ports like Havana, knowing that they would eventually end up as contraband arriving on the southern shores of the United States.

Prohibition, however, raised thorny international issues about the extent of the federal government's authority and power. While Prohibition encouraged an unprecedented expansion of the federal government to conduct the war on alcohol at home, ending smuggling in particular required the federal government to reach beyond the nation's borders and into the policies and practices of foreign countries.[29] Canada refused to prevent liquor exports to the United States and indeed profited from those exports, imposing a $20 duty on each case of alcohol exported to the United States. Smuggling there included not only bringing liquor into the United States but also doing so without paying the duty. The Bahamas capitalized on its colonial status with England and its proximity to Florida and profited enormously as a liquor distribution point for smugglers. In other relationships, however, America carried a bigger stick. Cuba in particular found itself in a more difficult situation than either Canada or the Bahamas. Cuba had well-established relationships with Europe and the rest of the world, and Havana in particular was a cosmopolitan, international city. But Cuba had complicated ties with the United States, whose imperial adventures began when it participated in Cuba's liberation from Spain. Trade and travel between the island and the United States, especially the South, was significant. Cubans embraced American markers of modernity from American brand names to baseball, while Americans consumed Cuban products and eventually the Cuban ethos as tourists. All these connections provided the makings of a significant traffic from Cuba in liquor, as well as other contraband like immigrants and narcotics. Nevertheless, Cuba's independence as a nation was compromised by the Platt Amendment to its constitution, which allowed the United States to intervene to protect life, property, and individual liberty. The United States intruded into Cuban affairs routinely over the course of the early twentieth century, both militarily and economically. Cuba's economy, moreover, was beholden to American business interests and almost entirely dependent on the sugar market, much of it held by American industrialists.[30] Cubans were ever mindful of the potential of American intervention, while Americans were considerably less mindful of Cuban interests. Like those of Canada and the Bahamas, Cuba's interests lay in continuing smuggling out of its ports. But allowing the trade to persist threatened the wrath of the American government, potentially even leading to intervention, which Cubans steadfastly did not want.

In Cuba, the drama surrounding questions about the extent of American state power was particularly acute. Cubans feared American intervention at the same time Prohibition made the U.S. government more invested in the expansion of its power, not just in the interests of empire but as a means to enforce its own laws. International law and custom allowed nations to enforce their laws within a three-mile limit on the waters surrounding their coasts. Ending smuggling required extending American power to enforce Prohibition much farther, well out to sea and even into the ports of foreign nations that supplied smugglers with their wares. The problem of smuggling thus became a problem of extending American law enforcement authority into international waters through the Coast Guard, including efforts to persuade or coerce other countries to help enforce a peculiarly American law. Over time, the United States consistently demonstrated that it could not enforce its own law and placed additional responsibility for doing so on the government in Havana, even as Americans expressed more and more disdain for the law at home. It was an awkward situation, one not lost on the American agents who were trying to end smuggling from Havana. Prohibition thus became a double-edged sword: it depended on American power over Cuba at the same time that it showed the U.S. government's confounding weaknesses. That the United States could demand Cuba's assistance in enforcing Prohibition was evidence of its imperial might, foreshadowing later efforts to prevent drug trafficking and illegal immigration. That it had to demand help in the first place was evidence of something else entirely.

This tale of the liquor traffic through the South presents a wide-ranging narrative tying smuggling along the southern coastline to foreign ports like Havana, to northern liquor markets, and to Prohibition policy made in the offices of federal agencies in Washington, D.C. It weaves enforcement efforts pushed by Washington with local officials in towns along the southern coast and across the seas to the streets of Cuba's capital. It is a southern story that is national and international in scope, though admittedly American in perspective. It opens by describing the liquor traffic itself, from wholesalers in Havana to the smuggling ships at sea to the transport of cases of alcohol from the beach to the final customer, a process that drew enterprising southerners into an international trade that promised significant profits. It then turns to the efforts of the U.S. Coast Guard to disrupt the traffic in liquor on the waters surrounding the South. The second chapter details the triumphs and frustrations of federal law enforcement's game of cat-and-mouse with smugglers on the high seas. In the process, it makes plain the extension of the power of the American government beyond the nation's boundaries. The third chapter returns to Havana, tracing the complicated dance among diplomats and a small band of U.S. Treasury agents to gain and fully exploit Cuba's cooperation to prevent the departure of rum-running ships from Havana. While those efforts achieved temporary success, smugglers expanded into other profitable illegal cargoes, including immigrants and narcotics, a parallel traffic discussed fully in the fourth chapter. The fifth chapter moves from Cuba back to efforts targeting not only smuggling ships but the "small fry" and "hip-flask toters" who bought, sold, and drank whatever intoxicating beverages they could find. It reveals how Prohibition mapped a modernizing southern commercial culture as well as how officials shared in the profits of the liquor market themselves. What is inescapable throughout, however, is the continuing demand for alcohol that fueled the black market in booze. Americans, and southerners with them, continued to drink, and the ways they did so shaped the social and cultural landscape of the 1920s, undermining any sense that drinking alcohol made one disreputable. From new patterns in where and with whom Americans drank to the rise in travel to destinations where liquor was readily available, as the final chapter argues, drinking shaped the ethos of the decade in ways that would continue long after the Eighteenth Amendment was repealed.

A Thousand Thirsty Beaches shows that smugglers capitalized on an increasingly unpopular law, advantageous geography, a modernizing South, and the region's historical sympathy to drinking to create an organized and profitable industry that served the interests of the nation's drinking population. It also documents the expanded federal power in the South and abroad that attempted to enforce the law. The story of this industry, and the attempts to stop it, provides a particularly colorful look into Prohibition, but it is not simply another look at the law's failure. It ultimately illuminates the social, economic, and cultural connections between the South and the rest of the liquor-drinking world, and the spread of federal power southward and beyond the nation's shorelines. *A Thousand Thirsty Beaches* depicts a South that was modern, enterprising, and connected to the larger international world. Like citizens of New York and Chicago, Americans nationwide, even in the South, resisted giving up their alcoholic beverages. They participated in sprawling smuggling networks and sought profit by meeting continuing demand. They drank what they could get their hands on; some made their own, while others put their lives in peril drinking poisonous concoctions sold by dealers eager to make a quick buck. But when they could, most drinkers preferred "the real McCoy," the finer forms of distilled spirits that storied distilleries around the world continued to produce for their American customers. Getting that liquor into the glasses of thirsty Americans took some effort, as numerous federal agencies and local law enforcement entities sought to prevent it, projecting their authority across the sea. But with continued demand, rum runners were eager to please, running rum in wherever they could. The southern coast became a destination of choice for rum runners, with a ready supply of enterprising locals eager to participate in the trade, enough demand to mitigate cutthroat competition and forestall violence, and enough coastline to give every small outfit a chance. With so many operators, so many customers, and so much coastline, it is little wonder that the liquor traffic was impossible to stop.

{ *Chapter One* }

THE TRAFFIC IN LIQUOR

✳

I N 1925, IN THE FACE OF A FLOOD of booze from Cuba, the U.S. government sent Captain Peter A. del Valle of the U.S. Marine Corps to Havana to investigate the smuggling industry in Cuba. He eventually submitted a forty-page report outlining an extensive smuggling network for liquor as well as companion cargoes of immigrants and drugs. During his investigation, del Valle posed as a businessman hoping to start a smuggling operation and met with a successful bootlegger at a local Havana café to learn the trade. Getting into the smuggling business, he was assured, was quite simple. One needed only a schooner, a relationship with a liquor wholesaler in Havana, and a relatively modest amount of capital to become a rum runner. Vessels that could carry 8,000 cases could be had for about $8,000, and the old hand in the trade even offered to locate a ship for a small commission. The smuggler also recommended a local liquor wholesaler, calling him a "square broker." Wholesalers, del Valle learned, were useful beyond merely providing the liquor itself. A good one also took care of "fixing" any inquisitive government officials and obtained the fake documents needed to enter and leave port. This helpful smuggler also suggested that Daytona, Florida, might provide a ready market for del Valle's smuggled goods.[1] In short, over the course of one evening and several rounds of drinks, del Valle was instructed in the intricacies of the liquor trade from equipment to supply to final customer. More than merely transporting liquor by boat from Havana to the southern coast, successful smuggling followed an established business model, with a little corruption, to ship liquor to its final destination in the glasses of thirsty Americans nationwide.

Rum runners operating out of Cuba fed a nationwide black market for booze. Schooners out of Havana traveled as far north as Boston, and liquor shipped from Cuba supplied the famous Rum Rows that developed off the coasts of major cities in the Northeast. They also served markets as far west as Galveston, Texas, and virtually every point on the coast in between. But rather than being concentrated on cities like New York, the liquor traffic was an adaptive trade. When federal authorities cracked down on the ships loitering off the coast in the Northeast, the traffic shifted south. It joined a fleet of southern smugglers plying southern waters whose cargo landed on southern beaches and traveled from southern railroad depots and on southern highways to markets like St. Louis, Chicago, and New York. Liquor smugglers from Miami to Mobile to New Orleans participated in a trade that spanned from foreign ports like Havana to the burgeoning towns and cities from the Southeast to the Northeast and the Midwest, providing liquor to populations throughout the eastern half of the United States. Southerners facilitated that trade at every step, drawing the South into an international business with tremendous profit potential created by federal laws against liquor.

The business model the smuggler described to del Valle in 1925 involved largely legal transactions, at least until the product reached American waters. Purchasing large quantities of liquor from a wholesaler in Havana was perfectly legal, as was shipping that liquor to a foreign port, just not one in the United States.[2] But it was no secret to U.S. officials in Cuba and to Cuban officials themselves that much of the liquor that left Cuba wound up in the United States. The traffic in liquor from Havana to those thirsty southern beaches veered from legal to illegal trade and built on existing trade relations established between Cuba and the United States. In many ways, the liquor traffic was a modern international business, using technological innovation, a focus on efficiency, and the delivery of a reliable product, in which southerners played no small part.

Despite America's Prohibition laws, numerous enterprising men, along with a few women, saw the money to be made in bringing booze to American shores. The high demand and limited supply virtually guaranteed a tidy profit for anyone who could successfully land liquor on shore and transport it to customers. One "rum king" made enough money to retire in 1927 after only a few years in the business. He willingly shared his business secrets with a reporter. What lured him into the smuggling business, he recalled, was opportunity. At loose ends at the end of his military service, he was offered a bottle of scotch by a fisherman while walking on the beach. Surmising that a more organized effort could yield a significant return, he decided to put his education in engineering and his military experience to good use constructing a smuggling network. It was, in his view, merely a matter of exploiting the "values of cooperation, of applied efficiency, and long phrased dogma of big business" to turn a profit. His skills could supply what he saw as an inexhaustible market and enabled him to piece together an operation that would eventually bring large amounts of alcohol to the eastern United States.

He began by developing relationships with owners of rum schooners lying off the coast, with fishermen who owned small boats, and with truckers on land, contracting them to provide their services to his organization. He later chartered two schooners and a tramp steamer to provide his own supply of liquor from Cuba on a reliable schedule. He then amassed a sea fleet of speedy motorboats to bring liquor to shore and a land fleet of trucks, manned by fast, loyal drivers, to distribute his supply to his customers. Eventually, in a model of business integration that would make Andrew Carnegie smile, he cut out the middleman and purchased three ships to bring liquor to the United States directly from distilleries in Scotland. Within a few years, having built a considerable fortune, he decided to retire. He built homes on the New England coast and in Florida and set his sights on a respectable marriage. "You can't go to courting or raising a family with the smell of liquor on your coat-tails, or a gang of federal agents reaching after that part of your attire," he wryly quipped. "It really isn't done in the very best of families."[3] For this rum king, rum-running was a short-term business venture, after which he turned to more respectable pursuits. He represented only one of a growing number of suppliers who turned their attention to the Caribbean, and ports like Havana, to construct their illegal business empires.

And a considerable empire they created. Smuggling liquor was big business, worth many millions of dollars a year. Beginning with a few bottles smuggled aboard regular ferry service to the United States, it increased by 1923 and 1924 into a thriving, well-organized industry. Henry Kime, a man-about-town working as an undercover agent in Havana, outlined the financial aspects of smuggling in a 1927 report to prohibition officials in Washington, D.C. He estimated there were at least twenty-eight ships engaged in smuggling docked in Havana at any one time and forty-five or so that regularly smuggled liquor from Havana to the United States. These ships could carry 2,000 to 10,000 cases of liquor, averaging about 5,000 per ship per voyage. Kime

Havana waterfront, ca. 1920 (Library of Congress, Prints and Photographs
Division, F. Gilbert, photographer; reproduction number LC-USZ62-143716)

pointed out that Havana alone supplied the United States with approximately
500,000 cases of illegal booze every month, totaling 6 million cases per year.
The financial implications of the trade were staggering. One article reported
that cases of scotch that sold for $11 in Scotland went for more than $50 on
American shores.[4] In the warehouses of Havana's liquor wholesalers, cases
of liquor varied in cost depending on the type — $12 for good whiskey, $20 to
$30 for a case of fine wines, but only $8 for a case of gin because it was easily
concocted in American bathtubs. But even using Havana wholesale prices,
the smuggling business out of Havana brought in approximately $80 million
worth of high-end spirits every year to the southern and eastern regions of
the United States.[5] Once liquor landed in the United States, it generated more
extended profits. In the sheds and warehouses of American bootleggers, it
was diluted or "cut" with water; doctored with colorings, flavorings, and even
burnt sugar to approximate the look and taste of fine liquor; and rebottled.
Before Christmas 1926, for example, one bootlegger landed 96,000 bottles
of liquor near New York City. Those bottles were repackaged onshore into
nearly 750,000 thousand bottles of bootleg booze that would bring holiday
cheer to New Yorkers.[6] Havana was thus a central location in a booming
business enterprise.

Havana was well positioned to play a central role in the black-market traffic in booze. By the 1920s, Havana was a bustling international port. Located on the northwestern coast of the island of Cuba, it offered a beautiful
natural harbor used for European trade since the early days of the Spanish

empire. Havana also featured close proximity to miles of southern beaches on the mainland of the United States and hosted numerous offices for American business concerns. Regular ferry service had operated between Cuba and Florida since the nineteenth century, providing convenient travel options for liquor entrepreneurs seeking to do business on the island. As a city, Havana hit its stride in the sugar boom after World War I. As the price of sugar increased, money lined the pockets of Havana's elite. The town began a building boom that continued into the 1930s. City development expanded westward along with the Malecón, the oceanside walkway that connected the historic old city by the harbor with Havana Centro and the suburbs of El Vedado, home to a growing number of fine hotels, including the Hotel Nacional, a familiar landmark that captured the imaginations of American tourists when it opened in 1930. As the 1920s passed, the Malecón continued its march west, spurring development of Miramar, an elite residential area and home to embassies from around the world. The bridge over the Almendares River connecting Vedado and Miramar would eventually become the launching point for smuggling vessels of a different sort, bringing illegal cargoes of undocumented immigrants to the shores of the Gulf Coast.[7]

Smuggling, along with most businesses associated with shipping, however, concentrated around the narrow, winding streets of what is now Old Havana near the docks of the harbor. Smugglers rubbed shoulders with tourists and legitimate businesspeople along a wharf that hosted ships of a variety of sizes and designs. Local cafés and bars attracted tourists and also served as places to finalize business transactions or recruit crews. Local hotels housed Americans visiting the tropical isle as well as budding and established liquor entrepreneurs. Wholesalers and smugglers alike managed their trades through local offices, while the police, customs agents, and American embassy officials sought to gain a vantage point on the entire market. It was impossible to disentangle legitimate economies of trade and tourism in Havana from the illegal trade in booze as well as immigrants and narcotics.

While Cuba supported its own growing liquor industry and was known for its domestically produced rum and aguardiente (a distilled spirit), liquor imported from Europe provided smugglers the range of products their customers desired. European distillers, loathe to lose their American markets, were happy to comply and eagerly used Havana as a transshipment point from which their liquor traveled to its final destination in the United States. Shortly after the passage of Prohibition, European liquor makers began to flood the Caribbean with booze. Many Caribbean isles were happy to take it, themselves profiting from the increase in customs revenues from foreign products. Cuba was not alone in offering its ports as transshipment points, but it had one primary advantage over its island neighbors, especially the Bahamas. Cuba's customs duties on imported foreign distilled spirits destined for shipment elsewhere were $3 per case cheaper than those out of Nassau.[8] With American Prohibition laws in place, European liquor producers could not send their products directly to the United States, nor could they suggest that their products arriving in Havana were intended ultimately for the American market. The transit trade and Cuba's own export of Cuban rum offered European countries plausible deniability when their product wound up on southern beaches. They could argue that they shipped liquor to Cuba only for transshipment to other markets in the Western Hemisphere where liquor was legal. That it ultimately fed the American market, they would insist, was entirely beyond their control. Their protestations fooled no one. Records on liquor imports flowing into Cuba quickly suggested that European distillers and exporters sought to maintain their American market by shipping liquor to Cuba, knowing that it would eventually make its way into the United States. Two examples traced Havana's growing prominence as a smuggling port. While Scotland shipped 15,500 cases of liquor to Cuba in all of 1922, in the first three months of 1923 alone, it shipped 46,665 cases. Wales was similar, shipping 4,000 cases to Cuba in 1922 and approximately 53,000 in the early months of 1923. Little of this trade targeted Cuban consumers or even left the docks at the harbor. Import duties were much stiffer on liquor imported for consumption in Cuba, and there was little indication that Cuban customs received those revenues. To American officials, the numbers represented a new business model among European distillers to provide their products to Americans and suggested a growing smuggling effort from Cuba.[9]

There was no shortage of eager, slightly shady entrepreneurs willing to take advantage of the underserved market of liquor consumers in the United States. Liquor wholesalers ran thriving businesses in Havana, purchasing large quantities of European gin, scotch, vodka, brandy, and whiskey, most of which was intended for smugglers headed to the United States. Havana had become the home of several extremely profitable businesses whose sole function, despite protests to the contrary, was to facilitate smuggling liquor to the United States. These liquor wholesale and export businesses not only provided cargoes of liquor to smugglers; they also provided customs services and documents needed to move liquor out of Cuban ports for shipment abroad. When Captain del Valle posed as a budding entrepreneur hoping to start a smuggling operation, his informant not only described the business; he also provided the names of local liquor wholesalers who could supply the product. He mentioned several wholesalers and customshouse brokers in Havana, including two prominent men, Minor Guinn and Henry Levin.[10] He also mentioned a third. Mourice Roud operated one of the largest wholesaling businesses, and his dealings especially caught the attention of agents in Havana. His name appeared regularly in reports on smuggling. But he was equally well known along the southern coast. His advertisements and list of prices appeared in the offices of bootlegging operations in cities like Mobile. Over time, agents uncovered a detailed picture of his operations and the role of wholesalers in smuggling networks. Roud himself, however, also embodied the established business ties and ebb and flow of trade between Cuba and the United States that could be used to support the development and expansion of the traffic in liquor.

Mourice Roud, while notorious in Havana, was not Cuban. Described derisively by authorities as an American Jew, his early occupations in Cuba had nothing to do with liquor. He started as the Camaguey representative of a Havana company of commission merchants dealing in onions and potatoes. In late 1922 or early 1923, Roud switched employers and took a job in Havana with a produce exporting company headquartered in Brooklyn, New York. He would not be employed long; his reputation for "dissipation"

and his association with "notorious women" led to his firing. He then entered the onion and potato export business for himself. By 1923, he began to
dabble in liquor as part of his business, eventually attracting the attention
of Prohibition authorities in Havana. As his liquor business grew, so did the
information about him held by American authorities, helped immensely by
an eleven-page statement given by a disgruntled employee who described
Roud's operations.[11] According to the statement, Roud insisted often and
loudly that there was nothing illegal about his business and professed that
he had no fears of being prosecuted for violating the Prohibition laws of the
United States. He rightly noted that his business was conducted "under the
name of the Mourice Roud Incorporated, a Cuban company, and that he has
a right under the Cuban law to sell liquor to any person and is not responsible [n]or can he be held responsible in any way if these goods eventually find
their way into the United States."[12] Confident that he faced no legal risks, he
amassed the connections and the capital necessary to build a substantial exporting business. Liquor wholesaling required some initial capital. Distillers
in France, Great Britain, and other European countries did not readily ship
liquor to Cuba on credit. Hardly flush in the trade of potatoes and onions,
Roud acquired the financial backing to start his business among potential
customers along the southern coast where his liquor would eventually land.
Enforcement officials traced his financing to prominent liquor interests including a New Orleans liquor dealer and property owner named Hemming-
way and a man named DuBois out of Tampa, as well as Felipe Alvarez, also
known as Nistal, from Tampa, who owned the smuggling schooner *Artemis*.[13] Not only were Tampa and New Orleans wide-open towns where liquor
was widely available, but they hosted smuggling networks that shipped liquor into the industrial heartland and the urban Northeast. Authorities also
established Roud's financial ties to a woman named Hazel Cameron, who
was originally from Louisville, Kentucky. Long suspected of participating in
rum-running, she was the "notorious woman" with whom Roud lived in 1922.
Roud's business thus was perfectly legal in Cuba but depended on the money
of large-scale liquor dealers in the South who received their inventory from
Roud and delivered it to the rest of the eastern United States.

According to Cuban law and in the eyes of European liquor companies,
Roud's business was a legitimate concern. He operated openly out of offices
located on Lamparilla and Compostela Streets, distributing White Horse
Whiskey, Canadian Club, Martell Cognac, Gordon's Dry Gin, and John Haig

Scotch whiskey. Several large distillers extended him their exclusive export concessions for tropical ports as long as he did not sell his inventory in Cuba. In addition, he was listed as the sole and exclusive exporter of Cliquot Champagne, L. Garnier Special Liquors, Simon Aine Liquors, Luis Roederer Wines, and Hennessy Cognacs. Roud purchased his inventory of scotch, whiskey, wine, and other liquor directly from Europe, usually at a cost of approximately $8 per case. He then charged his customers $9 to $13 per case. He stored his inventory in bonded warehouses owned by the Port of Havana Docks Company and the United Fruit Company. His customers, who were almost exclusively smugglers, paid for liquor cargo in cash secured through loans against financial documents and arranged their transactions through a branch of the Royal Bank of Canada in Havana. Roud usually dealt with the captains of smuggling schooners operating independently or with American agents who arranged for shipments of liquor to be smuggled into the United States aboard chartered vessels. Roud sold his liquor primarily on a cash-and-carry basis, though a few favored customers might occasionally receive several thousand dollars in credit. Roud's business also arranged the necessary customs documents needed for his products to leave port. Cargoes of liquor were then loaded onto schooners from the warehouse at the Tallapiedra Wharf, from which they would depart ostensibly for a foreign port where liquor was legal. Most, however, headed for the United States.[14]

Angel Sanchez, Roud's disgruntled former bookkeeper, also included an estimate of the size of Roud's business and indicated its focus on smugglers operating along the southern coast. During the fourteen months that Sanchez worked as the head bookkeeper at a salary of $200 per month, he estimated that Roud sold over $3.5 million worth of merchandise, including more than $1 million worth of liquor to a man named W. Alsingham, a primary liquor dealer in New Orleans. He also arranged regular shipments worth several hundreds of thousands of dollars each to various bootleggers operating in New Orleans, Tampa, Dundee, Florida, and other parts of the Gulf Coast. There was no doubt, the bookkeeper insisted, that Roud's ostensibly legal merchandise became cargo on rum-running ships headed for southern beaches. "It was the general understanding," he said, "in the office that these vessels called 'whiskeros' or 'contrabandistas' (trans. a Cuban slang expression applied to vessels engaged in running contraband liquor cargoes to the coast of the United States) did not touch at their port of destination but discharged their cargo off the American coast."[15]

Despite the largely legal basis of Roud's wholesaling business, lurking within his trade practices were indications that his career had always teetered on the edges of the law. Over the years, Roud was embroiled in rumors of shady operations involving his financial arrangements and his bookkeeping. When he managed the office for the Brooklyn exporting company, he was initially paid a salary. But the office generated so little profit that the main office reduced his pay to commission. Still unmotivated to increase the office revenue, Roud, Sanchez reported, had him pawn jewelry and seek loans from prominent Havana businessmen to pay for office expenses. Most refused, one telling Sanchez that Roud was fundamentally "untrustworthy." Sanchez also reported that Roud had been involved in a scheme to sell worthless stock in a shady sugar corporation. The main office in Brooklyn eventually got wind of Roud's dubiously ethical activities — and that he lived with Hazel Cameron, to whom he was not married — and fired him. By that point, however, Roud had already taken $12,000 of company money. Roud continued his shady ways even in his profitable liquor business. Because Roud's inventory was held in bonded warehouses on the wharf and was ostensibly destined for consumers outside Cuba, he paid little in customs duties to the Cuban government. Sanchez reported, however, that when loading thousands of cases of liquor purchased by his customers, Roud routinely siphoned off a few cases and transferred them to his own warehouses in Havana. These he sold for his own profit, without paying import duties and without reimbursing his customers for the cost of each case. Roud also cheated his own employees. Sanchez claimed Roud still owed him $100 for his work. When Roud refused to pay, he quit, only to return when it appeared that Roud's liquor wholesaling proved to be profitable. In many ways, Roud was so successful because of Domingo Prado, an experienced customs broker who provided customs services for Roud's customers. Roud originally promised to split the profits with Prado but never did so. Prado eventually left to go into business for himself selling fraudulent customs documents.[16]

Dealing in illicit liquor headed for the United States provided a profitable business model for Mourice Roud. For several years, he was very successful. He became known as one of the largest and seemingly most reliable of wholesalers, able to provide his customers not only with a steady stream of high-end liquor from Europe but also with the customs chicanery that enabled that liquor to leave the port of Havana and make its way to the United States. His enterprise was not, however, bound to last. In 1926, Cuba and the

United States signed a treaty to coordinate their efforts to disrupt operations like Roud's that made smuggling out of Havana possible (see Chapter 3).
Unable to continue his business openly in Havana, he sought to relocate
where he thought the legal impediments facing liquor wholesalers would be
more manageable. By 1927, he and several of his compatriots had relocated to
Puerto Mexico, known today as Coatzacoalcos, along the southern edge of
the Gulf of Mexico, hoping to reestablish the business model that had been so
successful in Havana. Mexican officials, however, were not quite so willing to
allow customs duties on liquor to slip through their fingers, and Roud missed
his accustomed profit. After marrying an American woman from Houston in
May 1927 and seeking to clear his name and escape from his past, he offered
to forgo his illegal activities and work undercover for American Prohibition
enforcement officials. They turned down his offer, and he eventually set up
another smuggling operation in southern California.[17]

Obtaining cargoes of liquor from wholesalers like Mourice Roud was only
the first step in bringing liquor from Cuba to the southern coast. Operations like his supplied the liquor from Europe that smugglers brought into
the United States illegally. The transport of cases of fine wines and liquors,
however, involved a large and varied list of participants, from rum kings and
seasoned captains and crews to wealthy criminal concerns to pleasure sailors
seeking a thrill and continued access to their pre-1920 beverages of choice.
All of these characters jockeyed for a deal, sought out co-conspirators, or
bargained for cheap labor throughout the winding stone streets of Havana.
These criminal networks in the port city connected with criminal concerns
along the coasts of southern states who would transport liquor once it had
completed its sea voyage. The travels of the *Adeliza D.* provide one example.
This schooner was purchased for $4,700 by four men at the Monteleone Hotel
in New Orleans who had decided to go into the rum-running business. While
the *Adeliza D.* made its way from New Orleans to Havana, two of its owners
traveled to meet it on a United Fruit Company Steamer. Once there, they
purchased 1,300 cases of liquor from a wholesaler and had them loaded onto
the *Adeliza D.* The schooner then sailed back to a location near Jefferson
Parish, Louisiana. There, the liquor was unloaded into a dairy barn on the
eastern bank of the Mississippi River to await shipment northward.[18] These
men were caught, but thousands others like them slipped by officials. One
rum runner told a reporter that he estimated he was caught once for every five
trips he made smuggling liquor. Whenever his boat was seized by authorities,

he simply bought it back at auction. This rum runner cleared about $4,200 per load and paid about $500 for gas and crew, leaving plenty of profit to cover the costs of seizure and arrest.[19]

Beyond representing an important element in the overall Cuban economy, the trade in liquor was interwoven into the local economy and fabric of city life in Havana. Captain del Valle, for example, met with his informant bootlegger at a bar in what is now Old Havana. Smugglers utilized familiar cafés and hotels to conduct their business and took advantage of area roads and beaches. Some, like Mario Pelli, a successful smuggler originally from Tampa, Florida, began a business — Hotel Genova — to house his illegal activities. Other smuggling outfits became associated with particular Havana merchants. U.S. immigration officials listed the Hotel Aurora, the Hotel Domenico, the Centro Gallego, and the Grand Continental as businesses associated with smuggling syndicates. Liquor smugglers were regular in their lodgings so they could be easily located — George Schwartz, who owned several ships that brought liquor to south Florida regularly, stayed at the Lafayette Hotel when he was in Havana. Smugglers also operated out of Neptuno Bar on Neptuno Street, the Sazarac on San Rafael, and Del Barrios American Bar, often conducting their business over drinks unavailable in the target markets.[20]

The shipping of illegal liquor supported other aspects of Havana's economy as well. Shipping concerns, liquor dealers, and owners of vessels with a cargo to transport used the resources of the city and its port to facilitate their ventures. Dealers sought ships, owners of ships sought captains, and captains sought crews for rum-running ventures on the streets, on wharves, in bars, and in seedy hotels of the city. Any needed repairs to ships in the trade often occurred in Havana. All the provisioning of ships utilized Havana businesses. Clothing stores, dry dock concerns, bars, and hotels owed a significant proportion of their business in the mid-1920s to smuggling operations. Common sailors who worked on smuggling vessels earned $60 to $100 a month, much of which they spent in Havana when they returned from voyages. Captains made $300 to $500 per month, adding their earnings to the local economy. It was little surprise, then, that many Cubans had no interest in helping the United States enforce its Prohibition law. It was certainly not in the economic interest of many Cubans to do so.[21]

Havana's rum fleet was extensive. During the heyday of smuggling, agents mentioned almost 350 separate vessels that at one point or another were

British schooner the *Arcola* (National Archives and Records Administration, Photographs of Suspected Rum Runners, U.S. Coast Guard, RG 26RR)

implicated in the liquor traffic. These ships were of various sizes and types and used various forms of propulsion. Some were old-fashioned sailing vessels, usually differentiated by type and number of masts. The *Malahat* was unusual in that it sported five masts; more common were two-masted auxiliary schooners like the *Alida Bonnefil* or the *Arcola*. The Coast Guard also reported tracking steam trawlers like the *Metak* or boats like the *Kingfisher*, described as an American steam tug. Other smugglers used smaller motorboats described as gas screws — propeller-driven boats powered by gasoline combustion engines. By the late 1920s, newer boats plied the waters, designed and built specifically for the liquor trade. As one magazine in the United States reported, the boats were "broad, low-masted, and sit well down in the water so that they are difficult to see. They are powered by the most modern type of engines, provided chiefly by a well-known American firm, and are capable of operating at high speed."[22] This writer likely referred to Liberty engines, manufactured originally for aircraft use during World War I and widely available as surplus after the war. Most boats operated with far less glamorous gasoline engines, which were only beginning to be incorporated into smaller boats. Attaching a gas combustion engine to a boat was still a tricky, and potentially dangerous, proposition. The American motorboat *Amelia G.*'s smuggling career ended in September 1925 when the engine exploded. Many schooners also sought to utilize both wind and mechanical power. The U.S. Coast Guard destroyer *Saukee*, for example, recorded the position of the *Goia Nard* in Havana harbor loading cargo and noted not only its three masts but its two powerful engines.[23]

The Coast Guard, however, recorded a ship's country of origin more often than its size or form of power. Numerous smuggling boats hailed from Europe, especially Britain and France; others hailed from the Western Hemisphere, especially Honduras. But boats routinely changed names and registries as they were seized, auctioned, or sold back and forth among smuggling operators. For example, one Cuban pleasure yacht was sold to Frank Collazo, who transformed it into a rum runner named the *Julito*. He delivered cargoes of liquor to American shores until the vessel was captured in the Chesapeake Bay. The *Coco* was formerly the *Antonio Barba*, but its name was changed and its registry was transferred when it was sold. It foundered in Havana harbor during the 1926 hurricane and was sold again.[24] Some rum captains were even known to sail with several name boards and registrations on board, allowing them to change the vessel's name and registry mid-voyage, thereby confusing law enforcement authorities at sea. The country of registry was an important aspect of rum-running. Boats registered in the United States were required by law to uphold American laws at all times, even when they were in international waters. They could be stopped by the Coast Guard at any time. Foreign vessels, however, were expected to abide by American laws only when they were in American territorial waters. A vessel registered in Honduras or the Bahamas thus had much more freedom to carry liquor. And countries like France and Scotland, to the chagrin of American authorities, were not always particularly concerned when their ships appeared to be violating Prohibition laws.

The tangled ownership of the *Arsene J* illustrates some of the tactics rum runners used to evade these laws. The *Arsene J*, owned by well-known Cuban smuggler Facundo Sardinas, was a successful rum runner, making a reported nineteen successful voyages between Canada and the coast of Massachusetts in 1923 and 1924. Changing his operations, Sardinas began to charter the *Arsene J* to others seeking to bring cargoes of liquor to the United States, charging $2,500 per month when the ship carried cargoes and

$1,500 per month when idle. He eventually decided to move the *Arsene J*'s operations south. He sailed the ship to Havana and took on a load of liquor, which he sold off the coast of New Orleans and Biloxi. Sardinas realized, however, that running his vessel under a Cuban registry compromised his operations, giving the Cuban government too much leverage over his trade. After 1926, Cuban port officials had the authority to levy higher customs duties on his Cuban vessel and prevent his departure if they believed he intended to violate American law. He tried a subtle end run around maritime law by "selling" the *Arsene J* to a French woman named Suzanne Jeannot. Owned by a French citizen, the *Arsene J* could claim French registry. Sardinas apparently hoped that officials would not notice that Jeannot was his mistress and lived with him in Havana. While American undercover officials in Havana indeed noticed the dubious sale, there was little they could do. Henry Kime, the American agent in Havana, surmised that if the *Arsene J* had been carrying arms to Nicaragua or narcotics to the United States, the French government would have shown more concern and intervened. But since liquor was the cargo, the French were more interested in continuing sales of French liquor to the United States and thus turned a blind eye to the schooner's illegal activities.[25]

Facundo Sardinas's efforts to sidestep the inconveniences of registration showed one particular obstacle presented by maritime law. As Sardinas realized, smuggling required the appearance of strict adherence to maritime rules governing international trade. Ships were required to carry a registry indicating their nation of origin. In addition, when a ship left a port for international waters with a cargo intended for a foreign destination, the captain was required to maintain a cargo manifest showing the cargo's contents and a list of all crew members, among other papers. The captain also had to carry a series of documents, known as clearance papers, when leaving port, indicating the destination of the cargo. The Cuban government also required that shipping concerns place a deposit or "bond" on the cargo with the port of departure's customs officials before the ship set sail. Once the ship returned to Havana with papers stating that it had indeed unloaded its cargo at its indicated destination and delivered it to its rightful owner, the bond would be canceled and the deposit returned. Documents indicating that a cargo of liquor was destined for the United States represented a clear violation of American Prohibition laws, giving Cuban authorities the necessary justification to prevent the ship's departure for sea. Consequently, liquor ships could only leave port if they carried authorized clearance papers indicating that they were headed or "clearing" for ports where the trade in liquor was legal.

Smugglers needed documents indicating that their cargo had been unloaded at an appropriate foreign port, even if it had actually been unloaded off the coast of the United States, if they wanted to both retrieve their bond and continue to be allowed to clear from Havana. There were several ways around this dilemma. Some smugglers simply forfeited their bond, claiming that they had lost their clearance papers at sea. Such a strategy, however, raised suspicions among authorities, who could then seek to prevent that boat's subsequent departures from port. Other smuggling ventures kept the letter but not necessarily the spirit of the law. Alastair Moray, the superintendent of the cargo (also called the supercargo) on board the ship the *Cask*, learned another method, which he later recounted in his diary. Several days into his voyage from Scotland to the United States with approximately 25,000 cases of Scotch whiskey, the captain stopped in a French port and ordered the cargo unloaded onto the docks. At first Moray was confused and irked at the added labor. Only when he saw the clearance papers did he understand the purpose of the brief stop. Once unloaded, the clearance papers were completed. The cargo was then quickly reloaded, and the voyage continued across the Atlantic. The brief detour to France allowed the *Cask* to claim that the cargo had been unloaded at a port in which the sale of liquor was legal. According to the documents, the subsequent voyage from France to the coast of the United States represented the travels of ship "in ballast"— or empty, in other words.[26]

Corruption created yet another way to obtain completed customs documents. To be successful, however, this method required the participation of a third country, or at least the willing participation of one or two corrupt officials from a third country. After investigations into Havana's smuggling business, undercover agents pieced together an arrangement involving officials from Honduras that enabled smugglers to obtain seemingly legitimate clearance papers, complete rum-running voyages, retrieve their bond, and begin the process again. The agents in Havana noticed that a suspiciously large number of ships leaving Havana's harbor indicated that they were headed for ports in Honduras. Export records in Cuba compounded their suspicions. Between 1919 and 1924, exports of liquor from Cuba to Honduras had increased by more than 726,796 gallons. There was, however, no explanation as to why the market for liquor in Honduras had expanded so extravagantly. More importantly, officials learned that although ships carried papers indicating they were returning from the Honduran port of Limón, where they had unloaded cargoes of alcohol, there was no customs office in Limón capable of certifying clearance documents.[27] Nor was there any evidence of the thousands of cases of liquor that had ostensibly been unloaded there. While thousands upon thousands of cases of liquor left Havana ostensibly for Honduran ports, those ports could document only $1,822 worth of the more $500,000 worth that left Havana.[28] An enormous amount of liquor was apparently leaving Havana for Honduras but failing to arrive there. Not only was there no port and no liquor at the port; some voyages, as detailed in ships' papers, also defied belief. According to the documents, ships left Havana, traveled to the designated port, and returned to Havana in a mere handful of days, voyages that simply were not possible. Even more suspicious, some ships returned to Havana claiming they traveled to Halifax, St. Pierre, or Miquelon in Canada, unloaded, encountered bad weather, and sought aid in a Honduran port, all in a few days. Such a trek was impossible. The only conclusion U.S. officials could draw was that Honduras was supplying smuggling ships with fraudulent clearance papers indicating they stopped in Honduran ports when in fact they never sailed anywhere near Honduras at all. Officials suspected that before they even left Havana, rum runners held official-looking papers, stamped with counterfeit stamps and sealed with counterfeit seals, indicating their cargo had been unloaded at its intended destination, usually Trujillo, Limón, Guanaja, or Iriona in Honduras.

Interviews with crew members added to their suspicions. Thomas Joseph Wiseman, a crew member aboard the *Artemis*, described one routine voyage. A seasoned sailor having completed sixteen voyages aboard rum-running ships, Wiseman told investigators that never once did his ship dock at the ostensible destination port listed on the ship's clearance papers. On one particular voyage in 1925, his ship departed from Havana with 4,400 cases of mixed whiskeys, with documents indicating it was headed for British Honduras. It proceeded directly to a point twenty miles off Timbalier Lighthouse on the Louisiana coast. Once there, a lugger approached, requesting delivery of 350 cases of liquor, prearranged with the cargo's owner for distribution in New Orleans. Other luggers soon followed, also purchasing cases of alcohol. After three weeks, the ship moved to forty-two miles off Grand Isle Light and anchored for another few days. The ship then returned to Havana, and the ship's master presented the counterfeit clearance papers to port authorities indicating it had unloaded its cargo in British Honduras.[29]

Smuggling outfits, independent captains, and charter operators, however, did not need to master the intricacies of obtaining foreign customs papers themselves. An indication of the high degree of organization in the smuggling business, wholesalers like Maurice Roud handled the matter for their customers. They maintained relationships with export brokers who arranged all the documents as part of their services and even paid any bribes required to "fix" lower-level officials who managed Havana's port. Indeed, business was so brisk in the smuggling trade that by 1926, two shipping agencies in Havana, one of them run by Domingo Prado, Mourice Roud's former employee, devoted their efforts exclusively to rum-running concerns. They provided comprehensive services to their clients, including "putting aboard liquor cargoes, arranging details at Havana Customs, supplying clearance papers and a dummy shipper [who would take delivery of the cargo], supplying fraudulent return papers from Honduran ports, and paying the small graft demanded by harbor officials." By 1927, officials confirmed that virtually all of the customs documents submitted by ships carrying liquor out of Havana were fraudulent.[30]

The process had become largely routine by the mid-1920s. A vessel in the rum fleet loaded liquor in Havana and cleared for either a Canadian or a tropical port. The ship then traveled to a point off the American coast and unloaded its cargo into "contact" boats from shore. Returning to Havana, the ship presented its forged customs papers from Honduras to the Cuban port authorities claiming that it was arriving "in ballast" from its Honduran destination, where its cargo had been unloaded. Cuban port authorities then returned the ship's bond. All of this took place in as little as four days, enabling the ship to begin the process again.[31] As smuggling out of Havana increased, American officials expressed continual frustration with the seeming unwillingness of Cuban officials to address what Americans believed were clear and obvious frauds. Cuban officials responded to American complaints by throwing up their hands and insisting there was little they could do; the ships were not violating Cuban law.

American officials pushed repeatedly for Cuban customs authorities to prevent smuggling ships from leaving port, but with little success. In the meantime, they focused their efforts on intercepting cargoes once they left Havana. With the papers of the rum fleet "in proper order," the staff at the

American consulate watched the movements of these vessels and reported "their comings and goings in the hopes that they might be seized by the Coast Guard cutters when the schooners entered the territorial waters of the United States."[32] Ship movements in and out of Havana harbor were no secret. The consulate assigned a staff member to visit the harbor every morning at 7:00 A.M. to determine any arrivals, departures, or loading. Authorities in Washington, D.C., received that information by cable within two hours. Eventually, however, as traffic increased, the consulate relied on the newspapers. The *Havana Post*, one of the English dailies, reported all shipping movements in the port, and the embassy transmitted its information to authorities in the United States. Henry Kime could thus report to his Coast Guard contact in Washington that on August 1, 1925, the Honduran schooner *Josephina* finished loading its 1,500 cases of liquor and had cleared for Trujillo, Honduras, with a suspected destination off the coast of Tampa. The British schooner *Fannie Prescott* left the harbor with 5,000 cases of mixed liquors, while the British schooner *Radio* was ready to leave with 2,000 cases on board. American officials hoped that Cuba could one day be convinced to enforce their own harbor regulations or at least recognize obvious frauds. If only they would, Henry Kime lamented, they could "knock the bottom out of the booze trade."[33]

With fraudulent papers aboard, rum runners left port and turned immediately toward the southern United States. Schooner captains were well aware that they faced prosecution under American Prohibition laws if they sought to unload their cargo within the territorial waters of the United States. There was, however, some disagreement as to how far from shore American jurisdiction extended. In diplomatic circles, territorial waters traditionally extended three miles from land. American law enforcement authorities could arrest boats unloading liquor or traveling toward shore within those three miles. Beyond that point, foreign vessels need not abide by American laws. To American authorities, rum runners' ability to lurk only three miles from shore, beyond the reach of American laws, was intolerable. Three miles was an easy jaunt for many boats, allowing them to travel out to rum schooners for liquor with virtual impunity. Their exchanges at sea were even visible from land if the weather conditions were right. In response, American authorities pushed to extend territorial jurisdiction to twelve miles from shore. After considerable diplomatic maneuvering, most countries, and especially Great Britain, accepted American enforcement of Prohibition within twelve miles or an hour's run from shore. And as bootleggers developed ever-faster boats, the confusion over the limits of territorial waters could spell freedom for the boat and crew in court.[34] The *Fannie Prescott*, for example, which left Havana with 5,000 cases of liquor, used uncertainty over distances at sea to its advantage when it was seized in 1925. Described as a two-masted "Gloucester" type schooner with a seventy-five-horsepower Fairbanks-Morse semidiesel engine, the *Fannie Prescott* led the Coast Guard on a chase in the waters off Sombrero Light, repeatedly shifting direction in an attempt to elude capture. When the crew of the *Fannie Prescott* was brought to trial, the defense capitalized on the uncertainty over whether the schooner was seized in U.S. territorial waters. Much of the cross-examination of Coast Guard personnel concerned the distance between the *Fannie Prescott* and Sombrero Light when the ship was finally seized and the distance both boats had traveled in relation to the light during the chase.[35] Despite the fact that the *Fannie Prescott* had sold all but a fraction of its 5,000-case cargo by the time it was boarded, the charges against the crew were dismissed. The court expressed uncertainty as to whether it was seized in U.S. territorial waters and cited little direct evidence that its cargo wound up on American shores.[36] Most rum runners, however, preferred to avoid the *Fannie Prescott*'s ordeal altogether. They kept their cargoes well outside territorial waters, waiting for their customers to venture out in contact boats for a load of liquor.

For smugglers, location was everything in avoiding interference from law enforcement. Even if they carried large cargoes of liquor, foreign vessels outside territorial waters and holding proper papers could not be seized by American authorities. It was no surprise that they conducted their business well outside territorial waters, often twenty or thirty miles off the coast. Thus the British schooner *Agnes Louise* was seized eight and a half miles offshore in July 1925 along with its 3,145 packages of liquor; after a guilty plea, the ship was sold for $315 and its cargo was destroyed. The ship *Madam* however, despite carrying more than 23,000 gallons of assorted alcohol, was released. Captured twenty miles off the coast of Florida, it fell outside U.S. territorial waters.[37] Eventually, treaties between the United States and several foreign countries allowed the U.S. Coast Guard to seize vessels outside territorial limits if the Coast Guard witnessed the schooner unloading its cargo of alcohol into contact boats that ventured out from shore. Captains of schooners like the *Cask* and the *Arsene J* could remain free from the clutches of American law enforcement only so long as there was no direct evidence their cargo was headed for the United States.[38]

Most of the American public carried only a dim awareness of debates about territorial waters or fraudulent clearance papers. They likely were aware of smuggling, though for many, their understanding of rum runners was quite sympathetic. The popular press described rum runners as "booze buccaneers," "modern pirates" who led lives of adventure "abaft the port beam!" The press regularly crowned various rum kings and recounted their success for readers; one reporter called one rum king "a hero — of a sort." Popular magazines like *Collier's* and *Scribner's* printed reporters' accounts of ride-alongs with rum runners and contact boats that emphasized the ready profit available to bootleggers.[39] Yet life for the crew aboard a rum runner was neither romantic nor glamorous; it often was downright dull. For ships leaving from Europe with cargoes of liquor to sell, the trip could last months. Alastair Moray's experience aboard the four-masted schooner the *Cask* lasted from September 1923 to August 1924. Recurring problems on the voyage lengthened the trip to eleven months. The ship detoured into friendly ports to repair an unreliable engine. Rough weather at sea destroyed sails, anchors, and cables, which also needed repair, causing additional delays.[40] Most voyages from Havana to the American coast and back were of considerably shorter duration. Officials estimated from customs papers that the *Fannie Prescott* made three voyages to the U.S. coast in July and August 1925. The *Radio*, which was reported to be fully loaded and ready to leave on August 1, returned "in ballast," having presumably delivered its cargo on August 18. The voyage of the *Arsene J* in 1926 lasted considerably longer. The ship left Havana on July 1 and traveled north ten days to a position off the coast of Boston. Unable to sell its cargo, the ship weighed anchor and sailed for six days farther north to Nova Scotia, where the owner of the ship and its cargo, Facundo Sardinas with his wife, met the ship. The ship stayed in port in Yarmouth for two weeks before setting sail for the Bahamas. En route, the ship was caught in a hurricane and lost its jibs and top sails. After another three weeks in Nassau for repairs, the ship sailed west, passing Havana, and anchored off New Orleans for about five weeks. The crew managed to sell some of their cargo before they were seized by a Coast Guard cutter, which attempted to tow them into New Orleans. Bad weather interfered, however, and the ship broke free from its tow in a storm. Two weeks later, it finally reached Puerto Mexico on its own, and the crew was paid for its troubles.[41]

Bad weather was a continual danger for ships even sailing in the warm waters of the West Indies. Schooners navigated through "dirty" or rough seas, "freshening" or strengthening winds, and as the *Arsene J* experienced, even hurricanes. Often there was little indication of coming weather other than the direction of the barometer. Ships regularly limped into port in Havana and elsewhere with the visible markers of a rough round of weather. Several never returned at all. The *Jose Luis* foundered near the Dry Tortugas and was eventually declared a hazard to navigation. The *Cayman* was lost off the coast of Mexico in a storm, taking its entire crew with it.[42]

Profit, the goal of rum-running, dictated life aboard ship. Most smugglers maximized the space on board ship for cargo, meaning crew quarters were rarely spacious or comfortable. Close quarters, rough seas, bad food, and even nips from bottles in the cargo made tempers short. Ships and crews continually contended with limited supplies of gasoline for engines, coal for cookstoves, fresh water, food, and perhaps most important to the crew, cigarettes.[43] Captains continually found they had to replace crew members who were fired, quit, or simply disappeared onshore when the ship docked for any reason. Alastair Moray described a virtual revolving door of crew members, many of whom proved unreliable or unsuited for life at sea or disappeared as soon as the ship docked. The near-constant turnover caused scrambles to find enough crew before the ship could set sail. Continual labor shortages, in fact, created the opportunity for undercover agents to infiltrate smuggling networks as crew. One undercover agent in Havana obtained employment as ship's mate on the *Varuna* in 1925. Another signed on as ship's cook for a voyage on the *Exploit*. He had no cooking experience whatsoever, let alone cooking in the small confines of a ship's galley. Desperation for crew members, however, made experience unnecessary. While the cook of the *Exploit* faced withering criticism of his culinary skills, the cook on Moray's ship was apparently little better. Exacerbating the lack of experience of some cooks was the lack of supplies on board ship. Fresh meat quickly went bad at sea, leaving the crew a steady if monotonous diet of salted pork and salted beef. This diet was occasionally interspersed with fish that found its way on board, from flying fish that literally leaped onto the deck to dolphin, cod, and a fish Moray referred to as "ling" caught by the crew. When the ship was actively selling its cargo, they might enjoy provisions, including fresh meat, that were brought from shore by the contact boats, but rarely did these treats last long.

Despite the monotony at sea, managing the ship and its cargo required continual attention. Captains put crews to work repairing winches and the various motors that helped raise and lower the anchors and the sails. The cargo also required preparation for sale. While many ships sold entire cases, loading the wooden boxes onto the boats of their customers, others dealt solely in smaller, easier to handle packages known as "hams." A ham usually consisted of five or six quart bottles of liquor packed in straw and sewn into a burlap sack. The shape of the resulting package led to its name. Hams were easier to handle and load into contact boats, though the bottles within them were more likely to break. When a package rattled, it was tossed aside to be opened and repackaged with six intact bottles. Hams also had another important advantage. When tossed overboard, hams sank. Cases tended to float when jettisoned during a chase, making them easily retrievable by the Coast Guard as evidence.[44] Repackaging bottles of liquor from cases into hams was a standard business practice. Mourice Roud always included burlap sacks and packing supplies with the cases of liquor he sold to his customers, though his customers frequently complained that he provided them at unconscionably inflated prices. After the cargo was loaded in cases in port, the crew repackaged the bottles into hams during the voyage, a tedious process referred to by one crew member as "sewing circle time."[45]

Time still passed slowly at sea, and crews creatively devised entertainments. Moray got into a splicing contest with another crew member, competing over who could join the finest line. He eventually won by splicing two ends of silk thread used for suturing.[46] Other crew members used empty bottles for target practice or tried to catch fish to improve their diet. Moray reported a series of relatively philosophical conversations with other crew members about religion, the afterlife, and the possibility of life on other planets. He also taught himself to play several instruments, one of which he crafted himself on board.[47] The ship's cargo, however, provided a continual temptation. Crew members saw access to an occasional bottle from the cargo as an expected perk of the job. The schooner's supercargo, who was responsible for managing the cargo and the proceeds from its sale, had to balance the need to keep the crew happy with the need to keep the crew sober enough to sail the ship. He also had to ensure that enough cases survived without being consumed to make the voyage profitable.[48]

Voyages may have been boring for the crew but they also could be dangerous, and hijackers presented the most serious concern. While most smuggling outfits established a network that extended from wholesalers like Mourice Roud to retail establishments across the United States, others sought a more direct method of obtaining inventory or profit: they stole it from other smugglers. Smuggling ships carried tens of thousands of dollars in cargo and, if they had sold their cargo, tens of thousands of dollars in cash, a tempting target for robbery. Rum runners well knew the potential dangers at sea. Realizing that they had little recourse with the law should they be hijacked, they prepared accordingly. Most ships were heavily armed. Scattered around the decks were automatic pistols, shotguns, and even machine guns. Gertrude Lythgoe described in detail the safety precautions taken by famed rum runner Captain Bill McCoy on his voyages. "No buyer was ever permitted in the cabin alone. Everyone aboard was armed, and no order was ever filled until the cash had been paid in advance of the loading."[49] Successful hijackings nonetheless occurred, usually documented not in the courts but in the reports of abandoned ships. The Coast Guard vessel CG-9054, for example, reported in 1931 that while patrolling in Florida, it came across two abandoned skiffs. Both skiffs still contained at least part of their illegal cargo — about 150 hams — but no crew was in sight. The Coast Guard vessel towed the skiffs to its base, holding several hams as evidence of the suspected hijacking.[50] The *Patricia M. Behman* was discovered off Long Island with a dragging anchor and decks splintered by machine-gun fire. Authorities speculated that hijackers had killed the captain and crew, stolen the $190,000 in proceeds the supercargo had recorded from selling the cargo, and then abandoned the ship. The *Hazel Herman* was more fortunate. The crew reportedly repulsed an attack by hijackers, but the ship was damaged and the captain was shot in the stomach during the struggle. The schooner was towed into Savannah by the Coast Guard cutter *Yamacraw* with a full load of liquor in its hold.[51] Fears of hijacking were so significant that for a ship in distress, even the Coast Guard might be a welcome sight. The crew of the *Shirin* were delighted to see the Coast Guard vessel *Vidette* pull alongside them after dark in 1922. The *Shirin* had sprung a leak, had six feet of water in the hold, and was dead in the water. The mate told Coast Guard officers that he "feared that if the news leaked out ashore amongst the Bootleggers, they would come out under cover of darkness and try to steal the cargo."[52] According to popular media, during Prohibition, coastal cities apparently reported an unprecedented number of bodies washing up onshore that they speculated were the casualties of battles between hijackers and rum runners at sea.

While hijackers represented a constant fear to smugglers, the Coast Guard was primarily a regular nuisance. Foreign rum runners generally avoided prosecution as long as they remained outside U.S. territorial waters. But they did nonetheless find patrolling Coast Guard cutters to be generally bad for business. If Coast Guard crews could not observe a rum runner unloading its cargo to boats headed for shore, they nonetheless lurked nearby to watch the boat's activities. Their very presence made it unlikely that customers would travel from shore to do business. At sea, smugglers preferred to avoid Coast Guard vessels entirely; they were easy to spot as a puff of smoke on the horizon six to seventeen miles away, depending on air quality and visibility. The appearance of a Coast Guard boat often was enough for the captain of a rum runner to weigh anchor and sail to more optimal locations, hoping the Coast Guard would not follow. Even if trailed by authorities, rum boats frequently eluded pursuers on the open water. Bad weather, poor visibility, the darkness of night, or even the smoke created by an unreliable engine burning oil often provided enough cover for a rum runner to avoid the Coast Guard. Rum runners used every trick they knew to escape. They obscured the ship's name and port of hail on the transom, making it difficult for Coast Guard crews to identify known smugglers who warranted close watching. They might carry several nameboards on board, hoping to confuse pursuers by changing the ship's name mid-voyage. Smuggling vessels sailed without running lights, which made them virtually invisible at night, leading the Coast Guard to coin the term "black ships" to refer to schooners engaged in rum-running. And if a rum runner could get far enough ahead of a revenue cutter even in daylight, it could disappear from view over the edge of the horizon and escape to sell its cargo elsewhere on the open sea.

The contact boats that traveled from shore to purchase liquor from rum runners, however, were more vulnerable. Contact boats were the primary means by which contraband liquor made its way from schooner to beach, and they were clear targets for seizure. For the Coast Guard, witnessing a rum runner unloading cargo over the side onto a contact boat provided unambiguous evidence that the cargo was destined for the American market and justified seizure of both boat and cargo. Rum runners and contact boats thus avoided conducting business when Coast Guard boats were within sight. Nevertheless, contact boats faced the greatest danger of seizure when they traveled back into U.S. waters toward shore with contraband liquor on board. Despite the risks, the potential for profit made even law-abiding boat owners willing to take the chance. The proceeds from running a boatload of liquor to shore could quickly outpace the money that small boat owners could earn by fishing, so the switch to bootlegging was tempting indeed. One man who had turned to bootlegging confided to a reporter that as a hard-working fisherman, he made between $4 and $5 a day. On a bad night running booze, he cleared $50. It was little surprise that so many boat owners along the coast worked their boats honestly by day and turned to bootlegging when the sun set. Indeed, at virtually every level in the liquor traffic, money was a primary motivation to participate in the trade. Arrested crewmen aboard rum runners professed regular occupations ranging from wholesale fish dealer to real estate agent, but they saw smuggling as a "way to make some money to get on my feet," as one smuggler told authorities.[53]

Smugglers only realized their profit, however, if they could successfully sell their cargo. Some schooners had prearranged and prepaid contracts to unload their cargo to designated contact boats. In these cases, the entire operation from wholesaler to retailer was planned from the outset. Schooner captains and onshore representatives developed elaborate schemes to recognize who should receive the liquor and transport it to shore. Some utilized codes; others used tokens such as torn currency and letters to indicate the contact boat was part of the enterprise. Most schooners also "sold over the side" to independent operators who made their way from shore to ship. Rum runners frequently anchored in the waters off the southern coast for weeks at a time to wait for customers to come to them. Once a contact boat reached the schooner, the buyer would accompany the captain into the main cabin, where the captain would produce an inventory of his cargo and samples of his fare. Currency would quickly change hands, and loading from deck to contact boat would begin with a shout from below. Part of the preference for sewing bottles into burlap-covered hams was that hams were more easily tossed, were less cumbersome to handle, and could be stowed quickly. If a Coast Guard boat was spotted, the alarm was given, ropes connecting the two vessels would be immediately slashed, and the contact boat would speed off. Usually it would return within a few days to retrieve the remains of its purchase.[54] More often, however, the loading proceeded without incident, and once the contact boat shoved off for shore, the transaction was complete.

Knowing they were vulnerable to seizure if they were in the midst of unloading, contact boats usually cast off and made a run for shore if the Coast Guard appeared. Unsurprisingly, speed was a highly desirable commodity, and boat owners willingly made modifications to achieve it. One pleasure yacht in New York was refitted with four Liberty motors of 460 horsepower each and an armored cabin.[55] One reporter on a ride-along with a contact boat near New York said that the craft, which could make thirty knots, could

Motorboat *My Fagela*, equipped with 3 Wright T-12 650 hp engines.
It could cruise at 35 mph with 700 cases of liquor on board (National
Archives and Records Administration, Photographs of Suspected
Rum Runners, U.S. Coast Guard, RG 26RR, 26-RR-133-1)

easily outrun a slow-moving government boat.[56] Most small contact boats
had advantages that made it possible for them to evade larger Coast Guard
cutters. Speed was one advantage; size was another. Because smaller boats
were more maneuverable and had a shallower draft, with enough head start
they could outrun larger Coast Guard ships and disappear in the shallow
inlets and mangrove banks that dotted southern beaches. Leery of running
aground in shallow waters, the Coast Guard boats could not follow. Bootleggers also used darkness to their advantage, conducting business at night
when possible, navigating without running lights, and unloading liquor onto
unlit beaches.

Because they transported liquor from rum runners through U.S. territorial waters, contact boats faced the greatest risk of seizure. Most of the
smuggling cases that appeared in federal courts along the southern coasts
stemmed from seizures of boats caught running liquor to shore. Smugglers
did what they could to avoid arrest. It was not uncommon for crews to attempt to eliminate the evidence by throwing their illegal cargo overboard,
as did three men from Monroe County, Florida. Unfortunately, they had

acted in full view of the Coast Guard officer who soon boarded their craft, and he also retrieved several cases as evidence. They were arrested and their motorboat was seized.[57] Efforts to jettison liquor were so widespread that southerners routinely walked the beaches looking for booze in the surf when they heard a smuggler had wrecked a boat or dumped cargo in an attempt to escape.[58] Those who could not escape faced possible conviction in federal district court. Local officials, for example, were probably suspicious of anything that the motorboat named *Home Brew* carried, but being captured with 132 cases of liquor near Pompano, Florida, made conviction of its owner more likely.[59] A smuggling operation in the mid-1920s was derailed when four contact boats were spotted by the Coast Guard. The group had arranged for the *Jose Luis* to transport 2,500 cases of assorted liquors, 300 cases of Old Dominion whiskey, 200 cases of Glenlivet Scotch whiskey, and 50 cases of champagne from Havana to the Timbalier Light and hoped to distribute the liquor in New Orleans. The boats were traveling back to the Mississippi River to store their illicit cargo in a dairy barn when they were caught.[60]

Those instances in which authorities interrupted landings revealed the reach of smuggling outfits along the southern coast along with the variety of spirits they provided. Some cargo was transported from beach to trucks or a railyard for transit north. Other cargo, maybe even from the same boatload, did not have far to travel, destined for drinking establishments or private purchase along the coast. The seized inventories of restaurant proprietors and soft drink stands in New Orleans indicated the tastes of the liquor market. Joe Masera, when he was arrested in February 1923, had an extensive collection of liquor that he sold through his restaurant on St. Louis Street in New Orleans. He carried Lawson, Louis Hunter, Atherton, Cedar Brooke, and Highland Green whiskeys, Gordon's gin, several kinds of wine, absinthe, champagne, and other unnamed assorted liqueurs. In court, he argued successfully that his premises were searched under an illegal warrant. When he was arrested again in April 1924, he had a similarly extensive collection of alcohol.[61] Albert Stander, the proprietor of a soft drink stand in Shell Beach in St. Bernard Parish, was arrested in October 1923 for possession of beer, wine, and Potio bitters, as well as seventy-six quarts of various liquors and twenty-three hams still bound in burlap containing their six bottles each. He was acquitted of the charges against him and demanded his liquor be returned to him. It was.[62] Other court cases described liquor being transferred from boat to barns along southern rivers; other smugglers used land-based travel, and some even utilized both. John Damonte, a well-known bootlegger in New Orleans, was arrested with members of his crew while attempting to load a fleet of trucks. They had already placed fifteen cases in a half-ton Ford truck, and two other Fords carried over twenty cases each. A Packard touring car and additional liquor sat behind one of the trucks waiting to be loaded. Each of the four men pled guilty and paid a $100 fine. A thousand miles away, two men near Key West unloaded 110 quarts of liquor from a skiff into their Chevrolet and proceeded from John Loews Dock to the intersection of Elizabeth and Greene Streets in Key West, where officers apprehended them. They too pled guilty and received a $100 fine.[63] The liquor might have been intended for local consumption or was on its way to the railyard for transit to more distant customers. Thomas Madden and Roger Pierce were apparently the leaders of an extensive conspiracy to transport imported liquor one case at a time to the city of Chicago using Pullman porters. They paid six Pullman porters between $7.50 and $15.00 per case to transport the whiskey on the Illinois Central Railroad in Pullman sleeper cars and deliver it to their compatriots in Chicago.[64] Another large group of conspirators used a similar business model near Jacksonville, Florida. There, the group stored liquor in a number of hotels in the area, including the Flagler Hotel, transported it to the train station in Jacksonville, and delivered it to Pullman porters, who transported the liquor three cases at a time to New York City and Washington, D.C. It was a model they used starting in 1921 and continued until 1924, when the group was arrested. By that time, they faced sixty-two counts against them.[65] Shipping liquor by rail, however, was not uncommon. Some smuggling organizations packed liquor into trunks for shipment from the coast to interior cities aboard express cars. It was a particular problem with rail traffic along the coast in Florida and Georgia and was maddeningly difficult for officials to detect. Until the late 1920s, railroads were reluctant to allow federal officials access to shipping records or to inspect railcars, and considerable amounts of smuggled liquor traveled north by train undetected.[66]

Rum-running's primary appeal, however, was profit. At heart, smuggling and bootlegging were about money, often substantial amounts of money. Like any business, bootlegging operations needed reliable financial mechanisms, and like any business, they often worked with local bankers to manage the cash flows required to purchase inventory and keep track of receivables. Many outfits maintained relationships with financial institutions to hold funds contracted for purchase until delivery; other banks even served as references for

Lumber truck stopped for attempting to smuggle
liquor, Tampa, Florida, 1927 (Courtesy of
the State Archives of Florida)

smuggling enterprises. One of the largest liquor and corruption trials in the
South revealed one organization's financial operations and the scope of their
business. This ring operated in Mobile, Alabama, and controlled the liquor
market in that city. It also regularly shipped loads of liquor to Chicago by rail.
The ring paid $5 per case in protection money to local officials and required
local retailers to sell only their product or risk raids by law enforcement.
The ring bought and sold liquor smuggled from Cuba and the Bahamas,
purchased in regular excursions to rum schooners like the *Artemis* hovering
outside U.S. territorial waters off the coast of Alabama. Each load of liquor
was substantial, worth between $10,000 and $20,000. The Mobile operation
was extensive, paying participants at every level from the main partners to
deliverymen, and it did so by checks drawn on regular accounts held at the

People's Bank of Mobile, whose president was a member of the smuggling ring. At trial, witnesses testified that loans from the bank provided the capital to obtain inventory, funded purchases from rum runners with money held in the ring's accounts, and used "New York exchanges"—a financial instrument similar to a cashier's check—to pay smugglers. Participants used the bank to deposit proceeds from liquor sales as well as their share of protection payments to officials and law enforcement. One witness even testified that proceeds from the sale of liquor were deposited into his personal account at the bank, which his wife then used for her regular housekeeping expenses and grocery purchases. The checks drawn out of the account at the People's Bank displayed the financial organization of the outfit. They showed payments for travel to Cuba by ferry, payments for telegrams, payments to railroad companies to transport liquor to Chicago, payments to Standard Oil Company, and payments to a local flour producer and fruit and produce company. Financial records even showed payment for the sewer service at the outfit's offices. They also detailed transactions between the ring's accounts at the People's Bank and three other local banks. The financial services provided by the bank made the operation of a large smuggling enterprise possible. Indeed, financially, it operated little differently from any business.[67] Until this particular business was disrupted by Prohibition agents brought in at the request of the local state's attorney, it was quite profitable.

As the Mobile ring's operations show, rum smuggling, even though illegal, was an international business. Successful operations managed their money and tried to maximize the laws of supply and demand; they worked to locate, train, and retain the skilled labor needed to be profitable. They also established business networks that stretched from Cuba across the South to markets in the rest of the country. According to one article, rum runners were less the romantic pirates depicted in popular media, but sober businessmen. They tended to be "mild" and "quiet," were unlikely to boast or swear, and focused on their work. When profits warranted, they looked to expand their operations, adding additional boats to run additional loads. Well-paid crewmen set out on their own once they had accumulated sufficient capital to buy a boat of their own. When they made enough money, they too might stay onshore and pay a crew to run the operation. Those crew members then would branch out on their own once they made enough money, and so the cycle would continue wherever profit and proximity to liquor converged.[68] Smuggling operations expanded because by the 1920s, railways and a growing network of roadways connected the southern coast to the rest of the country. Liquor that landed in Key West, Mobile, New Orleans, and countless places in between was loaded onto trucks or railcars to travel north or was unpacked at restaurants and soda stands across the South.

Utilizing well-traveled and well-known avenues of commerce as well as growing transportation routes linking the South to the rest of the country, liquor made its way from ports like Havana into the interior of the United States and to eager American customers. With the liquor trade legal in innumerable ports surrounding the United States and with a vast sea border that extended from Texas to Maine, smugglers recognized the potential profits the southern coastline presented in meeting virtually inexhaustible demand. In the process, thousands of dollars in economic activity fueled cities like Havana and lined the pockets of smugglers along the way. It was a well-organized business, with well-established transactions from wholesaler to customer. These entrepreneurs organized themselves soon after Prohibition became the law of the land and continued with a considerable degree of success until the repeal of the Eighteenth Amendment. But the enterprise did not exist unchallenged by authorities. In the face of a well-organized business, with supply chains extending across the country, government agencies developed equally well-organized, though perhaps less successful, methods of interdiction, and in the process expanded American law enforcement well beyond the nation's boundaries. The next chapter explores their efforts.

{ Chapter Two }

UNCLE SAM'S EFFORTS

✳

ESPITE HEARTY ASSURANCES that enforcing Prohibition would require little effort, the officials who would actually do the work knew almost immediately that they faced a near-impossible task. Soon after the Eighteenth Amendment passed, southern waters began to witness a burgeoning liquor traffic organized locally and abroad, and southern officials began to express their concern. J. F. C. Griggs, a customs collector in Tampa, made the difficulties clear to his supervisors a full six weeks before Prohibition even went into effect. Griggs was receiving reports from government officials in Florida, in the Bahamas, and in Cuba about the beginnings of a smuggling trade. "Dozens of vessels," he heard, made daily trips to Florida with liquor, and more whiskey was arriving on the east coast of Florida than there had been in years. "The Customs service," he wrote, "is absolutely helpless to prevent this smuggling." He reminded officials that the navy had ended its patrols of local waters at the end of World War I, and thus there were neither personnel nor boats available to keep smugglers from landing liquor on southern shores. More concerning, he pointed out that only five customs officers oversaw the nation's coastal borders between St. Augustine and Key West, a distance of some 500 miles. In his view, the Coast Guard was little better prepared. He reported that the Key West Coast Guard Station had but eight men, none of whom were familiar with the vessels or the waters of the Florida coast. Even worse, Griggs noted, when the Cuban secretary of the treasury cabled U.S. officials that a Cuban schooner had sailed for Miami with a load of liquor, the local Coast Guard officer replied that "he did not have a boat that was in running condition, and had only three gunners and three cooks available." "I am at a loss," Griggs stated, "to know what action to take to stop this illegal traffic."[1]

Griggs's letter conveys the concern among federal agencies as the start of Prohibition approached. When the Eighteenth Amendment was ratified, little real thought went into how to enforce it. When Congress created the enforcement infrastructure through the Volstead Act, it seriously under-estimated the magnitude of the task it would face. Temperance advocates and "drys," whether in or outside government, insisted that few resources would be needed. They cheerily assumed that once the initial disgruntlement about Prohibition had faded and existing stores of alcohol had disappeared, Americans would accept the law. Instead, a well-organized, persistent, and adaptive traffic in liquor soon developed that spanned from the southern coast and the waters that surrounded it to liquor producing and exporting islands like Cuba and the Bahamas to the south and Canadian sources of liquor to the north. The flow of liquor connected the coastal South to the rest of the nation and soon commanded the attention of the largest law enforce-ment effort by the government in the nation's history. Nevertheless, plans to prevent illegal importation of liquor from abroad were surprisingly sim-plistic and weakened by a lack of resources. The U.S. Customs Bureau, the U.S. Coast Guard, and the other agencies that would play significant roles in enforcement had neither the equipment nor the personnel needed to stop smuggling. Enforcement on the high seas along the entire eastern seaboard and Gulf Coast muddled along well into 1923, as disputes continued as to how and against whom federal authorities could and should enforce Prohibition. What was immediately clear, however, was that stemming the tide of illegally imported liquor and its distribution inland required the efforts of a number of federal agencies operating all along the nation's coast. Coordinating the work of the different agencies created continual frustrations that hampered enforcement overall. But at least theoretically, most officials agreed with a commonsense distribution of responsibilities developed in 1923. Much of the liquor arriving in the United States came by sea, giving the Coast Guard an outsized role in preventing smuggling "on the seas, the lakes or in the harbors of the United States, that is, on water." Its authority gave way to the Customs Bureau once water met land. The Customs Bureau's role was equally expan-sive, concentrated on the nation's "ports and borders, that is, on the docks, and on trains and automobiles entering the United States." Once goods had moved inside the nation's borders, the responsibilities for enforcement moved

General Lincoln C. Andrews (*left*) surveys the "war zone map" in the battle against smuggling, 1925 (Library of Congress, Prints and Photographs Division, photograph by Harris and Ewing; reproduction number LC-DIG-hec-44983)

to the Prohibition Bureau, a division within the Department of the Treasury.[2] A revised strategy for interagency cooperation appeared under General Lincoln C. Andrews, who oversaw Prohibition enforcement from 1925 to 1927.[3] Andrews's newly created Office of Foreign Control coordinated the efforts of the State Department and foreign governments to prevent shipments of liquor from leaving foreign ports. It also distributed intelligence to the Coast Guard when rum runners set sail with liquor cargoes aboard, allowing the Coast Guard to intercept shipments before they landed on the U.S. coast. The hope was that the efforts of the Office of Foreign Control, using diplomatic and other "proper" channels to obtain information, would "embarrass, handicap and render unprofitable the business of liquor smuggling from abroad."[4]

The Coast Guard's growing fleet throughout Prohibition would be distributed at nineteen Coast Guard divisions around the continental United States. Fourteen of those bases extended from the northern tip of Maine, down the eastern seaboard, around the tip of Florida, and west to the southern tip of Texas. While the Coast Guard also engaged in antismuggling activities on the West Coast, far more of its resources were concentrated, along with the bulk of the nation's population, on the eastern side of the country. The Coast Guard Intelligence Division, run by Commander Charles S. Root, would "collect, sift, classify, file and keep ready for immediate use . . . the latest obtainable intelligence concerning all movements of liquor ships and personnel engaged in smuggling at home and abroad."[5] Seizures of smuggling vessels and crew required the cooperation of several different federal agencies. When a Coast Guard boat made a seizure, the Coast Guard immediately notified Washington and turned the boat, along with any evidence, over to the collector of customs. The Bureau of Customs controlled jurisdiction over "every foot of land or water border of the United States" and formally enforced the tariff, trade, and other laws prohibiting entry of liquor and other illegal goods, like narcotics, into the United States. Local customs agents reported the seizures in their jurisdictions and cataloged all evidence that came into their possession. Their superiors then handed cases over to the appropriate U.S. Attorney for prosecution in the federal courts.

Ideally, enforcement plans promised seamless cooperation. In the event of a seizure, the Coast Guard would notify the local collector of customs, who would make contact with the U.S. Attorney and the local Prohibition agent, who would work with the Coast Guard to collect evidence. The Prohibition Bureau thus entered the case after the Customs Bureau and focused on obtaining evidence about the transportation and distribution of smuggled liquor within the United States. The Prohibition Bureau would "secure information and evidence of these various activities; to use the *information* to effect the elimination of the traffic, and to use the *evidence* to prosecute and punish those conducting it and responsible for it."[6] Whether the case was handled by the customs agent or the Prohibition agent, both would assist in the prosecution. The enforcement of prohibition laws thus required the cooperation of several agencies, agencies that were not always willing to work together. In 1927, the hope was that clearly communicating distinct lines of authority would lead to "harmony," ensure efficiency, and presumably end with victory in the Rum War. The creation of a ten-page statement about cooperation seven years into the Noble Experiment suggests that the obstacles to cooperation were indeed difficult to overcome.

At the same time, however, lawmakers envisioned Prohibition enforcement as a partnership between local and state law enforcement, on one hand,

and the federal government, on the other. Again, here too, the cooperation seemed straightforward. The federal government would concentrate its efforts on "control and the prevention of unlawful importations, while the States would naturally use their constituted police power for local enforcement in the respective jurisdictions."[7] Cooperation at this level would prove to be difficult as well. One state, Maryland, refused to pass concurrent Prohibition laws, which meant its law enforcement personnel had no authority to enforce federal Prohibition laws. Other states passed prohibition laws but allocated woefully few funds to enforce them, again tying the hands of state forces. Indeed, one contemporary source alleged that all forty-eight states allocated less than one fourth of the budget to Prohibition that they spent on maintenance of their monuments and parks. Cooperation worsened as Prohibition continued. Some states, including Alabama in the late 1920s, voted to cut budget appropriations for Prohibition enforcement entirely. Yet from the beginning, the role of the states in Prohibition enforcement was never clear. While the Eighteenth Amendment gave states "concurrent power" to enforce Prohibition, there was little agreement as to what that meant. There was absolutely no debate about state contributions to enforcement, which might have offered some guidance, as Congress considered the amendment. Some argued that "concurrent power" allowed states to continue to enforce their own liquor laws; other states insisted that it allowed states to help enforce the federal laws. All states, however, seemed to agree that the language did not impose any obligation to enforce the amendment. In any event, state and local forces might very well have been of little use. Lack of funding for local enforcement meant paltry levels of help in some states. And in many states, corruption among the very officials assigned to enforce Prohibition laws rendered their efforts less than worthless.[8] Federal government agencies and services like the Coast Guard thus faced uncertain assistance at the state and local levels when they caught suspected smugglers.

Regardless of the particular permutations of policy and the contributions of states, the Coast Guard, from the beginning, held primary authority to prevent the smuggling of illicit liquor in the nation's coastal waters and, eventually, well beyond them. This represented a considerable increase in the Coast Guard's responsibilities, and it turned its attention from lifesaving and navigation laws to the front lines of law enforcement. Only formally organized in 1915 when the Revenue Cutter Service and the U.S. Life Saving Service merged, the Coast Guard had yet to fully find its purpose when the United States went dry. During World War I, the U.S. Navy absorbed this fledgling agency. Its cutters spent the conflict either escorting convoys across the Atlantic or patrolling European waters around Gibraltar and the Mediterranean searching for enemy submarines. After the armistice, some suggested the Coast Guard should remain part of the navy, but it was eventually returned to the Department of the Treasury in 1919, with Commandant William F. Reynolds at the helm. When the Department of the Treasury received primary authority over the enforcement of Prohibition, fighting the Rum War became the Coast Guard's primary mission until 1933. The law enforcement mandate from Prohibition, however, continued, shaping the scope of Coast Guard activity thereafter.[9]

The Coast Guard initially focused surprisingly little of its efforts on stopping smuggling. While the U.S. Treasury reported that Prohibition enforcement was increasing customs activities, Coast Guard activity was not even mentioned. In June 1921, the Coast Guard reported that it assisted over 14,000 people in distress and boarded 18,000 vessels as part of its routine duties. Prohibition, however, apparently caused no significant increase in Coast Guard operations despite reports of seizures of some smuggling vessels. Regardless, little doubt existed that the Coast Guard was ill prepared for the task of patrolling for contraband. When Prohibition went into effect, the Coast Guard operated with a paltry fleet of some fifteen armed cutters, approximately fifteen smaller cutters, a small fleet of harbor cutters and launches, and some small craft and what were known as "surfboats" used at lifesaving stations around the country.[10] This fleet was laughably short of the vessels needed to patrol the thousands of miles of coastline that beckoned smugglers. By 1923, when the extent of the smuggling traffic had become evident and the nation's southern coastline was proving to be as porous as that of New Jersey, New York, and Massachusetts when it came to liquor, calls sounded to increase federal appropriations for law enforcement.

A 1923 report on national issues related to Prohibition laid out some of the concerns. "Four years of prohibition have both produced highly beneficial results and demonstrated the difficulty of enforcement." The report noted that Congress had appropriated only $8.25 million for Prohibition enforcement for the entire 1924 fiscal year, which provided for some 700 federal administrators, the operation of directorates in the states, and a field force of 1,522 agents. But there was little doubt such a force would be wholly inadequate. Acknowledging that the unlawful importation of alcohol remained the most persistent problem, the report called for additional vessels, cabin cruisers, motorboats, and other equipment that would target smugglers at sea. It also pleaded for additional personnel and additional funds of "not less than $20,000,000." The amount was eye-popping, especially compared with the initial $8.25 million that Congress had set aside for enforcement overall.[11] Secretary of the Treasury Andrew Mellon requested additional money to add 3,000 more men to the Coast Guard at a cost of some $28 million. Commandant Reynolds also requested that Congress appropriate sufficient funds, but he focused his request on equipment, asking to add 20 cutters, over 200 cabin cruisers, and almost 100 smaller vessels to his fleet. Such massive requests were well beyond the willingness and the ability of Congress to provide. Faced with a growing smuggling problem and noting the considerable time needed to build ships, Congress compromised, approving an increase in personnel and the transfer of decommissioned and mothballed naval destroyers to expand the Coast Guard's fleet. It increased funding for the Coast Guard by about half the amount that Reynolds and Mellon requested. Eventually, 20 destroyers, 203 cruisers, and 100 small boats would be added to the Coast Guard fleet at a cost of $14 million, representing the largest expansion of Coast Guard forces in the organization's relatively brief history.

Acquiring the kinds of seagoing vessels needed to keep up with smugglers was a primary consideration for the Coast Guard over the course of Prohibition. Two new categories of boats joined the Coast Guard fleet. Seventy-five-foot patrol boats, known colloquially as "six-bitters," were designed specifically with Prohibition enforcement in mind. With a speed of 17 miles per hour and a crew of eight, they could conduct extended missions 20 to 30 miles out to sea. Six-bitters kept cramped quarters for the crew, including a cook and a captain, and each tour was four days long.[12] Smaller 38-foot picket boats, designed for speed (up to 24 miles per hour if they were built without a cabin), chased the contact boats operating closer to shore. Eventually the Coast Guard also added larger 100-foot and 125-foot patrol boats, as well as 165-foot cutters. By the late 1920s, the Coast Guard had grown considerably, adding numerous vessels and expanding from just under 6,000 personnel in 1924 to more than 10,000 by the late 1920s.[13]

Despite the ever-more-apparent challenges to enforcement, the Department of the Treasury nonetheless expressed cheery confidence that the Coast Guard would be well able to prevent smuggling. In April 1924, as the federal government was still developing an overall plan for enforcement on the high seas, F. C. Billard, the new commandant of the Coast Guard, sought to buck up his troops. Projecting confidence in the Coast Guard's ability, the commandant called on the proud, if short, history of the Coast Guard and the spirit of its lifesaving men to convince his force to embrace the role of the organization in Prohibition enforcement. "It is not for us in the Coast Guard to question the wisdom of any law or order," he reminded them, acknowledging any possible dislike of Prohibition. "It is for us to obey, faithfully and loyally." He cautioned them that bootleggers might tempt them and that they would be "subjected to all sorts of insidious propaganda and influences and, indeed, attempts may be even made to bribe you," but he urged them to hold fast to their honor. "Pay no attention whatever to propaganda or talk intended to injure your morale, and if any man attempts to bribe you, treat him immediately as you would any man who has grossly insulted you." Reminding his forces that they would do well to avoid consorting with the enemy, he warned of grave consequences to those who succumbed to temptation. There would be, he insisted, "no room for traitors in the Coast Guard." He concluded by calling his men to render "zealous, efficient, and devoted service" in keeping with their splendid traditions. It was a pep talk to service, rousing in its call to duty and stern in its dismissal of those who failed to uphold the reputation of the Coast Guard. Unsurprisingly, it glossed over the very real challenges the Coast Guard faced.[14]

Preventing the illegal importation of alcohol, however, was an immensely complex task, well beyond the capability of the number of boats or personnel assigned to patrol the high seas. Even the extent to which the Coast Guard's authority to enforce this peculiarly American law extended out from shore was no simple matter. As Coast Guard officers soon learned, enforcement was a matter of both legal authority and international law. From the moment Prohibition went into effect, debate raged about the extent of American jurisdiction over the high seas. Most nations concurred that every country maintained the right to enforce its laws up to three miles out to sea from its coastline at low tide. Within that three-mile band of waters around American shores, according to this understanding, the Coast Guard had every right to board and search vessels for illegal liquor. But by the summer of 1921, the smuggling of liquor from nearby islands like Cuba and the Bahamas was a noticeable problem. Smuggling ships, aware of the limits on territorial waters, knew not to travel within the three-mile limit; they happily lingered just outside the three-mile line and let other boats transport their cargo to shore. Yet to Prohibition proponents, who bemoaned the presence of smugglers operating openly within sight of shore, this accepted tenet of international law was absolutely intolerable. They demanded that the federal government go after smugglers who used the three-mile limit to their advantage. After several notorious and contested seizures of British ships, the U.S. government sought to refine its policy toward seizures at sea, walking a fine line between adhering to accepted international law and not offending the vocal Prohibition zealots in Washington. Citing a precedent from 1888, it authorized the Coast Guard to seize vessels beyond the three-mile limit if that vessel's equipment — the dinghies and small boats most schooners carried — transported illicit liquor to shore. The extension of the ship's own equipment within the three-mile limit by proxy allowed the U.S. government to claim that the ship itself was within American territorial waters. Under this policy, smugglers faced legal consequences in U.S. courts if their crew or equipment traveled within the three-mile limit to unload cargo, even if the schooner itself stayed outside.

While this policy, because it better respected international law, appealed to the State Department, to dry advocates, it limited the Coast Guard's ability to seize smuggling vessels to only those boats that landed their own liquor. It did nothing to target smugglers who relied on contact boats from shore to unload their cargo and still limited enforcement to a three-mile limit. Supporters instead argued that an earlier precedent allowed seizure of foreign vessels up to twelve miles from shore if evidence showed that cargo was headed for American shores, whether or not the ship's own equipment was used to land it. While this approach was more to the liking of those who sought the most rigorous enforcement possible, it nonetheless violated accepted tenets of international law. Congress sought to give the twelve-mile limit more force by passing the Tariff Act of 1922, which authorized the Coast Guard to search and seize any vessel and its cargo within a twelve-mile limit whether or not evidence existed that the vessel was illegally unloading its cargo. The State Department disagreed with this effort, wanting to confine enforcement to only those instances in which a ship's own equipment brought liquor to shore. In pushing such a position, however, the State Department asked the Coast Guard to ignore countless ships suspected of carrying cargoes of liquor. As Rum Rows — the fleet of smuggling schooners hovering outside U.S. territorial waters selling their illegal wares to customers who traveled out from shore — became ever-more visible near metropolitan areas like New York City, Boston, New Orleans, and Mobile, the debates over the policies of enforcement against smuggling intensified. To Prohibition's supporters, any enforcement limit, whether three or twelve miles, seemed both arbitrary and counterproductive. A limit based on distance from shore merely advertised the point at which floating markets in liquor could begin.[15]

Faced with an inability to enforce its own laws and conceding that it could only do so with the assistance of foreign governments, the U.S. government finally resolved the matter through international treaties. These diplomatic agreements allowed foreign ships to maintain the liquor laws of their own countries while also enabling the Coast Guard to target vessels engaged in smuggling. Starting with the treaty with Great Britain and followed by similar agreements with Norway, Germany, Sweden, Denmark, Italy, Panama, France, and the Netherlands, foreign governments agreed to permit the Coast Guard to search vessels hovering up to twelve miles from shore in exchange for allowing foreign passenger ships to bring their own liquor stores under seal into U.S. territorial waters. By 1924, the Coast Guard adopted a policy to enforce Prohibition twelve miles from shore and to target contact boats that traveled to hovering ships to obtain liquor. Eventually, the twelve-mile limit was reconfigured, allowing the Coast Guard to search and seize ships suspected of liquor smuggling that were operating within an hour's run from shore as determined by the smuggling vehicle's estimated top speed.[16] The Coast Guard was less than pleased with the change, however. It required Coast Guard vessels to establish a vessel's speed during chase, not just its location at the time of seizure. Fuzziness in either speed or location measure allowed defense lawyers to contest a ship's seizure in court. As Intelligence Officer Charles Root dryly noted, "I might add that this is of no assistance whatever, but is considered a handicap."[17] The limit based on one hour's run from shore would remain in force with two additional modifications. The Coast Guard could board and seize vessels first identified within the twelve-mile limit that ran beyond the limit to elude Coast Guard pursuit. Subsequent capture by the Coast Guard, even if it occurred well outside the twelve-mile limit, was legitimate. This doctrine of "continuous" or "hot pursuit" resulted in numerous seizures on the seas surrounding the eastern and Gulf coasts of the United States. The second provision allowed for search and seizure if there was clear evidence that the rum runner was unloading cargo onto contact boats destined for American shores, provided, of course, that the Coast Guard could overtake and board the rum runner in question.

In August 1924, the Coast Guard began to record its overall efforts through weekly Notes on the General Situation. The first such report laid out the legal parameters the Coast Guard used to patrol the nation's coasts, as treaties made enforcement less clouded by diplomatic and legal disputes.[18] By 1924, the report noted that tariff laws extended U.S. authority twelve miles from shore, while the provisions of the Volstead Act extended it three miles. Indeed, the Coast Guard noted that it preferred smuggling ships not be cited for violations of the Volstead Act, since it classified smuggling violations as misdemeanors, with a penalty of six months in jail and a $500 fine. Penalties for violations of tariff laws were more stringent, and most smuggling cases in federal courts in the South charged captains and crews with those violations. The Coast Guard possessed the authority to board and search any American vessel at any time and any foreign boats within an hour's run from shore. It also had the right to board and search vessels outside the twelve-mile limit given evidence that the ship had sent its cargo to shore on smaller boats, even if those boats were not connected to the ship. In short, the Coast Guard was confident that its "authority was unquestionable" up to twelve miles out provided there was evidence that cargo was headed to shore.[19] Once that cargo was within the three-mile limit, the Coast Guard could assume that the cargo had been illegally smuggled into the United States. By 1924, then, not only had the U.S. Coast Guard received new law enforcement authority in the waters surrounding the entire nation, but that authority extended well beyond limits previously established by international law.

While diplomats discussed international law on the high seas, while the State Department and the Prohibition Bureau argued over enforcement at sea, and while drys and wets across the nation argued over the very merits of the law itself, the Coast Guard patrolled the nation's waters in search of smugglers, adding to its regular duties of aiding vessels in distress and enforcing the laws of navigation. Coast Guard ships routinely tracked, trailed, boarded, and seized boats suspected of illegally importing liquor from abroad into the United States. Crews sought to apply the laws of territorial waters to the best of their understanding, while perpetually grumbling about their inadequate resources. The Coast Guard tallied the number of black ships in its weekly Notes on the General Situation. As of 1924, the Coast Guard kept an eye on over 300 ships suspected of participating in the smuggling trade; this number, though it would decrease, stayed at approximately 240 vessels through the late 1920s. Not all of these ships hovered off the American coast at any one time, however. The number of vessels anchoring offshore with stores of liquor to sell was usually lower, running from as many as sixty-five ships to numbers in the teens and twenties as Coast Guard patrols intimidated smugglers. The rest of the suspected black ships, to the extent their locations were even known, were either in port loading another cargo or traveling to or from a selling point offshore. Together, these records sketch the ebb and flow of smuggling. Numbers of boats anchored offshore increased around the holidays, especially Christmas but also Easter, and decreased after announcements of enforcement offensives by the Coast Guard. During the worst of winter weather in the Northeast, smuggling ships often headed to more hospitable waters to the south. The tallies of rum runners also indicated the primary markets for liquor on the eastern seaboard and Gulf Coast. Hovering ships concentrated off Cape Cod and the entrances to New York City. The numbers fell off southward, with fluctuating numbers off the southern coast and in the Gulf of Mexico. While the numbers of boats hovering off the southern coast never neared the numbers located off New York or New Jersey, black ships also seemed to be more invisible in southern waters. The report for the week ending August 22, 1925, noted the movements of three smuggling ships from Cuba off the coast of St. Augustine, Florida. The report explained that sightings off the southern coasts were unusual, even though the Coast Guard received numerous reports from Havana about the smuggling trade centered there. "This is a rare incident," the report noted. "Few seagoing Blacks have ever been seen actually hovering off the Florida East Coast and the report of the 295 [a Coast Guard ship] is a complete confirmation of the information from Havana, the accuracy of which was doubted at the time." The author then went on to recommend that the Coast Guard contingent at Base Six near Ft. Lauderdale, Florida, should cruise the area as much as possible.[20]

The day-to-day effort to prevent smuggling occurred on board the boats of the Coast Guard in the seas surrounding the United States. In the early days of enforcement, when rum runners cheekily anchored in packs outside the three-mile limit, Coast Guard boats established a presence that they hoped would deter liquor sales and enable them to chase down and capture boats that sought to carry cargo toward shore. Rum runners, faced with a lurking Coast Guard presence, simply weighed anchor and moved to a more isolated site. After the imposition of the twelve-mile limit in 1925, better cooperation across federal agencies, and the Coast Guard's greater success in seizing suspicious craft, rum runners sought to elude capture by staying many miles offshore. Coast Guard boats would then search the seas off the coastline for smaller boats acting suspiciously. For members of the

Coast Guard, Prohibition enforcement meant long days at sea scouring the horizon for boats that might be involved in smuggling. A 1921 report from the commander of the Coast Guard cutter *Arrow* conveys a typical day of patrolling waters along the west coast of Florida. After having heard that smugglers intended to land a cargo of silk, whiskey, and immigrants from Cuba, the collector of customs notified the Coast Guard and asked that they go out on patrol. With the *Arrow* incapacitated by a broken gas line, the crew arranged to use the local naval reserve's sub-chaser. The crew left Tampa at noon and proceeded to the mouth of the Manatee River, having heard that the smugglers intended to land cargo either up the river or at Anclote Light. They then spotted "two small gasoline boats" acting suspiciously. The Coast Guard crew gave chase until the two boats escaped into shallow shoals where the sub-chaser could not follow. They changed heading and ran two miles up the Manatee River, found nothing, and returned to the mouth of the river to continue their search. Again, no luck. The crew then headed out to Egmont Key, through the South Pass, and on to Anclote Light, arriving after eight hours on the water. They spotted several boats, which they boarded and searched, belonging to sponge divers and fishermen. After spending the night in the vicinity of the light, they headed for home, finally docking after more than thirty hours on the water in a largely unsuccessful search.[21] While this particular voyage occurred early in Prohibition, it reflected voyages throughout the era.

Not long after Rum Rows appeared outside U.S. territorial waters, the Coast Guard established techniques designed to prevent the landing of illegal cargoes onshore. Because the Coast Guard could intervene only when evidence indicated a rum runner had unloaded its cargo onto a smaller boat headed to shore, crews hoped either to witness the transferring of cargo from ship to contact boat or to prevent it in the first place. "Picketing" or "trailing" sought to do just that. Destroyers and cutters took to sea for days at a time, patrolling around suspected rum runners, identifying suspicious ships, watching for the approach of contact boats, and where possible, boarding and seizing vessels. As one magazine described it, "Round and round the old ship, deep-loaded with a hundred thousand dollars' worth of contraband, scuttles a trim little seventy-five-foot patrol boat keeping a lonely sentry." Along with six-bitters, the Coast Guard clustered picket boats with destroyers acting as "mother ships," provisioning the picket boats to expand their range. This arrangement allowed destroyers to anchor far offshore outside well-known loading spots for liquor, while the picket boats pursued any vessels that sought to slip through. Destroyers cruised and notified picket boats when a contact boat tried to make a run for shore with a load of liquor. Picket boats might even lurk in shallow bays and inlets ready to give chase when a boat sought to land its illegal cargo. As one magazine colloquially explained, "The large vessels are the watchdogs; the smaller greyhounds are for the chase." It was labor-intensive work and required continued diligence on the part of a Coast Guard crew for the method to be effective. The Coast Guard's mere presence around suspected rum runners often deterred business enough for smugglers to try elsewhere. In January 1926, for example, the Coast Guard reported that the number of black ships picketed at a single location hovered from a low of four to a high of ten for a seven-day period. At times, the Coast Guard could even boast success. In August 1926, the commander of Coast Guard Intelligence included a report from a boatswain in Tampa who cheerily relayed the success of his picketing effort. He noted that the schooner *F. A. Maria* returned to Havana with its entire cargo still in its holds. The boatswain described why: "I kept a boat between this schooner and the shore until it became monotonous. I then boarded her and gave the master one hour to start home or start for Tampa. He chose home."[22]

The relative success of picketing methods forced many rum runners to change their tactics. The simplest evasion was to move their operations farther out to sea, essentially dispersing Coast Guard boats over more miles of water, making each individual rum runner less likely to be discovered and tracked. This was the most popular method, and one that broke up the Rum Rows near shore that characterized the early days of Prohibition. The Coast Guard reported with evident pleasure, "The Blacks have learned that they can no longer hover in the areas and do business. The only remaining method is either to remain far off shore and load American vessels, come in themselves or have American vessels go to American ports for liquor."[23] Other rum runners tried different methods. Some ships pulled far off the coast during the day and then came closer to shore under the cover of darkness to provide easy access for contact boats from shore.[24] No doubt a goodly number of masters of rum schooners merely crossed their fingers, hoping that they could sight a Coast Guard boat before the boat sighted them. Most of the time, however, rum runners merely needed to outlast the Coast Guard boat before selling their wares, waiting until the Coast Guard boat gave up and went elsewhere or returned to shore.

Suspected rum runner being trailed by the 125-foot patrol boat *Pulaski*, 1930
(National Archives and Records Administration, Photographs of Suspected
Rum Runners, U.S. Coast Guard, RG 26RR, 26-RR-58-1)

The Coast Guard well knew, however, that it had nowhere near the ability
to constantly picket every boat suspected of participating in the smuggling
trade. There were simply too many smugglers, contact boats, and miles of
coastline where they could operate. Coast Guard vessels also scouted the
waters between the United States and the primary foreign sources of liquor,
from Halifax and St. Pierre in the North and the Bahamas and Cuba in the
South, hoping to identify and disrupt rum runners well before they could
sell their cargoes. Each destroyer was responsible for an enormous amount
of coastline. The Coast Guard Cutter *Yamacraw*, for example, was the only
large vessel assigned to patrol the entire 450 miles between Savannah, Georgia, and Key Largo, Florida.[25] It was the duty of these ships to stop and board
vessels that they considered to be black ships that were already well known
participants in the smuggling trade, or whose suspicious movements or loading of cargo in a foreign port had been passed on to the Coast Guard. They
frequently stopped and boarded these vessels looking for irregularities in the

ship's manifest or clearance papers, or other violations of navigation laws that would allow them to seize the ship.

Whether it occurred after an extended period of picketing, a high-speed chase, or a chance encounter, boarding and searching a vessel could be dangerous business. The Coast Guard often described smugglers as "desperate" and thus prepared for resistance (which only rarely materialized), but it also knew that searches needed to follow recognized maritime laws if they were to obtain evidence that could be used in court. The Coast Guard established a standard procedure for identifying itself and asserting its authority and using escalating force to "overhaul" a vessel or "bring a boat to." Hailing a vessel initially meant gaining its attention using signals from a megaphone or by repeated blasts of a boat's whistle. If such efforts went "unheeded," the Coast Guard was authorized to "fire a gun as a signal to stop. If the vessel does not bring to after the Coast Guard pennant or ensign has been hoisted and a gun has been fired as a signal, the commanding officer of the Coast Guard craft may fire at or into said vessel."[26] In most cases, the initial shots were blanks, and live rounds were first directed "across the bow" or directly into the water in front of the boat in the direction in which it was headed. Once the vessel was finally stopped, a commissioned officer wearing only a sidearm could board the vessel and examine the ship's papers and cargo.[27] In 1921, Commanding Officer H. S. Browne Jr. of the Coast Guard cutter *Cygnan* reported events that led to the boarding and seizure of the smuggling schooner *Thritie* that illustrate the methods of hailing and boarding suspected vessels. The *Cygnan* left its Key West base at about 2:00 in the afternoon, proceeding along the reef until the early evening, when it spotted a suspicious vessel one mile east of Sombrero Light. The *Cygnan* changed course, increased to full speed, and headed for the small schooner. The *Thritie*, however, changed course and attempted to "dodge over the shoals." The *Cygnan* fired a blank shot before it noticed that the *Thritie* had run aground. Several Coast Guard men boarded the craft and were told the boat carried a cargo of gasoline. The men noticed, however, that the hatches of the *Thritie* had been nailed down. After running a line between the two craft to dislodge the *Thritie* from the shoals, they brought it alongside the *Cygnan*. After forcing open the hatches, they found a load of ninety-one cases of cognac and other liquors in the hold. Placing the crew under arrest, the *Cygnan* proceeded to tow the *Thritie* back to Key West, arriving in the wee hours of the morning. After placing the crew in the county jail, they delivered the liquor to the deputy collector of customs.[28]

Similar actions produced the seizure of the motorboat V-2774. The Coast Guard patrol boat CG-220 reported sighting two suspicious motorboats while on patrol. The CG-220 chased the first at high speed and sounded its horn repeatedly, but the boat failed to slow. The CG-220 fired three blank warning shots from its one-pounder gun, followed by three "service shots" fired approximately 100 yards from the boat. After the boat changed course, the CG-220 opened fire; but the boat never stopped, and the Coast Guard crew gave up the chase. A half-hour later, the CG-220 encountered another suspicious boat. Again the horn was sounded, and three warning shots were fired. Again the boat refused to stop even after three service shots from the one-pounder. Again the CG-220 opened fire on the boat and fired thirty-seven shots. The second boat, however, thought better of making a run for it and allowed itself to be boarded. While the search revealed some evidence that the boat was involved in smuggling liquor — the crew found burlap and straw used to tie quart bottles into hams strewn across the deck — it was not enough for arrest. Instead, the two men on board were brought to shore for navigation violations, specifically failing to heed a whistle while under way.[29] Another Coast Guard crew patrolling near the St. Augustine inlet gamely gave chase to a suspicious vessel, using "all possible means of sounding klaxon, and the waving of sombrero signal flags, to bring the felling vessel to, but without avail." At that point, the Coast Guard boat fired six blank shots from its one-pounder guns, followed by live rounds, "all of which were fired well clear of the vessel, and intended only to bring the vessel to." Throughout the chase, the crew observed the men on the other vessel throwing what appeared to be sacks of contraband overboard. Committed to the chase, the Coast Guard crew did not stop to retrieve any of the jettisoned packages. After an hour's chase, the fleeing vessel was beached, and the men on board leaped over the side, running for the sand dunes and the surrounding foliage. The Coast Guard boarded the beached vessel and found a case of assorted liquors as well as a single ham containing twelve pints of reserve whiskey similar to what they would recover from the surf. The vessel and cargo were taken into custody; the men on board escaped.[30]

Other seizures were more successful, though their descriptions were considerably less dramatic. The British schooner *Atwood W. Carson*, seized about twenty-five miles offshore from the mouth of the Mississippi River, for example, resulted in the forfeiture of the ship, fines for the crew of $1,550, and the destruction of its 2,100 bags of assorted liquor. In early April 1926, the *Madam*, formerly the *Island Home*, was seized off Egmont Key in Florida

Deck of the *Marion Adams* after seizure by the Coast Guard near Barataria
Bay, 1925 (Erik Overbey Collection, The Doy Leale McCall Rare Book
and Manuscript Library, University of South Alabama)

by the *Saukee*. The *Empress* was seized in 1925 twenty-six miles off the coast
of Miami. It was ostensibly bound from Bimini to Havana with a stated load
of fifty cases of liquor. The Coast Guard crew that spotted it noted that it had
more than 150 cases in its hold and only enough fuel to get from Bimini to the
Florida coast and back. They took the *Empress* into custody.[31]

Rum ships tried any measure to evade patrolling Coast Guard boats. Many
resorted to various forms of subterfuge, knowing that the Coast Guard still
maintained an obligation to help boaters in distress. The Coast Guard base
in New London, Connecticut, for example, received intelligence that rum
runners were planning to use false SOS calls to lure the Coast Guard away
from areas in which they hoped to land a cargo of liquor. The Coast Guard
in North Carolina received a call that the Frying Pan Shoals Lightship was
in trouble. When crews arrived, they discovered nothing was wrong. They
suspected, however, that the ruse had been designed to lure the Coast Guard
away from rum runners.[32] Some smugglers sought to outfit their vessels to

make them as unobtrusive as possible, painting them gray to blend with sea and sky. They took advantage of darkness, running without lights. Smugglers also sought gadgets, like "bombs of powdered charcoal" that created clouds of black smoke that could be used to locate one another or that could obscure sight of a rum boat long enough for it to escape. Newspapers reported on the tense dance executed between authorities and smugglers, with headlines like "Hide and Seek Adds Comedy to Rum Game" and with stories of suspected smugglers "braving the sharks and barracudas of the Gulf Stream by leaping overboard and swimming for it." More common than "swimming for it" were attempts to outrun Coast Guard vessels into areas in which Coast Guard boats could not follow. Most rum runners "drew little water" and could slip through shallows only three or four feet deep.[33]

Despite the Coast Guard's efforts, however, it frequently bemoaned the lack of equipment needed to stop smugglers. In addition to repeatedly calling for faster boats, it also demanded boats with shallower drafts that could follow rum runners into shallow waters in the deserted inlets and mangrove swamps where they sought to hide. It also considered various strategies to disguise its boats and confuse smugglers. At one point, the Coast Guard even considered relettering the registration numbers on the bows of its vessels to make them look more like those of the navy. The navy was not in the business of intercepting smugglers, and many Coast Guard boats were originally part of the naval fleet. Coast Guard men also pleaded for technology to aid in the search for rum runners, specifically more powerful searchlights and, the latest in technological development, the wireless radio. Most Coast Guard vessels were equipped with large flashlights or searchlights, one to sweep the water in search of suspicious vessels, another to light the Coast Guard pennant displaying the boat's authority. Even so, the lights had only limited life at sea, able to burn steadily for only ninety minutes before the carbon arcs used to generate illumination needed replenishing. Nor were the lights nearly powerful enough to provide detection during a high-speed chase. Intensity diminished the further the object of pursuit pulled away. If a rum runner could get far enough away from a picket boat in the dark, it could be "literally swallowed up in the night." Eventually the Coast Guard would develop radio outposts, enabling it to listen to radio conversations among rum runners, gaining advanced information about their operations. But initially, the Coast Guard worried that bootleggers were winning the race for technological advantage.[34]

One aggravating reality, however, bedeviled Coast Guard efforts throughout Prohibition. It was speed: the speed of rum runners and contact boats
and the lack of speed of Coast Guard ships. Seizing rum runners was only
possible if Coast Guard boats were fast enough to chase suspects to the three-
mile limit and overtake and board them. This was no sure thing. As a Coast
Guard report noted, "We cannot follow an American motor boat . . . with
anything we shall have available in the future and hope to remain alongside
or within gun range during a run of 9.1 miles."[35] Most Coast Guard boats
could not maintain enough speed over a nine-mile chase from the twelve-
mile to the three-mile limit to keep up with most contact boats. Faster Coast
Guard boats were a necessity. According to a story in the *Saturday Evening
Post*, in the early years of Prohibition, "rum runners availed themselves of
any kind of water craft that would float and carry a few cases of liquor." Once
Coast Guard cutters began patrolling and capturing ships with some regular-
ity, runners learned that "the only way to avoid capture was to operate only
swift motorboats having sufficient speed to outrun their pursuers." While
there was variation in size and type of smuggling crafts and contact boats
over the course of Prohibition, they tended to be about thirty feet in length
with speeds between twenty and thirty knots. Initially, few government boats
could match this speed. Coast Guard cutters topped out at sixteen knots.[36]
After considerable experience, Coast Guard officials insisted that any vessel
that could not make sixteen knots was virtually useless. Destroyer forces,
whose ships tended to move at slower speeds, also faced problems of maneu-
verability. Smuggling boats took advantage of a destroyer's limitations as they
sought to elude arrest. One officer noted that it took destroyers so long to
change heading that "speedy blacks can get from 2500 to 3000 yards away."[37]
Such gaps made trailing and apprehension impossible. Speed thus gave contact boats a decided advantage over the Coast Guard and was the justification
for continuing efforts to provide the Coast Guard with new ships that could
equal the speed of contact boats. The Coast Guard at one point announced
the development of its fastest boat, the *Bullett*, with a race off the Louisiana
coast "to impress the rum runners" that authorities had a boat able to match
the rum runners' speed.[38] Nevertheless, as the Coast Guard stepped up its
efforts, it noted corresponding efforts by smugglers to develop increasingly
fast boats. Indeed, one journalist described the fastest rum runners as nothing more than "a pair of powerful engines surrounded by a shell of wood to
keep the engines afloat," with minimal space for crew and the maximal space
for contraband cargo.[39]

Faced with limited appropriations for Coast Guard forces and the time it took to commission, bid, and build Coast Guard craft, authorities had to make do with what they had. They called on the ingenuity of Coast Guard mechanics to take materials that were available and use them to increase the speed of Coast Guard craft. Some hoped that the Coast Guard could do what rum runners had done and convert surplus Liberty aircraft engines to marine use, using their power to propel boats. Rum runners had some success doing this, but after some attempts, the Coast Guard abandoned the effort. Extensive mechanical changes were required to make aircraft engines reliable in salt water. The first attempt to place one aboard the Coast Guard vessel *Sea Gull* resulted in very quick cylinder wear, requiring upkeep beyond the capabilities of most Coast Guard mechanics. Engineer in Chief R. B. Adams surmised, "I am beginning to believe that there is something in the claim that our bases cannot operate these high-speed engines, and the only efficient boats we have are powered with Sterling or Speedway engines." Rum runners may not have been any more effective at keeping Liberty engines running; they may merely have been able to replace them more often. One reporter noted that rum runners ran their boats wide open for hours at a time, almost invariably wrecking the engine. He estimated that most smugglers had to replace their engines every three months at a cost of $4,000 each. Coast Guard appropriations were too paltry to permit such frequent replacements. Local mechanics at bases nonetheless used whatever came their way to their advantage. Ensign Shaw, stationed at Base Six near Ft. Lauderdale, hoped to use his mechanical skills to outfit a 125-foot boat with sea skiffs hanging from boat booms. He had one skiff in hand and hoped another would soon be caught. As for motors, he acquired a Liberty engine in Miami for spare parts to use in other engines: "I can get enough stuff to make a young machine shop and can get enough spare parts from the bootleggers to keep the engines up. . . . I can fix up any kind of engine and do any kind of hull repairs. . . . I would very much like to get just one more crack at those scoundrels around Miami," he told his superiors.[40]

As Ensign Shaw keenly noted, however, the best source of boats capable of catching rum runners came from rum runners themselves. Initially, when a boat was seized and "forfeit" in court, it was sold at auction by the Bureau of Customs. Not infrequently, the winning bids were rum runners themselves, often the very smuggler who had turned it over to authorities. For a few hundred dollars, which might very well be available from previous profits, a rum runner could buy back his boat and return to business. The Coast Guard's growing success at seizing vessels and forcing their forfeiture ironically only made the problem worse. The deputy collector of customs in Tampa reported in 1927 that auctioning Coast Guard seizures had flooded the market for small boats, driving prices down considerably. He noted that arrested rum runners allowed their cases to proceed through the courts knowing that they would be able to buy their boat at auction "at very small expense and the whole business will be reduced to a joke." Eventually, instead of auctioning seized boats, the courts instead turned them over to the Coast Guard for patrolling. In 1928, J. H. Smith of the Department of Justice reported that five motorboats had been seized in Florida, their liquor cargoes destroyed, and the vessels turned over to the Coast Guard, all in the month of March. Seized boats provided considerable assistance to enforcement efforts on southern coasts. One Coast Guard commander in Florida reported that nearly half of their seizures were accomplished with previously seized boats. Speed, however, was not the only advantage, as another officer noted. "The advantage of these boats is enormously increased by the fact that they are of nondescript appearance and would be able not only to make seizures but to spread consternation in the ranks of the enemy because of the inconspicuous appearance."[41] Simply put, they did not look like Coast Guard ships.

The Coast Guard confidently insisted that concentrated patrol and picketing of suspecting smuggling ships along the eastern seaboard and in the Gulf of Mexico was having a measurable effect. "The work of maintaining constant watch over foreign liquor-laden vessels arriving off our coast is steadily reducing the number of smuggling craft, and driving them out of business," reported one squadron commander. "If steady pressure is maintained, it will have the desired effect of eliminating the smuggler." News reports from abroad supported his optimism. Reports from Europe stated that "fifteen million dollars is the estimated loss sustained during the past year by English financiers" hoping to profit from smuggling. "The general impression in London is that whiskey runners are having a thin time owing to the tightening of preventive measures along the United States coast." Reports from the Bahamas sounded the same notes a few years later, noting a "trade depression" among liquor merchants in Nassau because of financial losses created by Coast Guard seizures.[42]

Few things suggested success more than watching schooners return to port with their liquor cargoes intact. The captain of the rum runner *Athena*, who operated out of Nova Scotia, returned to port with 1,200 cases of mixed liquors remaining in his hold. He reported that "conditions on rum-row is hard on business, owing to the stringency of the American blockades." After being at sea for more than two months and selling only a handful of cases, he lowered a boat to catch some fresh mackerel for his crew. A Coast Guard cruiser trained its gun on his ship and immediately approached. The captain gave up and returned to port. And recall the boatswain in Tampa who forced a schooner back to Havana with its entire cargo still in its holds. The American consul in Montreal estimated that the cost of re-storing unsold liquor in bonded warehouses seriously ate into the profits that smugglers expected from their trade. One skipper allegedly reported that "two seizures out of five attempts to run rum would [still] leave a fair profit, but the percentage of seizures has become higher, and it is not a profitable business."[43] In the face of what they hoped was increasing and potentially permanent success, the Coast Guard advocated vigilance and continued pressure on the rum forces.

The rum forces themselves took a different view. Reports reached the Coast Guard that most smuggling outfits believed any offensive harming their business was only temporary and destined to end. To gauge the level of commitment to enforcement, smugglers carefully watched the political infighting over maritime enforcement, the legal debates about the extent of territorial sovereignty, and most importantly, congressional appropriations. While they conceded changes in Prohibition leadership, especially when General Andrews replaced Roy Haynes, probably made concentrated offensives against smuggling possible, smugglers did not apparently expect offensives to last. One enforcement official on vacation posed as a bootleg purchasing agent in Halifax, Nova Scotia. While there, he learned that "there are many vessels standing by to load and proceed as soon as the Coast Guard 'runs out of fuel due to lack of money' and as soon as it begins to take vessels off duty for repairs, which will be in August they think. He has a letter from a hand on a schooner which specified August as the period when the smugglers expect to have a 'merry old time.'"[44] Rum runners understood they merely needed to outlast any eruptions of zeal for Prohibition enforcement to get back to business as usual.

Indeed, there were indications that Coast Guard patrols represented a real threat to business. Smuggling outfits certainly did their part to disrupt Coast Guard operations. One officer in Cape May, New Jersey, reported attempts to bribe Coast Guard men, citing offers of $10,000 and $5,000 to two crewmen. He himself had been "offered $20,000 for one free night" to land liquor without Coast Guard interference. Dismissing the offer, he boasted, "Send me one of your Intelligence Operatives and will catch some of those bribers red handed."[45] His experience represented only one of the many attempts to bribe the Coast Guard crews. However, there were other indications that smugglers took measures to prevent the Coast Guard from performing its duties. Smuggling outfits, for example, sought to incapacitate Coast Guard vessels and make them unable to leave shore to patrol. Local bootleggers in Florida paid mechanics to delay repairs to machinery aboard the boats "to keep them from operating." At another base, a crew went to perform their morning routine before setting out and noticed several inches of water on the boat's floorboards. After they pumped the water out, "it was found that the packing around the stern post was missing which apparently had been pulled out maliciously." Until the boat was rendered seaworthy again, it could not be used to patrol. A Florida base noted several instances of sabotage: a gas line removed, water poured into the oil tank of a Liberty engine, and ignition wires cut on a patrol boat. None of these actions caused more than a mechanical inconvenience, but they did keep boats at the dock. More ominous were more dangerous attempts at sabotage. In Florida, the Ft. Lauderdale base received a distress call, and the Coast Guard prepared to send out one of its faster boats. When a crew member touched the starter button, the boat exploded. After an investigation, the commander concluded that "it was the work of some mischief maker, probably in the pay of liquor runners as [the boat] was a fast boat and well suited for a chaser." Sabotaging a Coast Guard vessel was on the desperate end of a desperate trade. But not all smugglers resorted to violence to dissuade the Coast Guard from doing its duty. One rum-running ship simply added prostitutes to its crew, offering their services to the crews of Coast Guard picketing boats at no cost. The picket boat apparently left half of its crew at a time on board the smuggling ship to enjoy the women's favors while the other half continued to appear to be patrolling. By providing such entertainment, the rum runner hoped to ensure that the speedboats that arrived to unload cargo would not be noticed or harassed.[46]

But as the use of prostitutes as distraction indicated, a service primarily composed of young men could present other difficulties as they sought to prevent smugglers from successfully landing their cargo. With the effort to increase the size of the Coast Guard service, many men had been pulled into service with little experience and training. Not all seemed committed to service at sea or to Prohibition itself and could be led astray by distractions on land. Two officers in Florida, for example, faced reprimand for entertaining women in the officer's mess at 4:00 in the morning, when they were supposed to be on watch. A Miami newspaper reported that Boatswain Mate Williamson brought a woman to base in Florida with him, claiming she was his wife, while his actual wife was apparently still in Brooklyn. The resulting scandal was apparently "extremely damaging to the morale of the personnel" on base. Boatswain Anderson reportedly kept a mistress in New Orleans, not far from his base on Barataria Bay, and had a tendency toward drunkenness.[47] Similar scandals were frequent disruptions in a force manned largely by young men.

Many Coast Guard men had little experience on the seas, little experience with the waters they were intended to patrol, and little experience enforcing the law against rum runners. But the larger issues had to do with the task at hand. Law enforcement represented a new responsibility for the Coast Guard on the front lines of Prohibition enforcement. High-speed pursuits of suspected smugglers sounded exciting, but most day-to-day operations were more mundane. Coast Guard men often found patrolling and scouting for rum runners boring, requiring long hours at sea only occasionally punctuated by the thrill of a chase. Coast Guard commanders noted that they sometimes worried about lax discipline and halfhearted efforts on patrol boats. When the cutter *Mojave* sighted six black ships sixteen miles off Fire Island, it radioed for assistance. The Coast Guard ordered three six-bitters to the location, but none arrived. The local commander cited mechanical troubles but hinted that the crews simply could not be bothered to rush to the scene.[48] Indeed, throughout Prohibition, there were concerns that some Coast Guard crews were reluctant to enforce the law at all. In 1931, the Coast Guard sent out requests to retrain recent officers after learning that one commissioned officer had never stopped and boarded a suspected rum runner in over two years of service.[49] Numerous other patrol boats completed entire cruises without sighting any suspected black ships whatsoever. Commanders worried that these empty reports may have been more a function of the crews' inattention than the lack of targets to trail. During an eleven-day patrol, one particular captain decided to place some of his officers aboard his picket boats. He noticed that all the picket boats containing officers reported activity among rum runners, and some even recorded arrests. The boats without officers neither reported sightings nor made arrests. More troubling, the officers noted that several of their arrests were made only after contact boats approached the picket boats and asked outright if they could land a load. It most surely suggested that smugglers had asked that question before and received an affirmative response from Coast Guard crews. The same report also noted concerns about the trailing efforts of picket boats. In one case, when the captain returned to check on the boats trailing rum ships, he found they had allowed the prey to drift a considerable distance away, even though it was dark. To his dismay, one picket boat was almost three miles from its intended target. At that distance, there was simply no way to prevent a contact boat from successfully loading cargo and making a run for shore. The failure to maintain close surveillance suggested no desire even to try to prevent smuggling. By 1931, the Coast Guard commandant believed most patrols' efforts were halfhearted. He chided the Gulf Division in particular for patrolling routes that would "show good tracks on the chart" rather than focusing where they knew black ships tended to concentrate.[50] As a result, while the Coast Guard's role during Prohibition represented a new venture into law enforcement and a broadening reach of American federal authority beyond U.S. borders, it was not an unalloyed success. The Coast Guard's efforts were hampered by a lack of equipment and resources and occasionally even by a lack of commitment. The larger national context in which the Coast Guard sought to carry out its mission, one in which many Americans opposed Prohibition, played an important role in the ability of the Coast Guard to achieve its goals.

Bootleggers and enforcement authorities were locked into an ongoing game of pursuit, using both fair means and foul, nautical and just plain underhanded, to gain advantage. Some strategies involved simple mechanics, such as trying to gain an advantage of speed or reliability in watercraft or to use the limitations of watercraft to one's advantage. Beyond trying to elude or outwit Coast Guard pursuers, smuggling syndicates used whatever strategies they could to undermine federal authorities. As more picket boats were utilized off the east coast of Florida, rum runners concentrated their landings on areas of the coast that they estimated to be beyond the range of picket boats, well north of Miami, or between Miami and Key West.[51] But rum runners also sought to assert their advantage onshore as well. In areas in which smugglers had cozy relations with local land-based law enforcement, they used the legal system to harass Coast Guard men. One particularly brazen rum runner in Florida tried to charge the Coast Guard crew that arrested him with assault and battery. After he had been placed under arrest and brought on board the Coast Guard boat, he was given a meal. While eating, he attempted to conceal a knife, prompting a scuffle to disarm him. He complained to the local sheriff that he had been assaulted by the crew, and the sheriff sought to arrest them. The Coast Guard refused to turn the men over because the alleged assault took place on the high seas, well outside the jurisdiction of the local sheriff. The charges against another group of officers were more serious. When two bootleggers were killed by Coast Guard fire in two separate incidents in the Miami area, the local courts charged the crewmen involved with first-degree murder. Even after they were cleared of charges, the persecutions apparently did not stop. One Coast Guard officer in Ft. Lauderdale transferred to the Customs Border Patrol after what the Coast Guard called repeated attempts at assassination. Another informer reported that he had overheard six men at a restaurant plotting to assassinate Ensign Shaw, the enterprising engine mechanic stationed near Miami. They apparently knew where Shaw lived and were familiar with his movements, so it would be "an easy matter to waylay him, drag him into the nearby dense wood and kill him." Shaw was temporarily reassigned to another station. Smugglers were not even averse to using scandal to their advantage. The U.S. commissioner in Miami, Sidney Praeger, was the victim of a "badger" game in 1926. Praeger received a phone call from a woman in distress who asked him, "as a gentleman," to come to her hotel room. The moment he entered the room and shut the door, local police entered to arrest him on a morals charge. While newspapers covered the case with interest, Coast Guard authorities dismissed it as an attempt to discredit a Prohibition official. Despite his protests of innocence and local reports of a frame-up, Praeger was forced to resign.[52] However ham-handed, such efforts attempted to prevent or at least obstruct the ability of authorities to enforce Prohibition laws.

A final factor that frequently contributed to authorities' frustrations was the lack of support from the general public. This took a variety of forms, from outright opposition to Prohibition to impatience with enforcement efforts to dismay at Coast Guard tactics. Some opposition suggested widespread dislike of the Coast Guard itself, as the men at Base Six near Ft. Lauderdale experienced. There, officers reported that many local residents were "boycotting" the base and charging outrageously high rents for officers who lived off base with their wives. Machine shops reportedly would only do work for the Coast Guard at exorbitant prices, and "marine railway work" was impossible to manage because no one would do the work. No one in town was willing to supply the base with potable water. The base even reported that its electricity would be shut off "at any time." The only recourse, it seemed, was to make the base entirely self-sufficient. The base commander reported that a friend had told him that "the bootleggers have decided it was up to them to run me out one way or another, that we were too active and getting too many boats." He was, however, unfazed.[53] Smuggling outfits apparently sought to accentuate public displeasure with the Coast Guard to give themselves more room to maneuver.

For members of the public who supported Prohibition or just the efforts to end traffic in alcohol in their communities, the persistence of open criminal activities caused considerable frustration. Some residents along the southern coast believed the Coast Guard was deliberately ignoring obvious illegal activity. The "Citizens of Golden Beach," Florida, wrote the commander of the Coast Guard base in Ft. Lauderdale and complained that "one to four boats unloaded [liquor] per week," with little apparent attempt by the Coast Guard to stop them. The citizens promised that "unless something is done immediately to stop rum boats from unloading every few nights large quantities of liquor on Golden Beach, within a few minutes of your base, we propose to go to Washington and lodge a complaint with the Government." A community on the west side of Florida also came to federal authorities to complain about law enforcement in their area. The residents of Punta Gorda, Florida, sent a delegation of citizens to the collector of customs in Tampa complaining about the lack of effort to control the widespread liquor smuggling in their community. Their local police force had refused to respond; they had come to the federal authorities for help. The federal authorities did little more than throw up their hands, informing the citizens that "it was obviously beyond the power of the federal Government to intervene in every small community where conditions were unsatisfactory."[54]

Other communities felt that the Coast Guard's efforts to stop smugglers were too aggressive, putting innocent bystanders at risk. A *New York Herald Tribune* article in 1925 noted that Coast Guard crews in south Florida had opened fire on an innocent fishing trip. The Coast Guard, in its defense, noted that the boat was running at night without lights — usually an indication of a black ship. The paper high-handedly concluded the article by insisting that "reckless or lawless law enforcement is worse than possible non-enforcement." More loud complaints occurred after a Coast Guard boat near Miami chased a suspected rum runner close to shore. The Coast Guard boat opened fire on the boat when houses onshore were within range.

While no one was apparently injured, the firing of over 200 rounds from the boat's machine gun caused considerable local outrage. Even worse, the crew did not even capture the crew of the fleeing rum runner, who escaped onshore.[55] The local news media were not shy about complaining about what they termed "Enforcement Outrages." After the incident involving officials firing on the fishing expedition, the paper complained that residents of south Florida knew that "the federal government will do nothing to protect the lives of the people, when attacked by prohibition officers." They warned that continued outrages would scare off tourists to Miami. The Coast Guard was thought to be so undisciplined that the Exchange Club of Ft. Lauderdale set up a commission to investigate what it determined to be twenty-one cases of misconduct in the past two months involving Coast Guard men. The alleged misconduct ranged "from petty larceny and illegal possession of liquor and intoxication to attempted statutory offenses against minors." Though the local commander had appeared before the commission to attempt to calm tempers, his appearance had the opposite effect. The local media claimed that the base commander had admitted that he could not enforce discipline of the men under his command.[56]

Indeed, the relationship between the Coast Guard and the general public around Miami was apparently rocky at best, and the Coast Guard complained that the news coverage of conflicts between Coast Guard personnel and local citizens represented "considerable misrepresentation and unreliability." Nevertheless, such reports both reflected and shaped the local view of Coast Guard servicemen who appeared to many as unwelcome interlopers enforcing an unpopular law. Coast Guard men complained that they were arrested and charged with ridiculous infractions, such as spitting on the sidewalk, and were insulted and taunted on the streets or in local theaters. Some even suggested that there had been attempts to deliberately run them down on the streets. Local newspapers in turn published stories of "immoral escapades" by Coast Guard men with women of ill repute. Other locals complained that Coast Guard men were drunk. One Miami man who signed himself as "an Honest Fisherman" reported that he had witnessed three to four Coast Guard seventy-five-foot patrol boats anchored off Gun Key in the Bahamas, with the officer in charge "so intoxicated, I dare say, that he hardly knew of his whereabouts, and in a rude, drunken manner, insulted several of my party with whom he had spoken." Other crew on board attested that the officer was "always drunk" but that he would sober up when higher-level officers showed up on base. A notation scrawled at the bottom of the report by the chief intelligence officer noted that the officer referred to "does not drink."[57]

The Coast Guard surmised that the reports of drunkenness, immorality, and lawlessness of Coast Guard men, while concerning, were little more than an effort to discredit the service as a whole and undermine its efforts to enforce Prohibition. In Florida in particular, the Coast Guard believed such reports reflected its relative success in the area. "Imported liquor is now hard to obtain in Florida and that which is available is of such doubtful character that many people are afraid to use it." Out of desperation, Charles Root surmised, many people in the area were turning to "Moonshine corn liquor." But that very scarcity pushed the smuggling interests and their supporters to more concentrated efforts. "There is now a campaign of intimidation underway against Coast Guard and Customs officers and that this campaign is due mostly to the desperate straits in which the smugglers and the bootleggers find themselves." He went on to add, "Part of the local law-abiding element had joined in this campaign because of skillful propaganda published by the bootleggers which led these good people to believe that Government officers are utterly reckless of human life."[58] These complaints from frustrated citizens expressed concerns over the traffic in liquor, to be sure. But they also reflected the newly visible efforts by the Coast Guard to participate in law enforcement in local communities. Prohibiting alcohol through a federal amendment had supposedly been a response to the evils of alcohol, but southern communities along the coasts were discovering that the cure could be as bad as the disease. The Coast Guard efforts at law enforcement pleased no one.

Cooperation across all levels of law enforcement and between federal agencies, however, was frequently rocky, as bureaucratic procedures created in Washington failed utterly when put into practice. One continuing bone of contention was the failure of witnesses from government agencies to appear in court to testify. Criminal trials required testimony from the Coast Guard officers who seized the boat, but they were frequently at sea patrolling for smugglers. The Coast Guard received one blistering complaint from a U.S. Attorney in Florida that made plain the bureaucratic inefficiencies. The district court in Jacksonville, attempting to bring indictments in several smuggling cases, sent a list of Coast Guard witnesses to the Bureau of Customs at Tampa, Florida, with instructions that customs should make arrangements to have the Coast Guard officers in Jacksonville appear in court. On the day Coast Guard officers were scheduled to testify, the court learned that the Bureau of Customs had never notified the Coast Guard that the officers were needed. As a result, the court dismissed eight to ten smuggling cases.[59] The failures of cooperation hampered efforts to enforce Prohibition at the same time it made the federal government visible in southern communities in new ways.

The Coast Guard reports, however, continued to express optimism that eventually the organization could end smuggling. After the Coast Guard initiated its plan of trailing or picketing suspected rum ships, rum runners did have more difficulty anchoring just outside the legal limit and delivering liquor to contact boats from shore. In response, however, smuggling vessels merely moved their operations farther into international waters and spread out, thus becoming more difficult for the Coast Guard to track. But sprinkled throughout the pages of weekly Notes on the General Situation were indications that the Coast Guard faced an insurmountable task. The traffic in liquor was simply too extensive and profitable. While the Coast Guard did happily report vessels returning to port with their loads intact, as well as the number of suspected black ships that it picketed, it also acknowledged the considerable number of black ships that slipped through its grasp on the open sea. Virtually every week, the intelligence officer dutifully noted multiple ships that had been sighted but were now "unreported," like the *Ocean Maid*, which was spotted on September 16, 17, and 20 but that had apparently vanished by September 24.[60] In the summer of 1927, the situation was little improved. The *Zelda* had been spotted but disappeared the same day, while the *George and Earl* had been trailed but let go. It was located again a few days later but altered its course and disappeared. The *I'm Alone*, which several years later would cause a diplomatic crisis when sunk by the Coast Guard, was clearly adept at losing the Coast Guard in 1927. It disappeared from surveillance on June 30, only to be found again on July 1. It soon escaped again. The Coast Guard spotted and trailed it a week later, but because transmission of its position was garbled, the ship was never seized.[61] Despite Coast Guard efforts, numerous smuggling ships continued to elude capture.

At the same time, Coast Guard officials also noted that even their best and most concentrated patrolling efforts merely pushed the trade into other areas. While Canadian officials were enforcing customs laws near Halifax in an attempt to stem the liquor traffic, authorities in St. Pierre and St. Johns were not so cooperative. Traffic out of Halifax had dropped precipitously, but the traffic out of St. Pierre especially was booming. The situation was little different along the southern coast. In the spring of 1927, when the Coast Guard that patrolled the Gulf of Mexico moved to the Mississippi River to respond to historic floods, bootleggers moved into the waters the Coast Guard had vacated. That same year, efforts to stop the liquor traffic in the North had merely pushed smuggling south, where "activity in the Gulf Coast . . . has grown rapidly until now it rivals the old New England rum row." When the Coast Guard focused an offensive on the western coast of Florida, it drove smugglers "farther to the westward and they are now centering on New Orleans and the northern most part of the Texas coast." When the guard concentrated on Florida's eastern coast, traffic merely moved north to Georgia and South Carolina. Within six months, after the Coast Guard had moved toward Savannah to patrol Georgia and South Carolina waters, rum runners moved back to beaches near Fernandina, Florida, to land their cargoes.[62] Whatever force the Coast Guard could bring to bear only pushed the liquor traffic to other locations.

Even worse, despite the best efforts of the Coast Guard, liquor slipped past it even in areas with consistent patrols. The British steamer *MacHinery*, for example, left Halifax with a full cargo of liquor bound ostensibly for Bermuda. Coast Guard destroyers trailed it for three days until they reached the edge of their jurisdiction. They abandoned their pursuit, and within a week the *MacHinery* arrived back in Halifax with empty cargo holds. The Coast Guard base near Ft. Lauderdale reported that two schooners operating out of Havana had landed their cargo seventeen miles north of Cape Canaveral. And when a Coast Guard crew managed to stop and board the *Gemma*, all they found were a handful of broken liquor bottles and some bundles of straw. Yet barely a week earlier, this ship had cleared Yarmouth for Havana with 246 kegs of malt and almost 1,700 cases of liquor on board. At the end of 1928, the Coast Guard noted that it had seized a total of 370 domestic craft, 174 of which had been captured off the coast of Florida.[63] It was a significant number, but the rum fleet nonetheless continued its thriving illegal trade despite the Coast Guard's best efforts.

Coast Guard officers felt outmanned, unsupported by the public, and under-resourced. One commander likened the Coast Guard's efforts to "lion hunting with a peashooter." He went on: "We have bagged quite a number of lions so far and have scared a good many more, but I believe we could do better with a gun." As late as 1932, Coast Guard officers continued to complain that their forces were woefully inadequate, noting only two large offshore patrol boats, the cutters *Patriot* and the *Nansemond*, both commissioned in 1926 to combat smuggling, were stationed on the waters between New York City and Ft. Lauderdale, Florida. Some officers felt that the courts tied their hands, and others claimed that Congress had failed to provide them the necessary legal structure to effectively target rum runners. One commanding officer in the navy complained that while black ships were easy to identify—"by their hours going out and returning, by the smell of liquor in the hold, by straw from bottles, by equipment, by crew, by running without lights"— and while some courts would convict on such evidence, other jurisdictions would not. Unfortunately, passing legislation to clarify what evidence was required for prosecution, in their eyes, was "hopeless."[64]

Even the effort to extend American law enforcement authority into international waters remained controversial. Federal courts continued to question whether the United States in general and the Coast Guard in particular could enforce American laws outside traditional definitions of territorial limits and whether ships seized more than twelve miles out to sea were legitimate targets for the Coast Guard's antismuggling efforts. One Coast Guard officer reported that several federal officials in Florida insisted that "it was not legal for the Government to make seizures beyond the twelve-mile limit." Yet he also noted several other district court cases that upheld seizures of vessels suspected of smuggling beyond the territorial waters of the United States. "I therefore desire to know," he wrote plainly, "whether or not it is lawful for Coast Guard vessels to seize American vessels or boats laden with intoxicating liquors beyond the territorial waters." While the customs collector he spoke to stated that the Coast Guard could successfully win the forfeiture of vessels on other charges, including engaging in trade without a proper license or for failure to have an accurate manifest on board, he nonetheless wanted to know the exact scope of the Coast Guard's law enforcement role.[65] His concerns were not idle musings. Indeed, his letter was likely spurred by the attempt to win the forfeiture of the American motorboat V-3044 in Tampa weeks earlier. The V-3044 had been captured seventy-five miles west of Egmont Key carrying a cargo of liquor valued at over $10,000. At a hearing before the U.S. commissioner, the defense had won a dismissal of charges against the crew and promised to defend against the vessel's seizure in court vigorously, arguing that the "Coast Guard had no authority to seize American vessels beyond

the territorial limits of the United States." Commander Root, writing to the
U.S. Attorney in Tampa, insisted that such an interpretation was "entirely er-
roneous" and pointed out that such a ruling would "establish a precedent and
make every seizure of American vessels outside of territorial waters a waste of
time." Root insisted that the Coast Guard's expansive authority should not be
questioned. He knew that all efforts to prevent smuggling by the Coast Guard
would likely collapse without such a mandate. Adding to his frustration was
the identity of the defense attorney making the case. He was none other than
the former U.S. Attorney from Tampa who had now switched sides and was
defending rum runners and using concerns about the expanded reach of
federal authority to do so.[66] Indeed, others were apparently uncomfortable
about the expanded footprint of federal law enforcement in the region. The
special deputy collector of customs in Tampa, Florida, in a meeting with the
head of Coast Guard Intelligence, related an incident in which two carloads
of customs agents were detained by local police for alleged traffic violations
as they sped to a landing site to prevent the landing of a well-known smuggler
outside Miami. They were eventually allowed to proceed after proving their
authority, but the interchange highlighted lingering tensions nonetheless.[67]

As a Montreal newspaper reported as early as 1925, "Where there is supply on one side and a demand on the other, with an opportunity for large
profits, . . . the dry fleet, however vigilant, cannot make a rum-proof coast
unless it can first remove these three conditions, which is impossible."[68] The
experience of the Coast Guard bore this out. It fought a largely losing battle
in the waters off the southern coast. The potential for profits in smuggling,
the continued desire for alcoholic beverages by many Americans, and the established methods of smuggling together created an enormous black market
in booze that resisted efforts to stop its operation. With Prohibition, the U.S.
Coast Guard, however, received unprecedented authority to take on a direct
enforcement role and extend the authority of the federal government beyond
the accepted limits of American territorial waters. In Florida especially, there
were questions about the effectiveness of federal efforts, resentment about the
visibility of federal law enforcement officers, and even debate about the very
ability of the Coast Guard to extend American authority abroad. As support
for Prohibition diminished nationally, these concerns became more acute.

Florida was unusually hostile toward Prohibition, to be sure. But the concerns raised during Prohibition did not end with Prohibition's repeal. While
Prohibition would eventually end, the expansion into law enforcement for the

Coast Guard continued for the rest of the twentieth century. The fight against Prohibition solidified the Coast Guard as a partner in law enforcement and laid the groundwork for procedures that would be used to prevent smuggling of illegal drugs in the 1930s and unsanctioned immigration thereafter.

The Coast Guard did not face the battle of enforcing Prohibition on its own, however, and neither were efforts to disrupt the liquor traffic concentrated solely within American federal agencies. While the Coast Guard sought to prevent liquor from entering the United States by sea, other agencies sought to disrupt the source of supply more directly. To examine their efforts, the story now moves to Havana, Cuba, where a small band of quasi-official agents took on the liquor trade in the port where smugglers purchased their cargoes. In the process, this group further cemented the effect of Prohibition enforcement on the expansion of federal power south of the southern coast.

{ Chapter Three }

BOOZE COPS IN CUBA

＊

I N OCTOBER 1926, the editor of the *Country Press and World Press News* of Bogota, New Jersey, sent a letter to the American consul in Havana, Cuba. The paper was curious as to whether rum smuggling had indeed decreased as General Lincoln Andrews claimed in the press. Hoping to run an article on smuggling and unable to interview smugglers or bootleggers themselves, the newspaper requested a brief description of the view from Cuba. In exchange for some "interesting facts," they offered $25.00 for the consulate's troubles.[1] Vice Consul Charles F. Payne replied, composing a four-page summary of the positive effects of the antismuggling treaty signed by the United States and Cuba earlier that year. Payne noted that it had been an "open secret" that numerous schooners had been operating out of Havana's port, many of them flying British flags or carrying provisional registrations from nearby Central American countries. They took on liquor cargoes in Havana and headed out to sea with the stated intention of traveling to ports in the Bahamas, Honduras, or Canada—places where the importation and sale of liquor was perfectly legal. Instead, however, they unloaded their liquor onto the beaches of the southern United States. Because these schooners carried customs papers that appeared legitimate, Payne said, there was little the American consulate could do, other than report the departures of well-known smuggling schooners to authorities in the United States in the hopes that they might be seized by the Coast Guard once they entered American territorial waters. While the government achieved occasional success in seizing smuggling ships and prosecuting their owners and crews for violating American laws, in Payne's view, it failed to stop the illegal importation of liquor to American shores. It was this situation that led authorities in the

United States and Cuba to negotiate the antismuggling treaty, or Rum Treaty, as it came to be known, to coordinate their efforts.

In Payne's view, once the treaty went into effect, it had almost immediately ended the liquor traffic. Because there had never been firm numbers of the amount of liquor that landed illegally on American shores, Payne looked to another measure to support his view: the number of schooners attempting to clear from the port of Havana with cargoes of liquor on board. Before the treaty, several such schooners cleared Havana each week. Within a few months of the treaty's implementation, those departures had decreased to a virtual trickle, from eleven in July 1926 to just three in September, and one of those three was traveling in ballast or without cargo. Perhaps most heartening to the American diplomats in Cuba was the seeming willingness of Cuban officials to enforce the treaty. In the optimistic view of the consulate in Havana, Havana's thriving traffic in smuggling had come to a screeching halt. The harbor was full of idle schooners and their crews. "Each day that passes makes it more apparent that their day in Habana is over."[2]

While American officials in Havana freely expressed enthusiasm for the effects of the Rum Treaty with Cuba to the New Jersey paper, officials in Washington, D.C., were less pleased. The State Department took a dim view of consular officials providing seemingly official reports without first obtaining its approval. It discouraged the New Jersey paper from publishing any article on smuggling and chastised Carleton Bailey Hurst, the consul general in Havana. It reminded the officer that Foreign Service officials were prohibited from corresponding with newspapers on matters of public interest without the consent of the State Department leadership.[3] Despite the hand slap that the consulate in Havana received, it is hard to miss Payne's optimism about the success of the treaty. According to his short analysis of shipping activity in Havana's harbor, by 1926 the game for smugglers there had changed. He was, unsurprisingly, a bit premature with his declaration of victory. The treaty, in and of itself, altered rum-smuggling out of Havana, but it did not end it. It merely represented a particularly successful moment in the ongoing Rum War. At least initially, the U.S. government's efforts to stretch law enforcement into foreign governments had some effect, as Cuban officials prevented suspected smugglers from leaving Cuban ports. Smugglers faced much more difficulty loading cargoes of liquor with the intention of delivering them to the United States. Liquor smugglers would have to be more cagey, their liquor cargoes disguised as, or hidden within, other goods they exported from Havana. Indeed, while the Rum Treaty slowed smuggling out of Havana, ingenious smugglers merely worked around it, transferring their operations to other ports. It nonetheless represented the high-water mark of international cooperation with smuggling between Cuba and the United States. The success of the treaty, however, would not have been possible without the efforts of a band of American agents in Havana who promoted the need for Cubans to help with American law enforcement and provided the intelligence on the smuggling industry needed to stop it. Their ongoing efforts with both Cuban and American authorities made any successes attributed to the treaty possible. That success, however, would not last, as much a result of the failures of American policy as the determination of smugglers themselves.

Not long into Prohibition, U.S. officials realized that high-minded calls for national temperance alone would not convince Americans to abandon their taste for liquor, especially the high-end spirits distilled around the globe. Despite the efforts of the Coast Guard to prevent liquor from landing on U.S. shores, the flow of spirits continued from Europe to ports near the United States, from which it could be clandestinely landed on American shores. Distillers in France, Great Britain, and elsewhere were determined to continue providing their wares to American customers, and as the trade in intoxicating beverages remained legal in numerous foreign ports near the United States, a lively black market in booze seemed almost inevitable. Distillers merely shipped their wares for the American market to nearby countries with the full expectation that their products would eventually wind up in the hands of thirsty Americans. If liquor suppliers could reasonably claim that their liquor was destined for ports other than those in the United States, who could blame them if their products somehow landed in American glasses? More pointedly, what right did the U.S. government have to interrupt legal trade among willing international partners? They had a point. Prohibition was an American peculiarity, making illegal what were common transactions elsewhere. Other nations had little interest in harming their own liquor industries to cater to it. And most were squeamish about allowing American law enforcement authority to extend too far outside the territorial limits of the United States. The treaty that the United States eventually negotiated with Great Britain, which was followed by similar treaties with other European countries by early 1925, sought to find a middle ground.[4] The treaties gave American enforcement agencies the ability to interrupt transactions they had reason to believe would violate American law, and they sought the assistance of foreign countries in preventing the export of cargoes likely headed for the United States. The United States thus sought through diplomatic means to extend its authority beyond its borders to end efforts to bring high-end spirits to a black market in America.[5]

The diplomatic concerns with closer American neighbors, however, were a little different. Both Canada and Mexico shared long borders with the United States, and in both countries the transport and sale of liquor was legal. It came as little surprise that, after Prohibition went into effect, the borders with Canada and Mexico became increasingly porous, allowing alcohol to flow into the United States in substantial quantities. While treaties with far-flung liquor producers like Great Britain and France were clearly needed, so were treaties focused on contraband from America's closest neighbors. By early 1926, the United States had successfully negotiated antismuggling treaties with Canada and Mexico, even though export of liquor from Canada to the United States broke no Canadian law as long as a $20 duty per case was paid. While these treaties addressed the peculiarities of moving contraband across a common land border, they were only of limited use in providing the template for a treaty between Cuba and the United States. For both Canada and Mexico, illicit contraband found crossing the international border could be assumed to be traveling to the United States. There was simply nowhere else it could be going, and officials could assume the intention was to violate American law. Enforcing Prohibition in this context merely required the free flow of information about the nature of cargoes entering the United States, which could be useful in Prohibition enforcement and was thus required by the treaty.[6]

Cuban smuggling, however, represented a different dilemma. Cuba's relationship with the United States in the early twentieth century was unique. The Platt Amendment to the Cuban constitution allowed American intervention into Cuba to protect life, property, and individual liberty. Over the course of the first twenty years of the twentieth century, the United States undertook military and political intervention under increasingly broad interpretations of that mandate. The limits that the United States and the Platt Amendment placed on Cuban sovereignty aggravated many Cubans, but political factions nonetheless manipulated the potential for American intervention to promote their own partisan purposes.[7] Nevertheless, the possibility of American intervention cast its shadow over discussions of cooperation with the Cuban government in the enforcement of Prohibition, something the Bahamas, the other main location of Caribbean smuggling and a British colony, did not face. Discussions about Prohibition, however, were vastly overshadowed by concerns about the Cuban economy. Indeed, the American press seemed more concerned about the stability of the Cuban government than it was about Cuba's significant role in smuggling.[8] By 1920, American businesses held billions of dollars of interest in Cuban land and sugar production, and the well-being of sugar determined the well-being of Cuba's economy overall. Economics dominated discussions of Cuban-American relations at the highest levels, even though smuggling promised revenues that Cuba desperately needed. Prohibition thus put Cuba in a uniquely awkward position. One newspaper in Havana questioned why Cuba should become "near-policeman for the United States" to "enforce an internal law of the United States, which does not affect us and with which the immense majority of the people of the United States disagree."[9] One might think it had a point. Since the turn of the twentieth century, the United States had strutted its power around the region with a big stick. By the 1920s, those efforts had scaled back in favor of more neighborly relations, but Cuba in particular still felt a heavy hand. Ultimately, while the profits of smuggling did not protect the Cuban economy from catastrophe when the sugar market crashed, they did nonetheless undermine the seemingly impenetrable nature of American hegemony. The inability of the United States to enforce Prohibition in its own backyard, and its persistent demand that Cuba do so, had the potential to diminish Cuban perceptions of American might, as American agents in Havana realized.

The Platt Amendment encouraged some American officials to argue that direct military intervention in Cuba was the best approach to stop smuggling. When Peter del Valle came to Havana to investigate the smuggling business in 1925, he commented that the Cuban government had no apparent interest in preventing the departure of rum schooners. Indeed, he noted that members of the Cuban government not only owned and operated distilleries themselves but colluded with smugglers to profit from the illicit liquor trade. He insisted that the efforts of American officials in Havana to report ships' movements would not be enough to diminish Havana's prominence as a smuggling port. Believing that the Cuban government was "in the hands of an unscrupulous and predatory combination of irresponsible persons headed by the dictator Machado," del Valle argued that American control over the Cuban government should be increased. After his full investigation, he recommended strong diplomatic or even military action to shut down the liquor traffic. He even suggested that the U.S. government replace the Platt Amendment, which placed an extraordinary amount of American surveillance and control over the Cuban government, with an even stronger law. He envisioned a law that would permit the United States "to maintain a force upon the island at the disposal of the Ambassador, and permit our Coast Guard service to operate upon the harbors of Cuba for the apprehension of vessels" suspected of smuggling liquor into the United States.[10] Suggesting a military presence on the island was not unprecedented; beginning in 1903 the United States maintained a naval base at Guantanamo, Cuba. It would, however, vastly extend the reach of the U.S. government into Cuba in an effort to enforce one particular American law. Del Valle's recommendation for more intensive intrusion into Cuban affairs, however, never received serious consideration. Instead, the U.S. government hoped to convince the Cuban government to prevent the departures of loaded rum runners from Cuban ports and hold ships intending to engage in smuggling for violations of Cuban laws.

Havana, as we know, was an ideal smuggling port. Liquor could be legally shipped from Cuba to every country in the hemisphere except the United States. Suspicion that a known rum runner loaded with alcohol was headed for the United States was in and of itself not sufficient reason for the Cuban authorities to prevent the ship's departure from port. There was no way to prove that the intended destination was the United States until the cargo landed on a southern beach. The Cuban government, moreover, had very good reasons to take rum runners' customs declarations at face value and turn a blind eye to the likelihood that liquor cargoes were headed for the American coast. Each case of liquor that arrived in Cuba to be shipped elsewhere brought money in the form of duties into Cuban coffers. Cuban authorities faced a considerable quandary as they contemplated interfering in businesses like that of wholesaler Mourice Roud. The Havana businesses responsible for provisioning, loading, and clearing cargo for the rum fleet insisted that they were not violating U.S. liquor laws because their transactions occurred in Cuba, where they were legal. It was not their concern where cargo actually landed if the ships themselves claimed to be headed to destinations where the importation of liquor violated no law. Cuban public opinion was also in their favor. Smuggling liquor represented a trade of approximately 500,000 cases of alcohol per month, or about $80 million per year. The Cuban government collected export duties on much of this trade — especially on highly desirable Cuban rum and aguardiente. Moreover, the vast majority of the trade occurred through the port of Havana. The ships were provisioned in Havana, the crews often spent their wages in Havana, and repairs were contracted, completed, and paid for in Havana, all at a time when the larger Cuban economy buckled under the low price of sugar. It was no surprise that Cubans, and especially those in Havana, the seat of the national government, resisted U.S. demands that Cuba end the smuggling trade.[11]

No ships, however, left Cuban ports with illegal cargoes openly destined for American ports, at least according to their customs documents. A treaty like those with Canada and Mexico that required sharing cargo manifests was virtually useless. Instead, the attorney general recommended treaty terms that would direct Cuba to furnish information about shipments "where there is reasonable ground to suspect that the merchandise involved is to be smuggled or illegally introduced into the United States." With advance notice of the departures of suspected rum runners, American authorities might intercept the ships before they landed their cargo on American beaches. The United States hoped to expand American law enforcement authority over Cuban boats into international waters by authorizing American authorities to board them beyond the U.S. twelve-mile limit. American officials, of course, assumed that the only ships likely to be boarded were those known to engage in smuggling as their sole purpose and business. The Cubans, however, were less sure but ultimately withdrew their objections.[12] By the spring of 1926, the provisions of the treaty had been negotiated. Cuban authorities agreed to "raise no objections to the boarding of private vessels under Cuban flag outside the limits of territorial waters." And, specific to the Cuban treaty, if there were reasonable grounds among American authorities to believe that a vessel had cleared from Cuba and had committed or was attempting to commit an offense against the Prohibition laws of the United States, it could be seized and brought to a U.S. port.[13] American officials had successfully expanded American enforcement authority to police Cuban shipping.

These stipulations in the treaty were all very well and good, but in some ways they failed to address the heart of the problem of smuggling out of Havana. The treaty only addressed Cuban vessels, not those flying the flags of other countries. In addition, smuggling ships out of Havana, regardless of their country of registration, often had clearance papers that appeared to be perfectly in order, indicating that their liquor cargoes were headed for a port where the trade in alcohol was legal. They returned to Havana in ballast with documents indicating that they had unloaded their cargo as directed. American authorities in both the United States and the embassy in Cuba had strong suspicions that someone in Cuba was providing rum runners with forged clearance papers. They surmised that rum runners probably possessed fully completed papers indicating they had unloaded their cargo in the proper port before they even left Havana. This was the primary problem that authorities needed to solve to end smuggling from Cuba, and it was largely unaffected by the terms of the treaty. But to solve this larger problem, Americans needed the cooperation of Cuban officials. They needed the Cuban government to direct Havana port officials to prevent ships from departing in the first place.

Payne obviously did not go into these details when he relayed the astounding success of the Rum Treaty to the small New Jersey newspaper. Instead, he cheerily conveyed the willingness of the Cuban government to notify American authorities when a suspected smuggling vessel left Cuban ports. He quoted the treaty at length, including the basic cluster of factors that might tip off authorities that a vessel was engaged in the liquor traffic. Ships were suspicious if "tonnage, size, type of vessel, length of the voyage, period or conditions of navigation or transportation" suggested their planned voyage was impossible. Authorities could also target a ship that had "repetition of alleged accidents in prior voyages," such as claiming clearance papers had been lost at sea during a storm, or if "information concerning the vessel furnish[ed] evidence" that its cargo would enter the United States illegally.[14] These factors, of course, required someone interested in stopping smuggling to identify a ship meeting these characteristics, notify the American authorities, and pressure Cuban officials to prevent the ship's departure. If that failed, the information needed to reach American authorities with enough time to intercept the ship before it reached the southern coastline.

This last proviso proved to be particularly difficult. As early as 1921, well before talk of a treaty, Americans knew that timely notice of the departure of a smuggling vessel determined the Coast Guard's ability to intercept it. From the beginning, the framework to report ship departures was cumbersome at best: information was relayed from the Cuban customs offices to the American consulate in Havana, who then reported to the Bureau of Customs in Washington, D.C. From there, the information had to make its way to the customs inspector or Coast Guard station closest to where the ship might be headed. Little wonder that the information often arrived too late, almost laughably so, to be of any use. Indeed, shortly after the treaty went into effect, the collector of customs in Tampa wrote to Carleton Bailey Hurst, the consul general in Havana, arguing that the customs office needed notification within twelve hours of a ship's departure from Cuba if it were to intercept the vessel. The current reporting times were nowhere near that efficient. "In many instances," he noted, "it has been learned that a vessel leaving Habana with a cargo of liquor that has been cleared, say, for some port in Honduras, has been landed on the coast of Florida, and the vessel back in Havana for another cargo before the notice of her clearance sent out from the consulate has been received in this office." He begged the consulate to telegraph his office directly rather than rely on "another department of the Government" to provide the information in time. He was even willing to pay the cable charges himself.[15]

It would have been simpler, of course, to place an official at the consulate in Havana to monitor shipping traffic at its port. But American agencies could not agree who might undertake this task. Some argued for a naval attaché, while others favored a member of the State Department staff. Shipping traffic in Havana was heavy. Knowing what was loaded on each ship, monitoring the efforts of smuggling networks to conduct liquor sales in Cuba, and maintaining relations with the appropriate Cuban authorities to convince them to prevent a ship's departure was no small task. It also required familiarity with various entities around Havana, from the telegraph offices to the customs office to local police and harbor police to the consulate itself, all of whom interacted in various ways with the smuggling trade. No one in the federal government fit the bill. Rather than create a new bureaucracy in Havana, the federal government, through the Intelligence Division of the U.S. Coast Guard, funded and fostered a small group of civilians who acted, as they jokingly referred to themselves, as "Uncle Sam's Booze Cops" in Havana.[16] It was their efforts that shut down smuggling from Havana, if only temporarily.

The booze cops in Havana were recruited and led by an American named Henry J. Kime. Kime himself is a bit of a mystery. He was an expatriate living in Havana who appeared to have some financial resources. He did not work, yet he funded his group's operations when government reimbursements and salaries were slow in arriving, as they almost invariably were. And he apparently drove a canary-yellow car. By the time his efforts appear in the records of the Coast Guard Intelligence Division, he had already established friendly working relations with most of the American embassy staff and officials in the Cuban government, along with the various police and customs agencies in Havana. While he talked little about himself, his correspondence revealed he lived in the nicer and newer neighborhoods of Havana, first in Vedado and then in Miramar, two areas that developed along the Malecón, west of what is now Old Havana. He employed a Chinese cook and enjoyed few things more than Turkish cigarettes (Turkish *stinkeros*, as he referred to them in one letter) and long drives in his car under the Cuban moon. He was resourceful and good-humored, joking that vaudeville experience was vastly preferable to military training when it came to Prohibition work.[17] His compatriots were a varied bunch. Mary O'Kane was the Venezuelan-born wife of an American engineer working in Havana. She developed a special talent for encouraging people — Cuban government officials, tourists, and local grocery store owners, among others — to give her information. Another, Salvador Pena, had grown up Havana. He had a wife and a young child but was nonetheless willing to undertake risky undercover operations when needed. O'Kane and Pena formed the backbone of Kime's "gang." However, a revolving cast of characters, some sent down by authorities in Washington, D.C., and some recruited in Havana from the mass of people involved in greater or lesser ways with the smuggling industry, aided their efforts.

The work of the entire group was narrated in a series of letters between Kime and the head of the Coast Guard Intelligence Division, Charles S. Root, in Washington, D.C. Kime and Root's correspondence covers the period between late 1925, when the U.S. government began to focus on the liquor traffic out of Havana, to the end of 1927, when Kime and Root, after initial success, became worried that the liquor traffic was resuming. They communicated through the diplomatic pouch that traveled twice weekly between Washington and Havana, and their correspondence showed the easy camaraderie that had developed over several years of work. They griped about government bureaucracy, vented their frustrations about their superiors, and talked about sharing "barrels of red ink"— their euphemism for booze — under the tropical sky. Kime usually requested that Root send his regards to other officials, like Peter del Valle, who visited Cuba in 1925 to report on smuggling. Root often reminded Kime to take good care of O'Kane and Pena, who depended on him for their livelihoods. Root saw his correspondence with Kime as something friendlier that his usual official communications. One day when Root found himself tied to the office after 8:00 in the evening, he called his letter-writing to Kime "a breathing spell."[18] Together, their correspondence paints a surprisingly personal portrait of the American effort to stop liquor smuggling in Cuba, an effort that was equal parts diplomacy, intelligence gathering, subterfuge, and frustration.

Kime coordinated antismuggling efforts with members of the U.S. diplomatic staff in Havana and with the judicial police and local judiciary in the Cuban government. Root handled much of the bureaucratic framework around Kime's work and acted as a liaison between Kime, an informal and untitled Treasury agent, and the rest of the federal bureaucracy. Both positions provided a detailed view, though by no means a comprehensive one, of the efforts of the American government to enforce an American law at one of its most important international locations. And while it is likely that Kime's and Roots's perspectives on enforcement were sometimes dead wrong, their perceptions of the situation reveal a great deal about how Prohibition enforcement was reshaped by reality when it was implemented in a foreign country. What officials envisioned in Washington rarely worked as expected in Havana, and despite the expansion of federal power the law encouraged, as well as the U.S. government's hold over Cuban affairs, enforcement abroad was no sure thing. Together the two men formed a significant partnership that ultimately worked, at least for a time, to foil the large-scale smuggling of liquor from Cuba to the United States.

Officials in the United States long suspected that smuggling ships loaded cargoes of liquor in Havana that landed along the American coast. But they were unable to intervene because rum runners carried clearance papers that seemed in order. Kime and his group proved that these ships cleared Havana's port fraudulently; the customs documents indicating that the ship had unloaded their cargo in legal ports and not on the beaches of the United States were forged. This evidence convinced the Cuban government to start preventing the departures of loaded rum runners from Havana and hold them for violations of Cuban law. Kime and Root suspected that the fraudulent clearance papers originated with the Honduran consulate in Havana largely because so many suspected smugglers carried papers that indicated they had delivered their cargoes to Honduras. To gather information on exactly how these transactions took place required the work of an undercover operative. Salvador Pena took on that role, agreeing to sign on as a crew member on a British smuggling vessel, the *Varuna*, to gather information. The *Varuna* was a 300-ton, two-masted rum schooner with auxiliary engines. It had come to the attention of American officials for claiming to unload liquor in Limón, Honduras, a port with no customs office authorized to accept imported goods.[19] Claiming to be wanted by the Cuban police, Pena obtained work as an engineer on the *Varuna*, hired by the ship's master, Captain Charles E. Bodden. Pena boarded the boat, and until the boat sailed a few days later, Pena was left to his own devices on board. He proceeded to "ransack [the vessel] from bow to stern." In the captain's quarters, he discovered a complete set of clearance papers indicating the ship had unloaded its cargo in Honduras. The papers were already signed, with the seals of the Honduran customs agency at the destination port already affixed. The dates for the ship's voyage, however, were left blank. The papers provided strong evidence that smuggling schooners did indeed leave Havana with their completed customs papers already on board. The papers alone could not fully prove customs fraud, however, until they were presented to Cuban customs officials in Havana upon the ship's return from its voyage. Pena marked the papers with three pinholes in the corner to identify them as the papers on board before the ship's departure, a subtle identifier unlikely to catch the attention of the captain.[20]

After being appointed ship's engineer, Pena set about learning the operation of the ship's engine. Engines, whether powered by steam or gas combustion, were relatively new additions to schooners, and their operation was tricky and unreliable. Pena realized that disabling the engine could prove useful if the ship encountered the Coast Guard on its voyage. Pena hoped that if the Coast Guard seized the *Varuna* at sea while it was selling cargo to contact boats, the fraudulent papers could be used as evidence. And a ship unable to outrun the Coast Guard was more likely to be seized. Pena discovered he could use spit to render the engine temporarily inoperable, a strategy he had mastered by the time the ship set sail. The first few days of the voyage were difficult, as the ship encountered rough weather heading to a point off Mobile, Alabama, where the captain hoped to sell part of his cargo. He then planned to travel to Indian Rock Beach to unload the rest. Six days into the voyage, sailing slowly under one sail, the *Varuna* spotted the *Comanche*, a Coast Guard boat. Worried that Bodden might try to outrun the *Comanche* and that spitting might not be enough to stall the engine, Pena urinated on the carburetor, rendering the *Varuna* temporarily dead in the water. The Coast Guard boarded the ship and demanded to inspect the cargo. Seeing that some cases were missing, the officer sent the ship's papers over to the *Comanche* and informed Bodden that the vessel was being seized.[21]

The *Comanche* towed the *Varuna* to Mobile, where the crew was arrested and placed in the county jail. While leaving the dock, Pena heard the Coast

Guard men commenting on the fine quality spirits the *Varuna* was carrying. The following day the *Varuna*'s crew was photographed and fingerprinted, and Pena was questioned. He disclosed that he was an undercover agent and eventually showed officers the chart and the travels of the ship, pointing out that the vessel had never headed toward Honduras, its supposed destination. He also noticed the ship's condition after the Coast Guard took control. "The ship was strewn with empty champagne bottles and beer bottles — all the bottles we had were full when we left Havana. The ship looked as if somebody had been having a good time." All the personal belongings of the crew were also nowhere to be found. Not long after, Bodden bailed out the entire crew and gave Pena $100 for new clothes. Pena returned to Havana, his undercover identity intact, with an offer of employment on Bodden's next smuggling voyage aboard the *Exploit*. The *Varuna* was eventually released along with its cargo, and the charges against it and the crew were dismissed. Bodden returned to Havana and used the forged clearance papers on a subsequent voyage six months later. Another of Kime's agents retrieved a copy of the forged papers, clearly identified by Pena's three pinholes, from the port office.[22] Charles Root later lamented that it was almost unfortunate that the *Varuna* was "pinched"; the ship's capture prevented Pena from learning more of Bodden's smuggling connections in New Orleans.[23]

In some senses, Pena's mission aboard the *Varuna* was a success; he located the counterfeit clearance papers on board before the ship departed for sea. His efforts clearly established the role of forged clearance papers in the operations of smugglers, a considerable achievement. Nevertheless, while the treaty provided the broad outlines of procedures for stopping smuggling, ending smuggling also required the willingness on the part of Cuban officials to interrupt seemingly legitimate trade. Both Kime and Root expressed considerable frustration at the unwillingness of authorities in either Cuba or the United States to take effective steps to end what they believed was obvious lawbreaking, even after Pena's discoveries aboard the *Varuna*. Kime diligently obtained and copied the manifests of departing schooners in the hopes that if the ships were seized by the Coast Guard, the information would be sufficient to allow the courts to confiscate and auction the ships. But his efforts were frustratingly inadequate. Kime wrote Root that the *Elena* and *La Isla* had been released by the federal courts despite clear evidence that the boats carried cargoes of liquor and suspicions that the vessels were unloading their cargo to boats headed for the United States. "Too bad they can't hold them after they catch 'em," he wrote. "Thought the manifests I sent on these vessels would be enough to hold them — seems it was not."[24] His frustration at this point focused on the inability of American authorities to disrupt rum runners' operations. His disdain for Cuban authorities, who were unwilling to question the clearance papers of suspected schooners, revealed itself a few weeks later. Writing to Root that the schooner *C. M. Lawrence* (formerly the *Radio*) had returned to Havana after unloading its cargo, he noted the ship's "record-breaking voyage." "She went from here to St. Pierre [off the coast of Canada] — then to Trujillo [a port in Honduras] — then to Habana — all in six days. It just proves that the days of the fast clipper ships are not over — seems like a rum cargo surely does put speed to a vessel."[25] The evidence Kime's gang supplied did not convince Cuban officials that boats like the *C. M. Lawrence* carried fraudulent clearance papers from the start, smuggled liquor, and should not be allowed to leave port.

Pena did eventually uncover the racket in fraudulent clearance papers but through a much simpler operation. He bought a set of papers himself. Henry Kime gave Pena $200 and told him to purchase a set of forgeries from the Honduran officials suspected of selling them. Pena called at the Honduran consulate at the end of August 1926 and told a Mr. J. Cobo that he intended to go into the business of smuggling liquor into the United States and wanted to register his American vessel under the Honduran flag. Cobo said a foreign registry could not be accomplished without the boat actually traveling to Honduras. He nonetheless offered to take Pena to a man who could sell him a Honduran registry and forged clearance papers, though for a considerable price. Several days later, Cobo introduced Pena to another man at the Honduran consulate named Du Bouchet. After hearing Pena's plans, Du Bouchet stated "that things were bad now on account of the American government" but that he could still arrange papers for Pena's smuggling business. Du Bouchet agreed to supply Pena with forged clearance papers from any Honduran port for the sum of $200 per set. After several days, Pena returned to the consulate to pick up the papers for a fictitious ship named, with no small irony, the *Carrie Nation*. When Pena left the official's office, he carried not only the completed, forged papers but also a receipt signed by Du Bouchet stating that Pena had paid $200 to obtain them. Ten minutes after Pena left the consulate with papers in hand, he watched Cobo and Du Bouchet divide some money in a café near the Honduran consulate.[26]

Pena's clearly forged papers made their way to the Cuban and American authorities. Cuban government officials questioned Cobo about the papers,

Rum runner beached by tropical storm, Daytona, Florida, undated
(Courtesy of the State Archives of Florida)

but he denied he had ever seen them before. Nevertheless, especially with
the signed receipt, the evidence that smugglers carried forged papers was
indisputable. Honduran consular officials had been providing forged customs documents to rum-running ships for a fee. From that point forward,
the Cuban government found it much more difficult to argue that vessels
carrying seemingly legitimate documents were operating legally. Ultimately,
the treaty with the United States, printed in full in Havana newspapers, as
well as the clear evidence that the clearance papers of liquor-laden vessels
were fake, gave the Cuban government sufficient justification to take action.
Cuban officials began to prevent the departures of ships loaded with large
cargoes of alcohol claiming to be headed to Honduran ports. This action
represented a substantial victory against the liquor traffic and, in combination with the ability of the U.S. Coast Guard to board suspected boats outside
U.S. territorial waters, began to curtail the smuggling traffic out of Havana.

By the fall of 1926, with the evidence of Kime's undercover efforts and the
adoption of the Rum Treaty by Cuba, the tide seemed to be turning. When
Kime provided information about the *Alida Bonnefil*'s history of smuggling
voyages to Secretary Walter T. Prendergast at the embassy, Prendergast notified the Cuban state department that the ship was engaged in smuggling and
asked that it and its cargo of 200,000 gallons of liquor be held. The Cuban

government complied. Not long after, the *F. A. Marie* returned from the U.S. coast, having been unable to unload its cargo. The crew replaced its stores and made preparations again to head to sea. Kime again notified Prendergast that the *F. A. Marie*'s papers were fraudulent, and Prendergast again notified the Cuban state department to hold the ship. There was some mix-up by the Cubans, and the boat left the harbor, "only to be chased by a police boat after she passed Morro and [was] ordered back."[27] Prendergast, at Kime's urging, then asked that the Cuban government hold every vessel loading in Havana under a Honduran registry. Kime suggested that the embassy ask the Cubans to detain ships flying British flags as well, but the embassy was "not willing to go too far with that." But because of their efforts, ships loaded with liquor were no longer leaving port. Kime was ebullient. He chided smugglers who seemed surprised at the turnaround in the business. They "were so sure that the treaty didn't amount to a good damn that to this moment not one of the gang on Havana Rum Row has thought maybe it is the Treaty going into effect that has caused the trouble."[28] A few days later, his spirits had not dropped. The *Akola* had entered port with half its cargo on board, the other half being lost overboard in bad weather. Prendergast promised to have the boat held in port. He also promised to hold the *Melissa S.* and the *Thelma H.*, which were awaiting cargo. Charles Peters, owner of the *Alida Bonnefil*, had been forced to sell another of his ships, the *Cayman*, in order to pay the fees for the *Evylin D.*, held in Savannah. The *Evylin D.* eventually set sail but was immediately captured again by the Coast Guard. By mid-September, the port in Havana was holding thirteen vessels suspected of smuggling. Several wholesalers, including Mourice Roud, were making plans to transfer their operations to Mexico, where they hoped to find a more welcoming environment. And fewer than 1,500 cases of liquor had been cleared from the port in the past six weeks. It was a fairly spectacular victory. "We have walloped the smugglers and have them on the run," Kime boasted. By January 1927, only five ships remained anchored in Havana harbor, largely because they were prevented from leaving. In 1925, there had been twenty-eight vessels floating in Havana's port, all of them smuggling ships.[29]

Kime, the Cuban government, and the U.S. embassy in Havana had created a relatively workable system to prevent smugglers from leaving Cuba for the shores of the United States. Kime and his crew provided members of the staff at the consulate in Havana evidence that a ship was engaged in smuggling. The chargé d'affaires then contacted Cuban port authorities and requested that they hold the ship in port. For ships that left Havana for ports in the Bahamas, Bimini, or Mexico to take on liquor cargoes, Kime and his cohorts notified authorities in the United States of those ships' movements, providing what they hoped was sufficient information for the Coast Guard to intercept and seize the vessels. And when ships left with full cargoes headed toward the U.S. coast and were seized by Coast Guard patrols, Kime obtained evidence of the ships' fraudulent clearance papers and sent them to law enforcement officials in the United States. Kime's evidence was not always sufficient to obtain the convictions of crews or shipowners or to confiscate the vessel, but the information that Kime provided was, according to Root, "priceless."[30]

The success of Kime's band of "Booze Cops in the West Indies" was the result of a successful treaty "with teeth." Kime believed Cuba's passage of a domestic tariff law to support the treaty helped, as did a major hurricane in October 1926 that sank five schooners in Havana harbor and severely damaged an additional four.[31] Cuba and the American embassy were pushed to take action against smuggling ships because Kime's groups provided clear and convincing evidence of violations of international law. They obtained their information through old-fashioned undercover sleuthing, of which Pena's turn as a ship's engineer was only one part. The efforts of Mary O'Kane, whom a Secret Service agent once called "one of the finest detectives he had ever seen," played a role as well. Describing O'Kane's efforts to track down Mourice Roud's former bookkeeper in Florida to obtain information on Roud's operations in Havana, Kime likened her to a "professional Dick." When the bookkeeper disappeared from Tampa, she tracked him down in Jacksonville within twenty-four hours. When she found that he and his wife were broke, she convinced them to return to Havana with her. Not only were her interrogation skills at a level to convince an insider in the smuggling business to fully describe operations, but she saw the potential for information-gathering in the most mundane of encounters. On one occasion, she struck up a conversation with a female passenger on the ferry from Havana to Tampa. When the conversation raised her suspicions, she copied the woman's name from her suitcase and turned it over to authorities. It turned out to be "a clew [sic] of vast importance which uncovered a crooked U.S. official whose duplicity had not been hitherto suspected." Months later, when Kime wanted to know the exact nature of one smuggler's relationship with a woman living at the same address, O'Kane approached the owner of the corner grocery store and inquired into the couple's habits. Though the smuggler, Facundo

Sardinas, was married, he lived with his French mistress, to whom he had transferred title of a farm and one of his rum-running schooners to put it out of reach of Cuban authorities. O'Kane even took a job herself in Mourice Roud's office to gather information, a move that the Secret Service agent conceded took "iron nerve." O'Kane paid a certain price for her efforts. Despite her alleged toughness in the face of crooks, she was vulnerable to slights to her virtue. Kime wrote to Root in outrage when a onetime ally accused Kime and O'Kane of being lovers in a Havana gossip rag. Later, in her dealings with Cuban judicial officials, she was reminded several times that this was no work for a lady. She nevertheless commanded respect because of her effectiveness. Eventually, the Cuban judicial authorities began to refer to O'Kane as *nuestra embajadora* (our ambassador), as she was more successful working with the Cuban government against smugglers than was the American embassy.[32] Ultimately, she was a critical part of Kime's operations. Indeed, she achieved gains that likely no other member of the group could manage.

Pena's skills were of an entirely different variety. As a relatively young man, he used his employability to go undercover, working as crew on two sailing vessels. Eventually, U.S. enforcement authorities sent him to Puerto Mexico, Nassau, and other suspected smuggling ports to infiltrate smuggling operations. His efforts were by far the most dangerous as he worked directly with smugglers and pretended to be a member of their fraternity. Kime worried regularly that the bumblings of U.S. government agencies would blow Pena's cover, and both Kime and Root believed that U.S. officials treated him poorly. When he was arrested with the crew of the *Varuna*, it was Bodden who had provided his living expenses and paid for his passage back to Havana, something the federal government failed to do. Pena was arrested on several occasions with his smuggling companions. On only one occasion was he forced to flash a badge indicating that he was a U.S. government agent. But Kime worried about his safety continually.[33]

Kime himself was equally cagey in his work as an undercover agent. He spent many an evening loitering at Havana cafés, eavesdropping on individuals he suspected of being in the smuggling business. Late in his correspondence with Root, Kime reminded him to send him a particular brand of cigarettes in the diplomatic pouch, as they were one of the best ways to obtain information. "My tables at the various cafes I am forced to visit almost nightly is very popular [on account of] my cigarette case."[34] Kime was undoubtedly a man with a very cool nerve, and he used his quick wits in the

Facundo Sardinas (*right*), owner of the *Arsene J*
(National Archives and Records Administration,
Internal Revenue Service Prohibition Unit,
RG 58, box 52)

service of his mission. One night, driving over the Almendares River at what
was then the edge of the city, Kime noticed a gathering at the Miramar Café.
He stopped and entered the café, suspecting some kind of smuggling operation was preparing to leave from the bridge. When a man who was clearly
involved mistook Kime for a "jewish shirtmaker" who operated a shop in
Old Havana and was a partner in the venture, Kime took on the role without missing a beat. He spent the rest of the night posing as the shirtmaker,
watching the events around him. It turned out that the shirtmaker and his

friend planned to smuggle immigrants by boat to the Florida coast. This particular venture was foiled by rough seas, but Kime nevertheless obtained the names of two Cuban police officers who accepted bribes to ignore the boat's departure. When he could not get the U.S. embassy to intervene, he called the Cuban police. The schooner was towed to the police dock, where it remained.[35]

Kime's agents also leveraged the relationships that they formed with a variety of Cuban officials in Havana. They befriended port officers who collected the clearance papers of ships returning to port and, with well-placed bribes as incentive, took suspect papers and cargo manifests from the port office to be copied by "photostat" by American officials. They also tracked almost all the communications between the crew and captains of chartered schooners, local wholesalers, and bootlegging operations in the United States. For a monthly bribe, they received copies of virtually every suspicious letter and telegram that arrived in Havana. By early 1926, Kime crowed to Root that he had "control of all lines of communication," except the mail, which shortly followed. At the telegraph office, Kime had made a deal with the night manager that if Kime provided the name of the person in which he was interested, the telegraph employee would pull all the telegrams associated with the person, both to and from, and have them available for Kime to pick up within twenty-four hours. All it cost was a mere $150 a month. Kime eventually established a similar arrangement with a "queer duck" at Western Union for a similar amount. He eventually arranged to get summaries of smugglers' incoming and outgoing mail as well. The cost was "cheap at that price in this land of high pay for sin."[36]

Throughout Prohibition, Kime translated a vague implication that he was an American with influence and power into a considerable amount of information, miraculously without blowing his cover. Once, pointing out the necessity of deception, he admitted somewhat facetiously that he had "represented [himself] as being everything including a brother of a congressman and the daughter of the president." He played a tricky game. To some, he implied he was an American engaged in the smuggling business. To others, he claimed to be affiliated with U.S. government agencies from the Secret Service to the Treasury Department to the State Department. Kime pointed out that he needed some leeway in describing his agency affiliation because Prohibition agents had so little credibility on the island. As he told Root, "The Cuban and the American crooks here may be dumb but they would have the laugh on a person who was foolish enough to attempt to do all the above business ["immigration, fake money, dope, white slave, bunco, search for fugitives, deal with Havana customs, and fool the booze rings"] under the authority of the Prohibition Act alone. Can't be done." Root gave Kime an informal okay to impersonate whatever agency official suited his purposes. "You're the boss there and should claim to be the first cousin of the Secretary of State if conditions warrant. You should be a dollars-a-year man for every Department."[37]

All told, his gang of booze cops almost entirely wiped out the smuggling of liquor from Havana during 1926 and 1927. Aside from being a difficult task, it was also dangerous, something that the light tone of Root and Kime's correspondence often obscured. Threats against the group, however, were not uncommon. Charles Root received reports that smuggler Facundo Sardinas had offered Salvador Pena a $10,000 bribe with the warning that he should take the bribe or be bumped off. Men working for Sardinas also threatened to find out where O'Kane lived and beat her in an effort to force her to flee the country.[38] Early in his correspondence with Root, Kime described carrying a pistol, even though it violated Cuban law. Once when he was arrested, he attempted to convince the police that he was an American agent, showing them an improvised shield. The Cubans remained dubious until Kime had a friend telephone General Pablo Mendieta, Havana's chief of police, on his behalf. Mendieta called the police station and "gave the police captain hell," and Kime left the station with his gun. Not long after, Kime asked Root to investigate the possibility of obtaining a special gun permit through the embassy that would not require a photo and full identification. "We will go armed however regardless of permits," he warned Root. "I'd sooner that my men and [myself] take a chance of getting picked up once in a while by the police for carrying arms without permits than to have anyone get bumped off without a chance of defense on account of conforming to Cuban laws."[39]

Despite the seemingly happy picture of success in shutting down the smuggling industry in the Havana harbor, the American team faced a host of challenges, few of them having to do with the determination of smuggling outfits to stay in business. The U.S. government, in fact, created their biggest challenges. Ultimately, those obstacles, which remained unresolved, would spell failure in permanently ending smuggling from Cuban ports and of Prohibition as a whole. For though Kime and his group determined the mechanisms by which rum runners left and returned to the port of Havana and rooted out the corrupt system of fraudulent customs documents that made those departures and returns possible, the relatively functional relationship Kime and his gang shared with Cuban authorities was never matched by easy relationships with authorities in the United States. Kime and Root routinely butted heads with American officials, and the bumbling attempts by the U.S. government to control Kime's operations and Prohibition enforcement efforts in Cuba ultimately doomed their efforts. The inefficient and bureaucratically inept efforts by multiple U.S. government agencies to work together and extend their operations into Cuba undermined enforcement at every turn. The difficulties that Kime faced were legion, from incompetence to turnover up the chain of command to arcane accounting policies. But they represented a greater obstacle to successful enforcement of Prohibition than did rum runners themselves.

One of Henry Kime's greatest aggravations was the seemingly endless turnover in the men to whom he reported. Captain Peter del Valle recruited Henry Kime during his investigation in 1925, and initially Kime reported to him. When Root assumed oversight of the surveillance of smugglers, Kime sent his reports to him in Washington, D.C. It was likely during this time that the two developed their close relationship. Not long after, however, Kime was instructed to report to a series of officials in the Prohibition Bureau within the Department of the Treasury. He first reported to a man named Treadway, then to Jim Corcoran, followed by men named Moberly, Bruff, and Topham — revisions to a reporting structure that all occurred within a single year. As Kime wrote to Root, "If the smugglers would change their plans and bosses as frequently as this department, they would be easy to beat — and that is the chief reason why we are so easy to beat."[40] Each supervisor had his own agenda and his own expectations. Peter del Valle's investigation into smuggling from Cuba resulted in the antismuggling treaty with Cuba, and Kime supported his efforts by providing del Valle with contacts in Havana. Treadway urged Kime to focus on the suppliers. Under his watch, Kime placed O'Kane in Mourice Roud's wholesaling operation for twenty-seven days. Jim Corcoran insisted that Kime break into the actual smuggling ventures and infiltrate the communications of smuggling groups. Kime placed Pena aboard the *Varuna* and arranged to intercept telegraph and mail communications. Moberley focused on coded communications but accomplished little, given his short tenure, while Bruff was more willing to take action without permission. When Pena was arrested with nothing but a shirt when the

Exploit was seized, Bruff apparently did not consult with Washington before buying him a new suit. Bruff's supervisor "raised hell" about it, but Kime appreciated his decisiveness in small things. When Topham took over, he criticized the organization of Kime's reports, complaining that reports on multiple vessels should not be on a single page. Kime bought cheap paper and complied, despite his irritation. Not long after, Topham insisted that Kime only communicate with Topham's office in Jacksonville, Florida, instead of both Topham and Charles Root in Washington. Kime's frustration boiled over when Topham moved his office to Miami and neglected to provide Kime with his new address. Kime and Root speculated that Topham suffered from a desire to claim credit for diminishing smuggling from Cuba. He sought to isolate Kime's operations under his own command, leaving Kime largely in the dark about developments elsewhere. Summing up his feelings about being cut off from the larger antismuggling operation, Kime maligned, "The Habana office is cut off from any direct communication with Washington in the matter of reports, correspondence — money — first aid — weather reports — stock reports — fashion hints — good cheer — and thanks." At least Kime kept his sense of humor.[41]

Worse than the different habits and preferences, frequent turnover slowed Kime's efforts considerably. Each new supervisor had to be brought up to speed on the situation in Cuba. Each had to be introduced to the main characters involved in the liquor traffic, educated on the process by which ships evaded American law, and schooled on the peculiarities of Cuban government officials and law enforcement procedures. Both Kime and Root felt these hassles undermined their overall mission. Reporting on another turnover in the enforcement hierarchy, an exasperated Root wrote, "If we ever get where we can have the same system for more than three months at a time, I shall be glad," which was a very great understatement.[42] Indeed, venting about their frustrations with the chain of command was a common feature of their correspondence.

Unhelpful meddling in his operations also drove Kime to distraction, particularly when government officials sent him additional personnel without his approval. Two of them, though initially helpful, were sent back to Washington for insubordination and an alarming lack of discretion. One tried to claim credit for the success of Kime's overall operation; the other refused to recognize Kime's authority. The worst transplant from Washington, a man named Hugo, initially seemed like a hopeful addition to the team. Originally from the Philippines, he was a native Spanish speaker, no doubt a useful attribute in Cuba. But Kime and Hugo failed to establish a productive working relationship. As Kime complained to Root, "He is a cooky pushing punk. He didn't even try to make good." "Cooky pushing" was Root's and Kime's euphemism for focusing on bureaucratic procedure and kowtowing to higher authorities, even at the expense of the larger mission. Nimbleness in action was far preferable to adhering to bureaucratic rules, and in Kime's eyes, Hugo was useless. Hugo, however, earned Kime's enduring enmity with his method of departure. Unhappy in his work, Hugo contacted Kime's superior, who at the time was Bruff, and stated that he would like to be transferred to Jacksonville because of "Incompatibility with his chief." However, he sent the message over an open telegraph line to Bruff's government office address. Kime received a copy of the message from his source at the telegraph office and became immediately concerned that his cover was blown. "The boys at the [telegraph office] don't think we are a bootleg syndicate sending code messages about booze shipments anymore—they know we are government agents now after Hugo's message. Fine, what!"[43]

As Hugo's ill-advised departure suggests, the frequent turnover among personnel involved with enforcement represented a particular hazard to Kime's operations. Pena, O'Kane, and Kime operated best when their relationship to both smugglers and the U.S. government remained murky. Little annoyed them more than loose lips or ill-considered communications that could expose them as U.S. government agents working to stop the liquor traffic. Yet time and again, their positions were placed in jeopardy by the careless actions of American officials. Root was particularly frustrated, having more interaction with the higher level of enforcement than did Kime. He was often baffled by how little their superiors recognized that Kime and his group played a precarious game. "When I saw [government officials] in Florida," he wrote to Kime in 1926, "I was shocked by the open way in which they talked of matters which should never have been mentioned above a whisper." Cognizant of the possibility that allies of smuggling syndicates could be watching at any time, Root held his information close. Not so the men he worked with: "They are a lot of parrots," he concluded. Even Harry J. Anslinger, who was given authority over efforts to prevent smuggling from international ports and who had served as the consul general in Nassau, had to be reminded by Root to be more discreet. After Anslinger requested copies of the forged clearance papers for the *Carrie Nation* that Pena had obtained,

Root "cautioned him not to give the game away as he might be playing with safety and usefulness" of the team in Havana. Root, however, was not sure that his words of caution would do any good. "He promised, and perhaps he will be careful," Root concluded.[44] Kime's superiors might have been excused for being thoughtless when they were stateside. Communications with agents in Cuba was another matter. Root insisted that all communications with Kime should be sent either through the diplomatic pouch or encoded, in case they were intercepted by smuggling outfits or Cuban officials in their pay. Yet he was quite sure that the code used by Kime's superior, Topham, would provide little cover. "Anyone who knows the first thing about breaking ciphers could read them as easily as plain text. It is neither his fault nor mine, just some of the d__n stupidity of this Washington office."[45]

Intercepted communication was problem enough; indeed, Kime suspected that all his mail was being opened and occasionally swiped by someone in the Havana post office. Being exposed by the red tape of government bureaucracy was quite another matter. On several occasions members of government agencies, in their efforts to get proper documentation, put Kime's efforts uncomfortably in the spotlight. After both Salvador Pena and Henry Kime received official letters about employment policies from the U.S. Civil Service Commission in official envelopes mailed directly to their office in Havana, Kime snidely remarked, "I guess they believe we're in uniform down here and that it would be all right to use the regular mail." Stateside officials also requested forms be completed and submitted that could blow the covers of Kime's sources of information. At one point, for example, to provide the necessary documentation for payment, the government tried to require that everyone Kime paid for information sign a formal "informer's contract," including Kime's Cuban sources at the telegraph offices in Havana. Aside from the possible exposure such a document created, Kime insisted it would wreak havoc on the morale of his forces. All of them participated in his efforts out of a sense of adventure or a desire to have some official role, perhaps with a bit of attached glamour in working undercover for the U.S. government. Kime even spent a fair amount of his correspondence urging officials in Washington to devise some sort of impressive-looking, if largely meaningless, badge, which Kime's agents might carry, complete with gold foil and red ribbons. They most surely would not have been pleased to learn that in the eyes of the U.S. government, they were little more than stool pigeons and snitches, as the informer's contract implied. Indeed, Kime worked very hard to convey a sense of stature and pride to his agents. When one seemed to be doubtful that his services were official, Kime took him to the embassy and had a secretary there have him swear an oath. According to Kime, the agent took it so seriously he "looked like he was getting married." But it did the trick; the agent "believes that he is an honest to God officer of the U.S.A."[46] This man's belief that he worked in an official capacity was both a source of pride and a promise of loyalty; undermining both to meet the needs of bureaucracy ultimately harmed Kime's operations. Asking undercover operatives to jump through demeaning hoops like the informer's contract were continual reminders that officials residing on American soil had little real understanding of the work Kime and his gang did and the risks they faced.

Nothing, however, was a more persistent source of aggravation and bureaucratic ineptitude to Kime than the inability of the U.S. government to compensate him and his crew for their efforts. Indeed, accounting matters, referred to disparagingly as "Jew business" or trying to get Kime and his agents some "kale," formed a persistent drumbeat in their correspondence. When Kime began his work with Peter del Valle investigating the smuggling situation in Cuba in 1925, they agreed that Kime would receive $200 per month, a $5.00 per diem, and reimbursement of his expenses. By April 1926, Kime was $2,000 in the hole and found himself routinely using his own personal savings to support his agents. A mere month later, Kime was awaiting some $4,000 in payments, a combination of his salary for several months, the salaries of his gang, and unpaid reimbursements for his expenses. "I haven't seen any money for so long that I am beginning to wonder if they have moved the Treasury," he wryly noted.[47] Despite Root's continual work to track down pay vouchers and speed Kime's deposits along, the situation never improved. Occasionally money was forthcoming from Washington but never at a predictable rate that could prevent Kime's personal financial hemorrhage. Kime dutifully totaled up his accounts for Root and gamely sent his vouchers to whichever superior officer he was told to report to. But the government was always several thousand dollars behind in paying the agents manning its Havana operation. At various points, Salvador Pena took on side jobs as an illustrator to be able to provide for his family, and even O'Kane threatened to take a second job as a stenographer to make ends meet.[48] By mid-1927, Kime had put more than $7,000 of his own money into efforts to prevent smuggling from Cuba. Kime repeatedly noted that the entire operation in Havana would have been impossible had he not had a "small bankroll to fall back on," and he found the lack of attention to what should have been minor details of compensation profoundly frustrating. At times he responded with humor, as he did when he sent Root a note "to let you know that we are still alive and determined to not surrender to the Accounting Department — and have born the rigors of the Accounting Department's blockade of Havana most nobly to date." Warning that his agents were reduced to mere shadows of themselves, he told Root not to worry. If Topham were unsuccessful getting his pay through, Kime would send the remains of the Havana crew to Root via diplomatic pouch. He ended his letter by noting that Mourice Roud, the liquor wholesaler and their nemesis, enjoyed his dinner at one of the finest hotels in Havana.[49] At other points, Kime was plain angry, threatening to walk away, insisting that he was "beginning to wake up" and realize that the persistent denial of pay was in fact a veiled message that the government wanted him to quit. Root did his best to resolve the situation, but he, too, found himself largely stymied. The situation was not merely a problem of the Havana operation. Another of Root's operatives in Halifax, Nova Scotia, discovered that a turnover in his chain of command meant he was not paid for five months in a row. Root agonized over his agent's welfare, fearing he was "sitting on a corner with a tin cup and selling lead pencils because he has no Henry to help him between payments," affirming how Kime's personal wealth largely kept his operation in Havana going. Root's Miami operation faced similar difficulties. It had to suspend activities for lack of pay at a crucial moment in its investigations.[50]

Incompetence in the payroll department certainly provided a constant irritation, but the issues were more systemic. Policies regarding compensation and reimbursement changed without warning and without grandfathering already submitted requests for payment, throwing Kime's operations into confusion. Abruptly in 1927, Kime was informed that he would no longer be paid a per diem for his efforts. He was informed that the telegraph and telephone charges associated with the operations of his office also would not be covered by the government, despite the fact that timely notification of the movements of rum-running ships required Kime to send telegrams to the United States regularly. (Root was able to get the telegraph expenses approved after some pushback on his part.) Then to add insult to injury, the accounting department changed the policies on expenses. After being promised reimbursement for his expenses and receiving reimbursement for several months, they suddenly stopped. At one point, Kime even pointed out to Root the one-year anniversary since he received his last reimbursement, adding "God Bless the patient and long suffering." He was then informed by Root that the government would no longer reimburse him for his payments to telegraph and mail clerks for information about smuggling operations and the other various small gratuities that greased his informational wheels. The justification was an obscure law that the accounting office interpreted to mean that money paid to corrupt officials of a foreign state with which the United States was at peace could not be reimbursed. Not long after, Kime received an official notification that O'Kane had received payments amounting to over $1,200 in error and requesting that she return the money to the U.S. government immediately. Already operating without payment for several months, O'Kane was in no position to reimburse the government. Kime refused to ask her, and he was incensed the request was even made. He also knew that similar expenditures constituted a significant part of his operation; as he told Root, "I bust out crying every time I think about [it]." Root, as always, intervened to support Kime's group. He buttonholed officials up the hierarchy of Prohibition enforcement and earnestly pleaded with them to solve the pay problems or they risked losing the Havana team. Root even ventured to criticize government operations, telling Kime that he scolded Anslinger that "his pay department had ceased to function altogether (and Henry, that is the God's truth)."[51] But the money problems never ended.

The heart of the problem, however, was that Congress simply refused to appropriate enough money to enforce Prohibition. Prohibition proponents had promised that enforcement of the Eighteenth Amendment would be easy and inexpensive, as Americans would soon surrender their desire for alcohol. Congress took them at their word and appropriated minimal dollars for law enforcement, amounts that proved to be hopelessly inadequate. Enforcement unsurprisingly foundered. Extending that effort abroad, while it seemed necessary to Prohibition's success, only spread those scarce funds more widely. Foreign operations, however, were costly to maintain, and if the accounting office could find ways to disallow expenses, they did so regardless of the effect on Prohibition overall. Little matter that Kime's operation was reportedly a bright spot in Prohibition enforcement. Root tried to take money appropriated for other aspects of enforcement to fund the Havana operation. He proposed shutting down one of the Coast Guard's wireless stations to use its funds elsewhere. These radio stations, whose utility in locating smuggling operations had not yet been proved, were in their infancy. Eventually the Coast Guard's use of radio transmission and interception would highlight the usefulness of the technology for strategic purposes, but in 1927 Root would have rather used the money for other purposes. Closing one of the stations, in Root's estimation, would provide enough "kale" to fund Kime's operation without having to rely on an accounting department that Root was "convinced . . . is incapable of running even a corner grocery store."[52]

Root's idea was never adopted, but its suggestion laid bare the continual funding problems every agency charged with enforcing Prohibition faced. Eventually Root informed Kime that the situation had become so tenuous that the Prohibition Bureau, which was apparently in charge of all the funds, was conducting an audit of more than $200,000 in enforcement expenses. Root conceded the possibility that all expenses would be disallowed, leading to requests to return what little money Kime had received. If that happened, Root reassured Kime, the best course of action was to take the matter before Congress and ask for more appropriations. Apparently that dire event did not happen. But one irony lingered: as Kime found it ever-more difficult to be paid for his work, the federal government nonetheless continued to demand that the scope of his work expand. His success despite the obstacles he faced spurred the federal government to try to extend its efforts even further, both geographically and in terms of contraband. As it became clearer that his efforts had reduced rum-running out of Cuba to a trickle, he was asked to use his methods to shut down other black markets as well. He was told that his area of operation included not just Cuba but all of Central America and the entire West Indies. And his efforts should not merely focus on preventing the smuggling of booze but the smuggling of immigrants evading the new quota laws and narcotics and opium as well. As Chapter 4 will show, as he did with the liquor traffic, Kime developed procedures with the Cuban government that severely reduced the number of would-be immigrants departing Havana for the deserted beaches along the southern coast. But payment for his efforts never followed. Indeed, Kime fully expected that in return for his success, the government would find ways to further reduce his compensation. As he ruefully joked, "After we smash the alien running business here I suppose we will be rewarded by having our salaries reduced. We were rewarded for closing the harbor to rumrunners by having our expenses disallowed so I suppose something like that will happen. . . . What a nasty joke — on us."[53]

The financial failures of Prohibition enforcement were hardly helped by personnel failures. Careless comments and communications were compounded by the personal foibles and petty rivalries of the men in positions of authority. Root and Kime chafed under Topham's insistence that he and he alone control Kime's communications about his operations. Even the U.S. embassy in Havana was not immune. In one pointed example, in late 1927, Secretary Prendergast declared his refusal to ask Cuban officials to hold any more rum-running ships because he believed he had been denied a promotion.[54] Embedded in many of these issues, however, were hints that American officials were not very enthusiastic about Prohibition at all. Many of them were eager to upend illegal liquor traffic and bring American policing abroad to do so, but that did not mean that they were opposed to the pleasures of alcohol themselves. Kime clearly enjoyed alcoholic beverages, as he occasionally made note of them in the letters to Root, at one point mentioning that he was closing his letter to make a highball that he wished he could share. Root himself also clearly enjoyed alcoholic beverages, though they were theoretically more difficult for him to obtain. He nonetheless wrote about his desire to travel to Cuba and its possibilities for relaxation, telling Kime that he planned a visit to Havana as part of his trip to Florida and hoped "to see you and a barrel of red, red ink." Notably, no Prohibition official practiced temperate habits in Havana. Even Root's superiors were not immune. When high-level Prohibition officials visited, Kime promised to show them around Havana. Kime promised on one occasion to make one of them "forget he was ever Chief Prohibition Investigator, and I know he would love me for that alone!" Yet there was always the possibility that drinking by officials could disrupt enforcement efforts. When one of Root's superiors visited Kime to observe his operations for several weeks, he immediately asked for vacation leave upon his return. His absence delayed his promised efforts to facilitate compensation for Kime and his group. There may very well have been no relationship between his activities in Havana and his need for a vacation, but Root made the connection nevertheless. A month after the visit, with Root's superior still not back in the office, Root asked Kime, "What in the h--l did you do to him?? I fear that you have concealed something."[55]

The foibles of other officials were far more concerning and potentially detrimental to operations. Such concerns extended from the officers and enlisted men on Coast Guard cutters that stopped in Havana all the way up the chain of command. When the Coast Guard cutter *Saukee* voyaged to Havana in late 1927, American and Cuban officials noticed its sailors disembarked with American cigarettes to sell and reboarded with bottles of liquor hidden around their waists and in their pant legs. The Cuban police even chased off a small motorboat that pulled up alongside the *Saukee* with ten cases of liquor to load. Kime considered having the Cubans hold the vessel in port to search for contraband that would violate U.S. laws, but he thought it would be too embarrassing.[56] The problems with liquor went to higher levels of the bureaucracy, however. Kime and Root exchanged concerns about rumors that one new superior in the seemingly endless chain had a tendency to get "pickled" and talk too much about his past.[57] Kime and Root continually lamented the inability of the federal courts to obtain convictions in smuggling cases and confiscate rum-running ships. They attributed failures to incompetence and duplicity, especially among law enforcement in Florida. But access to alcohol and downright laziness seemed to contribute to the problem. Root reported that he had learned that whenever the U.S. District Court held its term in Key West, the judge would adjourn the court on Thursday afternoons to allow the judge, the marshal, the U.S. attorney, and all their assistants to "proceed to Havana for a grand time." These same court officers officiated at the trial of Horace Alderman, who was accused of killing several enforcement agents aboard a rum runner, convicted, and later executed. Root observed that when the officials returned to hold court in Miami one Monday morning, they were all hung over, having returned from Havana late the night before.[58]

Similar concerns could damage the effectiveness of embassy officials in Havana itself. When General Enoch Crowder resigned as ambassador and left Havana in June 1926, he was temporarily replaced by a chargé d'affaires named Winslow. Kime almost immediately questioned Winslow's abilities, pointing out that the two-week delay in reporting on one particular rum runner was caused by Winslow's failure to request the necessary papers from Cuban authorities. Kime "didn't want to go over his head" but nevertheless obtained them himself from his Cuban contacts. Kime's opinion of the man, however, did not improve, and both he and Root took to referring to Winslow with a nickname that suggested his vapid character: "Smoke Goes Up the Chimney," "Smoke," or "SGUTC" for short. Within a year, Winslow's behavior was causing more widespread concern at the consulate. Prendergast, who ranked just below Winslow in the embassy hierarchy and who openly sought Winslow's job, asked Kime how to handle the situation. Winslow "seemed to be having a real good time" in Havana "and is getting rather wild to put it mild," Kime reported to Root. Kime did not want to interfere too openly but worried that the situation was becoming perilous. "Prendergast saw some of SGUTC's fun and is horrified. Thinks it may get us into trouble." Kime urged Root to handle the information carefully, as he feared it could destroy his operation, but he was worried nonetheless. Less than a month later, Winslow had resigned his post. He had apparently been carousing with some questionable characters. Late one night, before Winslow's wife was to arrive in Havana, Prendergast phoned Kime at his home and asked Kime to help him find Winslow, "as it would not do to have him in the street all night." Kime and Prendergast found him at "a rather lousy bar" with some "English chaps." Winslow tendered his resignation almost immediately. Kime was relieved with his decision, fearing "he might say something someday that would cause the Cubans to believe we are not sincere when we claim to be crusading against Demon rum."[59]

Kime's words struck at the heart of Prohibition enforcement in Cuba. Concerns about lost pay vouchers and bureaucratic snafus aside, the unmistakable incompetence among American officials raised concerns among Cubans that Kime sought to avoid. The constant bungling suggested that the United States was unwilling to put forth the effort to stop liquor from coming onto its shores and preferred Cuba to do the work instead. This indeed was the larger conundrum that pushed Kime and Root to vent endlessly about the failures of U.S. government officials. In their eyes, the Cuban government seemed to bear more of the burden for preventing smuggling and more of the expense as well. Once the treaty was in place and operating in conjunction with Cuba's own tariff laws, the Cuban government stood to lose considerable revenue by severely reducing its exports and transshipments of distilled spirits. The city of Havana also lost considerable economic activity when the forty or so rum runners departed Havana looking for more hospitable ports to continue the liquor traffic.

Yet, in the eyes of Kime and Root, who together had clear pictures of the operations in both the United States and Havana, Cuba's efforts were far more effective. Root complained that the United States had too many different agencies engaged in different pieces of the operation to make it effective. Using a term from his days at sea, he described the situation as "everyone's mess and no one's watch."[60] No clear accountability or responsibility for ensuring success existed, and no consistent plan of action emerged. The U.S. government, moreover, seemed to continually churn its strategy for enforcement. When the government decided in 1927 to create a Division of Foreign Control headed by Henry J. Anslinger to coordinate antismuggling efforts, Root pronounced himself baffled by the idea. "Whatever the h--l that means. The Foreign Control belongs to the Coast Guard and can only effectively be used by us and why we didn't get it is more than I can figure out." While the Coast Guard had authority to extend U.S. law enforcement to the high seas, the desire to extend it to places like Havana was entirely more problematic. Not only did the U.S. government demand cooperation from the Cuban government that seemed counter to Cuba's own economic interests and not only was the extended reach of U.S. Prohibition enforcement beyond Kime's group laughably inept, but it placed responsibility for enforcing an American law at the feet of officials in Cuba. To add insult to injury, while efforts in Havana seemed, at least for a while, to be effective, the same could not be said for Prohibition enforcement on American soil. When Root informed Kime that the *Evylin D.* had been released from federal custody because prosecutors could not obtain sufficient identification of the Florida co-conspirators involved in its voyages, Root threw up his hands. "The trouble lies with our Florida gang. With all the chance and time they have had this doesn't look good to me." Kime evidently concurred, insisting that their efforts would be far more successful if stateside enforcement was on the ball. "If they [the U.S. federal courts] would do business on the other side, we could give them two ships per week," providing a far more effective deterrent to smugglers.[61]

Kime and Root also lamented the lack of coordination among the various jurisdictions in the United States that allowed suspected smugglers to slip through their fingers. When the Cubans arrested American Charles Peters, who had established himself in the bootlegging market in Daytona, Kime could not determine if there were outstanding warrants for his arrest that would justify his deportation to the United States. In another case, Cuban authorities arrested George the Greek, another known smuggler, but the embassy did not receive timely reports about his outstanding warrants in the United States. Kime thought George had already been deported back to Greece because the Cubans assumed he was not wanted in the United States. By the time Kime received information that the man was wanted in Texas, Mississippi, and Alabama, it was too late. Eventually even the Cubans became frustrated when the United States did not take advantage of their efforts. Kime, for example, worked with Cuban authorities to have the *Thelma H.* held at port in Havana after receiving information that it was engaged in smuggling. Cuban officials prevented the vessel's departure for almost three weeks before they let it go, even though it had become a popular tourist destination as an actual "contrabandista." It was carrying over 700 cases of assorted liquors and was the first booze ship to clear Havana in two weeks.

"We had 'em licked but Washington took too much time thinking about it," Kime reported. Indeed, once the Cubans began to prevent the departure of suspected rum-running ships, they realized that the U.S. embassy had no clear plan for how it wanted to proceed.[62] Eventually the Cuban government assessed fines from the schooners for customs irregularities that went a small way toward recouping their revenue losses from the export trade. They then held vessels until the fines were paid and the papers were sorted out. For some vessels, it meant a long stay tied to a Havana dock. The *Pauline B. Mosher*, a familiar vessel in the smuggling trade, spent a year in port. Kime suspected that its bottom was starting to rot and it would no longer be seaworthy.[63] But the *Thelma H.* returned to Havana within a few months with fewer cases but no evidence that it reached its stated destination. Again, Kime planned to ask the embassy to request that the boat be held.[64]

Kime speculated that the Rum Treaty in Cuba seemed to be successful in large part because it created the possibility for Cubans to regain some of the revenue lost from smuggling while simultaneously making Havana a far less attractive location for smugglers themselves. By 1927, Kime had developed a routine for dealing with smugglers that allowed the Cuban government to use violations of Cuban laws as a way to obstruct the operations of rum runners. Kime and his group gathered intelligence about who was planning a smuggling venture and fed this information to a Cuban judicial police officer named Alfonso Fors. Fors arrested the suspects and charged them with violations of harbor rules. The men would be released on bail, and if they decided not to incur the expenses of waiting six months for a trial in Havana, they would flee Cuba. If they left the country on bail with charges still pending, however, they could not return without heading immediately to jail. Either outcome "raises the devil with their business" and fueled Havana's growing reputation of being inhospitable to smugglers.[65] But fines for customs violations did not nearly replace the lost revenue from duties on the liquor traffic.

Kime noted that he would not be surprised if the Cuban government secretly wanted to restore the liquor traffic. Kime hoped that this would be unlikely, as wholesalers like Mourice Roud, who had upended their businesses when the liquor treaty went into effect, would be unlikely to place any faith in the protection of their businesses by the Cuban government again. "Without the wholesale liquor dealers there can be no big business!" he insisted.[66] Yet to Cubans on the ground, American efforts to enforce Prohibition looked intrusive but also foolish and inept. On numerous occasions the U.S. government asked Cuban officials to arrest suspected criminals who had recently been in the United States. The Cuban government could not understand why the United States could not arrest seemingly known criminals while they were still in the United States. One case in particular galled Fors. Mario Pelli was a smuggler who carried cargoes of booze, undocumented immigrants, and narcotics to the west coast of Florida. Pelli, however, was an Italian citizen, and the United States had the authority to arrest and deport him back to Italy for his smuggling crimes. Pelli apparently also had highly placed connections in the Florida state government and among municipal officials in Tampa. American officials had asked the Cubans to arrest Pelli if he came to Cuba for another cargo, rather than arrest and deport him from Florida. Fors questioned Kime as to whether the American government intended to have the Cuban government pay to deport Pelli so the American government could avoid doing so. In another instance, Kime had requested that Cuban officials arrest nine suspected smugglers who had left Miami in their yacht days before. It was unseemly, in Kime's view, for Americans to insist that the Cuban government arrest Americans on Cuban soil rather than in the United States, where they were actually breaking the law. As Fors eventually complained, "Why in Hell should Cuba try to help the U.S. enforce a law that people didn't like and was making the Cuban people lose a lot of money!"[67]

Fors had a point. Despite the treaty promising cooperation in smuggling enforcement and despite the demands by Americans that Cuba take on a law enforcement role against its own interests, in many ways America's enforcement efforts seemed halfhearted at best. The lack of urgency on the part of the U.S. government likely eroded willingness on the part of Cubans to uphold the treaty. It also prompted Cuban officials to push back on demands for help. And even though the United States could conceivably coerce cooperation with threats of intervention, the failures of Prohibition enforcement made plain the limits of American power and authority. After all, the United States could not even enforce its own laws. Kime warned, "We can't fool [Fors] any more by looking wise and mysterious and telling him we are watching these folks — to see that they don't catch cold! The joke is on us and we are rapidly losing all the prestige we had gained. This is too bad and I am inclined to weep — with some of the yeggs that are laughing at us." There was little doubt in his mind that Prohibition was damaging Cuban perceptions of American power. Root wrote that the Cubans no doubt thought the United States was "a nation of fools and crooks," which was "bad for our prestige."

Kime hoped that things would change and indeed believed they had to if Havana was going to continue to be closed to smuggling. "I may be dumb from the neck up," he wrote, "but I still believe that if there was ever a time that the U.S. should show the World — and particularly Latin America — that we are able to take care of ourselves and our laws — it is just about this day and date."[68] He accepted the right of the U.S. government to extend its authority into Cuba to enforce Prohibition. But the failure to do so effectively at home or abroad ultimately brought American might into question.

Kime's comments may have been little more than frustrated talk, though he certainly was well-placed to gauge the sentiments of lower-level Cuban officials. How far up the chain of leadership in Cuba these attitudes went is difficult to say. The extent to which the concerns about Prohibition enforcement seeped into larger discussions of Cuba's overall stability and its relations with the United States is also unclear. Enoch Crowder never mentioned Prohibition in his correspondence, other than obliquely through his mention of personal liquor orders. But by the late 1920s, American officials questioned whether the threat of intervention in any form helped or harmed the Cuban government. Gerardo Machado, Cuba's leader who negotiated the rum treaty with the United States, was looking more and more like a failure.[69] But the fiasco that was Prohibition enforcement was hard to miss. Kime picked up on growing frustration with the United States among Cuban officials, frustration that stemmed from the sense that the United States was asking Cuba to police a law that the American government should have been able to manage on its own.

Despite the initial success in thwarting smuggling in 1926, both Root and Kime sensed that Cuba was growing increasingly frustrated with its treaty partner. They suspected that if Cuban officials fully understood how poorly the United States was managing to enforce Prohibition at home, Cuba might very well decide to reopen its ports to smuggling. At the same time, smugglers themselves decided not to wait. Kime noticed signs that the liquor traffic in Cuba was picking up again. Several smugglers, for example, were arrested with bags of fake documents and Cuban customs seals, both tools of the smuggler's trade.[70] Occasional small cargoes of booze handled by small unknown operators continued to leave port and head north. Other smugglers turned to hiding liquor in cargoes of other commodities. Officials reported finding liquor amidst cargoes of grapefruit, tile, scrap metal, and even beef tallow after the treaty went into effect.[71] Kime also received reports that liquor cargoes departed for the United States from smaller ports and beaches outside Havana, including Marianao, Santa Lucia, and Mariel, among others. As Kime reminded officials in the United States, he could not "watch them all — all the time." But the return of smugglers connected with larger operations caused considerably more concern among Kime's operatives. In September 1927, Kime reported to Root that two major leaders of smuggling syndicates had returned to Cuba, were buying several thousand cases of liquor, and were looking for possible vessels to transport them.[72]

European and especially British distillers were also frustrated with the U.S. insistence on Prohibition and its Rum Treaty with Cuba, though for different reasons. They recognized the growing dislike of the treaty among Cubans and hoped to capitalize on that sentiment to revive the smuggling trade in Havana. Kime believed the Europeans subtly pressured public officials by reminding the Cuban people that the antismuggling treaty was more costly to Cuba than it was to the United States. Kime wondered if there was perhaps a connection between the apparent slackening effort to enforce the Rum Treaty, a concerted effort by European distillers to shift public opinion against the treaty, and the Cuban newspapers. He noticed a growing number of advertisements by British liquor companies as well as more news articles criticizing the cost of the treaty to the Cuban economy. And while the treaty ostensibly created policies to prevent the smuggling of immigrants and narcotics, which the Cuban people supported, as long as the press kept its focus on the suppression of liquor exports, it encouraged resentment among the Cuban people.[73] Indeed, there was even a commission designated to present a petition to the Cuban treasurer to amend both the antismuggling treaty and the Cuban tariff law that gave it teeth.

These developments were not lost on rum runners. Kime reported that they "smelled" the possibility that the treaty might be loosened and the rum trade in Havana might open again for business. While the commission was apparently not successful, Kime feared that revival of the rum trade was only a matter of time. Fors had finally become fed up with working with the Americans and had taken a bribe from a man trying to smuggle liquor in barrels of asphalt. Kime speculated that he accepted the money to provide a nice Christmas for his family, and he might return to the fold in a few weeks. But when a bureaucratic foul-up between different divisions of the State Department allowed two loaded liquor vessels to leave Havana, Fors's return appeared unlikely. By Christmas 1927, Kime was writing letters that even he thought sounded "mighty pitiful." His efforts to prevent shipments of booze from leaving Cuba faltered because, as he put it, "there is too much money in sight"— money for bribes, for captains and crews, and for anyone interested in bringing high-end booze to thirsty Americans. Kime was dispirited but not yet willing to give up. He nevertheless realized the cards were against him, in large part because he believed the cards themselves were marked. When he received news that the military officer assigned to patrol Mariel beach to prevent ship departures had been pulled off the job, he stated his conclusions bluntly. "The old gang is back in the saddle again and the place is wide open. This all fits in with [one returning smuggler's] statement that business looks good for the future."[74] Antismuggling efforts did indeed deteriorate in Havana. Eventually even Al Capone himself would try to get in on the Cuban rum trade. In 1930 he traveled to Havana and was rumored to be interested in a bankrupt distillery with large stores of liquor on site. Within twenty-four hours of his arrival, however, he was visited in his hotel room at dawn by fifteen to twenty members of the Havana police, who took him to meet with the head of Cuba's secret police. Capone left the country after spending less than forty-eight hours in Havana. While he never set up shop in Cuba, perhaps finding authorities unaccommodating, his visit indicated that smugglers again saw Cuba as a profitable location for business.[75]

The U.S. government nevertheless continued to crow about the success of its treaty with Cuba. Indeed, officials tried to make it a model for other antismuggling agreements. Confounded by the failure to stop smuggling along the Great Lakes and the border with Canada, American officials hoped to transfer the success of the treaty with Cuba to other countries. Root was included in the negotiations and informed Kime that the United States wanted the antismuggling treaty with Canada amended to read the same as the treaty with Cuba, as though the success in Havana resided in the magic of language. Root surmised that the secretary of state was dubious — mentioning that the man looked amused as Root explained how well the treaty was working, largely because he "now understands all about it." Kime did not discuss whether or not he supported the efforts to amend the Canadian treaty; he merely wished Root luck with it. But he then reminded Root that "it takes a lot more than a treaty to stop smuggling."[76] In Cuba, it took the passage of another tariff law and the willingness of the Cuban government to act according to the wishes of the United States. In many ways, Cuba had little choice but to accept American law enforcement efforts within its borders.

Most other nations were not so accommodating, despite the hopes of American officials. It also took a crew of operatives on the ground who provided information to Cuban officials and who were willing to bridge Cuban and American government agencies and grease the wheels to make both sides enforce the treaty. These were conditions not easily replicated everywhere. More to the point, however, even Cuba became less willing to cooperate when it realized that it bore a disproportionate share of the burden, largely because American Prohibition enforcement was so ineffective. Indeed, that ineffectiveness brought the limits of American power to light.

By the time the American government held up Havana as a success story in preventing smuggling, the success in Havana was already starting to unravel. Havana never returned to its heyday of smuggling, when schooners openly loaded hundreds of cases of liquor and set sail with forged Honduran clearance papers for the American coast. But the tenacity of smugglers to work around law enforcement efforts was striking. Profit beckoned, and rum runners were enterprising. When authorities picked up efforts in one area, smugglers merely moved to another. In the mid-1920s, many of them left Havana, if only temporarily, and set up shop in places like Puerto Mexico or Ensanada. Even Mourice Roud, by the late 1920s, was reportedly engaged in a successful smuggling operation around San Diego, California. Authorities in Havana continued to pressure smugglers, and authorities in the United States continued to pressure officials in Havana to apprehend more smugglers operating out of Cuba. In 1929, the secretary of state in Washington, D.C., chided the Havana consulate for growing lax in its enforcement efforts and reminded its personnel that "Habana is reputed to be the center of operations of certain persons engaged in smuggling." Havana never entirely lost its reputation as a smuggling port.[77] Despite the successes in 1926 and 1927, the numbers of schooners suspected of smuggling never seemed to diminish appreciably. In 1930, the consulate in Havana received a list of 115 vessels suspected of smuggling liquor into the United States. Several familiar names, including the *F. A. Marie*, were on it, including two ships that Kime had reported sunk in Havana's 1926 hurricane. In the face of American efforts, the liquor traffic was resilient indeed.[78]

{ Chapter Four }

SECOND ONLY TO BOOTLEGGING

❊

A S HENRY KIME STRUGGLED against rum runners, he grew increasingly aware that liquor was not the only illegal cargo that left Havana for the United States. Indeed, immigrants also sought passage across the waters that separated Cuba from the southern coast. One of them was listed as Ching Jack in subsequent court records. Barred from immigrating legally by the Chinese Exclusion Act, he went to Havana, Cuba, where he and approximately forty Chinese men arranged to travel to Florida illegally aboard the *Viola*. The voyage, however, did not go according to plan. After the immigrants sailed to the Florida coast, the boat intended to ferry them to shore never appeared. Over the next five days, the weather turned rough. While the Chinese men huddled seasick and "packed like sardines" in the hold, the motor died, the mainsails ripped from their moorings, and the *Viola* sprung a leak. The food supply ran low, and even the drinking water turned sour. The boat's occupants resorted to drinking the boat's other illicit cargo, whiskey, which was being smuggled into the United States. Without an engine or sail and taking on water, the captain beached the *Viola* near Pensacola. Within days, the *Viola*'s passengers were arrested and detained, and the crew was charged with violating both Prohibition and immigration laws. After testifying against the crew, Ching Jack was probably deported back to Cuba.[1]

Ching Jack was one of many people seeking to evade American immigration restrictions through Cuba. In 1923, the *Atlanta Constitution* warned "Rum Smugglers Find New Trade in Immigrants."[2] Cargoes of undocumented immigrants from China, Europe, the Middle East, and elsewhere comprised a companion cargo that traveled with illicit liquor to southern shores to the consternation of American observers. Indeed, as early as 1921, southern newspapers reported that smuggling immigrants was a growing sideline of rum smugglers. It was "an infant industry which bids fair to become secondary only to bootlegging . . . and it is said the two operations are carried on in conjunction in many cases."[3] "Bootlegging aliens" dovetailed nicely — both operationally and rhetorically — with efforts to smuggle alcohol to the southern coast. For some smuggling outfits, narcotics and other illicit drugs also joined liquor as contraband cargo. Smuggling of all varieties, as well as the efforts to stop it, pulled the waters and coastline of the southern United States into debates about Prohibition, international trade, and the extent of American authority outside the nation's borders. These companion contraband cargoes of migrants and drugs, however, brought debates about immigration and drug policies south as well. New laws that created these other prohibited cargoes created similar black markets that sought to meet growing demand in the United States and around the world. For would-be immigrants, the option of clandestine travel to the United States fostered global migrations south of the South and exploited the southern coast's proximity and connections to the Caribbean. In the process, it made efforts against smuggling that much more complicated. Expanding cargo beyond liquor to immigrants and drugs drew additional federal agencies into enforcement efforts in the waters off the southern coast, the landing point of much of this illegal cargo.

To Henry Kime, Charles Root, and members of the consulate in Havana, "bootlegging aliens" quickly became yet another reason why Havana was a particularly troublesome smuggling port. While the smuggling of Chinese persons into the United States was not new, bringing "illegal aliens" from around the world into the country increased and became more organized in response to new laws restricting immigration that passed shortly after Prohibition went into effect. Those restrictions created a growing number of would-be immigrants seeking "underground" ways to reach American shores, and they became a new category of potential customers for smugglers. Unable to immigrate under increasingly restrictive regulations, would-be immigrants utilized their status as profitable cargoes to sidestep the law. Smugglers seeking additional revenue streams easily accommodated demand for smuggling immigrants and narcotics. All forms of smuggling linked the United States and Cuba, all plied the waters and traveled the roads of the South, and all bedeviled American officials. "The smuggling of aliens is second only to the smuggling of liquor in this vicinity," one Florida customs official reported, "and the two are so closely aligned that the inspection of aliens forms an appreciable part of the activities of Customs officers in the Florida district."[4]

Immigrants and liquor had long been connected in the American imagination and became only more so during national Prohibition. Many white, native-born Americans associated particular immigrant groups with alcohol — Germans with beer, Irish with whiskey, Italians with wine — and had invoked those associations in temperance debates for years. Anti-German sentiment during World War I had accelerated the push for a federal prohibition amendment. Pairing immigrants and liquor continued once Prohibition became the law of the land. Americans assumed that the vast majority of liquor violations were perpetrated by immigrant groups. One writer, in the early 1920s, connected the two directly, arguing, "It is stated by those who ought to know that 75 percent of the bootleggers are aliens."[5] The so-called criminal tendencies of immigrants, including drunkenness, contributed to calls that immigration overall should be reduced.[6] Contrary to such claims, statistics showed otherwise. Immigrants were arrested for bootlegging in line with their proportion of the population, as much because economically insecure families sold liquor to help make ends meet. During Prohibition, their communities were more likely to suffer from zealous enforcement efforts. Police were far more likely to arrest immigrants and the children of immigrants than they were native-born Americans. Indeed, immigrants suffered so disproportionately that the experience eventually pushed them, according to one analysis, away from the Republican party, with its dry reputation, toward the Democrats.[7] Nevertheless, the synergy between urges to limit alcohol and to limit immigration was not entirely surprising. Nor was it particularly surprising that both laws created black markets to meet ongoing demand. What is interesting, however, is how the markets converged. The liquor traffic provided a ready-made organizational structure to facilitate the smuggling of immigrants. They often used the same boats, utilized similar businesses to fund operations, and traveled the same routes. There was one important difference, however. For many Americans, while the traffic in liquor might be tolerated with a wink and a raised glass, the traffic in immigrants was not. Anti-immigrant sentiment remained strong among many Americans. With the passage of Prohibition and the passage of restrictions on immigration between 1917 and 1924, the seas off the southern coast became host not only to rum runners seeking to land cargoes of illicit alcoholic beverages but to immigrants as well who leveraged their mobility and Cuba's more lenient immigration enforcement to circumvent American law.

To counter this multicargo smuggling network, seemingly unrelated government agencies and law enforcement operations tried to collaborate to enforce two laws that on their faces seemed entirely distinct. The effectiveness of a legal framework welcoming some immigrants and disallowing others depended, as it did with alcohol, on enforcement. Immigration restrictions and Prohibition laws created a crisscross of agencies tasked with enforcement, from local deputies and sheriffs in the communities along the coast and along the roads and railways leading north, through the bureaucracies focused on immigration and Prohibition in Washington, D.C., and into the federal courtrooms sprinkled in southern cities. Those efforts extended beyond the nation's borders and required the assistance of undercover agents like Henry Kime, working on the ground in foreign cities like Havana, and the officials of countries like Cuba, on whom American authorities applied pressure to cooperate. The large geographic space over which smuggling operations occurred both on land and at sea and the fractured bureaucracies sharing enforcement responsibilities created the cracks through which smugglers could maneuver.[8] The bureaucratic confusion created by both laws and both forms of illegal cargo, not to mention prohibitions on the traffic in narcotics, allowed smuggling to continue with only occasional interference. For Ching Jack, bad luck and federal authorities in Florida spelled the end of his attempt to immigrate, though perhaps only temporarily. But to officials, the willingness of immigrants to take their chances with rum smugglers and of rum smugglers to see profit in carrying both immigrants and drugs along with liquor complicated efforts to enforce the laws related to each. In the end, the federal government, like smugglers, saw immigrants and drugs as parallel contraband and elected to approach both as law enforcement problems in the same way it approached the liquor traffic. That decision, while perhaps reasonable in the context of Prohibition, would shape American policy toward both unsanctioned immigration and narcotics from that point forward.

Efforts to limit immigration dated back four decades at the start of Prohibition. Beginning in 1882, the Chinese Exclusion Act prohibited the Chinese from entering the United States; the infamous 1907 "Gentlemen's Agreement" followed, effectively halting Japanese immigration. Specific classes of "undesirable" immigrants, such as paupers, prostitutes, the mentally "unfit," and persons convicted of crimes of moral turpitude, had been prohibited from immigrating through a patchwork of restrictions since the 1890s, enforced through inspections by immigration officers at U.S. ports of entry. Finding piecemeal restrictions ineffective, however, and troubled by the entry of those they determined to be undesirable, by the 1920s Americans sought a more comprehensive solution. The immigration laws that followed in 1921 and 1924, rather than targeting "unfit" individual immigrants, sought to stanch the flow of immigration overall through increasingly strict quota systems based on national origins. Potential immigrants needed to obtain a visa from American consulates abroad, hoping that their country had not met its yearly quota.[9] Unsurprisingly, quotas for countries considered undesirable were very low. While the primary task of preventing so-called undesirables from entering the United States occurred at American consulates abroad, their efforts were supported by the Immigration Service within the Department of Labor, which manned immigration inspection points at ports of entry into the United States and processed immigrants within the quotas available for each nation. With the laws in place, immigration agents around the nation's periphery, with the help of state and local law enforcement, pursued and apprehended immigrants who entered the country without the approval of an immigrant inspector. Thus, just as the Volstead Act sought to reduce the flow of undesirable beverages to a trickle, so, too, the quota laws sought to stanch the flow of undesirable immigrants. As the *Washington Post* noted in 1924, "A cargo of rum in the wrong hands can do a lot of damage. But a cargo of undesirable aliens can easily become a national calamity."[10]

Just as Prohibition did not end Americans' thirst for liquor, the laws restricting immigration did not necessarily reduce the numbers of immigrants who desired to come to America. Indeed, soon after the passage of the 1882 Chinese Exclusion Act, smugglers devised methods for bringing Chinese into the United States despite the law. As other restrictions targeted European immigrants, they, too, looked for alternate routes, turning to the services of *padrones* who arranged entry into the country as well as employment as laborers in the nation's expanding industrial economy. Still other immigrants crossed the land borders with Canada and Mexico alongside Canadian whiskey and Mexican tequila.[11] Thousands of others, like Ching Jack, made their way to Havana in the hopes that they could be successfully smuggled into the United States aboard a rum runner. In precisely the same way Prohibition created a black market for booze, immigration restrictions spurred the development of an underground economy to meet the demand among immigrants for transportation to America for a significant price. Cuba's smuggling industry easily absorbed a new form of human contraband. Indeed, federal agencies speculated that smuggling aliens provided a potentially lucrative addition to smugglers' bottom lines. These agencies, however, also found their authority in enforcing the law expanded as well.

Cuba was a hospitable location for immigrants to congregate. Only ninety miles south of Florida and exempted from U.S. quota restrictions, Cuban citizens were free to travel without passport to the United States for up to six months. Growing numbers of tourists from the United States traveled to Cuba for vacations, arriving aboard ferries that operated regularly from Florida, New Orleans, and New York. Cuba also had long-standing economic and trade relationships around the globe and was itself a common destination for visitors from the rest of the world. Cuba had the second-largest community of Chinese immigrants in Latin America and had long absorbed numerous émigrés from Spain.[12] Cuba, in short, was an international crossroads with a multicultural population. International tourists and migrants were nothing unusual on the streets of Havana. Cuban immigration policies facilitated the country's establishment as a depot for undocumented immigrants hoping to head to the United States. After American intervention in the war for Cuba's independence from Spain, Cuba adopted immigration codes similar to those in the United States and moved to encourage the entry of populations they viewed as desirable: white immigrants from Europe.[13] Foreigners arriving in Cuba were subject to inspection upon arrival. Nevertheless, American officials reported it was common practice for immigrants to bribe officials to circumvent inspection, allowing virtually unimpeded access to the country for whoever could pay.[14] Unsurprisingly, propaganda in European countries targeted individuals who desired to go to America by touting Cuba as an alternate destination with fewer quota restrictions than in Europe.[15]

Intercepted immigrants admitted to a variety of origins and destinations, indicating the far reach of Cuba's attraction as a smuggling staging point. Individuals from China could request legal entry into Cuba as students and merchants and joined an established Chinese community. Other immigrants testified that they hailed from Russia, Greece, Lithuania, Portugal, Spain, Italy, and the Middle East, as well as throughout Asia.[16] Cuba's own immigration reports suggested that the adoption of quotas in the United States in 1924 increased the number of foreigners arriving in Cuba, ostensibly to use it as a way station for travel to America. Comparisons between immigration by country in 1923 and 1924 showed a substantial increase in travel to Cuba from Germany, Austria-Hungary, Greece, Japan, "Checo-Slovak," Lithuania, Yugoslavia, Syria, Turkey, and Palestine, in many cases more than doubling and in some cases even tripling the number of migrants in a single year. In 1924, more than 60,000 of the 85,000 immigrants entering Cuba came from countries subject to quota allotments in the United States.[17] To American officials, these numbers suggested a growing industry. In December 1924, just after the enactment of the most stringent quota law, Carleton Bailey Hurst, American consul general in Havana, wrote to the secretary of state in Washington, D.C., about the growing problem of immigrant smuggling in Havana. "It is well known that Habana is probably the most important center of the smuggling of immigrants and rum into the United States." By 1926, the smuggling of undocumented immigrants was a well-established business.[18]

"Bootlegging aliens" and rum-running were easily combined as smuggling ventures. Some of the most well-known Cuban smugglers, including Facundo Sardinas and Miguel Sastre, not only transported cargoes of immigrants and booze but occasionally dabbled in the smuggling of narcotics as well.[19] Testimony and intelligence information occasionally placed both illegal booze and illegal immigrants on the same boats that came surreptitiously to U.S. shores. The schooner *Parkir*, for example, took on 3,500 cases of liquor in Havana and then sailed to Cojimar, where it loaded an additional cargo of would-be immigrants before it proceeded to the east coast of Florida.[20] Arrested immigrants confided to authorities that they were forced to unload liquor on southern beaches, as smugglers used one commodity to move another.[21] And stateside distributors who wanted only to deal with one commodity could be forced to deal with both. One bootlegger in Florida, interested only in alcohol, testified that he was forced to bring aliens to shore before he was allowed to offload cases of booze from a rum runner.[22] That these two smuggling enterprises might join caused little surprise among officials.

Henry Kime, as well as the American government officials he worked with in Havana, Florida, and Washington, traced intricate immigrant- and alcohol-smuggling networks as well as the strategies used to enter the United States. Reports of smuggling attempts, both foiled and successful, abound in the records of the Immigration Service as well as in the files of the U.S. Coast Guard Intelligence Division. Henry Kime's correspondence with Charles

Root, increasingly focused on the movement of undocumented immigrants as the efforts to prevent the smuggling of liquor achieved more success. Together, these sources present a picture of an extensive network of smugglers, freely exchanging one cargo for the other, operating out of Havana with contacts and transportation networks along the southern coast from Texas to Florida and as far north as New York. As they did with liquor, officials and informants traded information about likely smuggling rings, the evolving strategies smugglers used to evade law enforcement, and reliable or corrupt officials involved in their effort. They also targeted stateside businesses — Chinese laundries, restaurants, sugar refineries, or fishing outfits — that were suspected of dabbling in smuggling or housing, employing, hiding, or moving cargoes of both varieties on the U.S. mainland. Indeed, the same report that laid out the liquor-smuggling operations in Havana in 1925 also described the most common methods of smuggling undocumented immigrants.[23]

Authorities estimated that approximately 200 immigrants per week were successfully smuggled into the United States from Cuba. This translated into an influx of more than 10,000 immigrants per year, each paying on average between $180 and $250 for the trip.[24] There were four principal strategies for transporting immigrants to the American coast. First, some immigrants entered the United States as stowaways on board the ferries or steamer ships that regularly ran between Cuba and the United States, the source of much small-scale liquor smuggling as well. Customs, for example, reported in 1927 that it discovered 19 immigrant stowaways and 115 quarts of alcohol being smuggled aboard the SS *Munleon* ferry on one trip between Havana and Tampa.[25] Immigrant stowaways were usually brought on board by complicit crew members. Passage to the United States was rarely pleasant as a stowaway; they were reportedly hidden in the ship's coal bin, in the coal pipes, in tunnels and holds, among the cargo, in the water tanks wearing life preservers, in the airshafts, in anchor compartments, or if they were lucky, in the crew quarters. Other would-be immigrants traveled as regular passengers, carrying falsified Cuban citizenship papers or birth certificates. Those without documents were smuggled off the ship via rope ladders as the ship waited in quarantine before docking, or they impersonated crew members helping passengers unload their baggage. Immigrants posing as passengers or crew, who held fraudulent papers, traveled in relative comfort and, unsurprisingly, paid the highest price for passage, around $300 to $400 per passenger.

Second, a substantial number of male immigrants entered the United States illegally as fraudulent members of ships' crews. These men paid large sums to take the place of crew members after the ship had cleared from port and headed out to sea. As evidence, officials pointed to the growing number of unemployed seamen who loitered around Havana, suggesting they either sold their crew spots to would-be immigrants for a profit or could not find work because ships "hired" undocumented immigrants willing to pay for passage to the United States as crew even if they had no seamanship skills. Once they reached an American port, all seamen received temporary shore leave. Many immigrants disembarked as seamen and simply never returned to the ship. Smuggling aboard American-bound ferries or as crew involved handfuls of immigrants at a time and could be done on an ad hoc basis, in much the same way that crews or passengers of the ferries brought small amounts of liquor into the United States.

Third, a far larger number of immigrants sought entry into the United States aboard smuggling ships that plied the waters between Cuba and the southern United States. Ships bringing in booze or immigrants might be sailing schooners that spent several days at sea or high-speed motor launches that could make the trip to the U.S. coast in a matter of hours. Schooner smuggling represented the most dangerous method of travel "owing to uncertainty of the weather, the leaky condition of the average smuggling craft, and the unscrupulous character of the schooner captains and crew"; it was also, unsurprisingly, the cheapest, averaging $100 to $180 per person.[26] High-speed gas launches offered a speedier trip and could take fifteen to thirty immigrants per trip. They usually could outrun Coast Guard vessels or lose them in the shallow waters offshore, especially near the Florida Keys. Operators made easy money, charging about $180 per passenger. Whether by sailing schooner or motorized launch, this nautical method commanded most of the attention of authorities and resulted in the largest numbers of apprehensions and prosecutions in U.S. courts. One such ship was the *Reemplazo*, seized by the Coast Guard in May 1920 as it lay at anchor off Clearwater, Florida. It was charged with landing 17 Chinese as well as carrying 3,000 quarts of whiskey and 15 demijohns of alcohol. The captain and crew faced charges in separate cases of violating the Prohibition laws and the immigration laws. They were acquitted of smuggling immigrants but convicted on the liquor charge and sentenced to a year in prison.[27]

Fourth, several networks of immigrant smuggling capitalized on expectations of family structure and gender roles, targeting female immigrants, though their business model resembled human trafficking more than simple smuggling. A few women entered the United States posing as the wife of a

Crew of rum runners, undated
(Courtesy of the State Archives of Florida)

crew member or passenger on a ferry from Cuba, paying a substantial sum
for the comfort of a cabin but also running the risk of unwelcome attention
from their "husband" while in transit. Word also reached authorities about
a scheme by which American men would come to Havana, marry a Greek
woman there, and travel with her as husband and wife to the United States.
Once the woman reached her family in America, she would sue for divorce.
She thus successfully entered the United States, while he could repeat the ruse
after the divorce. It could be a lucrative business. One man was promised $800
by his supposed bride.[28] Another network transported women, though not
always willing ones, to different cities in the Western Hemisphere. Captain
Gelabert, who was well known to officials in both Cuba and the United States,
created fictitious families for illegal entry into the United States. Gelabert

was an American citizen with a wife and children in Tampa and a mistress in Havana. But he specialized in traveling to the United States with women he claimed were his female family members. Apparently, he made at least thirty such trips, all with different women posing as his family. Authorities suspected that the steamship offices had colluded with him in his scheme, as he apparently never had difficulties arranging passage for his group.[29]

Gelabert's operation, however, had a darker side and identified its niche market through the international moral crusades against prostitution. Investigations in Havana had led authorities to believe that the majority of the women who posed as Gelabert's family members were prostitutes. Some were reportedly French and had worked in Havana until a morals campaign by the Cuban government had forced them from the country. Gelabert apparently charged these women $1,000 each for passage to the United States. Investigators believed he also smuggled Russian and Polish women who had worked as prostitutes in Argentina and Brazil.[30] Pushed out of Latin America, the women were trafficked to Cuba, where they were prostituted to Cuban men. Gelabert reportedly partnered with a Jewish woman in Havana named Mariam Speiss in this trade. Speiss recruited Jewish travelers to Cuba who wanted to immigrate to the United States. Young women who took advantage of her offer found themselves forced into a world they did not anticipate. Gelabert and Speiss insisted that young women interested in traveling as one of Gelabert's daughters abandon their friends and family and move into a house associated with their business to avoid arousing suspicions. There, young woman were forced to provide sexual services to young Cuban men from prominent and wealthy families. The prostitution allegedly provided an important financial component of the operation. Gelabert and Speiss would threaten to expose the young men and their families to scandal by publicizing their relations with the so-called prostitutes. The families of the Cuban men paid for silence, and the extortion money provided Gelabert and Speiss sufficient funds to "pay" for the women's transport to the United States.[31]

One young woman named Olga who eventually arrived in New York wrote a letter describing her experience as one of "indescribable suffering." Upon her arrival in Havana, she was "sold" to a lawyer and his young friends. He submitted her to the "worst sufferings" for a month at a house in Vedado. When Olga finally boarded the steamer for travel to the United States, Gelabert shared a cabin with her and "tried the most immoral acts." When they reached New York, she was delivered to another Jewish man, who paid

Gelabert money. Eventually, the letter said, she was able to escape.[32] Gelabert was eventually arrested in Laredo, Texas, for attempting to cross the U.S.-Mexican border with yet another family, but within two years he was back in Havana trying to revive his smuggling business.[33] Mariam Speiss, whom Kime and his associates viewed as little more than a brothel owner, seemed immune from prosecution or deportation. She was arrested numerous times in succession at the request of the American consulate, but she apparently had friends in high places. One high-placed Cuban official insisted that she was merely an innocent, hardworking girl. Kime was furious: "The Jewish pimps and Mariam Speiss are laughing at Uncle Sam. Maybe the Cubans are laughing also."[34]

Kime's frustration is no doubt familiar by now, though Gelabert's operation inspired particular disgust. To U.S. government officials, however, immigrant smugglers were frustratingly successful at their trade. One smuggler, Mario Pelli of Tampa, was well known for smuggling liquor and immigrants. He boasted that in 1923 alone, he single-handedly landed over 1,400 immigrants on Florida's shores. By all accounts, Pelli ran an efficient, successful, and profitable operation. With two boats under his command in 1923, he allegedly ran four full cargoes of immigrants to the United States per month. In 1924, he added four additional boats to his fleet. In 1925, he consolidated his operation by opening a hotel and restaurant, the Genova, that also served as his Havana headquarters. Like all good businessmen, Mario Pelli succeeded because he delivered a reliable product. He virtually guaranteed his customers safe landing on American shores, assuring them he had purchased the protection of officials in both Cuba and the United States.[35] According to Kime, by 1926, Pelli had a widespread and well-deserved reputation in the United States, Cuba, and Europe. "He has many hundreds of recommendations and references of Italian families. His fame is great and reaches Italy and even France. He never cheated an alien and when his attempts of contraband failed, he always very honestly returned the money aliens paid him in advance and suffered all the losses himself."[36] To drum up additional business, Pelli even traveled to Europe to recruit potential immigrant customers and arrange for their transport to Havana.

Pelli's operation was unusual in its comprehensive business model. Most smuggling outfits allowed European steamship lines' emphasis on Cuba's openness to immigration to do their marketing for them. One advertisement even pointed out that "you will clearly see that Cuba is a logical and ideal New World destination for those Old World Immigrants who are eager to avail themselves of the wide opportunities and advantages and the broad equality of America, but who are, because of filled quotas or other misfortunes, denied admittance to the United States." This 1922 advertisement for the French Line that appeared in Europe was forwarded to the Department of State. Embassy officials also learned that steamship companies frequently provided the names of well-known smugglers in Cuba to their passengers.[37] Once in Cuba, foreigners from countries with small U.S. immigration quotas recounted being approached by recruiters in Havana's parks or seeing flyers around the tourist areas of the cities. Two Jewish men who were captured on a train in Florida told authorities that they had traveled to Cuba after having attempted to obtain visas legally in Russia, Germany, and France. While sitting in Central Park in Havana, they overheard two other Jewish men talking about a smuggling operation and collected the business card of the leader.[38] Other would-be immigrants spoke of being approached by fellow countrymen who offered their services. Jim Glico, a Greek man traveling from Greece to Mexico with a stopover in Havana, recalled being approached by another Greek man who asked if he would like to go to the United States. After an initial reluctance, Glico decided he would.[39]

Concerned officials in Cuba and the United States noted the flood of foreigners entering Cuba, alarmed that many of these so-called tourists ultimately made their way illegally into the United States, since they seemed to disappear from the population in Cuba. Where else could they be? officials reasoned.[40] Eliminating the immigrant-smuggling economy, however, required that officials distinguish between potential immigrants and legitimate tourists in Cuba. It was a murky distinction, as many future immigrants "passed" as tourists until they could secure passage to the United States. Complicating matters further, organizations focused on the smuggling of both alcohol and immigrants were intertwined with the larger tourism industry in Havana. Smugglers utilized familiar cafés and hotels to conduct their business and took advantage of area roads and beaches. Some, like Mario Pelli, began businesses to house their illegal activities.[41] Coast Guard Intelligence officers estimated that another group, the California Hotel Gang, had smuggled approximately 800 aliens from Havana's Hotel California.[42] Would-be immigrants who utilized Hotel California's services traveled through the Hotel la Union at Sagua la Grande, about 250 miles east of Havana on the north coast of Cuba. The Hotel la Union at times housed more than seventy eager immigrants awaiting transportation to the United States, segregating migrants from regular hotel guests at a special rate. At the appropriate time, small groups of immigrants would be transported by car to the beach at Isabella and placed aboard a speedy motor launch, which transferred them to a craft hidden beyond the reef.[43]

Most immigrants seeking passage to the United States did not have to travel quite so far out of Cuba's capital. Many of them boarded the boats that would take them across the Straits of Florida at the mouth of the Almendares River on the outskirts of Havana. By 1927, however, Cuban authorities, thanks to the undercover investigations of Henry Kime at cafés in the area, had clamped down on smuggling ventures departing from the Almendares, driving operations elsewhere.[44] Miguel Sastre, who operated as part of Mario Pelli's operation, leased a small farm at Boca de Jeruco, on the north coast of Cuba about forty miles from Havana, which authorities believed he "used as an immigrant station and storage place for contraband liquor cargoes."[45] Intelligence officers went so far as to suspect that the Pelli/Sastre organization had achieved an "understanding" with the smuggling operation run by Facundo Sardinas to divide the beaches around Havana for use by their respective enterprises. The small beaches and ports to the west of Havana, including Bahia Honda, Mariel, and Jaimanitas, among others, would be used solely as loading ports for the Sardinas operation. The ports to the northeast of Havana, including Cojimar and the large port of Matanzas, would be used by the Pelli/Sastre gang.[46] Boats would load their liquor in Havana and then travel to more deserted locations to take on their immigrant cargo. The *Fannie Prescott*, for example, loaded 5,000 cases of liquor at the docks in Havana harbor and then proceeded to a predetermined location offshore from Marianao Playa to pick up twenty immigrants, an arrangement that had been finalized at the Aurora Restaurant in Old Havana.[47]

Smugglers utilized established financial procedures to conduct their business. Financing the smuggling of illegal immigrants was largely a cash business. Would-be immigrants paid varying rates for transport to the United States depending on their perceived risk as cargo. By about 1925, the market was established enough to charge largely standardized prices. The understanding among prospective immigrants that a standard service should command a uniform price presented problems to smugglers who cobbled together cargoes of immigrants from different sources in Havana. One group of Italian would-be immigrants raised a ruckus as they transferred from the dock to the schooner for transportation to the United States because they discovered that they had been charged different prices.[48]

Cost, however, varied by race. Invariably, Chinese immigrants paid the highest prices, usually between $800 and $1,000, likely because of simple discrimination and because they were so readily identifiable and thus a risky cargo. Europeans paid an average of about $200 per person. Passengers usually paid smugglers a portion of the transport fee in Havana before they left and then deposited the rest with specific Havana businessmen. The two Jewish men who found their way to a smuggling outfit after overhearing a conversation on a park bench received the card of Dr. Jamison, an optometrist at the Anglo-American Optical Company in Old Havana. Jamison held deposits for smuggled immigrants and paid their smuggling outfit upon their safe arrival — after subtracting a small fee for himself.[49] A report to the embassy in Havana detailed similar arrangements. Noting that two establishments, a grocery store and a café in Havana, handled deposits for immigrants, authorities traced the financial transactions. "The proprietors of these stores are given in deposit the amount of $200 for each alien and they charge $20 for their services. The officer of the crew taking charge of the alien receives $50 in advance payment. If the Alien lands safely upon the return of the vessel he receives the balance $150, if the alien is caught and deported to Habana he gets back the amount of $150."[50] The Bureau of Immigration outlined the general practice with more detail. "When the aliens are landed they give receipts to the smugglers and the smugglers return to Cuba and present these receipts" to obtain the deposited balance of cost of transport.[51] U.S. Coast Guard ships and U.S. immigration officials occasionally captured would-be immigrants and deported them back to Cuba. The immigrants merely retrieved the balance of their payment and waited to try again. American officials frequently expressed frustration that they had little ability to prevent immigrants from making multiple attempts to enter the United States, noting immigrants who had made the trip across the Straits of Florida three and four times unsuccessfully only to return to Cuba to try again.[52]

Bureaucrats saw undocumented immigrants as law violators, along with the smugglers who provided them passage. The language in these sources betrayed little sympathy for either smugglers or the people who sought transportation to the United States. Indeed, government officials tasked with enforcing American laws rarely viewed would-be immigrants as the victims of traffickers. But the media presented undocumented immigrants as a particularly dangerous and malevolent threat with the potential to contaminate the wider American population. An *Atlanta Constitution* editorial called immigrants "worthless human scum," while George Creel characterized them as "a broad and turgid stream [that] floats little more than human wreckage."[53] Article titles like "Breaking into the United States" constructed immigrant smuggling as a violation not just of immigration laws but of the nation itself, and the immigrants as undesirables whose arrival represented a home invasion.[54] The *Saturday Evening Post* ran several articles in the 1920s arguing that the "[smuggled immigrant] came in by the second story . . . instead of by the front door of the quota. He really sneaked in. . . . He comes in like a burglar yet he wants U.S. to give him an engraved guest invitation."[55] While many Americans looked on booze smuggling with a wink and a smile, the idea of unauthorized immigrants entering the United States was an entirely different matter.

Yet many of the foreigners who sought entry into the United States did not fit the negative descriptions common in the media. Many were single men, but there were also women, like Fannie Tunic, who traveled alone from Russia to Tampa to live with her brother-in-law.[56] A few families and single mothers even managed to make their way with their small children in tow to the United States. Some of them had been U.S. residents apparently successful enough to afford a trip to visit their country of origin. They then found themselves unexpectedly caught in the web of restrictions created by the new immigration laws and unable to return. Adolinae Marcinskas, for example, traveled with her two children from Lithuania to Cuba and then to Florida, where she was arrested. She, however, was not new to the United States. She had lived in New Jersey from 1907 to 1921, and her children had been born in the United States. In 1921, her husband sent her and her children back to Lithuania promising her he would follow. He never came, and she apparently decided to return to America to find him. By that point, the law had changed, transforming her from an immigrant to an illegal alien.[57] Tom Koronas, after living in Detroit for twelve years, returned to visit Greece in 1922. Upon his arrival, the U.S. consulate in Piraeus assured him that he would have no trouble obtaining a visa for his return. In 1923, however, he was drafted into the Greek army, extending his stay in Greece for twenty-eight months. When he sought to return to the United States, despite his efforts to do so legally, he was unable to obtain a visa because Greece had reached its quota limit. He decided to take his chances with a smuggler.[58] These immigrants had arrived initially at a time when restrictions on immigration were few. Despite long residence in the United States, their decision not to become naturalized American citizens meant that when they traveled to their country of origin and then sought to return, they were treated as though they were coming to the United States for the first time. They could not enter unless they could be accommodated under their country's quota limits. For them, smugglers represented a welcome alternative means of entry.

Arrival in America, however, was neither easy nor guaranteed. Numerous hopeful immigrants were caught as they landed, watched their smugglers be arrested for conspiracy, and then were held until they testified at trial before being deported back to where they began (usually Cuba, though occasionally Europe), as Ching Jack experienced. Others faced uncomfortable and even dangerous circumstances once they landed on Florida beaches. Some smugglers dropped their passengers off in remote locations on the shore, requiring them to fend for themselves. Immigration officials found bedraggled, mosquito-bitten, and starving would-be immigrants who had been dumped on deserted beaches in the Florida Keys. One group was shipwrecked miles from shore and rescued by a commercial ship. Another group reported being left to spend two uncomfortable days out in the open in April in Key West before being transported to a train bound for Miami.[59] A report even described a discovery in Florida of thirty-five skeletons of people who had starved waiting for a boat that was supposed to transport them to the mainland.[60] For children, the situation could be particularly trying. One mother attempting to make her way to the United States with her young children was caught only because she flagged down a police car. Her children, after four hours on the road, could walk no farther.[61]

Other immigrants paid for passage but never made it to the States. Fraudulent smugglers would request payment, stow would-be immigrants in the hold, and sail along the coast of Cuba for several hours until they arrived at a deserted spot. They then unloaded their cargo, claiming they had reached the United States, and deserted them with a cheery wave.[62] Even worse, smugglers might very well jettison illegal cargo, whether it was liquor or immigrants, when Coast Guard ships appeared. Because immigrant cargo could potentially testify against smuggling rings, some were thrown overboard or were killed outright when smugglers believed they spotted authorities.[63] While the black market in smuggling created by Prohibition and immigration restriction offered a way for immigrants to sidestep American laws, it did so by casting them into the arms of potentially violent criminals who, when fearing their businesses were threatened by law enforcement, could become desperate.

Prohibition laws and immigration quotas thus collapsed people and liquor into similar smuggle-able commodities and allowed smuggling operations to utilize the same organizations, businesses, and transportation networks for both. The two forms of contraband, however, did present some differences. Alcohol required transport directly to the customer, and the files of law enforcement are filled with incidents in which liquor successfully made it to southern shores from Cuba, only to be confiscated on the highways or railroad cars while it traveled to its market. Illegal immigrants, at least in theory, could move themselves. As one government official reported, immigrants were usually "landed and then left to their own resources."[64] Once these immigrants reached the United States, the experience of being smuggled was transformed according to the immigrant's ethnicity. Smuggling European immigrants, many smugglers insisted, was much easier. Able to blend with local populations, they could make their own way to their final destinations, where they often disappeared into the existing immigrant community.

Chinese immigrants, by contrast, faced different challenges. They were physically distinct. Knowing that many Americans viewed all Asians with distrust, smugglers believed they would inevitably be viewed as being in the country illegally. This was not entirely the case. Restrictions on Asian immigration allowed several exempted groups, including students and merchants, to remain in the United States. Also, the most convenient route from Asia to the Caribbean, parts of Latin America, and perhaps even Europe was through the United States. Many Chinese sailed from Asia to San Francisco, disembarked, and then traveled by railroad through the United States to Florida to reach ships that would take them to places like Cuba. Nevertheless, knowing that their mere presence in the United States raised suspicion, Chinese seeking to be smuggled often drew up their contracts with smugglers to stipulate that they would be delivered to a particular location, usually a large city on the east coast with a substantial Chinese population that made it easier for the immigrant to assimilate and "pass" as legal.[65] Networks focusing on traffic in illegal Chinese immigrants thus had to extend their operations beyond the coast into the interior of the United States.

Most smugglers nonetheless coordinated the movements of immigrants beyond landing them along the shoreline. Once in the United States, smugglers tried to attract as little attention as possible. Some organizations utilized train lines to transport would-be immigrants or alcohol to a larger metro-politan area. Others utilized cars driven by hired drivers. Groups weighed the dangers of being spotted on the road by a noisy local with the dangers of being spotted by an immigration official on a train.[66] Smugglers agreed that often the most difficult part of their journey was from the beach north to what officials called "the bottleneck" of northern Florida, where there was a finite number of possible routes north. Immigration or prohibition officials often waited at well-used bridges and roads, stopping "suspicious" vehicles possibly carrying either liquor or immigrants.[67] To avoid attracting attention, most smugglers divided their cargo into small groups for travel within the United States.[68] Reports of intercepted vehicles indicate the diverse destinations of immigrant groups, many of whom sought to go their separate ways across much of the country. In a 1923 report, one inspector in New Orleans noted that twenty-six Chinese immigrants who landed in St. Andrews, Florida, and were apprehended in Dothan, Alabama, had a variety of final destinations. Some intended to go to Philadelphia, Boston, Buffalo, or Youngstown, Ohio. Several others were bound for the mines in Thomas, West Virginia.[69]

Southerners, however, were less accustomed to immigrants in their midst. Cities like New York and Boston on the east coast and San Francisco in the West had hosted the nation's largest share of hopeful new Americans. But pockets of immigrant communities dotted the South. An enclave of Greek immigrants came to Tarpon Springs, Florida, in the 1890s and made their liv-ing as sponge divers. By the 1920s, the expanding industrial base in cities like Birmingham had long beckoned immigrants, who worked in the foundries and factories or began the restaurants that fed growing urban populations.[70] Even West Virginia, as the destinations of captured Chinese migrants indi-cated, drew new residents from foreign lands. Yet while many Americans might profess support for Prohibition in public and drink in private, their attitude toward unsanctioned immigrants was not so flexible. Indeed, the attitude toward the smuggling of immigrants, officials suggested, was almost entirely a function of one's relationship to the incoming immigrants them-selves. While folks along the coast might turn a blind eye to smuggling, the further removed from the trade, the less sympathy smuggling evoked. Move away from immigrant communities and inland away from the coast and any toleration evaporated. "The ordinary 'Florida cracker' or 'countryman' is very much against the foreigner," one customs official wrote, suggesting that in that particular area — inland from Pensacola in very rural and sparsely settled country — most smuggled immigrants had been apprehended by vigilant locals.[71] Hostility toward immigrants appeared frequently in letters sent to various government agencies from around the country as well as from communities caught in the traffic. They protested the appearance of foreign workers or assumed any Asian must be in the country illegally. One business owner in Fort Pierce, Florida, took his concerns directly to the White House, writing President Warren G. Harding prior to the passage of restrictions in 1924. It was too easy, he argued, for "skilled runners" to land unwanted immigrants and "chaperone [sic] up into the North where they can go in hiding." Tougher immigration laws, he insisted, would prevent enclaves of ethnicities "within our midst, made up of unassimilated and unassimilatable [sic] material."[72] Americans in Florida protested the presence of what they called "undesirables and paupers" arriving from Cuba. Others pointed out that Cuba provided an easy entrance to "the kind of immigrants that the U.S. would like *not* to have come to this country," suggesting that the smuggling of immigrants was common knowledge in the area.[73] In response, southerners worried about the presence of unfamiliar nationalities as they watched local and federal agents patrol southern roads and rail lines.

Many would-be immigrants traveled with the intention of joining well-established immigrant communities already in the United States; indeed, some had even been members of these communities before they returned to their country of origin. Their ability to evade immigrant laws depended in large part on their ability to blend into immigrant communities in the United States. Those communities helped facilitate networks that aided immigrants, sent them money in Cuba, or helped with the fees smugglers charged for transportation. Officials frequently looked with suspicion on particularly visible immigrant groups that they believed helped to smuggle their compatriots. They kept a wary eye on the Greek sponge divers who made their living from boats off the coast of Tampa and Tarpon Springs, Florida. Sotirios Targakis, for example, was captain of a sponge boat when he was accused of smuggling nine immigrants into the United States in 1925. When the prosecutor cross-examined Nicholas Amourginos and Nick Janeskis, two witnesses for the defense, the only question he asked them both was whether or not they were Greek, implying their support for the defendant stemmed from their common ethnicity.[74] Officials were no less attentive in their tracking of networks supporting Chinese immigrants. They investigated businesses, such as Chinese restaurants and laundries, that they believed harbored undocumented immigrants.[75] They did not doubt, and indeed often confirmed, that immigrant groups frequently were sympathetic to the efforts of smugglers and thus were little help in attempts to thwart their business.[76]

Henry Kime, tracking smuggling operations from Havana, understood that a willingness to smuggle one illicit commodity, like liquor, frequently encouraged a willingness to smuggle immigrants and drugs if the price was right. And as the Rum Treaty looked increasingly successful at thwarting the departure of liquor cargoes, Kime's superiors encouraged him to focus his undercover work on the traffic in smuggled immigrants and on uncovering the illegal market in narcotics that crossed the globe from China through Europe to Cuba and eventually the United States. As with unsanctioned immigrants, smugglers took on small cargoes of narcotics of various sorts if they believed it would increase their bottom line. The international community had sought to control the movement of opium and opium derivatives since the beginning of the twentieth century. In the United States, like the association of liquor and bootlegging with immigrants, particular drugs were associated with so-called undesirable groups: opium with the Chinese, heroin with the urban underclass, and cocaine with black men. These associations helped spur efforts to control or ban the substances outright.[77] Yet morphine had long been used to treat familiar kinds of pain, from menstrual cramps to hangovers, among Americans of all classes. The development of the hypodermic needle to deliver the drug, however, drew regular users into dependence. Many Americans found themselves ensnared in addiction, driven to locate drugs illicitly when they could not obtain them legally, and they were rendered criminals when they used drugs outside a doctor's care.[78]

The United States passed the Harrison Narcotic Act in 1914, which regulated the importation and sale of narcotic drugs. Under the law, importers, manufacturers, wholesalers, druggists, and physicians were required to register on an annual basis with the Treasury Department, pay an occupational tax, and keep clear records of all drug transactions. The law did not prohibit the sale of narcotics, but it rendered any traffic in those drugs, other than through registered purveyors, illegal. Efforts to regulate the international traffic in drugs, however, created a black market in drugs that spanned the globe. Opium from the Far East was refined into morphine and heroin in Europe. From there it made its way to the United States, often passing through Cuba and Mexico, where it was transshipped to American ports like New Orleans or Tampa. And as with the traffic in liquor, smuggling narcotics into the United States was a profitable business. One hundred ounces of morphine sold for $500 to $800 in Europe. That same amount reportedly had a street value of over $50,000 in the United States.[79] Once the Volstead Act passed outlining Prohibition enforcement, enforcement of the Harrison Narcotic Act was transferred to the same agency, a decision that solidified drug policy as a matter of law enforcement rather than public health. The Narcotics Division became a branch within the Prohibition Bureau under the Department of the Treasury. It would not be separated into its own independent bureau until 1930, with the development of the Federal Narcotics Bureau. For a full ten years, enforcing alcohol and narcotics laws represented parallel operations. Further uniting the approaches to both kinds of illicit substances, the first head of the Federal Narcotics Bureau was Henry J. Anslinger, a former Prohibition official and the first head of the Division of Foreign Control. Anslinger, who had been in favor of harsh penalties for liquor violations, took a similarly harsh enforcement approach to the battle against narcotics, focusing efforts on criminal prosecutions rather than the problem of addiction. Bureaucratically then, efforts to stem the traffic in drugs was closely tied to efforts to enforce Prohibition, though the overall amount of drugs smuggled was far smaller than the amount of smuggled liquor. Importantly, however, the procedures established to target liquor violations during Prohibition formed the foundation of drug policy under Anslinger and continued well into the 1960s, when Anslinger stepped down.[80]

Based on the 1925 investigation done by Captain Peter del Valle, illegal drugs constituted a "parallel" smuggling traffic between Havana and the southern coast. According to his sources, considerable stores of opium, heroin, cocaine, morphine, and other drugs were systematically stored, sold, and replaced in Cuba. Within Havana itself, many "peddlers" sold drugs to local addicts, who apparently were spread across the class spectrum well beyond the Chinese who were often associated with drug use. Many of the drugs that arrived in Cuba were then shipped in bulk to the United States, using the routes, the techniques, and even the cases used in rum smuggling. Kime, for example, reported that a Dutch steamer, the *Spaardam*, entered Havana carrying 400 packages of "dope." Prevented from landing, the ship sailed for Mexico and then returned to Havana, where it was allowed to land. The dope was moved into the warehouse of a liquor smuggler and repacked in Canadian Club whiskey cases and loaded aboard the *Alida Bonnefil*. The cargo was reportedly destined for Texas, where the *Alida Bonnefil* had been chased away by the Coast Guard on the previous trip. The *Alida Bonnefil* unloaded its cargo of drugs on its next trip, but it was spotted by the Coast Guard before it could unload its liquor cargo.[81]

The *Alida Bonnefil* carried a substantial amount of narcotics as cargo in addition to liquor cargo, but it was not unusual for many smuggling ships to carry small amounts of narcotics as additional cargo. They merely labeled the several cases loaded with drugs slightly differently to distinguish them from the cases of liquor.[82] Other smugglers focused their efforts on moving drugs exclusively. Kime, for example, reported the seizure of the Cuban schooner *Carmina*, carrying a load of drugs, off Boca Grande, Florida, in October 1930, as well as the arrest of three of its crew. Other smugglers who had been forced out of one smuggling trade expressed willingness to expand their cargoes into drugs if it might speed their return to a profitable business. Charles Peters, for example, was the leader of a large bootlegging organization in Daytona, Florida, at one time owning several schooners that made regular runs from Cuba to Florida. Two of those ships were sunk in the 1926 hurricane, and a third had been held by the Cuban government and was eventually sold by Peters to obtain money to pay a fine to release still another of his ships. Peters was arrested in Daytona, but he reportedly skipped out on his bail and went to seek his fortune in Tampa. When it appeared that Cuba might reopen as a smuggling port, he returned to Havana. Hoping to revive his business, he made it clear around Havana that he would be interested in smuggling opium in addition to liquor. Kime had him arrested and urged his deportation back to Daytona.[83]

Dealers in Havana seemed willing to sell drugs in amounts from a few ounces suitable for personal use to hundreds of pounds for selling wholesale elsewhere. An agent in Havana (probably Mary O'Kane) posed as a dealer at a German pharmaceutical importing business that promised her that, with thirty minutes' notice, they could supply 10 pounds of morphine at $315 per pound. A customs official whose office was located nearby promised 100 pounds of opium at $60 per pound and cited a Cuban senator as his supplier.[84] Still another supplier told an informer that he could "supply drugs in any amount and that he has as his associates two Cuban Senators. He also claims that another of his henchmen is an officer of the Cuban Secret Police."[85]

The alleged participation by Cuban government officials in the drug trade frequently appeared in the discussions of American agents. According to del Valle's sources, complicity in the illicit traffic in drugs was present in the highest levels of the Cuban government. Whereas liquor could be transported into Cuba legally from Europe and exported to other countries by numerous companies and wholesalers to supply the bootleg market in the United States, the same could not be said for drugs. The restrictions on narcotics importation in Cuba were similar to those in the United States and seemed quite restrictive. The regulations about sales of narcotics within Cuba were also strict. Narcotics had to be smuggled into Cuba or illegally diverted from pharmaceutical purposes for them to be sent to the United States. The primary sources of smuggled narcotics, according to del Valle's report, were members of the Cuban government. Violations of narcotics and importing laws "by the wholesale by the Cuban government officials themselves are of constant occurrence."[86] Both del Valle's diary and report identified several Cuban senators and representatives organizing large-scale efforts to smuggle narcotics into Cuba to supply the illegal drug trade; they capitalized on their positions in government to avoid detection. The report cited several instances in which these members of government traveled on diplomatic passports to Europe carrying large amounts of cash. The report also noted that as members of government, Cuban officials were largely immune from arrest. They made arrangements with the commissioner of customs to remove obstacles to their return to Cuba and trusted that, as officials, their luggage would not be searched. They returned to Cuba carrying large amounts of drugs in their luggage and then stored their supply at the residences of members of government, where they were immune from search and arrest. The report cited one Cuban senator in particular who had a brother in the Cuban consulate in Barcelona. Drugs were sent from Barcelona to Cuba under diplomatic immunity. The senator's house in Cuba was located on an island, so shipping the drugs to the United States was very easy. And as the customs inspector at the port near the island residence was a relative of the senator himself and owed his job to the senator, there was little worry about his interference. Not only were Cuban government officials apparently willing to participate in the illegal importation of narcotics into Cuba, but they also freely offered "protection" for those who sought to enter the drug smuggling business, promising that they would face no impediment to their business.[87]

"Every trail we followed in the drug business in Cuba led to some person of official prominence who was immune," del Valle reported. And indeed the presence of official members of government in the drug smuggling business virtually guaranteed that all cases would end without prosecution, as one Cuban detective informed del Valle when they "became chatty." As illustration, this detective recounted one investigation in which he received a tip that a large amount of narcotics was being unloaded at Jaimanitas, a beach near Havana. Taking four detectives with him, the officer traveled to the site and determined that crews were unloading what looked to be narcotic packages onto shore. When the detectives went to seize the cargo and arrest the crew, the crew merely laughed and pointed to the boxes. They were labeled "Machinery, SENATOR CELSO CUELLAR." With immunity from his political office, the senator's boxes could not be seized, his illegal drug business could not be shut down, and neither he nor his crew could be arrested and prosecuted. The only risk to drug dealers that del Valle could see was that of purchasing "phoney" substances, usually chalk disguised as morphine, as the quality of illicitly purchased drugs could be unreliable. It was a potentially serious risk. He noted, with some understatement, that "it was dangerous to try and peddle bad stuff on the U.S. side, because the people who bought there knew when it was bad and they were dangerous people to fool with."[88]

The legal infrastructure existed, however, to disrupt the traffic in drugs, as well as in immigrants and liquor. Cuba's antimuggling treaty with the United States covered all three illicit cargoes — liquor, immigrants, and narcotics — theoretically uniting efforts between the two countries to stop all forms of illicit traffic. It was a fact often obscured by frequent references to the treaty as the "Rum Treaty." And while many Cubans opposed efforts by the Cuban government to help the United States enforce its Prohibition laws because they believed liquor sales should be legal, they disliked immigrant smuggling and drug trafficking. Cuban views toward unsanctioned immigration and narcotics trafficking more closely aligned the purposes of the treaty. Henry Kime was not afraid to use Cuban opposition to immigrant and drug smuggling if it helped support the enforcement of the treaty in general. In 1927, when there was a move to encourage the Cuban government to amend the treaty, Kime pushed the Cuban press to publish stories about Cuban efforts to disrupt the traffic in drugs and immigrants and remind the Cuban population that the treaty prohibited smuggling of all three cargoes. By persistently referring to the antismuggling treaty as the Rum Treaty, he believed, the press focused the public's attention on the aspects of smuggling interdiction that the public opposed. Reminding them that the treaty also prohibited aspects of the smuggling trade that Cubans supported, Kime believed, would ultimately help shore up support for the treaty overall.[89]

Kime's efforts to thwart smuggling of immigrants did face one particular obstacle that was not an issue with the smuggling of liquor and drugs. There was no legal way to export opium from Cuba to the United States. While sending liquor abroad was legal, Cuba's tariff act of 1926, as well as the anti-smuggling treaty, gave the Cuban government the legal means to prevent the departure of suspected smuggling vessels. The travel of foreigners to and from Cuba, however, was legal. While Cuban law regarding the arrival of persons from China mimicked aspects of American laws prohibiting immigration from China, Cuban laws were more open regarding immigration and tourism from other areas of the world. Cuba had no quota laws like those passed in the United States. There was thus no obvious legal structure by which Cuban officials could refuse to allow would-be immigrants to enter the country, even if there was good reason to believe that the migrants intended to travel illegally to the United States.

Kime, however, was determined to prevent the smuggling of individuals he believed were undesirable. He was, in fact, a product of his time, with the corresponding bigotry that implied. He revealed his anti-Semitism in his casual references to the "jew business" in his conversations about accounting and compensation with Charles Root. When he caustically noted that O'Kane was thinking of obtaining a stenographer's job because the U.S. government would not pay her or reimburse her expenses, he noted that the extra income would enable her to "live like a white woman."[90] He thus internalized the assumptions and stereotypes about marginalized groups that were common among white Americans at the time. His tactics for forcing the Cuban government to take action against immigrant smugglers also traded on assumptions about the likely political beliefs of particular ethnic groups. Kime argued that the immigrants who sought to be smuggled into the United States were primarily political radicals, "Communists" and "anarchists" from groups that were as unwanted in Cuba as they were in the United States. He emphasized these suspect ideologies as he convinced the Cuban government to take a stronger stance concerning immigrants. Kime insisted that the immigrants he spoke with "undercover" "have Anarchistic or Communistic tendencies."[91] His tactic proved remarkably successful, especially in a country concerned about the stability of its government, which was closely tied to American business. "This new idea that all aliens are Anarchists or Communists has been keeping us all busy," he wrote, suggesting that the politics of immigrants could provoke authorities in ways that their mere presence could not.[92] Kime was not alone in his assumptions. Many native-born, white Americans in the 1920s worried that immigrants from eastern and southern Europe brought dangerous political sympathies with them to the United States. Such assumptions provided the impetus for such notorious aspects of the Red Scare as the Palmer Raids and the execution, eventually, of Nicola Sacco and Bartolomeo Vanzetti. Yet Kime believed that such fears were shared in Cuba and used them to encourage Cuba to help enforce American immigration laws.

Kime utilized this tactic in his attempts to stop Miguel Sastre and his partner, a man Kime referred to as El Catalan, from running regular immigrant smuggling trips between Cuba and western Florida. Sastre was an American citizen who worked with Mario Pelli out of Tampa aboard the *Sunbeam*, a fast launch that traveled with two registration numbers and two demountable masts.[93] Kime arranged with the State Department to have Cuban police arrest El Catalan, but he was released the next morning because of what one Cuban official claimed was a judicial error. Again, U.S. officials asked that El Catalan and Miguel Sastre be arrested, and they were. The Cuban judge complained, however, that there was no Cuban law to prevent the smuggling of immigrants out of Cuba, especially if they were in Cuba legally. The crime only occurred when the would-be immigrants landed on American shores. Kime searched the Cuban legal code for the means to prevent immigrant smuggling. He found three technicalities he used to his advantage. The first focused on registration, declaring if a pleasure vessel or fishing vessel that was clearly not a commercial vessel left a Cuban port carrying paying passengers, it had committed perjury in its registration. Since most would-be immigrants paid for their passage, the boat's owner could be held liable. It was also illegal for anyone to leave Cuba without paying a tax on the currency the traveler carried out of the country. Finally, Cuban vessels were prohibited from traveling to foreign countries without first clearing from an official Cuban port and could not return to a Cuban port without official health papers from the foreign port from which they returned. All of these legal requirements could be mustered to make the lives of immigrant smugglers uncomfortable. While the maritime laws that were violated usually only merited a light fine, Kime's legal maneuvering apparently provided some rationale for holding persons suspected of smuggling immigrants.[94] It was easier, however, for the United States to encourage Cuba to simply remove smugglers from the country. O'Kane apparently successfully convinced the Cuban government, according to Kime, to deport suspected immigrant runners. She used the persuasive argument that immigrants, as well as those who smuggled them, were political dissidents whose ideas posed a threat to Cuba. With that logic, and in light of the fact that many leaders of smuggling operations in Cuba were not Cuban themselves, the government was free, as the U.S. government desired, to deport foreigners who were believed to be smuggling immigrants. At one point in 1927, the Cuban government held eleven men suspected of immigrant smuggling with the intent to deport them to their home countries.

Deporting suspected immigrant smugglers solved one problem but merely created another. Once again, the Cuban government bore the burden for enforcing an American law. Kime realized that Cuban government officials were increasingly irritated that Cuba bore most of the cost of preventing the smuggling of unauthorized immigrants, as it paid the cost of return passage for deported foreigners. The United States, despite Kime's best efforts, was unwilling to chip in, even though controlling immigration through a quota system was an American innovation. Kime hoped that the mere threat of deportation, and the potential difficulty returning to Havana with charges pending, would cause many an interested smuggler to think twice about carrying a cargo of immigrants.

As with liquor, Kime did not believe even deportation would fully and completely end the illegal landing of would-be immigrants on southern beaches. He conceded that even though his "alien stunt"—claiming that all immigrants were anarchists and communists—"worked out fine," he suspected that immigrants continued to depart from Cuba and arrive in Florida. Kime faced the same problems with stopping the ships with human cargoes as he did stopping ships with liquid cargoes or cargoes of drugs. "They are still shipping aliens — don't worry — about twenty will leave before the end of the week," he wrote. "We can't stop the business at once — with four agents and no money."[95] His group of undercover agents was small, and money to fund their efforts was a persistent problem. While the treaty between Cuba and the United States focused on what Kime called the "Unholy Trinity" of smuggling — booze, aliens, and drugs — American enforcement was inefficient at best. Certainly, American law seemed equally determined to control human traffic as it did the liquor and drug traffic, and the American public at least seemed more willing to enforce immigration laws than perhaps it was with Prohibition laws. But enforcing three separate laws covering smuggling networks that ran parallel operations nonetheless faced bureaucratic obstacles that could not be simply swept aside. While the Prohibition Bureau, part of the Department of the Treasury, focused on liquor and drugs, immigration was under the Department of Labor, with its own attendant bureaucracy. The funds that Kime relied on to manage his operation to shut down liquor smuggling, even though they rarely arrived on time, had been appropriated by Congress to fight the illegal importation of liquor. Kime had no access to funds that had been appropriated to the Immigration Bureau to prevent the smuggling of immigrants. And even though Kime had been told that his antismuggling efforts should move beyond a focus on the smuggling of liquor, the much-maligned accounting office was not so flexible. In October 1927, Root informed Kime that the accounting office had disallowed expenses incurred in investigations into the smuggling of illegal immigrants. Kime had listed an item for $10 that was used in the capture of an "immigrant runner." Root noted that the appropriations under which they worked "were only for the purpose of enforcing the Prohibition and Narcotic Acts." "No one in the world could legally authorize the payment of anything that [was appropriated] for any other purpose," he derisively concluded.[96] While smuggling operations often worked together, and while investigations into smuggling revealed information about traffic involving all three forms of illegal cargo, the separate federal agencies charged with enforcement could only fund efforts to stop smuggling in the one category over which they had jurisdiction.

Root's admonishment might very well have caused Kime to throw up his hands in frustration, as it reflected the continuing stranglehold the accounting department and the divided bureaucracy had on enforcement in the face of a fluid and adaptable smuggling network. While congressional appropriations saw enforcing immigrant and liquor laws as entirely distinct, to smugglers they were seamlessly connected, even interchangeable. Root ultimately, however, took an entirely practical approach to this particular bureaucratic dilemma. He conceded that efforts to stem the smuggling of immigrants should rightly be charged to the Bureau of Labor, an impossible complication in terms of paperwork. Rather than even attempt it, he merely advised Kime to avoid mention of any immigrant smuggling whatsoever in his accounts. "As all of the hombres whom you are hunting are also interested in liquor and narcotics I can see no impropriety in so stating and in leaving out all references to aliens." Since most smugglers were willing to handle all three illicit cargoes, there was little need to distinguish among cargoes in the paperwork submitted for accounting purposes. For practical purposes, they were intertwined enough to justify erasing references to immigrants.[97]

With this bureaucratic sleight of hand, Kime continued his efforts to thwart smuggling of all varieties.

As with liquor smuggling, while Kime developed relatively effective strategies to discourage the departure of ships carrying unsanctioned immigrants and narcotics from Cuba, neither he nor the Cuban government nor the American consulate ever stopped the smuggling traffic entirely. Cuba simply had too many beaches to watch effectively all the time and hosted too many persons who were interested in continuing the trade. Most importantly, there was simply too much money to be made. Immigrants who were prevented from entering the United States under the new quota laws sought other ways to arrive in America and were willing to pay for the opportunity. At the same time, there was a growing appetite for illicit drugs in the United States that made the illegal importation of heroin, morphine, opium, and cocaine profitable. The locations in the South that welcomed alcohol, like Tampa and New Orleans, also hosted large markets in illicit drugs. The transportation networks that facilitated shipping smuggled liquor also took immigrants to their stateside destinations. The same reasons that made the South hospitable to smuggling liquor worked for the other cargoes as well. And the same efforts on the part of the federal government to stem traffic in all three cargoes demanded the extension of American law enforcement across international boundaries and into Havana.

It is perhaps little surprise that efforts to stem smuggling faced nearly insurmountable obstacles. Smugglers saw profit and were adaptive in their strategies, including in the contraband cargoes they were willing to carry. The bureaucracy of the federal government was less adaptive and less able to foster cooperation among agencies whose focus was on only one illegal cargo. Nevertheless, the methods of enforcement developed during Prohibition were durable, even if Prohibition itself was not. The Coast Guard's role in enforcing the nation's laws began with Prohibition but continued with the smuggling of narcotics and the increasing numbers of immigrants no longer able to enter the United States because of quota restrictions. The nation's drug policy centered on criminal prosecution rather than treating addiction. And the problem of smuggling in all its guises enabled the Coast Guard, the Bureau of Customs, and the Immigration and Naturalization Service to expand their authority beyond the nation's borders, across international waters, and occasionally into the internal affairs of foreign countries. At the same time, smuggling became a problem that bedeviled the southern coast. With it, southerners who had escaped most of the fierce debates about immigration for the previous four decades found themselves at the forefront of the issue that would consume immigration debates for the foreseeable future: what to do about would-be immigrants who circumvented the law when they entered the United States.

In the meantime, however, the efforts to enforce Prohibition on the other side of the Straits of Florida, in the United States, faltered. As Root and Kime repeatedly complained, they were hopelessly ineffective. And to those efforts we turn our attention next.

{ *Chapter Five* }

THE LIQUOR MARKET

✳

HERE WAS NO DOUBT that Miami, Florida, cared little for Prohibition. After a vacation there in 1929, a resident of Maine wrote the governor of Florida, Doyle Carlton, disgustedly describing Miami as a "wide open" town where gambling, racing, drinking, and all manner of carousing were hard to miss, even for the most law-abiding visitors. It was, the writer concluded, "a shame to ruin a good winter resort this way."[1] For much of the population of Miami, it seemed, Prohibition merely disrupted a good time, and for tourists, the good time brought them to town and encouraged them to open their wallets and spend. No surprise, then, that enforcing Prohibition was a tough sell, especially as the exploits of bootleggers were part of the promised entertainment. In 1927, however, Miami was in an uproar after several well-known bootleggers had been killed by the Coast Guard. One of the best known of them, Red Shannon, was shot and killed during a high-speed boat chase that moved from Biscayne Bay to the canals that snaked into Miami itself. The Coast Guard men opened fire in full view of Fleetwood Hotel guests who had been peacefully enjoying the evening when the chase came into sight. Witnesses to the killing swore that Shannon had his arms raised in surrender when he was struck by the fatal shots.[2] His death fueled public outrage that the Coast Guard put innocent bystanders in harm's way. Soon after, the five crew members on the Coast Guard boat were charged with murder.

The killings incited a vitriolic editorial in the weekly newspaper, *Miami Life*, a publication known for its support of Miami's wild side and its disdain for Prohibition. Shannon had died, it lamented, "because he supplied thousands of good citizens . . . with liquor. The victim, we might say further, of a farce of law, a law whose enforcement is a farce, a law enacted in the first place by a farce of a Congress." The anonymous author went on to declaim the failures of Prohibition: it was largely ignored by much of the population and encouraged crime. Even its initial supporters were dismayed by what the law had wrought. The problem was not merely "bootleggers flourishing and liquor dealers of all kinds flaunting the law." More concerning were the failures of the law that the public saw all around them:

> They see policemen and deputy sheriffs and federal agents driving about in Packards and Cadillacs and they hear reports of "protection" and "hush money." ... They see prohibition officers getting drunk. They sit in roadhouses and see raiding squads come in drunker than the most inebriated patrons. They see policemen off duty buying drinks from the most notorious bootleggers. They see Coast Guardsmen, revenue men, enforcement agents sitting about in cabarets sipping strong highballs. They see "bone-dry" congressmen sneaking copious drinks out of large flasks. They see treasury department officials standing on supper club tables reciting childhood poems. They see great men whose names could not be mentioned getting tipsy and begging for more drinks.[3]

What everyone saw, in short, was the corruption spurred by Prohibition. Such extensive corruption was possible because, despite the law, the market for liquor never disappeared. From cities like Miami and New Orleans, which showed no intention of going dry, to the smaller towns like Mobile, Alabama, to the more secluded areas along the coast and inland, the commerce in liquor continued. The liquor traffic, as we know, proved to be organized, adaptable, and persistent. It was also supported by large sectors of the population, in the South and elsewhere, who might not necessarily participate in the illegal trade themselves but gleefully ignored the law in their own drinking habits. To do so, they patronized liquor retailers of all varieties in locations throughout the South.

While much of the South remained rural and agricultural, in the growing numbers of cities, small towns, and even country crossroads, a commercial landscape took hold that enabled the liquor market to flourish. As liquor smuggling and retailing provided the possibility of large profits, southerners' eagerness to participate in the trade reflected their own embrace of commerce and enterprise. The local businesses and retail outlets that enabled southerners to buy more of their necessities also allowed them to buy alcohol if they wanted it. For officials in these communities, the temptations were too much to resist. They, too, quickly saw how a developing interest in commercial enterprise, leisure, and entertainment dovetailed with a continued desire to drink. Unsurprisingly, some of them used their official positions to join the liquor market, from accepting bribes to allow retailing to flourish to controlling their own extensive marketplaces of vice.

The extent of the retail market in liquor in the South comes into focus through the efforts to disrupt it. Prohibition agents and local police recorded where they sought and successfully purchased alcohol. Those efforts, however, faced virtually insurmountable obstacles because of a confused and inconsistent federal bureaucracy and inadequate resources on the ground. Well into the 1920s, even the relationship of Prohibition enforcement to the rest of the federal government remained in question. First placed under the Treasury Department, Prohibition enforcement joined the arm of revenue enforcement. Secretary of the Treasury Andrew W. Mellon, however, made little secret of his personal dislike of the amendment, and ardent Prohibitionists later insisted his lack of enthusiasm contributed to its ineffectiveness. More concerning, however, the relationship between disrupting the liquor traffic, the job of the Bureau of Prohibition, and prosecuting violators in courts, housed under the Department of Justice, was fuzzy at best. Only in 1930, in an effort to streamline both law enforcement and the judiciary, was the Bureau of Prohibition moved from the Department of Treasury into the Department of Justice. Incredibly, a full ten years into the Noble Experiment, the federal bureaucracy asked to enforce Prohibition remained in flux.

The leadership and enforcement priorities at the highest level were no more consistent. John F. Kramer was named the first chief Prohibition enforcement officer. He was replaced within a year by Roy A. Haynes at the insistence of Wayne Wheeler, head of the powerful Anti-Saloon League. Haynes was described as little more than Wheeler's puppet.[4] He genially assured the public that enforcement was proceeding splendidly and conveyed unceasing optimism about the government's ability to stop the liquor traffic. In his view, it was only a matter of time before bootleggers and smugglers of all kinds were pushed out of business. Haynes concentrated his efforts on education and propaganda to persuade Americans to quit drinking, employing numerous female agents to tour the country giving speeches on the public's moral obligation to obey the law and the dangers of bootleg booze. His detractors derided Haynes's perpetual cheery reports on the success of

Prohibition enforcement, which they deemed "virtually all fiction." Despite Haynes's efforts as a "crusader for the moral cause," by 1925 it was abundantly clear that many Americans refused to refrain from drinking.[5] Haynes was pushed aside in the summer of 1925, replaced by General Lincoln C. Andrews, who was named assistant secretary of the Treasury. Newspaper accounts reported that Haynes had been "shelved," that Andrews had taken his "mop job" away from him and "shorn" him of his powers.[6]

Described as a soldier of "singularly diverse and rounded training," and known for his focus on military discipline and as a scholar on leadership, General Andrews promised to unify the efforts to stem the continuing flow of intoxicants into the country.[7] His appointment was greeted with enormous optimism, despite growing skepticism about the law. He had supervisory authority over not just the Prohibition Bureau but also the Customs Bureau and the Coast Guard. Under his leadership, Andrews promised the government would end Haynes's propaganda efforts, derisively called "side-show stuff," and focus not on persuasion but on enforcement. He turned his attention to streamlining the organizational structure of Prohibition enforcement "on a business basis," well in line with the worship of business that characterized the decade.[8]

Using corporate language touting efficiency to frame his vision, Andrews forcefully argued that the enforcement bureaucracy should be built on merit and ability. He fully intended to divorce Prohibition appointments from state-level political patronage, even wanting potential agents to take civil service exams. Andrews thought it eminently logical that the appointment of Prohibition officials should be done on the basis of experience, training, and morality rather than on political "pull." He forcefully argued that political interference in the appointment of officials impeded his ability to enforce the law effectively. Well-connected patrons of politicians, he insisted, were not necessarily successful law enforcement officers. He faced considerable opposition, however. Members of Congress considered it their "duty" to advise and recommend candidates for Prohibition jobs in their states, often in return for political favors. The Anti-Saloon League, not pleased by Andrews's appointment from the start, also looked askance at this proposal. In the league's view, only men who supported Prohibition in all aspects of their private and professional lives should serve in government on its behalf. Andrews himself freely acknowledged that he had "taken many a drink" since Prohibition went into effect, though he promised to be "on the wagon" once he took his official position.[9]

In order to "clear the decks" and rebuild an enforcement structure based on merit, Andrews planned to require the resignation of every current Prohibition agent, replacing them with agents who met his criteria.[10] Agents across the country were warned they had no guarantee of reemployment; state and regional administrators who oversaw Prohibition agents in regional districts faced ouster as well, as Andrews envisioned administrators who were organizational experts, perhaps even with experience in big business, who understood how to manage large organizations. He faced opposition at every turn, however. Even Secretary Mellon opposed his suggestion that Prohibition agents take civil service exams.[11] Over the course of his tenure in office, he also contended with the apparent "crookedness" of federal enforcement forces as well as insufficient funds. Ultimately, he only lasted two years in the position. Many voiced suspicions that he was forced out because he had crossed swords too openly with the Anti-Saloon League.[12]

Andrews resigned in the summer of 1927, replaced by Seymour Lowman, a Republican from New York who described himself as "a politician and proud of it." Dr. James Doran, a noted chemist, was appointed as Prohibition commissioner and oversaw the Prohibition Bureau. Lowman promised "sound, business-like law enforcement without spectacular fireworks," forgoing special campaigns in favor of "diligent, conscientious work." Like Andrews, Lowman highlighted the need to attract effective, honest men to positions in Prohibition enforcement. His primary challenge, he told the public, was to "find skilled men who can withstand the temptations that beset enforcement officers."[13] Lowman intended to maintain most of Andrews's organizational structure, but he immediately called for civil service reform, requiring that all Prohibition officials formally apply and have their merits evaluated independent of politics to win a job, including taking the civil service exam. Again, the Anti-Saloon League balked, wanting only "friends of the law"—those who professed to be dry in their personal lives as well as their public lives—to be appointed to enforcement positions. Secretary Mellon and even President Calvin Coolidge resisted this time, noting caustically that "friends of the law" had not done a particularly effective job of enforcement up to that point. At their insistence, "belief in the law" and "teetotalism" did not become formal job requirements.[14]

Lowman immediately began cleaning house, loudly proclaiming that bribery and corruption were rampant among Prohibition forces. Eventually, one in every twelve Prohibition agents would be removed from office for cause over the course of Prohibition. Lowman certainly did his share. Noting the many "incompetent and crooked men" in enforcement positions, Lowman chortled, "some days my arm gets tired signing orders of dismissal."[15] Lowman, after being urged to tone down his rhetoric, did manage to enact civil service requirements for Prohibition jobs. While his efforts added some much-needed credibility to Prohibition enforcement, it nonetheless raised unexpected problems. Civil service requirements were imposed without exempting current Prohibition agents; all were required to take what newspapers colloquially referred to as the "Dry Quiz" to keep their jobs. Most failed immediately; 75 percent of agents, almost 1,500 of 2,000 agents currently on the payroll, could not pass the exam. Not a single agent in the Carolina district passed it. The numbers were dismal across the South, where 85 percent of agents failed. In New Orleans, 65 percent of agents failed, while 75 percent of agents in Alabama could not pass. Even college graduates and former officials received failing grades.[16] Of those who did pass, about 4,000 people nationwide, many were considered otherwise unfit to hold the job according to the Prohibition Bureau.[17] Prohibition Commissioner Doran put the blame squarely on Congress, which had passed the civil service requirement, and he urged more flexibility in qualifications. "Intellectual giants [are] not needed to smash stills," he insisted. "It is more important for an agent to be able to smash a bootleg joint than it is to spell idiosyncracy [sic]. . . . We don't want to hire a questionnaire, we want to hire a man."[18]

Lowman and Doran stayed in their posts for the remainder of the Prohibition Era and continued an enforcement strategy initially developed by General Andrews. That organizational structure balanced the different efforts of federal, state, and municipal authorities to target the market created by the laws of supply and demand. The federal government focused on the main sources of liquor supply, including illegal importation and the diversion of alcohol from industrial sources, and worked to disrupt major bootlegging operations, their protection rackets, and the banking procedures they used. Andrews envisioned that federal forces would confront wholesale suppliers, while state and local forces, with some help from Prohibition agents, would tackle local sources of supply—the dealers and retailers—as well as their customers, whom they called the "small fry" and the "hip-flask toter." State and local cooperation, however, was crucial to success. "We are not alone responsible" for enforcement, Andrews insisted. Federal Prohibition forces should not serve as "village policemen" if the problem of liquor traffic was to be addressed. To press home his point, in 1925 Andrews himself fired a federal

Prohibition agent in New Orleans who pursued, searched, and arrested a female motorist who was carrying "a pint flask, perhaps a third full." Arrests of average citizens engaged in the most mundane violations, Andrews insisted, only served to make federal law "obnoxious and cheap."[19] Better to have federal agents focus on more significant targets. With the large liquor operators attacked by federal forces, and small local distributors and retailers targeted by local sheriffs and police with occasional assistance from Prohibition agents, Andrews believed the cost of liquor would eventually increase beyond the willingness of consumers to pay. As he concluded, "The widespread 'casual' drinking, which is the most open indication that liquor is fairly easy to secure in the United States, is expected to fall of its own weight directly [as] supplies become scanty." And, he hoped, too expensive for most customers.[20]

Federal agents who could provide assistance to local officials, however, were far too few to manage the task in front of them. Each state was allocated only a paltry number of agents to police wide swaths of territory. Alabama was divided into three districts, each with only six Prohibition agents. The state government provided an additional thirty men focused entirely on Prohibition enforcement. Mississippi only had two districts, each with six agents. Louisiana was divided into two districts; the district containing New Orleans had fourteen agents and five investigators, while the other had a mere two.[21] Most states had far fewer federal Prohibition officers than needed to enforce the law. Nowhere was this more clear than in Florida. As one Prohibition official put it, "Nature is strongly allied with the Florida rum smuggler." Boasting more than 1,000 miles of coastline, "honeycombed with small inlets and keys," and only a short boat ride to Cuba and the Bahamas, Florida waged "constant warfare" against smuggling. Its resort cities like Miami and Tampa, with their "night clubs, transplanted from Broadway, luxurious gambling palaces, race tracks and boxing stadia," attracted a "free spending sporting class" fueling a booming market for liquor. The state's growing transportation networks not only made its tourist destinations accessible to northerners, but it also encouraged the flow of liquor north through smaller communities along the way. Yet Florida received only thirty-nine federal agents for the entire state.[22]

Florida residents who supported Prohibition railed to authorities about the obvious evidence of the liquor traffic, but officials felt hamstrung by lack of resources appropriated for enforcement. At one point in 1927, the deputy

Prohibition administrator in Jacksonville expressed his frustration to his superior in Savannah. After receiving a complaint about the lackluster efforts of
local law enforcement in West Palm Beach and a plea for the help of federal
agents, he noted that the complaint merely reflected the situation throughout
the state. The allegations, he was sure, were true, "not only in West Palm
Beach, but in every other city in the State of Florida, especially along the coast
where smuggling operations are carried on a large scale." He had similar
requests for help from across the state, "but with a force of only twenty-two
agents working in this state with an average expense allowance per agent
of only $119.68, it is an impossibility to give the necessary attention to these
letters."[23] No matter how ineffective local law enforcement was, federal forces
were too ill-equipped and underresourced to step in. At best, they could only
make occasional visits to troublesome areas. And when they visited, residents
complained they were little better than local forces. When Prohibition agents
moved in to Stuart, Florida, to enforce the law in the face of a reluctant sheriff, they apparently seized some liquor after a number of searches. But before
they could turn their seizures into court cases, they had a party and drank all
their evidence. They left town without making a single arrest.[24]

With federal enforcement officials spread so thin, and in the face of growing public disdain for the law, little wonder that law enforcement officials
at every level, from local constables to federal officials and even the Coast
Guard, might seek to join the retail liquor market. The temptation directly
in front of local, state, and federal officials was simply impossible for many
to resist. One constable in Manatee County, Florida, laid out the problem.
When he was elected, he wrote the governor, he intended to do his duty as
best he knew how. He "went into office clean and pledged himself not to
sell out to the bootleggers." He tried to do his best, but "since I have been in
office the bootleggers have constantly besieged me with offers to buy me and
my protection. I have refused to take one dollar of whiskey money and they
have constantly made threats that they would get rid of me by fair means or
foul."[25] In his view, officials could accept the money offered or be destroyed
personally or professionally if they chose not to. For many, apparently, it was
not a particularly difficult decision.

While officials along the southern coast sought to follow the structure for
enforcement laid out by General Andrews, their efforts merely highlighted
the thriving commercial world that took advantage of the public's continued desire for booze in the name of profit. Cities and communities along

the southern coast of the Atlantic and the Gulf of Mexico formed the front lines of Prohibition enforcement on every level, proximate to the seas where smuggling proliferated, home to interstate supply networks that shipped imported liquor north, yet beset as well by the local violations onshore that all communities faced. Over the course of Prohibition, enforcement extended its reach across the breadth of southern communities largely because alcohol and the traffic in it permeated so much of southern society. Despite the law, and despite exhortations to obey the law no matter how unpopular, many southerners continued to make, import, distribute, sell, purchase, and consume alcohol of every variety. The growth in retail establishments in the South of all kinds, from filling stations to restaurants, provided innumerable places where liquor could be sold, highlighting and accelerating the South's embrace of consumer culture. Enforcement efforts, whatever the level, merely demonstrated the broad reach of the southern black market in booze.

The extent of the liquor market in the South, however, belies the reputation of an abstemious South. Despite the loud exhortations of southern evangelicals, in practice, the South was far less committed to Prohibition than it seemed. While most southern cities were located in states that ostensibly supported Prohibition and even enacted statewide Prohibition laws before the passage of the federal amendment, the local tastes of many southerners indicated halfhearted support for completely eliminating alcoholic beverages. In fact, the existence of dry laws in southern states obscured significant support for drinking among many southerners. Mississippi's dry law, for example, permitted homemade wine. Alabama's Prohibition law was pretty leaky. It allowed citizens to import from "wet" states two quarts of distilled spirits or two gallons of wine or five gallons of beer every fifteen days. It prohibited selling alcohol within the state but certainly did not attempt to end drinking by Alabamians. And it was the votes of southern states in favor of repealing Prohibition that pushed the Twenty-First Amendment toward ratification.[26]

Southern distaste for bone-dry Prohibition was not entirely surprising. Alcohol had always played a significant role in southern socializing. Southerners embraced both sin and salvation, their behavior varying by location. Carl Carmer, a professor at the University of Alabama, summed up the elements of southern culture in Tuscaloosa: "Gossip, dancing, swimming, drinking, love-making, even religious observance, each has its niche in the structure of a day," acknowledging the light and dark side by side in southerners. He was not alone among southern writers describing a southern drinking culture that was more tightly tied to sociability than elsewhere. W. J. Cash, in his seminal treatise on southern culture, noted southerners' affinity for both sin and absolution. He argued that clandestine entertainments like drinking carried the "highest enjoyment," which helped make the South the hardest-drinking region in the nation. Southern socializing usually included sharing alcohol of some kind; among men especially, comradery had long included drinking alongside swearing, shooting, and fighting. While drinking was an important part of recreation, however, most men did not drink heavily in their homes or with ladies before Prohibition.[27]

Not all southerners agreed that alcohol-soaked sociability was a desirable aspect of southern distinctiveness. Certainly, many southerners abhorred drinking and advocated temperance. Many churchgoing southerners shared the view of many northerners that alcohol brought only misery and despair and should be eliminated, or at the very least reduced. Some southern communities had even tried several policies toward that end, including local option laws and dispensary systems to limit liquor's availability. Local option laws allowed individual counties to determine whether or not to allow the sale of liquor. Dispensary systems put the sale of liquor under state control. But the tide of southerners who traveled to wet counties or patronized state-run dispensaries merely highlighted the willingness of some southerners to continue to drink if alcohol was available in neighboring counties or states. Southern temperance advocates hoped that national Prohibition would render alcohol more reliably unavailable, making it largely out of reach nationwide.[28] Despite the fervent hopes of evangelical temperance reformers, however, not even federal law managed to dry out the South. Southern Prohibitionists failed to anticipate that just as consumers had previously sought liquor outside the counties or states where it was prohibited, they would seek it outside the nation's borders when it was prohibited nationwide. Nor did they anticipate that European distillers would seek to maintain their American market by flooding the Caribbean with products that would be smuggled to the United States. Finally, they never anticipated that so much smuggled liquor would travel to and through the South.

Many in the South applauded Prohibition nonetheless. They saw Prohibition as a means of racial control, and in their view, Prohibition would primarily serve to keep liquor out of the hands of those unfit to handle it. While many African Americans joined temperance efforts as a vehicle of racial uplift, whites believed they carried a special burden to protect the so-called inferior race from its frailties, including the dangers of drink. The writing of Archibald Rutledge, a white writer and the first poet laureate of South Carolina, embodied the paternalistic racism of white southerners regarding alcohol. Because "weaker races" were liable to succumb to the vices of "stronger races," whites had an obligation to prevent access to alcohol for African Americans. Many white employers, for example, hid their liquor to protect their household help. Prohibition merely offered a more comprehensive way to contain the problem. Whites, meanwhile, could resist the dangers of alcohol in ways that blacks could not. Outside circles of church organizations, Prohibition was never intended to apply to whites at all. "No one supposed that the white man would obey the law," Rutledge insisted. "Few white people in the South, as far as I can judge by what I myself see and hear at home, take national prohibition seriously insofar as it affects themselves."[29] Prohibition thus might serve as a tool of racial control or perhaps politics; it was not, however, a recipe for living. As Clarence Cason, an Alabama writer, noted, "The southern conscience is unruffled by the act of lifting a glass with one hand and gesturing for Prohibition with the other." Indeed, southerners were noted for their casual embrace of hypocrisy. Southerners, one popular publication noted, "think their whole duty is done when they believe as they are supposed to believe. . . . There is no requirement that their actions parallel their beliefs."[30] Sentiments like these may have been tall tales intended merely to amuse, and certainly many devout southerners of both races shunned liquor entirely. For others, however, such attitudes laid the groundwork for ignoring the law in their own behavior. And while racial attitudes shaped the South's landscape of liquor, they did so in ways more complicated than merely denying African Americans strong drink.

For officials in the South, the problems of Prohibition were broad indeed. In addition to the familiar smuggler and liquor dealer, one newspaper also described "the wine-drop man, the hip-pocket flasker, the drunk in the auto, and the family distiller" as Prohibition violators. The South was awash in retail outlets promising refreshment, sustenance, or a good time. Cities like Miami and New Orleans were only the most obvious and crowded examples. Liquor flowed freely in New Orleans throughout Prohibition, placing the city at the center of a far-reaching bootlegging network. Reputed to be the "wettest spot in America," New Orleans refused to end its historic romance with alcohol-fueled good times despite the Eighteenth Amendment. Liquor was openly consumed on the streets and readily available to just about anyone who sought it. Conveniently located near the Gulf, New Orleans received a steady supply of Caribbean liquor through Lake Ponchartrain, St. Bernard's Parish, and Barataria.[31] Some of the imported spirits headed north, but much of it served the local market as well. Officials did their best to bring New Orleans in line with the law. Prohibition agents from the Gulf Coast region including Mississippi and Alabama occasionally descended on the city and beyond its limits to target local retailers and cripple the supply routes that kept New Orleans decidedly wet. In one such raid, agents descended in trucks and cars on St. Bernard Parish, targeting "known resorts" and capturing several thousand cases of liquor that varied in quality from imported brands to moonshine.[32] Other times, agents focused only on local retailing, especially the small liquor purveyors operating soft drink stands and bootleg joints in the central business district, the suburbs, and residential areas. In 1928, agents raided over fifty establishments and charged their owners with possession of liquor for sale. While the amounts of liquor seized were reportedly small — agents noted that small establishments like soft drink stands did not tend to keep large amounts of liquor on hand at any one time — they nonetheless conveyed the pervasive presence of liquor on the city streets. Officials stated they had been spurred into action by the "scores of complaints from wives and mothers protesting against the unmolested presence of soft drink establishments in the business and residential districts of New Orleans."[33] Officials also proudly raided two supposedly "raid proof" clubs, the Ace Club and the Bat, that catered to the city's business and financial sectors. Officers confiscated and destroyed a "choice assortment of liquors" from a vault secreted behind an old-fashioned bar. News reports described the Ace Club and the leisure activities it provided its well-heeled, business-minded patrons. The club had several lounge rooms, a dining room, a service bar, bulletin boards, a stock ticker, and musical instruments, along with a room devoted to gambling. While the employees of the club, three white men and two black men, were arrested in the raid, the fifteen to twenty patrons who were enjoying the club were allowed to leave without charges.[34] Reports of these raids alone revealed the varied liquor market in the area. It offered retail options for those with little to spend or who only wanted a quick drink as well as venues for more refined clientele who sought a genteel and relaxing atmosphere where they could also monitor their stock portfolios.

Mobile, Alabama, also had a well-organized liquor market. Despite many of its residents' casual attitude toward Prohibition laws, it had its own champions of Prohibition, and its most notorious spectacle of Prohibition enforcement occurred in 1923 and 1924. It targeted an extensive local conspiracy to import liquor and distribute it among the city's local retailers and to the North as well. Located on Mobile Bay, in easy shouting distance of the Gulf Coast and the rivers heading inland, Mobile was a crossroads for liquor traffic. Boatloads of liquor would land on shores in and around Mobile Bay or be transported farther inland to be hidden in barns and swamps. Road and rail traffic connected Mobile to New Orleans to the west, where Prohibition tastes matched those of many Mobilians. To the east, the coast traveled along the Florida panhandle and then headed south toward Tampa's wide-open vice market and Miami's bootleg tourist culture. Roads out of Mobile also headed to the growing industrial centers like Birmingham and provided easy access to roads and rails heading to the thriving liquor markets of Chicago and the Northeast. Mobile's commonalities with its Gulf Coast neighbors and its own peculiarities provide the outlines of another liquor market.

In late 1923, more than seventy local men, including a state representative and former sheriff, the city's political boss, the chief of police, the county sheriff, several deputies, a local attorney, and a wealthy businessman, were arrested and indicted on charges of violating Prohibition laws. Federal officials also captured more than 10,000 quarts of liquor. The indictments alleged that these men operated a liquor wholesale business that stretched from the Rum Row in the waters off Mobile to the liquor markets in Chicago. At least once a month, a member of the operation traveled by boat to the fleet of rum schooners plying their trade in the Gulf of Mexico and returned with 500 to 1,000 cases of imported liquor from the Bahamas and Cuba. The cases were stored in garages around the Mobile area, and some eventually were packed in barrels, labeled as turpentine, and shipped by rail to Chicago. The rest supplied local liquor retailers who paid protection money to local officials and, as part of the bargain, agreed to sell only liquor provided by the operation. Business was so brisk and increased so rapidly that there were more customers eager to purchase the smuggled liquor than there was liquor to sell. The operation was also a model of organization. It kept its accounts at local banks; paid protection money to local, state, and ostensibly even federal agents; and allocated funds in its budget to bribe law enforcement and to cover the legal fees of its members. Realizing as well that politics would affect their profit, members of the operation also donated to the Republican National Committee to "steal the next elections."[35] Mobile's conspiracy blended smuggling with retailing

and trafficking across state lines. It placed Mobile at the center of an international distribution network, with spokes that extended around the South
and as far north as Chicago.

The Mobile Whiskey cases, however, were only the most spectacular evidence of Mobile's participation in the liquor traffic. Many other smaller liquor
operations moved liquor through the area. Law enforcement forces along the
southern coast often encountered boats loaded with liquor. Mobile authorities, for example, discovered thirty cases of "high grade" liquor, including
champagne, cognac, sherry, scotch, and Benedictine, aboard the steamship
Saccaroppa anchored at the Alabama Dry Dock. The liquor was sealed in a
specially constructed tank that was so well crafted it required a mechanic to
remove its steel lid.[36] Mobile also received many of the rum runners seized by
the Coast Guard. The *Francis E*, a British schooner from Nassau with $10,000
in wines and liquor from Havana on board, was seized off Cedar Key by the
Coast Guard cutter *Saukee* and taken to Mobile. Not long after, the *Agnes
Louise*, also registered in Nassau, was captured and joined it. These were but
a few of the rum schooners brought to Mobile as trophies. Ships themselves
were stored nearby at Chickabogue, adding "to the government's laid up fleet
of alleged rum-running vessels," while crews awaited trial. Eventually the
Madam, the *Wanderer*, the *Rhadamanthe*, the *Agnes Louise*, the *Marguerite*,
and the *Hazel Herman*, each captured with a large cargo, spent time tied
to docks near Mobile until they were released or auctioned. But the record
of convictions was poor. Of the major ships held in Mobile, four were sold
at auction, and their crews were convicted. Seven were released with their
cargoes intact.[37]

Despite the spectacle of federal court trials for suspected rum runners,
much of the day-to-day enforcement of Prohibition fell into the hands of
individual agents who operated alone or occasionally with informants along
the southern coast. Their efforts brought to light the reach of the liquor traffic
into the crevices, corners, and cupboards of southern communities. They
faced a daunting task, since there were far fewer agents than needed to enforce the law. To make up for scarce resources, local men contracted to work
with the federal government for a few weeks at a time to identify illegal liquor
dealers. The reports of these Prohibition agents in Mobile, a rare set of records, illustrate well how local law enforcement ferreted out the "small fry"
and the "hip-flask toters" and occasionally prevented smuggling from abroad
as well. Most of the work of Prohibition agents involved driving about the

Truck under guard loaded with seized liquor, Mobile, Alabama
(Erik Overbey Collection, The Doy Leale McCall Rare Book
and Manuscript Library, University of South Alabama)

area searching for suspected liquor dealers and making "test purchases" of alcoholic beverages that provided the grounds for arrests on charges of selling booze. Their records describe the various venues and establishments where booze might be sold. In December 1927, for example, agent Michael Guillera purchased alcoholic beverages at residences and restaurants around downtown Mobile, as well as at rooming houses and regular businesses, including a barbershop. Mostly men sold to him, and most of those men were black. He usually paid fifty cents for a half-pint but might pay as much as a dollar. He rarely turned in his half-pints as evidence. Instead, his records indicate that he "consumed on the premises"—in other words, drank them—to determine that the beverage was indeed alcoholic. O. D. Beard sought out liquor violators not only in Mobile and its surrounding areas but also in New Orleans, Birmingham, and Tuscaloosa. He spent his mornings in the office completing his paperwork, meeting with his supervisor, or interviewing informants. In the evenings he would go out in search of stills and rum runners. He made test purchases at Bill's Pool Room in Biloxi and at the Sugar Bowl and Pastione restaurants; he inspected seized boats; he even spent six hours one night watching the shore at Bayou La Batre after receiving reports that smugglers would be landing a load of whiskey.[38]

W. H. Barton, another Prohibition agent in Mobile, was a little more descriptive about where southerners might find liquor. He was assigned general undercover work in response to complaints in Jackson, Alabama, a small town approximately thirty miles north of Mobile. Residents there had reported that the mayor and the marshal "are both in sympathy with the liquor elements" and that others were "selling shinny." His undercover work took him first to Mt. Vernon, then to a tourist camp, and then to "see a negro by the name of Woodie on the west side of the road between Bilboe's Creek and Bates' Creek." He eventually went to the small hamlets of Hawthorn and Leroy before finally arriving in Jackson. He set out to locate small purveyors of liquor at a wide variety of commercial enterprises. He was unsuccessful at making a purchase at Barnes Mercantile Co., despite spending two hours in the effort. He was more successful at Miller's Café. At the depot, he could not make a sale but was directed to make a purchase from "the boy" who ran the Pressing Club. He tried to make a purchase at the Calvert Garage without success, nor was he successful at the Red Top Filling Station. He then took the supposedly corrupt marshal fishing in an attempt to make a buy, but again to no avail. The next day was little better. He could not locate a still in the swamp despite the help of a local tip. He then headed back to Mobile but stopped along the way at a fruit stand just north of Mobile, where he was directed to a "lady's house" where he bought three half-pints of whiskey. Despite only minimal success on the Jackson trip, Barton's other reports indicate he usually found many places where he could buy a drink, from the porter at the Arlington House hotel (a "yellow negro boy" named Leo) to filling stations, cook shops, and rooming houses, as well as at both hardwood mills and paper mills. And unlike other agents, Barton did not consume his evidence; he labeled and stored it.[39] Other agents found liquor being sold out of restaurants, soda fountains, and even a candy store. One Prohibition agent in Atlanta realized that hot dog carts were frequent retailers for alcohol, and he installed agents in a few to arrest their suppliers.[40] Agents like Barton, then, spent their days in search of booze, following tips or their own suspicions as to where they were likely to find it, which could be just about anywhere.

It was not uncommon for these agents to buy liquor from African American and white women who ran cafés, rooming houses, or "disorderly houses" sprinkled throughout the South. Providing alcohol fit seamlessly within women's traditional role of providing home, food, and sex and could be a source of social mobility for them and their families.[41] It was often in these businesses that women came to the attention of authorities. Pauline Nunnally, for example, was convicted of selling whiskey out of her house in 1925 in Savannah, Georgia. She received two years' probation, which was revoked when she was again arrested for selling whiskey in 1927. Bertha Bly and Virginia Raspberry were arrested for selling whiskey at their rooming house in Tampa. A search by officers had located "a dozen or more empty bottles and several empty fruit jars that had contained illicit whiskey" in a kitchen cabinet. Mabel Matthews reportedly stored her nineteen half-pints of whiskey waiting to be sold in her outhouse.[42] In some cases, women apparently even controlled the family liquor business, at least in the eyes of the law. Both Cleveland Burnes and his wife, Salina Burnes, were arrested at the same time in Birmingham in January 1927 for violating the state liquor laws. The charges against Cleveland were dismissed, while Salina was fined $56.[43] District courts throughout the South indicated that women violated the Prohibition laws or participated in the liquor traffic if it suited their purposes. They played roles in other aspects of the liquor traffic as well. They drove the cars transporting liquor because they were less likely to be stopped by enforcement officers, or they rode next to the driver, giving the impression the car belonged to a couple out on an innocent excursion. Women drove "cover vehicles" tasked with blocking policemen from catching the cars actually carrying liquor. Women had advantages that men did not, bootleggers believed. "She not only escapes detection more easily and for longer periods, but if she has a pleasant smile she has a ten times better chance of wheedling or buying her way out of trouble," one told a reporter. Some women even took over their husband's entire bootlegging operation when he died.[44]

Prohibition agent reports convey the ready availability of alcohol in the South, but they rarely made much reference to its quality. It was not unusual for agents like Guillera to drink the evidence or "consume on the premises" of the liquor retailers to determine whether the drink they purchased was alcoholic. Walter Rawnsley, a Prohibition agent in Key West, for example, testified in 1928 that when he purchased two bottles of home-brewed beer, he and his partner each drank one and "found it to be intoxicating." When cross-examined, he insisted that no chemical analysis was done to the beer and none was needed; he had "considerable experience in testing home brew beer . . . that he was able to tell by the smell and the taste of this bottle that it was intoxicating."[45] Nevertheless, the fact that Prohibition agents often drank their evidence suggested to the public, as well as to dry advocates, that Prohibition agents were little better than drunkards themselves. General Andrews conceded the difficulties but insisted that testing possible alcoholic beverages by tasting them at the point of purchase was an "unpleasant duty" at best. Even imported liquor from Europe was usually doctored once it reached the United States. Domestic alcohol sources included not only home brew and distilled products but also alcohol diverted from industrial sources. Prohibition agents routinely tasted alcohol reclaimed from antifreeze and even embalming fluid. "It's so poor, most of it, that no man drinks it willingly," Andrews averred. When challenged, he recalibrated his response: "I mean none of our men." Drinking the evidence nonetheless remained a public relations problem for Prohibition enforcement until 1931, when Prohibition agents were instructed that buying alcoholic beverages constituted sufficient evidence of a crime and that drinking was unnecessary. Indeed, agents learned they must have specific permission to do so.[46]

Seizing contraband liquor caused problems of a different sort. Some agents labeled and stored their purchases. Raids and seizures of smuggling vessels brought in considerably larger amounts of evidence. The 1923 raid in Mobile captured some 10,000 quarts of liquor. In September 1927, the Mobile newspaper announced that 7,000 gallons of the "finest grade of Havana alcohol," valued at $70,000, confiscated from a seized rum runner were to be unloaded at the customs warehouse in Mobile.[47] Officials initially stored seized liquor in the customshouse, but when that was full, they began to use a warehouse and even published the warehouse's location in the newspaper. Large warehouses filled with seized liquor represented an enormous temptation to bootleggers as potential sources of supply. The deputy U.S. marshal in Key West, Florida, Andrew Lopez, bemoaned the problems he faced guarding federal warehouses. In July 1925, the seizure room in the customs office in Key West was entirely full, and there was no additional space for liquor. He requested permission to destroy almost 1,500 bottles that he thought were unlikely to be used as evidence. He insisted that destroying seized liquor was almost a monthly necessity.[48] Seized liquor also attracted bootleggers and thieves. Not long before, Lopez had been awakened by a call that his liquor storage facility had been robbed of several sacks of confiscated beer from the *Fannie E. Prescott*. Lopez expressed his frustration in his report. The liquor was stored in a "place where I was certain it was impossible for anyone to tamper with." Nonetheless, the theft had occurred, and Lopez worried he might be held responsible.[49] Just two nights later, Lopez was forced to "shoot twice at

Police destroying confiscated liquor in Miami, 1925
(Courtesy of the State Archives of Florida)

Pirates" who once again tried to steal stored liquor. He sent a telegram asking permission to station four guards permanently over the seized evidence.[50] Other officials responsible for storing seized liquor faced similar difficulties. A collector of customs in 1926 asked for permission to destroy more than 1,000 bottles of booze that had been stored in Miami for over two years. By the time he wrote, warehouses in Tampa, Key West, and Jacksonville had already been broken into and had liquor stolen. He feared the same might happen in Miami.[51] Fearing bad press, federal officials considered other ways of handling seized alcohol. An agent in Denver poisoned the liquor he stored, hoping to deter thieves, but the possible manslaughter charges made this particular solution untenable. The Justice Department, concerned about "safe custody," advised that seized liquor should be destroyed rather than held for evidence in 1924. Officials were immediately ordered to destroy all their seized liquor wherever it was held, and thereafter they kept only small amounts of a liquor cargo as evidence for trial.[52]

Despite the pronouncements of increased or reorganized forces, and endless insistence on progress, liquor continued to flow onto southern beaches

across the South. The work of Prohibition agents mapped the changing landscape of the modernizing South, which offered growing opportunities for a
nexus between commerce and illicit consumption. Over the course of the
early twentieth century, cafés, restaurants, sidewalk stands, and lunchrooms
popped up in towns across the South. They provided refreshment for workers; spaces for socializing, discussion, or smoking for men; lunches for shop-
ping women; and dinners out for courting couples. They were accompanied
by dance halls, clubs, and "joints" that offered more illicit entertainments like
jazz music, dancing, gambling, and prostitution. It was little surprise that
they, alongside the blind tigers, also became purveyors of illegal alcohol as
well.[53] Changing travel created other commercial opportunities for enterprising southerners. Garages and filling stations represented other commercial
enterprises that proliferated across the South in the 1920s. The increase in automobile travel, the building of roads, and growing tourism created demand
for gasoline, motor oil, tires, and repairs in communities small and large.
General stores installed fuel pumps and maintained barrels of motor oil to
meet the needs of their motoring customers. These new customers often
sought refreshment while they waited, and enterprising mechanics and gro-
cers sold liquor along with car repair and snacks for the road. Travelers also
stopped at soft drink stands, produce stands, souvenir shops, and barbecue
joints to sample local fare. By 1927, roadside vendors were common on most
roadways in the South. Many of these establishments took advantage of the
increased profit potential in alcohol and sold it to their customers, something
Prohibition agents quickly learned.[54]

Certainly, many southerners in church circles bemoaned the liquor traffic
in their midst, and dry advocates continually pleaded for Americans to respect the law. Despite the efforts of agents like Barton and Guillera, many residents in small communities thought liquor joints and retailers were all too
obvious and disruptive. Many residents placed great hope in the law's power
to tame what they saw as the evil influence of alcohol, which they believed
destroyed orderly community life. They fully expected their elected officials
to do as the law required. When Prohibition failed to eradicate prominent social ills, they demanded officials redouble their efforts and sent handwritten
letters to their governors for help. Residents in the northern part of Escambia
County, Florida, for example, complained about "those who do not do anything but sell whiskey to the men and young boys." A letter signed by "the
voters of Bluff Springs, Florida," wanted the governor to know that "our little

town has become almost an open bar room" and hoped he could help. Similar complaints arose out of Calhoun County targeting a sheriff that residents believed had been a bootlegger before his election to office. The area had become home to liquor joints and prostitutes, a fact that was apparently known to the sheriff, yet there was "no effort made on his part to correct this evil."[55] Upholding the law, however, required southerners to forgo a beverage that not everyone saw as particularly immoral. Many officials, from local police officers through politicians in high office, also felt little commitment to the law. The black market in liquor tempted many of Prohibition's enforcers to trade on their authority to participate in the liquor traffic. The profit possible in selling liquor beckoned officials at every level.

The numbers alone suggested the extent of corruption among federal forces. Estimates would later suggest that one in twelve agents employed by the Bureau of Prohibition were dismissed for malfeasance. Corruption among federal officials was likely matched, if not exceeded, among local sheriffs, police, and state officials.[56] Of course, many officials did their best to uphold the law. In a 1929 survey of 104 judges, prosecutors, and sheriffs in Alabama and the panhandle of Florida conducted by the National Commission on Law Observance and Enforcement, 75 were rated good or excellent, with both interest and ability to enforce Prohibition. Only 29 were judged to be fairly indifferent or absolutely opposed to the law. The survey did not include lower-level officials like deputies or constables; nevertheless, it suggested that a significant proportion of the highest-ranking representatives of law enforcement and the justice system in local communities were not fully behind the law. After all, those 29 represented over 25 percent of leading officials. Similarly, of the 42 counties surveyed, in only 5 did public support for Prohibition top 75 percent of the population. In most (33), only 50 to 60 percent of the population favored enforcement of the amendment, which might explain why in 34 of the counties, the survey found conditions in which authorities there could not handle the traffic in their communities, the public refused to inform on law violators, and juries tended to acquit bootleggers. Across the region, communities were divided over Prohibition. In such an environment, not only was corruption among officials not surprising, but complaints about it by outraged citizens were not surprising either.[57]

The most commonly mentioned temptation for officials at every level, of course, was money. One agent who engineered more than a few corruption cases by posing as a bootlegger reported being told by one corrupt customs

official "that if I didn't make money as a dry agent I was a fool and that Prohibition was an unpopular thing." Why not make money off an unpopular
law?[58] Throughout the Prohibition Era, the low pay of federal agents was
a perpetual target of complaint and frequent explanation for why bribery
was so common. In many areas, the wages of Prohibition agents barely supported a family. Most federal agents earned a mere $150 to $200 per month.
Many a bootlegger was happy to supplement that income with protection
payments from $500 to $1,000 per month. The profits of bootlegging generated more than adequate funds to pay off officials, and officials needed, and
often wanted, the money. It was little surprise, then, that Prohibition agents
and law enforcement accepted it so readily and even sought out official appointments to do so. The potential profit the black market in liquor promised was enough, many in the popular press suggested, to make bootleggers
and corrupt officials some of the most ardent, if unlikely, supporters of the
Volstead law. Their revenue streams depended on it. Liquor as contraband
commanded much higher profits than it did as a legal commodity. For bootleggers and rum runners, paying protection money or bribes to officials was
merely another business expense, "just as fixed and calculable a part of over-
head as faked whisky, imitation bottles, and counterfeit labels."[59] It began
with the fake customs documents needed to ship liquor out of Havana and
continued all the way to the local precinct officer or sheriff paid to ignore
the operation of a speakeasy, allowing liquor to be a continuing presence in
virtually every city and town in the nation.

Taking bribes to ignore liquor violations was a common accusation against
officials. Allegations that they participated in smuggling and bootlegging
also crossed the desks of officials in Washington. Persistent rumors, for example, prompted an investigation into whether the naval radio station at Jupiter, Florida, was broadcasting information concerning the location of Coast
Guard vessels. The findings were inconclusive. Not long after, Jupiter Inlet's
light keeper was suspected of using his light to signal smugglers when it was
safe to land their cargoes. He apparently received $500 per month for his
efforts.[60] Other officials became involved in smuggling outfits themselves.
The case of Joseph E. Courtney, a federal Prohibition officer in Miami who
was accused of bribery and corruption, received only moderate attention in
the newspapers. Bill Kelly, an undercover agent in Miami who reported to
Charles Root, however, offered more details of Courtney's operations in 1925
and 1926, suggesting how the reach of the liquor market could ensnare those

who were supposed to stop it. According to Kelly, Julian Venable, who operated a retail liquor establishment in Miami, offered Courtney a proposition after being shut down several times because of federal raids. He would pay Courtney $300 per month to warn him whenever federal agents intended to raid his establishment. Their relationship grew from there. Eventually, Venable stated, Courtney contributed $1,500 to purchase liquor in the Bahamas, making him a partner in smuggling ventures. Courtney also offered Venable the keys to the government storehouse for seized liquor as well as the location of the most valuable liquor in storage, giving him the opportunity to steal and sell it. Venable soon described his arrangement with Courtney to other bootleggers in the area who also hoped to obtain Courtney's protection. Harold Jensen agreed to pay Courtney $500 per month, and four others did so as well, including Sue Kauz, who would later testify that Courtney was a partner in her liquor-smuggling business and received half of the profits. In return for the monthly payments, Courtney warned them of raids on their businesses with enough time to clear out their liquor supply. Each bootlegger confirmed that he or she made cash payments to either Courtney himself — Kauz reported that she left his share of profits on his office desk folded inside a pack of cigarettes — or to his wife. Despite the testimony at trial, however, a Miami jury acquitted Courtney.[61] Bill Kelly suspected that Courtney escaped conviction largely because of the corruption endemic in Florida's federal district courts.

The men of the Coast Guard also faced significant temptations. Their charge to prevent illegal importation of liquor from abroad put many ships and crews in direct contact with some of the highest-quality distilled spirits the world had to offer. Allegations of misbehavior unsurprisingly followed. Many involved relatively minor infractions, like drunkenness, that did not compromise the overall mission of the service. They indicated how the men in the Coast Guard were little different from other Americans; they still enjoyed drinking and did so when they could. More significant episodes of corruption occurred where the mission of the Coast Guard intersected with attempts to land smuggled liquor onshore. The crew of the CG-2345, for example, pilfered 80 of the 800 sacks of assorted liquors they seized from a motorboat off the coast near St. Augustine. They gave it to two men who then sold it to a bootlegger in Jacksonville. At some point in the transaction, one suspects, they shared in the profits.[62] A boatswain from Zack's Inlet Station started his own liquor business using Coast Guard equipment. He did not use

Prohibition raid in Miami, 1925 (Courtesy of the State Archives of Florida)

boats, however. He was caught using the base's horse and cart to transport cases of liquor inland from shore. His appointment was revoked. When he tried to be reinstated, he was refused.[63] Other men apparently gained the tools or the contacts to enter the smuggling business for themselves through their service in the Coast Guard. They could even use their connection to the Coast Guard as a claim of authority and trustworthiness to further their clandestine business. Customs agents, for example, quickly contacted the Coast Guard when they arrested Franz B. Janssen unloading burlap sacks from a motorboat into a rented sedan along the waterfront in Miami. This was not the first time that Janssen had rented a sedan. It appeared Janssen told the rental company that he was a member of the Coast Guard. Janssen had been dismissed from the service more than five months before, but claiming official status enabled him to rent the car.[64]

In areas in which the traffic in liquor was particularly heavy and, like Miami, where the local population profited from promoting drinking as tourist entertainment, Coast Guard crews were more likely to take a role in marketing and selling liquor. The Coast Guard men stationed on Base Six in Broward County, Florida, faced nearly endless opportunities to profit from their positions. Coast Guard officials in Washington conceded that the area around Miami and Ft. Lauderdale was "hostile territory," but the base's reputation in the area suggested that the men stationed there participated in bootlegging themselves. In 1927, Charles Root noted that the senior judge in Dade County had publicly branded the men of Base Six as "grafters, thieves, and hijackers." Root thought such characterization was unfair, but it reflected long-standing concerns about corruption on the base. Over the course of Prohibition, Base Six came under scrutiny on a regular basis for undermining Prohibition. The resulting investigations uncovered a dizzying array of violations. The first investigation into allegations of corruption on Base Six occurred in 1924, when rumors that some crew members were "suspiciously intimate" with known bootleggers reached the ears of the commander of the Gulf Division. Allegations also surfaced that one boatswain was "in the pay of liquor interests" and crew members were misbehaving onshore. The commander's investigation revealed no direct evidence of bribery, but he noted a persistent popular belief that the ability of Coast Guard men to purchase late-model automobiles indicated they were accepting bribes. This, in his belief, was a red herring, especially near Miami. He noted that many winter vacationers sold their cars to locals rather than transport them back north. "Almost anybody can get a good automobile in the spring for very little money," he took care to note.[65]

Car ownership may not have been evidence of corruption, but he nonetheless had other concerns. He suspected that some patrols refused to disrupt smuggling operations. One picket boat, for example, brought in a seized boat but reported that its crew had escaped. The boat, however, contained only half its cargo. The base commander suspected that the picket boat had allowed the crew to escape and then threw half the cargo overboard for them to salvage later. When the base commander tried to replace suspect members of the picket boat's crew with men he knew were reliable, the crew protested, claiming that they "did not want to go out [on patrol at sea] with any psalm singers." Frustrated and unable to locate hard evidence of corruption, the commander did note that discipline overall on the base was well below Coast Guard standards. He recommended that an additional officer be placed at the base, one who was "accustomed to driving with a taut rein." The commandant of the Coast Guard refused.[66]

Suspicions about collusion with smugglers did not diminish, however. In 1927, the commandant again received information about corruption at Base Six. This time, the allegation involved a bribery scheme, and the information came from a rum runner who indicated he had an ongoing arrangement with Coast Guard men to land his liquor onshore. Smuggler C. E. Conroy of Miami reported he had paid the men at Base Six $2 for every case that he landed onshore since 1925, delivering payment to Coast Guard members at their houses. Paying for protection was a significant operating expense; Conroy noted that the Coast Guard men "were making more than the bootleggers did." But it was, he argued, a necessary expense: "You had to be pretty square with them, for if they found out you were behind with them, they would knock you off."[67] It was notoriously difficult, however, for investigators to prove that picket boat crews were deliberately ignoring smugglers in return for their money. Coast Guard boats had numerous ways they could aid smugglers, most of which looked little different from their regular patrols. They might, for example, warn bootleggers in advance of their planned movements, allowing contact boats to dash to shore when the Coast Guard patrol headed in the opposite direction. The Coast Guard might "tear around fiercely and report everything in sight except the schooners it is paid to protect." The system was so easily organized that "crude acts of commission are seldom necessary."[68] Even identification of the guilty Coast Guard men could be difficult. When Conroy was asked if he could identify the men he paid, he replied that he knew some of them by sight, but not their names, and those he paid changed regularly as servicemen rotated among bases. Conroy noted the men would "just come and go"; he merely paid whichever crewmen were assigned to the Florida base.[69] Conroy's statement buttressed other allegations about problems on Base Six. Several "absolutely honest" men were stationed on the base, and they told authorities that there were serious problems, though they had little hard proof. In their view, Base Six maintained "a woefully deficient moral code as to looting cargo and a very poor standard of sobriety."[70]

The situation at Base Six hit bottom in 1929, when an incident with the crew of the CG-249 again brought the base under suspicion for corruption. Reported seizures had dropped precipitously, and there was also some suspicion that the machinists on the base were dragging their feet when it came to repairing engines and keeping boats seaworthy. In response, Charles Root sent yet another investigator to look into the matter.[71] In the course of this investigation, the CG-249 was thoroughly searched. The search revealed liquor concealed virtually "in every compartment on the ship." "Chains had been roused out, cases stored under them and then the chains run back in the lockers; the radio cabinet was stocked full, there was liquor in the lazerette, in the cabin, in the galley, and in the engine rooms, the floor boards in the crew compartment had been lifted and liquor stored in the turn of the bilge." This was not the haphazard effort of casual usage or a hurried job in the face of an imminent inspection. The investigator estimated that it would have taken the work of three men to hide all the liquor in all the various places on board. It was such a thorough job, there being no straw, sacking, or loose bottles remaining about, that he also speculated it could not have happened without the knowledge of the crew. And yet when questioned, each crew member "blandly state[d] that he saw nothing of the kind going on." Indeed, the statements of the crew were so similar that they "showed coaching and rehearsal." In the eyes of officers, the liquor on board the CG-249 suggested an ongoing practice among the crew of looting liquor cargoes of seized ships and selling the booze themselves. The commander of Base Six had also heard persistent rumors about the misbehavior of his men, but up to that point he had refused to believe such "gossip." The discovery on board the CG-249 caused him to reconsider. He had heard remarks that "Base Six runs the biggest bootlegging gang in the community." Another marketing phrase had become common in Miami liquor circles, he noted. Bootleggers assured their customers of the quality of their wares by saying, "You can depend on this liquor, it is Coast Guard liquor." He was crestfallen to learn of the activities of the crew, yet he could not escape the fact that the "ill-repute of the Coast Guard" in Florida was "well-deserved."[72] Base Six, of course, operated in the heart of an area known for its sporting life. Commander Root noted that Miami had "gone wild." "There are more booze joints already opened here and at Miami Beach than in any other part of the United States I have ever seen. Everybody with the price of a case of whiskey has set up a joint and is ready to do business."[73] The temptations Miami presented to even the most stalwart Coast Guard men could be hard to shake, especially when the "enemy" could offer "corruption funds dully equivalent to ten times our wage scale."[74] Apparently more than a few of the men on Base Six made no effort to resist temptation.

In response, Coast Guard commanders instituted a practice of more frequent rotations of crew around the various bases in the United States, taking quick action when concerns about a crew member arose. When a surfman in Barataria, for example, was suspected of unspecified collusion with boot-leggers, he was quickly transferred to another station.[75] The policy seemed to have some good effect, as did rotating the tours of the larger Coast Guard cutters. In 1930, a general summary of smuggling efforts from the Bahamas noted that liquor smugglers had suffered some significant losses to their busi-ness because of Coast Guard action. "The continuous changing around of the Coast Guard cutters" was "causing considerable difficulty and inconve-nience" to smugglers. "They never knew as to who they were likely to en-counter and whatever arrangements they may have made previously with one Coast Guard Officer, was, in the present conditions useless, as on their return with a load, this Officer would have been dispatched for duty to some other point."[76] If base personnel were corrupt, moving them away from their bootlegging friends could solve the problem.

While the Coast Guard faced particular temptations along Florida's coast, local officials throughout the state did so as well in their areas. Few states had such ready access to such immense quantities and varieties of forbidden liquor moving through the landscape. Alcohol flowed through Florida like a flood, whether it followed the roads north or the southbound stream of tourists seeking liquor-soaked entertainments. And not all Florida officials supported Prohibition. More than a few no doubt shared the sentiments of the sheriff of Titusville, who allegedly proclaimed that "he would not live in a community that would not sell liquor and lots of it."[77] Such pervasive sen-timents caused Charles Root to fear that Prohibition could not be enforced successfully in Florida at all. In a memo in 1927, he gave a hint of the extent of official corruption throughout the state. He estimated that only one or two counties in Florida were free from corruption in their law enforcement and judicial systems. He called St. Johns and Flagler counties "thoroughly rotten," noting that the editor of a St. Augustine newspaper dominated smuggling in that area. He reported that the sheriff of Duval County was "in the smuggling business and is a partner of one Paxton who is a notorious smuggler." Several Duval County judicial officers would eventually be indicted for offering a bribe to a federal agent in 1932.[78] Smuggling in Brevard County, he believed, was financed by a wealthy woman who was purportedly a niece of the local judge. Palm Beach County was "so rotten that I cannot attempt to describe the situation in detail. Even the Deputy Collector of Customs . . . [was] not above suspicion." Dade County was "absolutely uncivilized," as was the county surrounding Key West. Only Lee and St. Lucie county officials were described as clean.[79] Charles Root shared his concern with Henry Kime in a letter. "The more I learn of it the more horrified I am at conditions in Florida. Up to two months ago I did not dream that such a state of affairs could exist in any semi-civilized country, let alone the United States. Turkey in its worst days of misgovernment, was not as bad as Florida now is, and Cuba in its worst days was only a piker." In his view, if the U.S. government could not effectively "lick" the corruption in the state, it should get out and "leave it to its own devices."[80] The U.S. District Courts in Florida were apparently little better. Coast Guard vessels were instructed to tow seized vessels to either Mobile or Savannah when possible, because the district courts outside Florida were more likely to prosecute smuggling offenses successfully.

The duty of all sworn law enforcement officials was to enforce the law regardless of their personal beliefs or proclivities. Nevertheless, their discretion over how they enforced the law expanded the ways in which corruption could infiltrate the functioning of an entire community. Consider, for example, the sheriff of Stuart, Florida, a man named Marion McGee. He apparently liked his liquor, despite trying to abstain for his first few years in office. He regularly carried whiskey with him and openly drank his lemonade with a hefty dose of it in front of others. He had been discovered hopelessly drunk in a local drugstore as well as in his car in the wee hours of the morning. The justice of the peace and the local judge both apparently confronted him about his drinking, and he offered a short-lived promise to quit. But he reportedly was visibly intoxicated when he attempted to arrest a man from Detroit traveling on the Dixie Highway, dragging the man to jail on the slimmest of charges. His power as sheriff and his relationship with alcohol, however, shaped how all laws were enforced in the area. He had allegedly warned his deputies not to arrest anyone for a Prohibition violation without his approval. He required the same for charges of gambling as well. Eventually, no arrests of suspected criminals could occur without his express permission, and he threatened to fire any deputies who violated this mandate. In practice, this meant he targeted some people and allowed others to carry on their illegal business without interference. As one resident put it, "His supporters were not to be bothered under any circumstances and his enemies were to be hounded at any cost." He even sought to extend his selective enforcement to the justice system. He pilfered liquor for his own use from the cache of seized liquor under the control of the clerk of the court. He instructed his brother, who was the local jailer, to refuse to allow attorneys to visit their jailed clients

or receive messages from them. He only allowed his "favorites" among attorneys to have access to the jail and apparently steered potential clients in
their direction. When challenged, however, Sheriff McGee was intransigent.
He insisted "he was sheriff of Martin County and he would run the affairs
of his office as he damned pleased."[81] Eventually residents reached the limits
of their tolerance, spurring a movement to have him removed from office.
Until then, his corruption shaped the entire criminal justice system in the
community.

Failure to enforce the law fairly and equitably was one of the most frequent
complaints residents in Florida communities had about their law enforcement officers. And while McGee's preferential treatment of certain alleged
criminals seemed to cross over all types of crimes, other officials used their
positions to shape the liquor market in their jurisdictions. Accepting protection payments allowed some retailers to flourish while others faced official
action. One resident of Punta Gorda surmised that the only reason the local
sheriff had not closed the disorderly house operating nearby was because he
had been paid off. "It seems as if they don't care for they have not bothered
him yet and he has been running here three of four years" as a dance hall,
barroom, and "red light." No other explanation in her mind could justify the
sheriff's failure to shut it down. An anonymous complaint from Escambia
County also suggested that the local sheriff was paid to ignore liquor makers
and sellers and disorderly houses. Again, the evidence provided was thin —
"I have heard and it must be true"— but the persistence of lawlessness, the
petitioner believed, could be explained no other way. More reliable evidence
came from the owner of a coffee shop in Key West. He was arrested by the
local deputy sheriff for selling alcohol. In his letter of protest to the governor,
he did not deny the charge; instead, he complained that the only reason he
was arrested was because he had refused to pay for protection from local
officers. He reported that on three separate occasions officers demanded that
he pay to avoid raids. After his final refusal, he was arrested.[82]

Liquor dealers who participated in protection rackets, despite their illegality, nonetheless believed that they had established a clear contract with law
enforcement that allowed them to conduct their liquor businesses freely. If
they paid for protection from the law, they should receive it. One distiller in
Flagler County made his displeasure plain to the governor when local officials backtracked on the agreement. He was a long-standing resident of his
community, and during the 1928 election for sheriff, one candidate promised
him that if he worked to get the man elected, he would face no raids on his

stills. The candidate won, and the distiller confirmed his understanding of their agreement and even paid $100 in cash for additional consideration. He set up his still "at great expense," but not long after, it was raided by deputies, who took the man into custody and destroyed his equipment. When he complained about his treatment to the sheriff, the sheriff replied that he still had four years in office and the man would no doubt cover his loss. When he continued to complain, shots were fired into his house. With considerable understatement, the man wrote the governor that he "was very much displeased at my treatment by his force." He had "already paid for protection, which I did not get."[83]

Protection schemes, raids, and the ability to confiscate equipment gave local law enforcement officers an enormous amount of control over the liquor market in their area, from who could sell individual drinks all the way to the sources of supply. Henry Hidalgo, a constable in Tampa — a city known, like Miami, for its illicit entertainments — used a variety of tactics beyond simple protection payments to oversee the widespread liquor, gambling, and bolita (a type of lottery) market in the area. Tampa had more than doubled its size in the first five years of the 1920s. It had a thriving vice market along with, at one time, an estimated 142 businesses openly selling liquor.[84] Hidalgo took advantage of the opportunities these illicit entertainments offered, collecting monthly payments for protection. Hidalgo also planted whiskey in the cars of those who did not make their payments and arrested them for possession. One of his common tactics was to arrive to make a raid, agree to accept a large sum of money to "fix the case," and require the bootlegger to pay $10 per week in protection thereafter. He even required protection money — though only $5 per week — from the organizers of chicken fights. He used one additional method to control the local liquor market that profoundly irritated the liquor distillers in his area. When he raided establishments, he would confiscate the distilling equipment. He would then force distillers, once their case had been resolved, to buy back their own equipment. If they refused or were slow in payment, he sold the equipment to someone else. He thus determined who could produce liquor for the local market and simultaneously ensured he profited from those who did. Hidalgo was eventually arrested, and though he was acquitted by a local court, his federal case resulted in a conviction and a sentence in the federal penitentiary in Atlanta.[85]

Even in smaller communities, a bootleg industry controlled by local officials could not only thrive but come to influence much of the larger community, especially when its proximity to Florida's growing road networks provided a ready supply of traveling customers. Residents of Ocala, Florida, in Marion County found themselves in such a situation by the end of the 1920s. The western route of the Dixie Highway passed through Ocala, located south of Gainesville and north of Tampa. Ocala had grown considerably, from just under 5,000 residents in the 1920 census to more than 7,000 thousand by 1930. The population growth and tourist traffic spurred the development of commercial establishments that easily doubled as liquor joints. But the residents of Ocala itself were generally conservative. They had voted in the 1920s to prohibit movie showings on Sundays and voted Republican in the hopes that liquor laws might be better enforced. While the city of Ocala itself, with a strong marshal, seemed to keep bootleggers at bay, county officers did not. They were more intent on supporting a marketplace in booze that provided illicit entertainments, attracted tourists, and lined their own pockets. Notorious "liquor joints" and gambling sites, many of which were located on the public highways and frequently traveled roadways near local attractions, were sprinkled around the county outside the city limits. The most well known was the Dixie Filling Station, which offered not only alcohol but slot machines as well, located a mile north of the city center. While residents complained that most filling stations offered booze and slot machines, the Dixie Filling Station seemed unusually entrepreneurial. It carried a wide variety of liquors from moonshine and homebrew beer to three makes of whisky, including Canadian Club. It also boasted excellent customer service, bringing drinks on trays directly to customers in their cars. Other well-known liquor retailers were Charley Peoples's place, operated by a local African American man, and Josephine Sanders's "low dive saloon" near the fairgrounds. Peter Paul's was also commonly mentioned, as was Carrie Nix's place, located next door to one of Ocala's "old and respectable families." The easy availability of alcohol even spread to the streets. Taxi drivers apparently sold liquor by the bottle. The local booze market in Ocala and Marion County also crossed racial lines. Josephine Sanders, Charley Peoples, and Peter Paul were black; Carrie Nix was apparently white. But they welcomed customers of both races.[86]

While many Ocala residents did not participate in the gaming culture of the town or patronize its local dives, the existence and locations of suspect establishments were apparently common knowledge. As the editor of the local newspaper reported to the governor, though he himself did not frequent these places, it was nonetheless "common talk on the street and where ever men gather in social converse that liquor and home brew are being sold openly in many filling stations and 'joints' throughout the county." One did not need to be part of the culture to see its effects, he continued. "Most of the things we quiet homebodies learn about liquor selling is from hearsay evidence, but there is plenty of it circulating around and if liquor wasn't so easy to obtain, everybody wouldn't know where it is being sold and by whom and who is buying it." There were even suggestions that federal authorities recognized Marion County as the "wettest" county in Florida, a substantial if dubious achievement, considering the problems with Prohibition in the state as a whole.[87]

Residents who supported Prohibition complained to the governor that local law enforcement did nothing to enforce Prohibition laws. Officials apparently did not raid well-known establishments or attempt to put them out of business in any sustained way. As the local newspaper editor suggested, while they might occasionally locate a still, "they don't seem to work very hard at it." Other residents noted that local officials had "not raided nor made a single arrest of the most notorious dives which have been operating unmolested." The only attempts at cracking down on the liquor market were made by federal agents who occasionally conducted "spasmodic raids" within the county. One local automobile salesman who traveled throughout the county compared his experience in Marion County with those of his travels in the rest of the country. "I have never seen such open and flagrant defiance of the laws as evidenced by the promiscuous and unmolested operation of the numerous liquor and gambling dives in the County." Out of curiosity, he finally asked one of the proprietors of several liquor joints how he operated so openly. He was told that the local liquor merchants "were not afraid of being molested by the Sheriff or his deputies, nor from Federal Officers either, as they would be notified in advance of the Federal Officers' arrival by the Sheriff or his deputies." Occasionally local proprietors faced charges of violating Prohibition laws, but they usually escaped with minor fines if they were punished at all. Mrs. C. C. Lamb, arrested for operating one of the better-known joints, for example, was convicted in federal court but only of possession of liquor, not even its sale, and she received a $50 fine. Even when federal Prohibition agents arrested offenders at local blind tigers, the charges did not always stick. Two of the more notorious local dealers, for example, were released when the material witness in their case failed to appear in court. Residents had occasionally even taken matters into their own hands, staging their own "target buys" and turning over the purchased alcohol to authorities as evidence for prosecution. One ardent Prohibitionist tried to jump-start prosecutions by purchasing liquor to bring before a grand jury. In his telling, his actions resulted in the indictment of thirty bootleggers, but only one was convicted. The rest of the cases were not even prosecuted.[88]

Many local residents viewed Sheriff S. C. M. Thomas as the problem. He and his deputies operated a protection racket for local bootleggers. But his corruption spread further than the lucrative business of protection. He, like many others, liked alcohol. Community members reported that he drank and occasionally patronized the liquor joints in the area. He was not averse to exploiting his power in other ways. On one occasion, apparently, when a young man and young woman were arrested by Department of Justice officials and given over to the county authorities, the man was left in the jail while the woman was removed from the jail and held at a local hotel. Her stay there was paid for by the sheriff, and the town was set abuzz when the sheriff's wife caught him in bed with his supposed inmate. The community focused outrage on his infidelity less than the sexual coercion of his female prisoner. Nevertheless, the sheriff was apparently "paralyzed drunk" when he was caught.[89]

Local residents, however, did not believe that the sheriff alone facilitated the liquor market in town. Many also blamed two local judges. Both of them reportedly owned properties in which liquor joints operated. Some, like the local newspaper editor, argued that their ownership was little more than coincidence and that the judges could not be held responsible for the habits of their tenants. But others argued there was more deliberate collusion between landlord and tenant. One judge, a man named L. E. Futch, owned a property referred to variously as the Old Hartman Place, the Hawaiian Inn, and the Springway Inn. The establishment sold pint bottles of liquor and housed four slot machines. The judge rented the property to a man named Easterling. Over the course of a year, Easterling was arrested four times by federal agents and, on his fourth arrest, was convicted and fined $250. While many believed the four arrests offered sufficient cause for eviction, Easterling had been convicted of bootlegging even before he entered into the lease in the first place, suggesting the judge knew that Easterling might very well operate a liquor joint on the premises.[90] Another judge in town, Judge Bullock, also owned property that was rented to known bootleggers. He had rented one of his houses to Carrie Nix, who had been arrested for disorderly conduct several times. When neighbors complained about her activities, the judge was unmoved. He allegedly replied that the "sporting class paid good rent and that as long as Mrs. Nix paid her rent, he would not make her move."[91] Bullock's attitude was not uncommon. Federal officials noted that Florida landlords were notoriously willing to overlook liquor violations as long as they received their rent.[92]

The complaints about Prohibition enforcement in Ocala and Marion County stemmed from what many residents saw as a crooked sheriff who operated what was reputed to be a "central distribution point" for illegal liquor and a "notorious den of bootleggers,"[93] as well as local judges who rarely oversaw convictions of bootleggers and who themselves owned properties that housed liquor joints. Residents complained that the only efforts for any enforcement at all came from federal authorities. But the sheriff did make arrests for liquor violations, just not the ones that mattered. His targets were not liquor wholesalers or dealers. Instead, his enforcement efforts preyed on the smaller fish in the river of booze that flowed through the county, the least powerful people committing the least significant violations of liquor laws: the customers. The sheriff targeted the "unfortunates caught with a half pint of liquor in their possession or under the influence of liquor." And these perpetrators, according to a local merchant, received "excessive sentences and fines."[94] Another resident concurred. The only arrests made by the sheriff's office at the notorious dives were for "drunkenness or possession of a half pint of liquor, which is very frequent. Severe penalties are imposed for these lesser offenses."[95] Going after the smaller fish, the "hip-flask toters," was a common strategy for law enforcement. After all, federal officials routinely argued that efforts to enforce Prohibition against smaller offenders belonged with local officials. As Prohibition became ever-more unpopular, local small-scale consumers were the least troublesome to arrest. They usually did not employ high-priced lawyers for their defense or stretch out the legal process through appeals.[96]

Officials' targeting of low-level violators fell most heavily on marginalized members of the community. Joe Borden, the automobile dealer who was particularly disgusted by enforcement in Marion County, identified who came under the sheriff's eye. The sheriff's office, he speculated, had only made about a half-dozen arrests for liquor violations, and even fewer convictions — "probably two or three negroes with a pint or two."[97] His comments point to the ways that the discretion of white law enforcement structure could both

excuse and target African Americans during Prohibition. Officials oversee-
ing the liquor market in Ocala encouraged some of the liquor joints run by
African Americans but not all liquor violations by African Americans. African Americans throughout the South were easy targets. Pearlie Ezell, a black
man, for example, was convicted in Escambia County, Alabama, for violating Prohibition laws. He described the events leading to his arrest this way:
"While out working in a field, an officer raided my house and found a half-
pint of liquor which I have for my own use. I did not have any charge of selling
liquor against me." Having liquor in one's home for one's own personal use
was not a violation of the Prohibition laws, but Ezell's home was searched and
he was arrested nonetheless. Targeting drunken black men let white dealers
and drinkers off the hook, reassured whites that unruly blacks faced legal
consequences, and indicated that Prohibition operated as originally promised as a form of racial control. Similar allegations were made in other Florida
counties that suggest that preferential enforcement of Prohibition laws based
on race was not uncommon. They appeared in Alabama as well. Complaining about how enforcement was "poorly executed," an attorney pointed out
that most Prohibition arrests did not target the sources supplying liquor to
southern communities. "The result of all efforts seems to be the arrest of a
few negroes and worthless white people. . . . I have good reason to know that
the trouble is higher up."[98] If a sheriff wanted to make a few arrests to show
his bona fides on Prohibition, apprehending a few drunken black men would
do the trick. Indeed, in St. Petersburg, when the local sheriff came under
attack, his supporters noted his vigorous enforcement efforts; one even noted
the sheriff "carried on a relentless warfare against bootleggers and has found
them among the whites instead of bottle-toting negroes."[99] Surely, the letter
writer insisted, this represented evidence of his commitment to the law.

African Americans nevertheless saw the profit potential in liquor retailing, despite the risks. African Americans were well represented among bootleggers and frequently provided liquor to whites, as did the liquor joints in
Ocala. In some areas, they represented a majority of liquor dealers even as
small operators. Wherever they operated, they took the money of whites who
wanted a drink, occasionally even winning white admiration for their ingenuity. One black man was arrested after being discovered with a canvas belt
worn under his shirt that could hold up to nine half-pints of liquor strapped
to his chest, enabling him to sell by the pint and keep his inventory at hand.
The white officers who arrested him were apparently impressed with its

design, which explains why his case was mentioned in the newspaper.[100] So entrenched were white assumptions of black inferiority that whites refused to believe that African Americans could direct large liquor operations on their own. In 1928, state officers conducted a raid of a restaurant in Mobile where the officers found a "cleverly concealed cache" containing thirty-one quarts and forty-two pints of liquor. Two black men were arrested, yet officers doubted that the two men managed their liquor business on their own. As the newspaper reported, "Officers sought to obtain from them information about the white men who had employed them but they denied that they were working for a white man."[101] Whites interested in liquor, however, expressed no concern about supporting black criminal behavior, apparently accepting without question that African Americans would provide what they sought. And as whites assumed African Americans were more criminal by nature, they may have preferred that blacks take on any legal risk in purchasing liquor. Dinah Toombs, a black woman in Dothan, Alabama, did not hesitate to take advantage of those assumptions. When a white man gave her $20 to buy him whiskey, she simply took his money and kept it, making no effort to actually purchase what he sought.[102]

Throughout Prohibition, law enforcement paid less attention to the misdeeds of the better customers who patronized bootleggers, echoing claims that this was how Prohibition was intended to operate in the South. One sociological study noted that police officers in the South seldom arrested upperclass or upper-middle-class whites. But Prohibition made such attitudes ever-more apparent. The same study went on, "An upper-class individual may be drunk on the streets, and the police will either ignore him or escort him home." They might even keep him in jail overnight. But he would not be booked and tried for the offense. Such statements testified to the uneven landscape of Prohibition and continued support for drinking. And those charged with upholding the law understood that their positions depended on understanding where and for whom violations of Prohibition were tolerated, often allowing elites to violate the law with impunity. "The people would not stand for the arrest of men of standing in the community for violating liquor laws," insisted one sheriff. A probate judge was more specific: he stood no chance at reelection if he prosecuted an upper-class violator.[103] Nevertheless, the unwillingness of law enforcement to go after rich and poor alike helped to undermine the law. Such "arbitrary enforcement," where "we arrest the lowly wage-earner whose lot Prohibition was supposed to improve, and wink at the influential citizen who has such liquors as he wants and does pretty much as he chooses," undermined any value of the law throughout the country. Why were "banquets," "private dances," "golf games," "downtown clubs," and even wet "Easter egg hunts" spared the attention of authorities, while the liquor joints of the less elite were not? "Local option" had been redefined to mean that "each community is left to decide which people within its borders shall have the privilege of breaking the law."[104]

To many whites, however, the criminal possibilities that Prohibition presented threatened to undo any benefits it initially promised. Prohibition seemed to be turning otherwise innocent and humble racial inferiors into lawbreakers. Archibald Rutledge, who insisted Prohibition was only ever intended to apply to blacks, bemoaned at length the effect of Prohibition on the character of African Americans in general. Prohibition's corrupting influence was turning familiar blacks toward "slyness and evasiveness," he argued. "I find among my erstwhile simple and ingenuous Negro friends a growing furtiveness, a secretiveness, a disconcerting tendency to be serpentine. These children are getting wily." Equally concerning to him were the more entrepreneurial consequences of lawbreaking. African Americans were "appearing prosperous." Among southerners of both races, "formerly down-and-out families were moving into well-built homes, buying cars, and sending their children to school." While Rutledge understood that blacks routinely "imitate[ed their] superiors," this was going too far. "A vast underground business is going on, and its effect on the Negro I love is ruinous." The apparent threat represented by black bootleggers was more profound. It undermined the very mandates of white supremacy itself, as African Americans not only grasped the privileges of drinking and profiting from drink but saw themselves potentially to be above the law like whites as well.[105]

Prohibition shaped an underworld of liquor retailing, liquor dives, and gambling dens where racial lines might be blurry at best. That the complaints about Sheriff Thomas in Ocala noted that several liquor joints were run by black proprietors and served an integrated clientele suggests how uncomfortable such interactions made many whites. Such developments indicated that, despite the hopes of some whites, the law was not an effective means of racial control. Indeed, it seemed to be spurring the development of commercial entertainments that eroded the racial order. Some southerners seemed to embrace liquor as entertainment with gleeful abandon, and occasionally the very officials charged with patrolling orderly behavior were promoting the breakdown. While some communities might tolerate corruption among officials because the liquor traffic supported their own tastes and preferences, if officials violated other community norms, they might find that toleration evaporate, as a sheriff in Tampa learned.

Tampa, across the state from Miami, hosted a vice market that flourished with the apparent collusion of local law enforcement. In the late 1920s, however, several officials in the area came to the attention of the governor for allegations of corruption. Constable Henry Hidalgo, mentioned earlier, was only one of them. Other officials in Tampa also faced a wide variety of charges. One was accused of conducting court business while intoxicated. Another Tampa constable allegedly manufactured and distributed liquor, while a third constable sought out rum runners unloading liquor from their boats, demanded a payoff, and then took their liquor to sell himself. One smuggler, apparently relieved to escape arrest for a $300 payment, even helped the crooked constable load the twenty-eight cases of liquor into his patrol car. That same constable consorted with a woman of "ill-repute," plotted with her to make bogus raids on known bootleggers to loot their liquor, and apparently engaged in lewd acts at local parks. Finally, several justices of the peace faced accusations of accepting protection payments from local liquor dealers.[106] Corruption thus seemed to be almost the norm for the municipalities in Hillsborough County, and the complaints these official actions generated indicated the limits of community tolerance.

The local sheriff, a man named L. M. Hatton, played an outsized role in the vice trade in Tampa. He received weekly protection payments of $10 to $50 per week at bolita houses, roadhouses, and gambling houses, and even from individual prostitutes, numbering more than twenty establishments trading in vice. Those proprietors who paid could continue to conduct business; those who did not were quickly arrested.[107] Hatton shared some characteristics of other corrupt sheriffs in the Sunshine State as well. When asked by local residents to raid known liquor joints, Sheriff Hatton and his deputies would refuse. Hatton tolerated Tampa's liquor markets whether the proprietors were white or black. And he tolerated interracial liquor operations as well. When nineteen black men and one white man were arrested in January 1929, the sheriff released them all with no charges when the white man produced evidence that he had paid for protection. Hatton himself was no racial liberal — he allowed a lynch mob to remove a black man, who was subsequently killed, from jail — but he tolerated interracial interactions in the world of vice. He himself was known to frequent Nellie's Road House in the company of gamblers and bootleggers, to watch nude women dancing, and to take prostitutes to bed. Indeed, a number of residents complained that he tolerated houses of prostitution that contained both black and white prostitutes operating under the direction of an African American madam. After almost forty affidavits complaining about his activities were sent to the governor, the governor took action and removed Hatton from office. The interracial vice market that he tolerated was beyond the pale even for Tampa. That it continued as long as it did, however, suggested the cultural changes that the black market in liquor seemed to encourage.

Unwilling to slide quietly into obscurity, Hatton professed his intent to clear his name. He demanded to know who had spoken out against him and claimed that the governor's actions were driven by politics. He even challenged the governor's manhood, daring him to "act the part of a real Governor, and a real he-man. I am calling on your manhood."[108] But his actions as sheriff underscored the new modern culture that Prohibition had been designed to prevent. Rather than keeping liquor away from African Americans, it had enabled many of them to earn considerable profits from the law, allowing them to escape poverty, at least for a while. That whites patronized African American bootleggers or even worked with them to create thriving vice markets catering to both black and white customers suggested the outlines of a new, unfamiliar world in which commercial establishments provided sleazy entertainment to all comers in the name of profit. Traditional standards of moral conduct that temperance advocates supported, even when backed by the law, seemed helpless in the face of public demand for vice. But a world in which African Americans and whites partnered in and enjoyed criminal conspiracies that were largely above the law was, to many whites, unthinkable.[109]

The complaints of residents about the thriving liquor markets in their midst indicated the widespread failure of Prohibition. The failure and frustrations of Prohibition were not the stories that mattered, however. What Prohibition revealed was a South eager to embrace the benefits and profits a modern consumer society presented. Enterprising southerners took advantage of proximity to islands like Cuba to make money providing liquor to markets near and far. Southerners used the growing network of roads and rails to move liquor and a wide variety of commercial establishments to sell it to consumers. They supplied small retailers, drink stands, cafés, rooming houses, hotels, filling stations, and garages with liquor to sell. And they created liquor-fueled illicit entertainments that crossed color lines. Prohibition spurred and accelerated the development of a world of leisure around alcohol and even vice, where blacks profited from and with whites. Law enforcement officers not only failed to enforce the law; they actively subverted it, turning a blind eye, promoting some bootleggers over others, and developing their own venues where liquor was bought and sold. The corruption created by Prohibition brought the opposite of what respectable southerners thought it would deliver. Liquor soaked the South, from its beaches to the streets in towns small and large and along its rural roadsides; alcohol was shelved in the cupboards of restaurants and boardinghouses and alongside barrels of motor oil in general stores and garages. Prohibition, in short, helped the South become modern and accelerated the trend away from its rural, agricultural heritage toward a world of commercial leisure characterized by pleasure and consumption.

Liquor flowed, of course, because, Americans never lost their taste for booze. Many of them expressed little real concern about violating the law to quench that thirst. And despite the concerted efforts of the Coast Guard, federal Prohibition agents, and local police to deprive them of alcoholic beverages, Americans continued to consume alcohol, whether they purchased it at a local filling station or made it themselves. Chapter 6 explores the myriad ways they found to fill their glasses and raise a toast to a new, modern world.

{ Chapter Six }

COCKTAIL TIME

✳

A T THE END OF 1920, the Alabama conferences of the Methodist Epis-
copal Church were effusive in their praise of the first year of Prohibition. They declared that Prohibition "had proved itself one of the
most humanitarian and uplifting events of the whole Christian era," according to an early history of the Prohibition movement in Alabama. Drunkenness and crime had decreased, poverty had decreased, and homes were
happier with families better cared for. The change was "like a miracle of
God." By 1923, however, church organizations in the state expressed increasing alarm at the ever-growing number of liquor violations within the state.[1]
By 1927, there were full-throated warnings of efforts to bring back the evils
of the saloon and nullify the law. Throughout Prohibition, a steady stream
of southerners wrote their state officials bemoaning the continued presence
of alcohol in their midst. Many women in communities around the South
insisted that the liquor trade during Prohibition represented an ongoing
threat to young men in particular. One widow wrote to complain about the
"shinny maker" in her neighborhood. "He makes and sells it to everyone,
even to boys in knee-pants." The women of La Pine, Alabama, pleaded with
Governor Thomas Kilby in 1922 to "rid our town and people of the curse
that has fallen upon us, and make our town a fit place in which to rear our
boys to noble manhood." The ladies were vague about their specific concerns
but noted that the men in their community were setting a "terrible example
of lawlessness," and they bemoaned the fact that "our boys [come] home to
us reeling as they walk." In their view, alcohol stole ambitions, self-respect,
morals, and intelligence, thereby "dooming [young men] to lives of dishonor,
and in the end, the narrow darkness of the drunkard's grave." Sons were not

the only potential casualties. A concerned citizen in Enterprise, Alabama, expressed concern about the level of corruption among officers and the damage of widespread lawlessness to the social fabric, but his larger concern was the "steady degradation of humanity by shattering the morals of young manhood and lowering the virtue of the feminine sex caused by drinking." Some Mobile citizens, despite the city's long-standing opposition to Prohibition overall, worried about their streets soon after Prohibition went into effect. One anonymous letter to the governor in 1921 noted that "it has gotten so bad Ladies is [sic] not safe from insults in town on account of the shinny sellers and makers." After accusing the sheriffs and police of corruption, and they would indeed be tried on those charges a few years later, the writer noted the "blind tigers in the heart of the city" and "immoral houses" on almost every block.[2] These citizens were part of a steady chorus about the effect of alcohol on their communities and its influence on young people. They supported the Eighteenth Amendment but found themselves profoundly dismayed by its effects. Nevertheless, their complaints suggest the continued taste for liquor among their fellow citizens, something that had spelled the demise of previous efforts to control alcohol in southern communities. Their words represented a growing divide between those who believed alcohol led to ruin and those who increasingly saw liquor as a pleasurable pastime. Over the course of the decade, that divide sketched the outlines of a new social culture in the South, one that embraced drinking and the personal freedom to choose for oneself whether or not to imbibe.

The line dividing people who drank and people who abstained was seldom clear. As we saw earlier, drinking among public officials suggested a distinction between enforcing the law and supporting its intended purpose; drinking did not disqualify anyone from participating in Prohibition enforcement. Henry Kime continued to drink in Havana even as he sought to upend the smuggling industry. Charles Root, when he was in Havana, apparently joined him in sharing "barrels of red ink." Virtually every Prohibition official who went to Havana to investigate the liquor traffic drank while they were there. Coast Guard men from Maine to Texas drank as well, often siphoning their supply from the very liquor they seized from smugglers. Court officials were little better. In both Miami and Key West, federal court officials took advantage of the proximity to Cuba, closed court early on Fridays, and headed to Havana for the weekend, only to hold court on Monday morning hung over. Local enforcement officials imbibed as well. Police officers in Florida were reported to be drunk while on the job. One officer in Atlanta later recalled, "Back in those days [of Prohibition] the policemen drank a whole lot, nearly all of them did. Half of them did."[3] Prohibition enforcement no doubt placed men in close proximity to alcohol, and some could not resist the temptation. Nevertheless, throughout the era, the desire to drink in many quarters created the demand that kept bootleggers in business. While dry advocates continued to insist that drinking was a social evil, many Americans were coming to see it as something else: an escape, a bad habit, fashionable rebellion, or the key to sophisticated pleasure and entertainment. Indeed, as the 1920s continued, Americans embraced a new ethic of indulgence and personal gratification. The world around the consumption of alcohol contributed to new ways of socializing and new expectations for the pleasures life had to offer. Despite the legal risks, many Americans saw consuming alcohol as relatively harmless entertainment and drank accordingly. Linguists at the time measured a remarkable flowering in the terms used for alcohol, drinking, and drunkenness that colorfully illustrated the trend. Whether they were drinking corn juice, giggle water, monkey swill, panther sweat, tonsil bath, whoopee, or just plain something on the hip, Americans, and southerners with them, continued to drench the gizzard, hit the hotbozel, go on a bender or on the blink or on a spree, or get three sheets to the wind. They routinely got drunk, canned, coked, corned, fiddled, frazzled, jingled, Methodistconated, pickled, piffled, plastered, slopped, snozzled, soused, whipsey, and whoozey along the way.[4]

The extent to which Americans chose to drink, however, is not easy to measure. There were no large surveys of the general public or easy methods to gauge the numbers of Americans who consumed alcohol. During the 1920s, wets and drys debated endlessly whether drinking was increasing or declining under the law. Their use of statistics was entirely selective and largely for propaganda purposes, ending for all practical purposes in a draw. One modern analysis suggests that while drinking declined significantly at the start of the Noble Experiment, by the late 1920s it had climbed to between 60 and 70 percent of pre-Prohibition levels.[5] The instances of drinking that remain in the archives or in official records, however, are at best episodic. They might reside in court records, the result of individuals unlucky enough to be caught drinking. They occasionally appear in letters or newspapers, revealing persons cavalier enough to discuss their drinking habits openly or be described doing so by others. Court records of cases involving drunkenness also likely skew toward those whose private lives more often attracted the attention of local officials. Courts rarely documented the experiences of people who kept their drinking safely behind closed doors at home or in elite clubs immune to raids and who probably received every benefit of the doubt for their behavior. Nevertheless, the records that remain provide enough evidence to suggest that people of all social classes drank alcohol and that Prohibition encouraged them to drink in new ways. This was especially true with young people and young women, but the growth in tourism allowed even otherwise respectable Americans to travel to exotic destinations, many of which were in the South or near the South, where drinking was tolerated or encouraged. Throughout, this new modern world inspired both cheers and revulsion.

Dry advocates were not entirely wrong that drinking could be disruptive. Circuit courts were filled with people arrested by local authorities for drunkenness when they became disorderly in public. In the New Smyrna, Florida, municipal court, for example, in 1925, Tom Farmer was fined $10 for being drunk, Clyde Pace was fined $25 for a drunk and disorderly charge, and Bernard Harring faced a stiff fine of $100 for driving under the influence of liquor. His fine was doubled because he wrecked the car he was driving, which belonged to his friend. At the municipal court that day, nineteen cases came before the bench; eleven of them involved liquor, and six of those involved drinking. The local municipal court in Tampa faced a more crowded docket in October 1929 after what was described as a busy weekend for police. Of the 100 cases it adjudicated, 42 involved some allegation of drinking, either drunkenness or driving under the influence.[6] There are a few tallies that indicate the extent to which drinking factored in the Prohibition cases that appeared on court dockets. One relatively comprehensive count appeared in the *Mobile Register* in late 1925. After tallying all the cases the local circuit court faced so far that year, it noted that 874 Mobilians had been arrested for drunkenness, 720 of them convicted. Those numbers far outstripped the 376 arrests for other Prohibition offenses. Another indication appears in the list of offenses that the judge of the circuit court in Rome, Georgia, submitted to the National Commission on Law Observance and Enforcement, charged with assessing the extent to which Americans were abiding by the law. Between 1924 and 1929, the court in Rome prosecuted 343 violations of state Prohibition laws; during the same period, there were 163 public drunkenness charges. While not the majority of cases, as in Mobile, public drunkenness was not uncommon.[7] Together, these numbers indicate that arrests for drunkenness were far from rare and suggest that at least some southerners continued to drink alcohol in public and become impaired enough to attract the attention of authorities. But as we know, police selectively enforced Prohibition, focusing their attention on smaller, socially marginalized violators, many of whom were individual African Americans. Arrest records alone cannot provide a complete picture of the extent of drinking in southern towns and cities.

Other kinds of court records also support Prohibitionists' argument that drinking could damage cherished social institutions like marriage and the family. In many states, including Alabama and Florida, habitual drunkenness was grounds for divorce. Spouses suing to end their marriage used evidence of alcohol consumption to bolster their cases. Rosalind Green sued her husband of two years for divorce, claiming habitual drunkenness. For nearly nine months, she testified, he had been almost constantly under the influence of alcohol, and practically every night he was out until 1:00 in the morning. Her divorce was granted. A. A. Woods also petitioned for divorce from his wife, Inez, in 1925. While he had caught her with another man, he also noted in his petition that he had "seen my wife at various times . . . go into different houses and stay a great length of time at night. She has come home intoxicated numbers of times after the parties she would go on with men." Both aggrieved spouses not only blamed liquor but pointed to socializing around liquor as a factor in the demise of the marriages.[8] Charges of habitual drunkenness were not nearly as common as charges of adultery or cruelty in divorce petitions, but they were present nonetheless. And drunkenness tended to accompany charges of cruelty made against husbands, while it was more likely to accompany charges of adultery against wives. A judge in Tampa, Florida, in 1929 made a similar connection. He noted that liquor was "looming in the background" of many divorces. By 1929, Tampa was granting one divorce for every three marriages, for a total of 601 divorces between October 1928 and October 1929. While financial difficulties, infidelity, and desertion were the most common grounds for suing for divorce, this judge pointed out that in the 90 percent of divorces citing violent and ungovernable temper as a contributing cause, there were also allegations of drinking. "If a man strikes or beats his wife, he gets drunk first."[9]

Excessive and unruly drinking had long disqualified poor or working-class Americans from any claim to respectability. Numerous records documenting official intervention into the lives of poorer people often included

statements about their drinking habits underlining the connection. The superintendent of Alabama's State Training School for Girls, for example, ag-
onized over whether to return a fourteen-year-old girl to the custody of her
mother, speculating that the girl's mother was "addicted to drinking, having
been here under the influence of liquor." Similarly, when a white woman
in Andalusia, Alabama, reported that she had been raped by a black man,
state officials dismissed her allegations, noting that the woman was "very
much under the influence of drink."[10] The drinking habits of these women
excluded them from claiming authority as mothers and white women wor-
thy of protection. Nevertheless, notations like the two above were relatively
uncommon, and despite the claims of the judge in Tampa, divorce also remained uncommon. Allegations of drinking in cases of divorce were even
less so. But that such records exist at all suggests the continuing link between
drinking and autonomy for people with little influence.

One group that tried to systematically determine the effect of drinking on
the poor were the nation's settlement house workers. Working in many of
the nation's urban slums, they sought to provide help and assistance to the
poor. In an effort to assess the effectiveness of Prohibition for addressing the
social problems that Progressives attributed to alcohol — family destitution
and violence, among others — Martha Bensley Bruère conducted a survey of
settlement house workers around the country to ascertain whether Prohibition had had the salutary effects its promoters envisioned. The results were
mixed, and her conclusions suggested a changing social landscape. Settlement houses in Georgia, Florida, Alabama, Mississippi, and Louisiana reported that while family crises stemming from alcohol led to fewer requests
for services, they did not indicate the use of alcohol was any less frequent.
Indeed, in New Orleans, it seemed to have increased. Drinking was common
at dances, and liquor was readily available at roadside stands. More women
and boys and girls were drinking. Soft drink stands seemed to have replaced
saloons as sites of socializing where liquor was available for purchase. And
accompanying liquor consumption was a general lack of concern for breaking the law. In South Carolina, there was no "disgrace" attached to violating
Prohibition laws. In Alabama, it was considered evidence of "state independence" to show Alabamians "could still drink." More surprisingly, however,
settlement workers described fewer requests for aid not because families
spent less of their income on drink but because bootlegging provided better
incomes for poor families. Prohibition might have made families less likely to

need aid, but not in the way in which it was intended. Indeed, one reformer noted that regardless of where one lived, "well-to-do Americans" were "the most profitable customers of the bootleggers," pulling poor families out of destitution with their liquor purchases, an opinion that would be echoed widely.[11]

For many temperance advocates in the South and around the country, drinking among those "well-to-do Americans" provided some of the most concerning evidence that Prohibition was failing to bind dry habits and respectability ever-more tightly together. By 1930, as the failures of Prohibition were ever-more apparent, President Herbert Hoover created the National Commission on Law Observance and Enforcement — better known as the Wickersham Commission — specifically to examine Prohibition enforcement and the public's overall respect for the law. Among its investigations, it surveyed each Prohibition district to determine public attitudes toward the law and ranked those attitudes on a five-point scale, ranging from "excellent" to "bad." In Florida and Alabama, for example, most legal officials described the public sentiments toward Prohibition in their communities as either "good" or "fair." Only a handful of areas reportedly had "excellent" support for the law, defined as 75 percent or more of the population favoring enforcement of Prohibition; an almost equal number described their communities as having "poor" attitudes toward Prohibition, defined as less than a majority supporting enforcement efforts.[12] But more interesting were the letters from legal officials and law enforcement officers solicited by the commission requesting information about crime in their areas. The commission sent out a series of letters in the second half of 1929 to public officials — prosecuting attorneys, judges, and police chiefs, among others — asking them to submit their views on the state of law enforcement in their area. The first letter in July was quite broad, asking only for any information or advice the official wanted to give related to the commission's work. The two letters sent in October became more pointed. The first asked for ideas about how to better enforce the nation's criminal laws. The final letter asked for information about a number of specific areas related to the legal system, including the causes of crime, local crime statistics, the functioning of local courts, penal institutions, probation and parole, and Prohibition. The commission received boxes upon boxes of replies ranging from curt notes of less than a page to dense treatises extending to a dozen or more single-spaced, typed pages on issues related to Prohibition and respect for the law generally. In particular, they offered assessments of public attitudes concerning Prohibition enforcement. Relatively few of those letters came from officials in the South, yet their opinions are nonetheless instructive.[13]

Officials offered wide-ranging suggestions for improving citizens' willingness to abide by the law, suggesting that the widespread *unwillingness* of citizens to obey the law was a prominent problem with Prohibition. Several letters suggested that punishments for violating Prohibition laws were too lenient, undermining any deterrent effect of the law. Officials who described the conditions in their community as good often also reported that they took an unfailingly strict approach to liquor violations. But many more comments reflected the low esteem many citizens had for the law. A judge in Galveston, Texas, described Prohibition as "a joke," even among citizens who did not drink. The chief of police in Abbeville, Louisiana, concurred, writing, "Prohibition is looked upon as a farce"; its violation was honorable, not disgraceful. In many communities, the public simply looked on Prohibition with scorn. An attorney in Appalachicola, Florida, noted that the "average citizen" had little respect for Prohibition and believed the Prohibition amendment was an infringement on personal liberty. Violating Prohibition laws, in his opinion, was practically a national pastime. The circuit court judge in Gulfport, Mississippi, concurred, noting that crimes had steadily increased in his county. "Ninety percent of the men" in his area "who violate no other law, and a large percentage of the women, do not hesitate to violate the Volstead Act." The only exceptions to this statement, he believed, were ministers.[14] This was the crux of the matter: numerous citizens in every community gave little thought to defying Prohibition, even though they obeyed most other laws. While prominent members of society were less likely to be dragged to court for their actions, it was not because they were more likely to obey the law. Even they continued to drink and purchase liquor despite its illegality. There seemed to be no link between abstemious habits and respectability.

Public disdain for the law among otherwise upright and respectable citizens was perhaps the greatest obstacle to improved enforcement. One official was straightforward: "If the so-called best people and people who are in high society would obey the laws and refrain from patronizing the bootlegger," law enforcement problems would be solved. Others agreed that the behavior of local elites was a large part of the problem. A judge in Atlanta noted, "Social drinking, or non-law observance by our so called best citizens leads to disregard and disrespect" for laws in general. Bootlegging would continue, he believed, "as long as the bootlegger can find customers for his wares," a view shared by a number of officials.[15] It was thus the continued willingness of respectable citizens to drink that spelled the failure of the law, especially because they usually drank with impunity. Officials who responded to the Wickersham Commission's request for information usually painted their concerns about drinking in their communities in broad strokes. They addressed larger concerns of overall justice and good order in towns and on city streets and even gestured broadly toward the relationship between private consumption and attitudes toward Prohibition. But a consistent theme suggested that hypocrisy, especially among the "better" sort, went a long way to explain the poor attitudes toward Prohibition among all members of society. In their view, respectable members of society should provide a better example, thereby reinforcing the link between dry habits and the social order. That hypocrisy usually remained behind closed doors, either in private homes or in well-heeled clubs, known, one supposes, only to the bootlegger providing the liquor. One popular writer describing drinking in Macon, Georgia, noted that drinking was widespread among even those proclaiming dry sentiments. It merely "had become domestic." Southerners, he wrote, undoubtedly broke the law, "but when we break a law we do it, not with the brazen defiance of bawdy Chicago, but with due regard to the finest traditions of delicacy and of hospitality of the Old South."[16]

It became a public problem when the "better" sort got behind the wheel of a car. Driving drunk made even drinking by elites a public matter. The solicitor general in Forsyth, Georgia, for example, bemoaned "the men of good standing, who are unfortunately addicted to liquor" and took to "crowded paved highways while under the influence of intoxicating liquors."[17] Drinking while driving was a visible manifestation of drinking by the better-off segments of society. Drunk driving combined the new popularity of the automobile, the development of good paved roads, and prohibitions on drink to create a potentially combustible mixture. It revealed drinkers that might otherwise have remained out of sight of the community. Many cases of driving under the influence appeared on the dockets of local circuit courts. But complaints about drunk driving by respectable citizens appeared in the letters to the Wickersham Commission and in the litany of complaints that appeared on the desks of state governors. A resident of Jasper, Alabama, for example, wrote Governor Bibb Graves in 1929 relating the misdeeds of a local official who had, on separate occasions, driven his car into a swimming pool, demolished a buggy, run off an embankment, and driven into a ditch, all while intoxicated. While the litany of this man's mishaps at the wheel was almost comic, the writer connected his example to the larger good of the community. He asked the governor to "encourage decency and soberness and good citizenship" by removing the man from office.[18]

While many southerners, probably much like other Americans, expected Prohibition to remove the problem of alcohol from their communities, its continued presence seemed everywhere. Many, like Elmore Lucas, who was in jail charged with drunkenness and fighting at a barbecue, complained about the dire implications of drinking at social events. Residents of Akron, Alabama, were troubled when a white man appeared at the local school football game inebriated and cursed in the presence of ladies. One visitor to South Carolina commented that he was offered drinks "from morning to night" and noted that drunkenness in public no longer harmed one's social reputation as it had before. So embedded was liquor in social functions that the local sentiment toward Prohibition was "on the side of the gentleman who breaks the law in moderation."[19] The continued drinking among many southerners, like Americans elsewhere, concerned legal officials. Some believed Prohibition itself was the problem. Americans wanted to drink, and Prohibition should be reformed to allow the consumption of light beers and wines. "Temperance, not Prohibition, is what the people want," said a judge from Dublin, Georgia.[20] Don't throw out the entire law, they pleaded, but modify it to allow people to drink some alcohol if they wanted. Others doubted whether even modifying the law would work. Over the course of Prohibition, American drinking tastes shifted from beer to distilled spirits and cocktails. Modification seemed hopeless for a nation now accustomed to gin.[21]

The visibility of liquor at local community events contributed, in the eyes of many respectable elders, to the most concerning effect of Prohibition, and that was the encouragement of drinking in young people. Apparently, it was not uncommon for adults to express support for Prohibition while continuing to enjoy alcohol. As one official noted, "Too many Dad's [were] drinking wet and talking dry," failing to set a good example for their children.[22] That disjuncture was important, as many officials expressed concern that disdain for Prohibition had a particularly pernicious effect on the nation's youth. Many women apparently agreed, as in their letters to officials they frequently complained that grown men were destroying young boys by providing them alcohol. Girls, however, represented a growing worry. A police official in Abbeville, Louisiana, noted with dismay that at a recent local dance "nine-tenths of the young men and women dancing there [were] under the influence of liquor." More concerning, the effects of that liquor made them "indulge in all sorts of indecencies." The consequences for young women were particularly dire. Officials bemoaned that young women had come to view liquor as a necessary part of social relationships. One attorney in Texas relayed the following story as evidence: One boy took "a little girl out (considered nice) (of a good family) and the first thing she asked him was 'Have you a flask on your hip?' and because he did not, said she 'I would not have come with you had I known that.'"[23] Things had surely deteriorated if even respectable girls from good families expected liquor on a date. Officials blamed this sorry state of affairs on parents who were too focused on their own pleasure to teach their children proper respect for the law.

Young women asking to share a flask, however, were part of a trend. Over the course of Prohibition, young men, often with young women by their side, increasingly incorporated the consumption of alcohol into their social interactions.[24] As the official's letter bemoaning that even good girls expected liquor on dates shows, even courtship could not be separated from violating Prohibition laws. Concerns about drinking among local teens provided a steady drumbeat of concern in descriptions of local attitudes toward obeying the law. To many, the presence of alcohol during social activities of young people on the cusp of independence remained the most concerning aspect of Prohibition's failure. Young people driving drunk or carousing while under the influence was bad enough. That seemingly respectable young men and women were engaging in such activities together was even worse. This was a new and particularly troubling development, and one that promised certain moral decay, as the disturbed official suggested when he cited the high rates of drinking at a local dance and the apparent indecencies that followed. Older, more traditionally respectable women lost no time in identifying the connection between alcohol, new forms of nightlife, and the potential for sexual immorality. Mrs. Alexander Greet of Gadsden, Alabama, writing on American Legion Auxiliary stationery, lamented "the inroads being made upon our American Legion and Auxiliaries by booze." Her letter outlined the drinking at national conventions in New Orleans and San Francisco, as well as around Alabama. From drinking on the train to "quantities of [alcohol] in the bath tubs with ice for sale," she hoped the governor would act to protect "the men and women and girls" at the next convention. In her opinion, "More of our women are getting drunk now, and several, if not many of the young girls, as well as women, were drinking at Huntsville. There is nothing wholesome or uplifting about this Beauty Contest business." She was not alone. An anonymous student at the University of Alabama also connected drinking and sex when he informed the governor that a professor had enabled a student to obtain cash, knowing that the student intended to use it to purchase whiskey. He then noted that the same student "a few nights later went to bed with a coed in one of the Frat Houses."[25] Faced with what in their view was an effort to flout the law and engage in immorality, concerned citizens demanded that the state act to impose behavior that was both legal and respectable and, in the process, return the youth to the social standards of the past.

Dry advocates correctly identified an emerging trend. One of the long-term consequences of Prohibition, scholars argue, was that it made public drinking and socializing with men acceptable for women. And while the saloon had been a largely male institution, speakeasies (and cafés, roadside stands, and the other new retail sites for liquor) welcomed the gentler sex.[26] One of the principal blessings of Prohibition, one writer slyly wrote, was that it taught "our women to drink," though unlike men, some still were troubled about their potential misbehavior while intoxicated. Even in the South and even among the fairer sex, drinking was going mainstream, though most women "never forgot the decorum of the Deep South that dictates that even a lady in her cups must be a lady." In particular, drinking was an increasingly common aspect of socializing among college students. The casual exchange of a recipe for bathtub gin sent to Sara Mayfield, a young college woman from a prominent Tuscaloosa family, from one of her male college friends provides but one example. The recipe called for one pint of "Mr. Al K. Hall," one pint of distilled water, four to five drops of oil of juniper, and one tablespoon of glycerine, and it included the assurance, "I know there is nothing in this Rx that is poisonous." It appeared in an exchange of letters that described a whirl of social events that were key elements of college life.[27] College students across the country equated consumption of alcohol with sociability and youthful spirit. A survey of college seniors in 1927 noted that students associated drinking with "personal and social release," and that it was part of a "rebellion pattern," so much so that even students who drank infrequently were eager to be considered drinkers. And an overwhelming number of students surveyed preferred to repeal or amend the Eighteenth Amendment to legalize light wines and beer rather than enforce the existing law.[28]

Certainly male drinking was more accepted and expected among adults, but much of the popular culture associated with campus life, not just in the South but nationwide, depicted college drinking as an activity for men and women to enjoy together. Students traded jokes about alcohol at dances and drunken coeds in college humor. The 1924 inaugural edition of the University of Alabama's humor magazine the *Rammer Jammer* printed a small bit of humor that suggested that Sara Mayfield's interest in illicit booze was not unique. "The only time a girl does not want the spotlight on her is when she is on a wild party. All she wants then is moonshine, fifty percent moonshine and fifty percent moonshine."[29] Consumption of alcohol was indelibly connected to the pleasures and dangers of dating especially at college, and students drank heavily despite Prohibition, even in the South.[30] The Board of Public Health, for example, notified President George Denny of the University of Alabama that when it cleared a vacant field adjacent to campus, it found "several bottles of whiskey hidden in the vines," suggesting that the area was the headquarters of a local bootlegger, likely one who sold to college students. Many of the letters between President Denny and the parents of students concerned drinking and its effect on academic work. One mother's reply to the news that her son had been recommended for suspension because of his drinking was only unusual in that she blamed the university for "permitting whiskey to be sold to University students away from their Mothers."[31]

While drinking, and humor about drinking, was common, the extent to which women participated alongside their male counterparts is less clear. Some studies suggest that college drinking was a primarily male pastime and that campus rules prohibited female students from imbibing.[32] But what colleges prohibited and what students actually did are two very different things. Part of college culture was a gleeful eagerness to evade the rules imposed by administrators. In Alabama in the 1920s, both the University of Alabama and Auburn prohibited all their students from consuming alcohol. Nevertheless, student humor suggests that students believed such rules should be flouted. Definitive evidence of drunken coeds, however, is elusive. President Denny's correspondence occasionally expressed concern about women's behavior but did not contain any specific references to female students drinking. Rumors about a drunken female student being carried into a fraternity house at Auburn caused such a scandal that they reached the governor's office.[33] Both

Alabama and Auburn proudly reported that while there were some violations of the rules by women students, none was sufficient to merit expulsion, perhaps seeking to reassure concerned adults that alleged coed indiscretions were fears and fantasies rather than facts. Nevertheless, the sheer number of allusions in student publications to women students drinking and enjoying it suggests that women's participation in illegal alcohol consumption, even in the South, was an accepted part of college life. After all, Sara Mayfield may very well have requested that recipe for bathtub gin she received from a friend. And while humor might not be an exact representation of reality, as the *Rammer Jammer* suggested, it represented "the truth in an intoxicated condition"—meaning an exaggeration, but not necessarily a fabrication.[34]

The *Crimson-White*, the University of Alabama's student newspaper, for example, pointedly reminded men that when taking a woman on a date, "Thou shalt always be mindful of her hunger — and thirst." A joke in the *Rammer Jammer* played on generational differences: "Old Lady: Shame on you smoking here in a public place. Why, I would as soon be drunk! Hard-Hearted Hannah: Well, who wouldn't?" Other jokes pointed to the connection between women's access to alcohol and their relations with men. "He: Didja ever take a drink? She: 'Twas never necessary. They always offer it to me." Women usually shared men's flasks rather than obtaining alcohol on their own, another iteration of the troubling requirement that men provide alcohol for their female companions. And women did not merely sip politely. Some apparently got "tight," a 1920s euphemism for drunk. Fictional coed Ruby told her friend she had the grandest time the previous night even though she could not remember anything after 11:00 P.M. When asked how she knew she had fun, she replied, "Oh, I heard a cop tell the judge about it this morning." According to the *Glomerata*, the yearbook at Auburn University, the usual coed smoked, chewed, cussed, wore rouge and powder, danced, went out with beaus, attended dinner parties and shows, and craved silk "undies" along with bootleg booze. Most students likely agreed with the following version of the myth of Pandora's box, which suggested that modern girls, on their own initiative, drank. Pandora, of course, had been given strict instructions not to open the box, "but [she] was a modern young thing and didn't give a damn about orders. So she snapped the lock and took out the two bottles of Old Crow [a brand of whiskey]."[35] Perhaps flirting with evil, modern Alabama coeds snapped their fingers at the possible dangers of alcohol and enjoyed it with their dates.

The antics of young people on dates made drinking visible and demonstrated the claim of young, otherwise respectable women to new forms of socializing with men in public. Those activities, however, might also get them in trouble. One indication of this trend resides in the arrest records for the city of Birmingham, Alabama. These records demonstrate that drinking among women was not unprecedented before Prohibition. In the first six months of 1912, 90 percent of the arrests of women for alcohol violations involved drunkenness, but those numbers represented only 47 arrests. Under state prohibition laws in 1917, only 29 women were arrested for drunkenness, which represented 85 percent of all of women's alcohol violations. By 1928, however, arrests for drunkenness by women, while only 37.6 percent of their arrests for alcohol violations, represented 146 arrests. By the time many Americans were questioning the relative utility of the Eighteenth Amendment, Birmingham police were encountering not only more prohibition violations among women, but also growing numbers of drunken women in public as well. These records, however, also indicate that the social context in which drinking among women occurred had changed. In 1912 and 1917, women arrested for drunkenness were usually arrested on their own. Mattie Ellis, for example, an African American woman, was arrested at 10:30 P.M. on June 9, 1912, for being drunk. Laura Champion, a white woman, was arrested at 12:30 A.M. on August 20 for the same reason.[36] The arrests listed above and below each of these women's on the docket were at different times and by different arresting officers, indicating they were unrelated incidents. In short, the two women were arrested by themselves. A similar pattern holds in 1917. While hard to prove definitively, these arrests suggest that these were lonely women perhaps isolated by the very fact they drank in public.

By the later 1920s, while being arrested likely remained a dubious distinction, arrests of drunken women were often part of a sociable evening out on the town, as men and women were arrested together. Maud Swindle, a white woman, for example, was arrested at 11:30 P.M. on October 7, 1926, for being drunk, along with John William of Memphis, Tennessee, who faced drunkenness charges as well. Exia Hargrove and Mary Spencer, two black women, were arrested for being drunk on October 28 at 2:00 A.M., along with a white man and two black men who faced charges of being drunk and driving an auto while intoxicated. And Alma Gant was out with D. F. Winn at 1:15 A.M. on October 19 when she was arrested for public drunkenness and he was arrested for driving while intoxicated, speeding, and violating the liquor laws.[37] These examples are only a few that are spread throughout the arrest records in the second half of the 1920s, and they indicate a new public, sociable culture of alcohol consumption. Together, they suggest that the humor found in the *Rammer Jammer* may very well have contained some truth. While women still represented only about 12 percent of Prohibition arrests, more and more of those arrests interrupted the dates of couples for whom alcohol was part of an evening's entertainment. They are the visible manifestation of a changing social culture in which women and men drank together in public. The hours during which women were arrested strengthen this conclusion. More and more women were being arrested on the streets, in the company of men, late in the evening and during the wee hours of the morning. Public drinking for women was part of a new fashion of sociability and, despite disapproval among many quarters, no longer necessarily branded a woman as disreputable. By the 1920s, in the Deep South and even at universities like Alabama, dating and drinking went hand in hand, as it apparently did in cities like Birmingham as well.[38]

One might expect young people to be at the leading edge of cultural change, and flouting Prohibition was part of their rebellion. The extent to which their parents saw alcohol as part of normal social life, however, is more difficult to determine. As we saw earlier, law enforcement officials often turned a blind eye to liquor consumption by so-called respectable whites. Nevertheless, there is another indication that even respectable elders rejected the abstinence and secrecy that Prohibition mandated, and that was in travel. Americans traveled to destinations where they could freely indulge in activities they were prohibited from doing at home. Many crossed the nation's northern border for the "wet oasis" in Canada. Detroiters crossed the river to imbibe in Windsor, Canada.[39] Other Americans sought more extensive trips to fill their glasses. Wealthy Americans had long seen travel as a perk of their class status, and for many years Europe was their destination of choice. When World War I made travel to Europe impossible, southern destinations gained popularity as an alternate, and exotic, destination for American travelers. It was part of a growing trend in which Americans who could afford it used travel not for education and edification but for leisure and pleasure. The rising popularity of travel, along with increasing interest in travel to nearby tropical locales like Florida and the Caribbean, opened opportunities for more Americans to travel to locations where liquor proliferated. Indeed, the access to strong drink was likely a large part of the draw to balmy destinations like Miami and Havana.

Elites, however, were not the only tourists. Travel for pleasure became much more accessible to more Americans across the economic spectrum in the 1920s. The 1920s were a prosperous decade with a measurable increase in wages for most Americans. With extra money in their pockets for discretionary spending, increasing numbers of middle class Americans joined elites in embracing the concept of the vacation. The growing popularity of the automobile helped. With installment credit making the purchase of a family car possible to many more households, travel away from home no longer required access to railroads or the fares travel by rail required. That did not mean that the proliferation of railroads in Florida in the late nineteenth and early twentieth centuries did not contribute to Florida's increasing prominence as a tourist destination — it most certainly did — but the possibility of travel by car expanded the options of families with fewer resources. Paired with the rapid development of roads and highways in Florida, what became known as "tin-can tourism," or traveling by car and camping along the way, became increasingly popular. For many roving northerners, the South had particular appeal. Its romanticized ethos of moonlight and magnolias drew northerners away from the frenetic pace of urban, industrial life. Florida's siren call of beaches and excitement lured many. And of course there was always the weather.[40] Recognizing the benefits of tourism, Floridians rushed to build the roads and the travel amenities that, by the 1920s, brought Americans to the state in droves. Filling stations and general stores sprouted up along the main travel routes to cater to tourists' travel needs, creating an infrastructure for trade in alcohol along the way. Hotels mushroomed along coastal beaches; the opulent Ponce de Leon in St. Augustine and the Royal Poinciana in West Palm Beach were only the most fabulous and notorious. Alongside pleasure palaces that catered to the rich were numerous more modest establishments that saw the traveler of limited means as their market.[41]

Amidst the hyperbole about its real estate potential, Florida heavily marketed its attractions, hailing the sunshine and the warm breezes as a welcome respite from the bitter cold of winter in the North. One article summed up Florida's lure, after noting that approximately 15 percent of the U.S. population was economically able to spend part of the winter in Florida: "We are going to Florida — we fourteen million shivering eligible — to get warm." Highbrow publications like *Travel* magazine included Florida destinations in their seemingly yearly descriptions of winter playgrounds. But even more popular publications like the *Saturday Evening Post* educated their readers on the possibilities of "Florida loafing." While it conceded the problems of Florida's real estate fixation and pointed out the inflated promises of cheap and easy living in the land of sunshine, the *Saturday Evening Post* also celebrated the fishing, the beaches, the pretty girls, and the weather.[42] While the booming real estate market eventually crashed, it only dampened tourist travel. For many Americans, the lure of summer weather during winter was a primary draw, as the postcards travelers sent to family and friends back home make plain. "I wish you could enjoy a bit of this wonderful balmy air and sunshine," Mary wrote to her friends back in Battle Creek, Michigan. "Lots of sunshine and nice weather — you'd never leave if you once got down here," Dorothy promised her friend in Detroit. Emma was more pointed about the advantages of Florida weather to her friend Florence: "Think of us eating oranges and you snowballs," she taunted. Postcards home also attest to the variety of economic backgrounds of Florida travelers. One vacationer named Carolyn, who was "wild" about Florida, was "doing the state in our car" with her mother and two others. Adela recounted 280 miles of car travel from Daytona to Coral Gables to Cocoa to Stuart, West Palm Beach, and Miami, noting that West Palm Beach and Miami were "very interesting, especially Miami." Travelers recounted their sunburns and swimming, the rides on the beach, and the tropical trees and flowers. They also might describe things they did not like. "There may be warmer places but I doubt it," wrote one to friends back home. Others noted the downsides of Florida's popularity, especially in terms of numbers of people. One tourist noted that there were more people in Florida than she had seen on previous trips and more traffic accidents as well. "Every day there are a dozen or more auto smashes. There is to[o] much congestion."[43]

Along with the sunshine and warmth, tourists also marveled at Florida's good-time ambiance. "All the cities in Florida seem very much alive," wrote one traveler. Another concurred. "Something doing all the time," he wrote.[44] Few declared it openly to friends back home, but many Florida tourists sought easy access to the forbidden beverages that they may very well have treated with disdain at home. Indeed, the tourism industry provided an infrastructure within which the traffic in liquor could flourish. Whether through the filling stations and general stores that catered to tin-can tourists or the swank hotels in Miami and Tampa, providing amenities to tourists usually included providing alcohol to them as well. Liquor and tourism were so closely aligned that when the Wickersham Commission conducted Prohibition surveys of all fifty states, Florida's survey opened by noting that "the Florida crime barometer rises and falls with the migration and exodus of the winter tourist population." Making the observation that tourism revenue was critical to the state's ability to finance public improvements, the survey noted that many communities looked askance at "crusades or law-enforcement movements" that could disrupt that flow of funds. Florida depended on tourist dollars, and tourists expected alcohol as part of their vacation entertainments. After all, the Dixie Filling Station in Ocala, Florida, brought drinks on trays right to cars of their tourist customers. Cities like Miami, Palm Beach, Daytona, and Tampa on the Gulf Coast offered entertainments to which liquor was a natural accompaniment. Night clubs, "luxurious gambling palaces," race tracks, and athletic spectacles like boxing and jai alai drew tourists in droves, and as the survey noted, "The presence of a free-spending sporting class in these places creates a profitable liquor market" that eagerly sought the foreign liquors that were widely available. Other more popular sources of information also clarified the connection between tourism and drinking. As one newspaper clipping kept by the Coast Guard indicated, "Tourists come from all parts of the country to enjoy Miami's climate and liquor."[45]

Liquor was not hard to find. Bootleggers apparently openly advertised their wares in *Miami Life*, a weekly newspaper that made no secret of its disdain for temperance of any kind. Hotels like the Fleetwood, whose guests witnessed the shooting of Red Shannon by the Coast Guard, and the Roney Plaza in Miami Beach openly sold drinks in their dining rooms and were not shy about offering them to patrons. The Wofford Hotel did them one better, operating an open bar with five regularly employed bartenders and two waiters, promising "every drink known before Prohibition. . . . They served every and anybody, and the place was known and talked about all over the United States, and was advertised in all newspapers, daily and weekly, in Miami." Most hotels catered to the drinking preferences of guests and offered the procurement of liquor as as an amenity. "It is almost impossible to register at any of the hotels without being offered liquor by the bell boys," Bill Kelly reported.[46] Hotel employees were especially notorious for providing liquor, as Prohibition agents in Mobile documented numerous times. One helpful citizen wrote to Wayne Wheeler of the Anti-Saloon League from Miami in 1925 noting that even white bellhops worked with bootleggers to supply tourists with liquor. St. Petersburg, which supposedly catered to a more mature and sober clientele, nonetheless stocked up on liquor as the winter tourist season approached. An internal memo discussing the liquor traffic in St. Petersburg in 1927 noted that liquor was brought into St. Petersburg for the tourist season

Tourists at photo booth at Hardie's Bathing Casino,
Miami Beach, Florida, 1925 (Courtesy of the
State Archives of Florida)

for "local and tourist consumption." It was also shipped from there by express disguised as shipments of citrus. Miami's liquor supply also landed on
area beaches, usually between Coconut Grove and Marathon, Florida, sometimes even in view of tourist bathers on the beach. It was such a dependable
and profitable market that liquor wholesalers in the Bahamas worried little
about extending credit to smuggling outfits. One outfit that sold liquor exclusively to hotels in Miami was able to land $100,000 worth of liquor bought on
credit alone. Cracking down on liquor at hotels was such a notorious problem during Prohibition that authorities bemoaned their inability to solve it
as late as 1930. They noted that many hotel proprietors condoned providing

bootleg booze to their patrons rather than sacrificing their earnings or their customers' patronage.[47]

Apparently, hotels like the Wofford in Miami Beach provided a sought-after commodity. Tourists drank openly and excessively. They snapped photos of themselves posing at drink stands on the beach. Even Governor Doyle Carlton received a clipping from a New York newspaper from a New York resident suggesting "tragic" inefficiency and indifference on the part of local authorities when it came to enforcing Prohibition laws. The article described the experience of a tourist who traveled to Miami for the winter in search of rest. Instead, he encountered "so much drinking and carousing everywhere" that he moved on to Nassau in the Bahamas, where liquor was legal but the atmosphere was peaceful. In Miami, by contrast, "the drunks were reeling on the sidewalks," he told reporters, "and there was so much noise and carousing at night that he could not sleep. The town was full of liquor," he went on, "and everybody seemed to be imbibing."[48] Bearing out his assessment even several years later, Miami police reported 3,435 arrests for drunkenness in 1929 alone, far more than for any other offense, with an additional 930 arrests for driving under the influence. The next most frequent offenses were traffic violations, with 2,691. Those crimes alone represented almost 70 percent of the total arrests for the year. Tampa reported similar numbers. In 1929, police made 3,207 arrests for drunkenness and 249 for driving under the influence. Police there also made over 2,000 arrests for disorderly conduct, which could easily accompany both alcohol and a night on the town. Tourists did not even need to end their carousing when they departed for home. They could continue their drinking binges on the trains out of Miami. One disgusted local businessman wrote to General Andrews to report "that it doesn't take very long for northbound passengers from Miami to get on a good 'jag' after boarding the Pullmans." Officials conceded that open drinking on passenger trains remained a problem until 1927, but it took on exaggerated form with tourists in Florida.[49]

Everyday tourists were only one aspect of the problem. Florida drew convention traffic in the 1920s as well as regular tourists. Large groups came to Florida for conferences and meetings expecting readily available liquor. Despite Prohibition, alcohol remained a critical aspect of the annual gatherings of various organizations, and convention organizers went to great lengths to make sure that supplies were adequate. In 1928, men who claimed they were representatives of the mayor of Hollywood, Florida, and the president of the

Hollywood Shrine Club approached the Coast Guard in Ft. Lauderdale in the hopes that the Coast Guard men would, as the officer reported, "see that they were kept properly supplied with the necessary amount of liquor to handle their needs — they were rather short on liquor and thought I could keep them well supplied." The Coast Guard officer reported that he angrily refused. Concerns about conventions, however, were ongoing. Both the Shriners and the Elks were planning to hold conventions in Miami during the summer of 1928, drawing attendees in the hundreds of thousands. The Coast Guard in Miami reported to the commandant that they had received information that convention organizers had set aside $250,000 to procure liquor for attendees.

The Coast Guard's efforts apparently limited the availability of alcohol for Shriners and Elks in Miami, but those were not the only groups who saw liquor as a critical part of their annual gatherings. Banker's Union meetings in Memphis included events at local clubs that had "all the liquor you could ask for." When asked about the supply, organizers stated that "they had fleets of cars from the south all the time; also they lose one occasionally, which was just part of the game and expected." Even politicians expected good booze at their most glittering gatherings. A memorandum outlining the general situation surrounding Coast Guard bases in the summer of 1928 noted that "large amounts of liquor had been landed in the vicinity of Galveston for the Democratic Convention" to be held in Houston. Travel and convivial gatherings were incomplete without the social lubricant of liquor, especially during Prohibition. Indeed, any large attraction seemed to require its own supply for customers. A 1925 report on smuggling out of Cuba warned that 10,000 cases of liquor had been commissioned by the manager of the Giants, who was importing it for "five or six baseball teams which are now in Florida" for spring training. The deal had been arranged with the help of Mr. Ringling of the Ringling Brothers Circus, who also wanted some of the cargo.[50] Those 10,000 cases may have been intended for players and circus performers. More likely they would also be part of the concessions available to the crowds attending the events.

Liquor consumption, of course, was not prohibited by the Volstead Act. Prohibition only prohibited possession of alcohol for sale, transportation, selling, or importing. For tourists coming to Florida or attending the Democratic convention or the Republican convention in Kansas City, which was also awash in booze, or even the circus or a baseball game, some illegal act was involved somewhere along the line in the process that placed strong drink in the hands of travelers. For tourists who were a little more squeamish about openly violating the law, travel to Cuba might provide the answer. In Cuba, liquor was legal and drinking was encouraged. And during Prohibition in the 1920s, travel to Cuba skyrocketed.

Havana benefited from the overall growth in travel in the 1920s. Increasing numbers of American tourists made their way to Havana to enjoy its tropical delights. Cuba as a travel destination offered particular attractions. Its relatively low cost allowed average Americans to live like temporary aristocrats, enjoying luxury made possible by a poor country desperate for tourist dollars. It was also easy to reach by ferry and eventually by airplane. The island promised exotic scenery and beautiful weather. But it also boasted enticing nightlife and intoxicating pleasures, including the liquid variety, that were forbidden at home. Cuba's strangeness, its seemingly alien culture packaged for tourist entertainment, was a significant part of its allure.[51] Havana promised pleasure and marketed vice, and alcohol played a prominent role in how Cuban travel was advertised, much more so than travel to other alcohol-soaked destinations like Miami. Tourists in Miami enjoyed better access to good booze than they likely had at home, and one law enforcement officer noted that in Miami hotels "every bellhop is a bartender." But Cuba's open market for liquor was no secret, and it was likely a primary factor in its attractiveness as a travel destination. Bacardi advertisements during Prohibition, in fact, trumpeted the widespread availability of rum, showing a Bacardi bat carrying Uncle Sam, cocktail glass in hand, from a dry United States to Cuba. Dabbling in vice "in moderation" on the island allowed Americans to experience pleasure while still adhering to respectability and the law at home. While Cuba seemed alien and exotic, its ties to the United States were close. Businesses operated in both Cuba and the United States, and Cubans and Americans frequently traveled back and forth. Cuban shops promised a familiar experience. Los Precios Fijos, for examples, advertised Spanish shawls and mantillas as well as well-marked prices that required no haggling. It practiced, as its advertisement noted, "an all around American system."[52] Travel to Cuba for American tourists, then, was both pleasingly exotic and comfortably convenient.

Cuban tourism from the United States increased considerably in the 1920s. While only about 2,000 tourists enjoyed Cuba's warm winter breezes in 1918, by 1925 nearly 45,000 tourists strolled the revitalized Malecón in search of excitement during the four winter months of the tourist high season. Between

1927 and 1933, when the economic bottom fell out of the tourist market, around 400,000 tourists of all kinds traveled to the island. Popular guide books like *Terry's Guide to Cuba* promised that Cuba was "a winsome sunlit land of singular and abiding charm, where travel is cheap, easy and safe; where American money is used and much English is spoken; where the hotels are good, the food wholesome ... the people friendly and helpful; ... and where unusual and unexpected pleasures await the traveler."[53] The Cuban tourist industry targeted a broad swath of Americans across economic lines, and many Americans heeded the call, boarding the ferries that could transport tourists from the train station in Key West to Havana in six hours. Others traveled from New Orleans or New York, and after 1928, still others flew Pan Am's regular air service from Miami to Havana.

Tourists came from across the United States, recounting a bit of their experiences on postcards to friends back home in places like Marion, Pennsylvania; Romulus, Michigan; and Hamilton, Texas. Their experiences varied from the prosaic to the alcoholic. One female traveler on a brief stop noted that while Havana was "not as picturesque as St. Augustine," she nonetheless toured the town, visited a cigar factory, took in a jai alai game (which she called "very exciting"), and "had a wonderful drink made of pineapple juice." Betty Jane's Uncle Russell noted the "nice fruit, flowers and music," while Anne wrote her friend that Havana was a "great place — full of garlic and excitement."[54] *Travel* magazine reiterated the sophisticated attractions, naming Havana "Cuba's Vivacious Metropolis" or the "Paris of the Caribbean." *National Geographic* called Cuba "The Isle of Romance," while the *New Republic* suggested "Cuba for the Winter." Tourists seemed to concur. Tom wrote his friend in Syracuse, New York, that while he had not yet been to the races, his "trip is worth all I spent." Walt, writing to Miss Francis in Philly, said his trip to Havana "has been so wonderful, it seems like a dream." Even *Women's Home Companion* recommended "our gay neighbor Havana" for a December vacation, noting that Havana "is the most popular winter city in the modern world." *Women's Home Companion* assured its readers that steamship travel to the island was convenient and inexpensive, there were numerous "very good hotels," and "as long as you don't drink and don't gamble," a tourist could spend a week for about $100.[55]

Drinking and gambling, however, were a tremendous part of the allure of this so-called Pearl of the Antilles, and while many travelers were modest and restrained in their notes home, plenty took advantage of the widespread

Sloppy Joe's Bar, Havana, Cuba (Photo in possession of author)

availability of alcohol to enhance their travel experience. The entire town of Havana, one writer for the *Outlook and Independent* noted, was itself as "intoxicating as a cocktail." The *New Republic* assured its readers that unlike dry America, Cuba was "hot, it is 'wet,' it is, in its easy tropical way, Wide Open." Its pleasures were available to all travelers regardless of age, as "gray haired ladies cling to the bar rail in Sloppy Joe's," a well-known bar located near where the ferries from the United States docked. Even the restrained *Terry's Guide to Cuba* helpfully informed tourists that the most popular cocktails were the daiquiri and the George Washington.[56]

Basil Woon's tongue-in-cheek travel memoir and guide alluded to the centrality of alcohol in its very title, *When It's Cocktail Time in Cuba*. Woon warned the reader that he was not providing a travel guide per se; he recommended several other guidebooks, including *Terry's Guide to Cuba*, for that. Instead, he presented his nearly 300 page book as entertainment of its own: "I have merely amused myself by setting down on paper what the tourist to Cuba will see, do (and drink) in a land where personal liberty and climate are blended in just the right setting of beauty and romance." He reiterated the desire of Americans for the exotic and celebrated their realization "that only sixty miles from their own shores is a city so completely exotic that they may be as superior as they please." He listed four main appeals of travel to Havana: its foreign character, its commitment to personal liberty, its climate, and its romantic history.[57] This second appeal, personal liberty, anchored his attention to the availability of liquor. Personal liberty had appeared in the criticisms of Prohibition that came to the desk of the Wickersham Commission. It reflected the attitudes of individuals who, as an attorney from Apalachicola described, regarded "such laws as do not meet with [their] approval as an imposition and unwarranted infringement of [their] vaunted liberty."[58] The term came to mean resentment toward Prohibition's attempt to replace Americans' personal decisions about whether or not to drink alcohol with the force of law. Indeed, despite the reforming impulse that motivated temperance movements and eventually Prohibition itself, its moral high-handedness offended a significant proportion of the population. Personal liberty came to be a catchword for opposition to Prohibition based not necessarily on a desire to consume alcohol but on the belief that respectable adults should be able to make the choice on their own. Woon's summary of the definition of personal liberty in Havana reflected that understanding. Personal liberty in Cuba, in his view, meant the ability to make one's own moral choices. It involved alcohol surely — the ability to drink as much as one wanted and to buy as many drinks for friends as one wished. But it also included the right to indulge in every other form of vice, from gambling and the lottery to infidelity, if one chose to do so. Woon devoted attention to the wide variety of vice tourism that Havana provided, including horse racing, cockfights, gambling, prostitution, strip clubs, "hoochee-koochee" joints, and "'French' motion picture shows." They were all available for the interested traveler. Woon also celebrated Havana's more democratic playground. He skewered the snobbery of Palm Beach, noting, "You need no card of membership to Havana's attractions any more than you need a chemist on your staff to sample the champagne you drink." Social status was largely irrelevant in Cuba as long as one had the money to purchase its pleasures.[59]

Drinking in Havana was perhaps its most celebrated attraction. Even Woon gave prominence of place to access to alcohol in his witty guidebook, devoting his first full chapter on Cuba's attractions to alcohol and highlighting the popularity of cocktails in its title, "Where Everyone Is Drinking and Not a Soul Is Drunk!" Only after describing drinking in Havana did he follow with a chapter titled "But One Must Eat."[60] Woon described the favored drinks — the daiquiri, Planter's Punch, the presidente — and how to make them. He mentioned the most fashionable bars — La Florida, the Paris Bar, and of course Sloppy Joe's, owned by a man who used to be the barman at the Biltmore Hotel in New York. Sloppy Joe's did the largest tourist business, was always filled, and never closed, employing eleven bartenders. Well aware of that particular bar's appeal to tourists, Carleton Bailey Hurst, a member of the embassy staff in Havana, noted that virtually all Americans went there for a drink the moment they arrived, joking that it would almost be more efficient for the embassy to look for Americans there rather than at their hotels.[61] It was not the only bar with roots in the United States. The Café Sazerac was owned by two Greek men, one of whom was known in New York for his interpretation of the Ramos Gin Fizz when he worked at a bar near Times Square. But local establishments proliferated. Favored bars were virtually everywhere on the streets of Havana, from the fancy hotels catering to tourists to the local bodegas along the Central Plaza. Drinks were served on rooftop gardens at the Hotel Sevilla Biltmore and at the Hotel Plaza, which featured an evening show with a dancer whose mother was reportedly eaten by a shark. Bars might be structured as patios along popular thoroughfares, like the Inglaterra Bar and Patio, a favored spot for drinks after the opera. Regardless, drinks were omnipresent; there were no restrictions on when or what one drank. Even the daiquiri was described by Woon as "healthful," and he implied that any concoction of spirits, mixers, and ice was a cooling refreshment at any time of day. But importantly for Woon, alcohol was not an end in and of itself. It was an accompaniment, "an accessory before, during and after the fact. It easily and gently lubricates one's path through the fascinating labyrinth of Cuba's pleasures."[62] For him, Havana's draw was its larger culture and its exotic allure, be it cockfighting or the casino or even the Cuban characters one met along the way. But for all those attractions, one rarely did them without a drink in hand. Many Americans embraced Woon's approach to drinking while on vacation. For others, however, the drinking overshadowed anything else Cuba had to offer.

Few tourists boasted too openly about their drinking to friends back home. If they did mention it, it was looped in with the sights and sounds of Havana. One woman's postcard gave a sense of how the historic and the alcoholic sightseeing merged: "We visited Moro Castle, all churches, clubs and theaters, Tropical Gardens with plenty of Beer, free if you wanted it." The Tropical Gardens, a brewery, was a favorite tourist attraction, and more than a few tourists traveled home with respectable snapshots of themselves holding complimentary mugs of beer after their tour. This traveler, however, made certain to note the churches and historical sites she visited first. One tourist named Fred was unusually open about his gleeful pursuit of legalized drinking in

Havana. He eagerly described his alcohol-related sightseeing to his friend Charles in Ohio, highlighting noted drinking spots: "Going out to see Sloppy Joe today," he wrote, "located him yesterday and then to the Brewery — Tropical Gardens — 'oh boy.'"[63] While some tourists reported their promenade to the various celebrated liquor venues, others found word of their exploits made it home in other ways. In 1927, for example, William Beyersdorfer, a businessman from Milwaukee, traveled to Cuba and apparently enjoyed himself immensely. When he failed to return to work, his employer became concerned and wrote to the consulate in Havana inquiring as to his whereabouts. The consulate replied that Beyersdorfer had fallen in the street while drunk and been hit by a tram. While not badly hurt, he had nonetheless suffered injuries that kept him in the hospital beyond his planned departure date. His employer seemed either quite understanding or not entirely surprised by the painful end to Beyersdorfer's trip. He wrote to the consulate thanking them for the information and noted, "It looks as if our Mr. Beyersdorfer had just one or two drinks too many, as would be natural, having just gone to Havana."[64]

As the comment above suggests, the eager pursuit of intoxication was almost standard for tourists in Cuba. Little wonder that when responding to State Department requests as to the number of American citizens in foreign jails, the Havana delegation noted that its numbers were often higher than those of other foreign consulates. "The fact that the city is an important sporting center during the winter months and the absence of laws prohibiting the sale of intoxicating liquors in Cuba, all contributed to a larger number of cases in which American citizens are charged with crimes before local courts," it explained. Woon promised that local police were very understanding toward tourists who overindulged, telling potential travelers that in the event a tourist had "difficulty in navigating late at night it is quite likely that a friendly policeman will call a taxicab and himself conduct you to your hotel. There are even instances, they say, when they will take you to your room and put you to bed." But other sources suggest that Cuban authorities were not always so tolerant. Jeanette Jay of New York was one tourist who found herself in the crosshairs of the police during her brief stay in Havana. She and her party of nine were arrested for being drunk and disorderly in a Havana café. She strenuously disputed that characterization of her evening, though consular officials responded that her experience was not uncommon. "Of the large number of American tourists visiting Cuba, a certain number become

Tourists with their complimentary mugs of
beer at the Tropical Gardens brewery
(Souvenir photo in possession of author)

intoxicated and have to be arrested," they pointed out. Liquor consumption complicated the travels of many Americans. One traveler who came to
Havana on business spent the first two days of his visit "constantly drunk."
M. M. McIntyre of New York and Cecil Johnson are only two of many Americans who found themselves jailed on drunk and disorderly charges after a
night on the town. William Beyersdorfer's booze-soaked holiday ended with
a run-in with a tram. They all were more fortunate than Fred P. Newcomb, a
sailor visiting town, who was drunk when he boarded the launch to take him

back to his ship. He fell overboard and drowned.[65] Indeed, for many Americans, Havana's lure could not be separated from its more illicit pleasures. Americans came to Cuba to do openly, freely, and at times continually what they were prohibited by law from doing so openly at home.

It was no surprise, then, that Americans got in trouble. Some lost all financial restraint in the face of Havana's entertainments. As one newlywed bride noted, when seeking financial help from the embassy to get herself and her husband home, "Before they knew it their money seemed to disappear." Schuyler Merritt, a member of Congress from Stamford, Connecticut, cabled the American consul inquiring how on earth his son could be wiring for more money after his father had already sent him an extra $300. The consul in charge wryly replied that the son had squandered the $300 and now owed additional bills of $200. Apparently so common were money troubles among tourists in Havana that one souvenir guidebook contained a full page of advertisements for pawnshops offering loans in exchange for valuables, amidst pages advertising liquor. *La Ideal*, one of four advertisers, commanded reader attention with "Dinaro" in large letters and promised in English, "We lend money on jewels without any limit."[66] Other Americans occasionally took the idea of Havana as a wide-open town too far, forgetting that there were limits on what Cubans would tolerate in public. While Cuba's tourism industry traded on Cuba's reputation for the exotic, Cubans themselves were considerably less "wide open," and wild antics by tourists were not so tolerated outside Havana's main tourist areas. Two young couples who hired a car to take them to see the sights around town discovered the limits on public carousing. They found themselves in jail, charged with an offense against modesty when two local "vigilantes" reported that the "girls were sitting in the boys' laps, were embracing, kissing, and yelling, and that one of the boys had one of the girl's skirts up over her head." The two boys were fined, missed their ship's departure, and had to have financial help to get out of jail and get home. Similar resentment toward tourists arose in a case in which Albert Wright was jailed after a fight at a café. The consulate claimed that Wright had been beaten by a mob that gathered when he was accused of skipping out on his bill. Wright maintained he had already paid, and the consulate chastised the local police for overreacting to what was merely a "state of happy inebriation" on the part of a tourist.[67]

Havana's notoriety as a smuggling port was also an attraction, and tourists sought to witness the spectacle of rum-running firsthand. Once the Cuban government began to prevent the departure of known smuggling vessels from port in 1926, the ships themselves became tourist attractions as they floated fully loaded with liquor in Havana harbor. Indeed, some members of the Cuban tourist industry mourned when the *Thelma H.* was finally allowed to sail after being detained in Havana harbor for three weeks. It had become a sightseeing destination as an actual "contrabandista." The potential tourist revenue that rum-running might generate inflected the interactions between Cubans and Americans over Prohibition enforcement in other ways. Many American officials bemoaned that even when suspected smuggling vessels were seized, they quickly returned to smuggling when they were purchased at auction by smugglers. The vice president of the Cuban National Commission of Tourists in Havana contacted the Coast Guard in Miami hoping to capitalize on the romantic lure of rum-running. He suggested that several seized boats be sent to Havana to provide entertainment for tourists, though how, exactly, was unclear. Henry Kime assured Charles Root that the proposal came from a reliable source and insisted it was better to have the boats become tourist attractions in Havana than to "sell 'em back to American smugglers." All Root could do, however, was suggest that the Commission of Tourists make a request through appropriate channels in the State Department. Nothing apparently came of the idea, but it attests to the notion that the popular appeal of rum-running drew tourists to the docks in Havana to see the trade for themselves.[68]

While many tourists approached Cuba's illicit pleasures with relish, others were more leery and sought help to steer them to more respectable diversions. For these tourists, the American consulate offered guidance to avoid any potential danger in Cuba's exotic pleasures. One tourist hoping for a brief excursion to Havana from Miami wrote the consulate asking for hotel recommendations, as he wanted to stay in a "respectable, home-like place." C. W. Winstedt went a step further, requesting that a member of the consular staff meet his wife and son at the pier when they arrived, transport them to a good hotel at a reasonable price, and then escort them around Havana. He offered to pay for the staff member's time and efforts. The consulate obliged and only took reimbursements for actual expenses. And one elderly woman raised a fuss because she believed that the Cuban porter at her hotel had stolen one of her bags. The consulate discovered that she had never cleared her bag through customs when she arrived by ferry. Her age, the consulate surmised, contributed to her overreaction. Travel guides tried to reassure

Americans that Cuba was safe. *Terry's Guide to Cuba* insisted that thieves were rare and that Cubans as a people were extraordinarily honest. "One is never short-changed, flim-flammed, cheated or (rarely) overcharged."[69] But tourists assumed they were potential targets for Cuban criminals. George Irwin of Altoona, Pennsylvania, received a message from the consulate after Havana police found a pocketbook belonging to a member of his family at the Tropical Gardens brewery. When Irwin wrote back his thanks, he noted that the pocketbook had also contained some cash, "which I naturally did not expect to recover."[70] Another couple's travels turned sour when their evening of dining and dancing was interrupted by a scuffle with some Cubans at the rooftop restaurant of the Hotel Sevilla-Biltmore, one of the newest and most fashionable hotels along the Prado.[71] In each instance alcohol played a role.

Some American tourists sought Cuba precisely for its pleasures and indulged even to excess while on the island, while others were faintly repelled by its attractions, even if they might still tour the Tropical Gardens brewery. Many flocked to its hedonistic vibe that was a decided contrast to the ethos at home. Some sought the help of the consulate to steer them away from dangers. In other cases, the consulate became involved when dabbling in vice crossed the line from moderation to excess. Whatever their personal experience on the island, however, numerous tourists tried to extend their "personal liberty" from Cuba back home by smuggling small amounts of alcohol into the United States upon their return. Carmela Perez, who left Havana aboard one of the regular ferries, was charged with importing seven bottles of liquor, one bottle of wine, and seventeen yards of linen into Key West in 1922. Lucy Thistlewaite was returning from Cuba with her husband when the customs agent in Key West noticed that her overcoat looked unusually bulky. Upon inspection, they found she had hidden five quart bottles of liquor in two layers of overcoats. She pled guilty and was fined $100.[72] Even members of Congress were not immune to either the seductions of Cuba or the temptation to circumvent the law. M. A. Michaelson, a representative from Chicago, was arrested with the makings of virtually an entire bar in his baggage, including whiskey, crème de menthe, crème de cacao, and brandy. Charged with the intent to sell, he was acquitted, claiming that the alcohol really belonged to his brother-in-law. His arrest occurred, however, despite a telegram from Washington requesting he be given free entry privileges as a member of Congress.[73] Bringing booze back from vacation may have been more the norm than the exception, however. The docking of the Clyde Line ship the *Shawnee*, which traveled from Havana through Miami to New York City, caused a considerable stir when more than 200 of its 400 passengers were found to be carrying liquor when they disembarked. Liquor peddlers near the ferry dock in Key West even supplied liquor to those who left Cuba without it, offering, as one outraged tourist reported, "any kind of liquor I wanted and in any quantity desired." Not only would these purveyors provide the liquor; they would also provide trunks to pack it in and place them aboard whatever train the tourist was taking.[74] The tourist who made the report apparently supported drinking on vacation but Prohibition at home. Many others seemed to believe that the alcoholic pleasures of travel did not need to end in the land of Prohibition. Some invested in a store of liquor only to have it confiscated by the Customs Bureau in Key West. But one suspects that there were many others who passed through with their liquor undetected. Lucy Thistlewaite was caught because of her lumpy appearance. Congressman Michaelson was caught because his trunk was leaking. More subtle and careful packing likely spared many others the attention of authorities.

Taken together, the experiences of the local courts, police officers patrolling city streets late at night, college administrators, and tourists themselves suggest that, despite the dismay that some citizens conveyed to officials, a great many Americans had incorporated liquor into their expectations for social life and leisure activity. The connection between temperance and respectability had eroded considerably by Prohibition's end. Whether drinking was a troubling habit that ruined a marriage, evidence of new social interactions among the nation's young people, or part of the pleasure travel provided, alcohol's illegality did not constrain the actions of Americans, and they found a ready market to purchase what they desired. New commercial entertainments found in blind tigers, in dance halls, on dates, and during travel were among the modern, respectable pleasures of which drinking was an integral part. It represented a world no longer confined to large cities or to the wealthy or to the utterly disreputable. It was available to and embraced by Americans north and south. While alcohol had been presented as the consummate social evil, the actions of many Americans suggested otherwise. For them, alcohol was a beverage, an activity, perhaps an escape. Over the course of Prohibition, it became a signifier of sophistication and modern leisure, part of the new pleasure ethic that characterized the age. In the process, Americans rejected the vision of morality promoted by Prohibition's most ardent advocates. They opted instead for personal liberty and the right to choose to drink if they were so inclined. Little wonder, then, that the most prominent women's repeal organization evoked personal liberty in its motto, "the restoration of the Bill of Rights."[75] The embrace by Americans of alcohol in their homes and in public allowed a black market in booze to flourish, and enterprising providers sought ways to meet the continued demand for liquor. Whether it was a rural woman selling liquor by the drink out of her kitchen or a curbside liquor salesman waiting for passengers returning from Cuba, Americans of all varieties sought out those who might fill their glasses and show them a good time.

Americans' use of liquor during Prohibition involved a bit of rebellion, a willingness to flout the law or travel to exotic locales where liquor was legal but the ambiance was more edgy. That aspect of Cuba's allure faded with Prohibition's repeal, but travel to Cuba during Prohibition nonetheless laid an important foundation. It demonstrated Cuba's potential as a vice-soaked vacation paradise. Indeed, while the flow of liquor and tourists between Cuba and the United States diminished briefly in the 1930s, its glamour did not go unnoticed by Meyer Lansky, the infamous mob financier. Unable to corner the market on rum-running out of Cuba during Prohibition, the mob turned its attention to tourist vice in Havana in the years after repeal. By the late 1930s, the American mob conquered Cuban nightlife, controlling Havana's casinos, nightclubs, illicit entertainments, and sporting venues. Building on Cuba's allure from the 1920s, it created a high-end vacation paradise promising virtually any pleasure, which reached its zenith in the 1950s. Havana beckoned glamorous stars, musicians, and American investors, who turned a blind eye to the poverty, violence, and corruption around them. By the late 1950s, Cuba was a powder keg and Havana's hedonistic vibe helped create the conditions that led to revolution.

Conclusion

B Y 1930, THE FAILURES of Prohibition were hard to miss. Despite ten years of enforcement, the federal government had been unable to stem liquor traffic and indeed found itself in the midst of increasing complaints about the consequences of enforcing the Eighteenth Amendment. When the Wickersham Commission, established by President Hoover to examine the problems of law enforcement and observance, began its hearings that year, the growing list of problems was inescapable. The federal government had spent millions of dollars, and yet "in many cities large and small [there] are as many if not more places where liquor is sold." Officials had been corrupted, citizens had lost respect for the law, and the courts had been overwhelmed with individuals charged with crimes. The media had even accused Prohibition agents of outright murder in their efforts to enforce the nation's dry laws. Yet liquor remained plentiful virtually throughout the nation.[1] Despite a decade of effort, liquor continued to make its way to southern beaches where bootleggers transported it to markets near and far. Law enforcement agents struggled to enforce the law, while others found numerous ways to profit from it. Throughout, Americans continued to drink, creating the demand that kept bootleggers in business. To many observers, the traffic in liquor was simply too extensive, too profitable, and too persistent to ever be fully stopped, and they no longer saw the point in trying. It was clear that Prohibition had not eliminated any of the nation's social ills; indeed it had very likely created more problems than it solved.

While Prohibition had clearly failed by the time the Eighteenth Amendment was repealed in 1933, it fostered permanent changes across the landscape nevertheless. It shaped American responses to international traffic in illicit goods and people long after. Federal law enforcement efforts became more visible, reaching into southern cities and towns as well as across the Straits of Florida into Cuba. The U.S. Coast Guard embodied this effort on the seas, taking on a law enforcement role well outside the nation's territorial waters that continued for the rest of the twentieth century. Prohibition laws encouraged widely successful and profitable trafficking networks; unsurprisingly, similar prohibitions on immigration and drugs did the same, creating equally persistent criminal enterprises. "Illegal immigration" only became possible once laws restricted the entry of immigrants into the United States; it has been a focus of immigration policy ever since. Similarly, the Federal Bureau of Narcotics transposed Prohibition's approach to alcohol as a problem of criminal activity to illicit drugs. American antidrug policies that began for all practical purposes in the 1930s continued U.S. efforts to coerce Latin American nations to participate in the enforcement of American laws. The problems of international cooperation, the extent of U.S. authority beyond the nation's shores, and the diplomatic and law enforcement dilemmas created by prohibited substances and migration continue to bedevil federal authorities.

Within the South, the consequences of the thirteen years of Prohibition are equally profound. By 1933, many southerners had participated in and profited from the liquor traffic. Many more had evaded the law as they embraced emerging national trends in culture and social life. Smuggling networks that stretched from Havana to the southern coast and from there into cities like Chicago, St. Louis, and New York created economic networks that helped pull the South closer into a national embrace. Those same networks belied assumptions of a backward and isolated South as they demonstrated the international reach of enterprising southerners. Retail and entertainment outlets selling liquor mushroomed across the South, accelerating the development of a consumer culture that marketed new forms of leisure and social interaction in which liquor was a key ingredient. The willingness of wide swaths of the American population, southerners among them, to drink despite the law, and even to spite the law, ultimately eroded the link between temperate habits and respectability. These changes were eagerly embraced by the region's youth, though their parents found ways to participate as well. Travel to the South and through the South offered opportunities to enjoy liquor for those sheepish about imbibing freely at home. The new popularity of travel to southern destinations and Cuba would also have a lasting impact. Americans from across the nation would continue to travel to the southern coast for beach vacations or for more sinful entertainments in glittering tourist meccas like Miami and New Orleans. Many of them traveled farther south to the most glamorous destination of all. The American mob moved into

Havana after Prohibition's repeal, transforming neon lights, mambo music, organized gambling, and illicit sex into the world's most famous and most notorious vacation destination by midcentury. Prohibition, in short, helped make the South modern while it expanded the scope of American power and influence at home and abroad. This was no small thing.

After a year of investigation, the Wickersham Commission provided its conclusions in 1931. While the official report of the commission recommended maintaining Prohibition as it was, the message to the public was considerably more conflicted. The individual statements of the commission's members displayed widespread divisions over Prohibition's future. A majority of members themselves favored either modification or outright repeal of the Eighteenth Amendment. Their personal views aligned fairly well with those of the nation's college seniors, who also favored modification or repeal by wide margins. Those opinions likely matched the views of many Americans across the country. There was, however, widespread confusion as to whether repeal was even possible. No amendment in the nation's history had ever been repealed, and initially there seemed little likelihood that such extreme action was possible. Some observers raised the possibility that the Eighteenth Amendment should simply be ignored, nullified by ending all attempts to enforce it at the federal, state, and local levels. Many thought this seemed horrifyingly radical and downright disrespectful to the Constitution itself. But again, the South was pivotal in this argument. Felix Frankfurter, professor at Harvard Law School and future U.S. Supreme Court justice, as early as 1923 posited the possibility of simply ignoring the Eighteenth Amendment, noting that there was considerable precedent for doing so. Had not the South routinely ignored and failed to enforce the Reconstruction amendments to the Constitution? Southern states routinely violated the Fourteenth Amendment and had long enforced legislation that trampled the spirit if not the letter of the Fifteenth Amendment. Some argued that Prohibition could be handled in the same way. Frankfurter concluded that ignoring increasing numbers of constitutional amendments might ultimately undermine overall respect for the entire document, something that he believed would be dangerous. But others pointed out the option nevertheless.[2]

Eventually, the problem of Prohibition would be solved by repeal, facilitated by a massive economic depression that made the need for government revenue inescapable, which taxes on liquor could readily supply. In the midst of the Great Depression, the moral issues embedded in Prohibition no longer seemed important. The warm comfort of a legal drink seemed to promise some sustenance to a beleaguered nation. One of Franklin Roosevelt's earliest acts as president was to legalize beer, commenting, "I think it's time the country did something about beer." By December 1933, enough states had ratified the Twenty-First Amendment, ending national Prohibition once and for all.[3]

In many parts of the nation, however, the battle for Prohibition had been lost long before the Eighteenth Amendment was repealed by the Twenty-First Amendment. Many states had declared themselves out of the enforcement business by the end of the 1920s. By 1930, twenty-one states at state party conventions had placed demands for repeal in their platforms. New York repealed its state prohibition law in 1923, leaving enforcement entirely to federal officials. By 1930, another six states had followed suit.[4] None of those states was in the South, but Alabama's actions represented another option. In 1930, the governor disbanded the State Law Enforcement Department, which had provided state officers to assist federal officers in enforcing the Eighteenth Amendment. Part of the rationale for doing so was economic; the office was an "extravagance" in the face of a crumbling economy. But the governor also noted that the office was "a source of constant annoyance and irritation." From 1930 on, any Prohibition activities were the province of federal agents or local officers.[5] Even the crucial work of the U.S. Coast Guard Intelligence Division was not what it once was. There was still a chief intelligence officer, but it was not Captain Charles Root. Root did not live to see a time when he would no longer be chasing "red ink." He died suddenly in August 1930, hit by a taxi as he was crossing Massachusetts Avenue in Washington, D.C. Henry Kime continued his work in Havana, his distinct typewriter font continuing to appear in the files of the Coast Guard Intelligence Division. But his life after Prohibition is unknown. Salvador Pena, however, used his experience as Uncle Sam's booze cop in the West Indies to parlay himself into a career in intelligence. He would eventually retire from intelligence work in the 1950s.

It is easy to dismiss Prohibition as a silly law leading to a farce of enforcement, providing much of the fuel that made the Roaring Twenties roar. It nonetheless left additional lasting effects beyond those raised in this book, as other scholars have noted. As a result of Prohibition, Americans became accustomed to a federal government with a broader reach. They came to accept a government whose policies might affect their daily lives, one that carried a federal law enforcement arm. The battles over Prohibition and its enforcement created new political alignments, as marginalized groups who faced the brunt of enforcement efforts turned away from the Republican party and embraced the Democrats as more in line with their interests. Franklin Roosevelt benefited from these shifts. Americans also learned the limits of the voting power of specific groups. Prohibition had been passed in part as a nod to the new power of the women's vote, and women were seen as a powerful bloc in the dry arsenal at the ballot box. By the end of the 1920s, however, it was clear not only that women voted like everybody else, but that they now drank like everybody else. By the dawn of the new decade, the potential power of the women's vote was no longer feared.[6]

Other changes seeped into southern culture as they did the rest of the nation. In the South and nationally, Prohibition made women's public drinking acceptable, part of a larger cultural shift that embraced dating and commercial leisure and conceded the possibility of respectable drinking. Women, too, now could belly up to the bar alongside their male companions. Women too also took part in the business side of liquor, combining the selling of liquor with their other household tasks to make money for their families. And for African Americans as well, bootlegging became a means of social mobility at least for a while, providing a level of income for their families that was impossible before. Bootlegging remained a survival strategy well after Prohibition and the Great Depression. It did so because despite the South's evangelical reputation and the persistence of dry sentiment, and even the lingering alcohol control policies in southern states, southerners continued to drink. They did not always do so openly or at home or in front of their mothers, but drink they did. In this regard as well, southern culture was not so very different from the rest of America.

One last quip makes this point. The Wickersham Commission released its findings in early 1931. Its general report optimistically suggested that Prohibition enforcement was possible by transferring the Prohibition Bureau to the Department of Justice and changing legal procedures to facilitate the flow of cases through the courts. Its conclusions were largely greeted with derision. A popular ditty summed up the nation's view of the Wickersham Commission's work and illustrated the seeming contradictions between the commission's hopes for effective Prohibition and the reality that Americans saw around them every day:

> Prohibition is an awful flop.
> We like it.
> It can't stop what it's meant to stop.
> We like it.

> It's left a trail of graft and slime,
> It's filled our land with vice and crime,
> It don't prohibit worth a dime,
>   Nevertheless we're for it.

Attributed to Franklin P. Adams, it appeared in the *New York World* in 1931 and soon became part of the ethos of the movement toward Prohibition's repeal. It was not, however, entirely original. It followed the pattern of a ditty about dating that appeared in the *Crimson-White*, the University of Alabama's student newspaper, in 1921 and subsequently appeared in student publications at Centenary College in 1923, at both Massachusetts Agricultural College and Monmouth College in 1924, and at both Rawlings and what would become Bowling Green State University in 1925.[7] The college version, titled "Men — The Co-ed's Version," celebrated the new dating culture on college campuses:

> These men are simple folk.
>   I like 'em.
> They take me out until they are broke.
>   I like 'em.
> I like them naughty, tall and lean,
> And short and fat and good and green,
> And many other kinds I've seen,
>   I like 'em.
> They take me to the show.
> They take me to the candy store
>   I like 'em.
> But when they show that they don't care,
> And hug me roughly like a bear,
> And crack my ribs and muss my hair —
>   Oh man — I love 'em.

What are we to make of the travels of a humorous rhyme that first mocked new college dating norms and then mocked Prohibition? This short poem echoes the national ties created between south and north over the course of the 1920s. College students in Alabama, Massachusetts, and Ohio all got the same jokes because they understood relationships between men and women similarly. They all shared the same culture that grew from their experience as college students. The rhythm of poem, however, lent itself as well to contradictions that bedeviled Prohibition and were understood by Americans everywhere. But it does not merely suggest that college students in Alabama were part of a national college culture, though it does that. This poem connects the social changes happening at college campuses across the country, even in the South, with the world that Prohibition created. Dating humor paralleled Prohibition humor because both grew out of the same cultural shifts of the 1920s, shifts that were intimately related to the world of alcohol on college campuses across the country. But this world was evident everywhere, not just at college. Southern beaches welcomed loads of smuggled liquor from abroad, as did beaches in New Jersey and along the Detroit River, despite the Coast Guard's efforts to stem the tide. Southerners themselves participated in the black market in booze that Prohibition created, as did many Americans. They created networks that extended south across the water to Cuba and to liquor markets in the North as well and corrupted officials along the way. Despite the efforts of local, state, and federal officials in the South, at sea, and even in places like Havana, the traffic in liquor persisted. And Americans everywhere continued to drink. They did so on college campuses, in their homes, and at cafés, soda stands, restaurants, and blind tigers. They did so on vacation in Miami and Havana and in hotels all along the southern coast, all without the risk of a sullied reputation. Prohibition connected a modernizing south to a national and international market and to a national culture. When it came to booze, Americans, and southerners with them, "liked it," something that has not changed to this day.

Notes

Abbreviations

ADAH	Alabama Department of Archives and History, Montgomery
AUA	Auburn University Archives, Auburn, Alabama
BPL	Birmingham Public Library Archives, Birmingham Municipal Court Dockets, Birmingham, Alabama
DOJ	Records of the Bureau of Prohibition, Records of Officials and Organizational Units, General Records of the Department of Justice, RG 60, National Archives and Records Administration, College Park, Maryland
DOS	Records of Foreign Service Posts, U.S. Department of State, RG 84, National Archives and Records Administration, College Park, Maryland
DOT	Central Files of the Office of the Secretary of the Treasury, 1917–1932, Correspondence of the Secretary of the Treasury, General Files of the U.S. Department of the Treasury, RG 56, National Archives and Records Administration, College Park, Maryland
GCUSCG	General Correspondence, 1910–1941, Records of the U.S. Coast Guard, RG 26, National Archives and Records Administration, Washington, D.C.
INS	Records of the U.S. Immigration and Naturalization Services, RG 85, National Archives and Records Administration, Washington, D.C.
IRS	Prohibition Unit, Records of the Internal Revenue Service, RG 58, National Archives and Records Administration, College Park, Maryland
MBC	Records of the U.S. Bureau of Customs, Mobile, RG 36, National Archives and Records Administration, Southeast Region, Morrow, Georgia
NCLOE	Records of the National Commission on Law Observance and Enforcement, RG 10, National Archives and Records Administration, College Park, Maryland
SAF	Doyle Elam Carlton Papers, 1929–33, Series 204, State Archives of Florida, Tallahassee

USCGID   Records of the U.S. Coast Guard Intelligence Division, 1922–41, RG 26, National Archives and Records Administration, Washington, D.C.

USDCSE   Records of the United States District Courts, RG 21, National Archives and Records Administration, Southeast Region, Morrow, Georgia

USDCSW   United States District Court Records, RG 21, National Archives and Records Administration, Southwest Region, Ft. Worth, Texas

USMSKW   Records of the U.S. Marshall's Service, Key West, RG 527, National Archives and Records Administration, Southeast Region, Morrow, Georgia

WSHUA   W. S. Hoole Special Collections, University of Alabama, Tuscaloosa

Introduction

1. Letter from Aubrey Boyles to the Attorney General, January 23, 1926, then forwarded to O. D. Jackson, Prohibition Administrator, New Orleans, Louisiana, folder "Correspondence of the Other Offices and Divisions of the Bureau," box 55, IRS.

2. U.S. Congress, *Investigation of Prohibition Enforcement*, March 17, 1930.

3. Green, "What Price Bribery?," 148.

4. "M'Carthy Upbraids Liquor Agents," *New York Times*, March 4, 1920; "Threat to Seize Alien Rum Ships," *New York Times*, October 12, 1920; "Signs in New York Read 'Why Go to Cuba?,'" *New York Times*, December 3, 1920; "Rum Boom off Nova Scotia," *New York Times*, December 3, 1921.

5. Andreas, *Smuggler Nation*.

6. While few historians in general focus on rum-running, only Randy Sanders has written about rum-running in the South; see Sanders, "Delivering Demon Rum."

7. L. T. Chalker to Chief of Staff, Commander, Special Patrol Force, February 3, 1928, box 10, USCGID.

8. Lowe, *Calypso Magnolia*, 1.

9. "Bootlegging Heirs of the Buccaneers of Barataria," *New York Times*, October 23, 1921.

10. "Bootlegging Heirs of the Buccaneers of Barataria," *New York Times*, October 23, 1921.

11. "Haynes Sees End of Rum Running," *New York Times*, July 24, 1923.

12. "Secrets of the Rum Fleet and Its Freebooters," *New York Times*, July 22, 1923.

13. "Reports Increases in Liquor Running," *New York Times*, March 2, 1924.

14. "Trail of Smugglers Leads over the World," *New York Times*, August 3, 1924.

15. "Dry Navy and Army Are Stripped for Action," *New York Times*, July 28, 1926.

16. "Next Big Dry Problem Is to Stop Distilling," *New York Times*, March 6, 1927.

17. "Rum Running Is Shifting Back to Island Bases," *New York Times*, June 22, 1930.

18. "Alcohol: Its Use and Abuse," *Outlook*, October 24, 1917, 286.

19. Van Buren, *Gospel Temperance*.

20. Davis, "Race Menace in Bootlegging," 337–44, esp. 339, and Mandeville, "More Sin and Gin," 299.

21. Billy Sunday, sermon, Boston, Mass., November 12, 1916.

22. On the role of the Women's Christian Temperance Union and women's politics in the South, see Sims, *Power of Femininity in the New South*, 54–79, and Thomas, *New Woman in Alabama*, 10–40.

23. This story is well told in numerous sources. See especially Okrent, *Last Call*; Lerner, *Dry Manhattan*; Sinclair, *Era of Excess*; and Pegram, *Battling Demon Rum*.

24. Lewis, *Coming of Southern Prohibition*; Willis, *Southern Prohibition*.

25. Thompson, *Most Stirring and Significant Episode*; Coker, *Liquor in the Land of the Lost Cause*.

26. Ring, *Problem South*.

27. Murdock, *Domesticating Drink*, 89; Pegram, *Battling Demon Rum*, 152.

28. Murchison, *Federal Criminal Law Doctrines*.

29. McGirr, *War on Alcohol*.

30. Pérez, *Cuba under the Platt Amendment*.

Chapter One

1. Captain Peter del Valle, Secret Diary, pp. 19–20, Cuba Report 1925, folder "Cuba Volume 1, 1 of 2," box 64, USCGID.

2. In this regard, Cuba was actually more helpful toward American Prohibition laws than was Canada, the U.S. neighbor to the north. Cuba prohibited exporting liquor to the United States, where it was illegal. Canada did not. Indeed, the dominion took advantage of Prohibition to provide Americans with booze, though Canada charged a $20 duty on each case of liquor exported to the United States. Such a stiff duty put a crimp in exporters' profits and made legally exported liquor less competitive on the open market. Little wonder many Canadians chose to smuggle liquor to the United States rather than pay the duty. See Moore, *Bootleggers and Borders*, 56–73.

3. Karig, "Gold from Salt Water," 203–6.

4. "Booze Buccaneering along 'Rum Row,'" 52.

5. Cuba Report sent by Henry Kime to Charles Root, approximately June 1927, p. 1, box 68, USCGID. The report begins in earnest on the third page after Kime's facetious effort to recast his undercover efforts in Cuba as a crime drama with the title "Super-Snoopers of the Caribbean or With Uncle Sam's Booze Cops in the West Indies." The report is hereinafter referred to as "Uncle Sam's Booze Cops," USCGID.

6. Karig, "Gold from Salt Water," 206.

7. Cluster and Hernandez, *History of Havana*, 135–38.

8. Captain Peter del Valle, Secret Diary, p. 18, Cuba Report 1925, folder "Cuba Volume 1, 1 of 2," box 64, USCGID.

9. List of Shipments of Liquor, Wine, and Beer from Foreign ports, folder "Customs 1923 January–June," box 1458, 64, Various Service Cooperations, Correspondence 1910–1935, GCUSCG.

10. Captain Peter del Valle, Secret Diary, p. 19, Cuba Report 1925, folder "Cuba Volume 1, 1 of 2," box 64, USCGID.

11. Letter from Charles S. Root to Henry J. Anslinger, Division of Foreign Control, Bureau of Prohibition, April 30, 1928, folder "Correspondence Relating to Individuals, Rum-Running Era, 1927–30," box 56, USCGID. Root summarized the information in this letter from earlier accounts of Roud's operations, including the eleven-page affidavit of Angel Sanchez, who served as Roud's bookkeeper from 1923 to 1925.

12. Angel Sanchez, June 1, 1926, p. 11, folder "Special Agent Wm. Kelly's Reports, 1925–27," box 67, USCGID.

13. General Survey of Liquor Smuggling Cuba–United States, p. 1, folder "Cuba Report 1925, Reference g," box 64, USCGID. See also handwritten note, Cuba Report 1925, folder 1 of 2, and handwritten note, July 23, folder "Cuba Report 1925, Reference e," box 64, USCGID.

14. Angel Sanchez statement, esp. pp. 9–11, folder "Special Agent Wm. Kelly's Reports, 1925–27," box 67, USCGID.

15. Angel Sanchez statement, p. 4, folder "Special Agent Wm. Kelly's Reports, 1925–27," box 67, USCGID.

16. Angel Sanchez statement, pp. 2–4, folder "Special Agent Wm. Kelly's Reports, 1925–27," box 67, USCGID.

17. Marriage reported in letter from Henry Kime to Charles Root, May 18, 1927, Cuba Binder, box 68, USCGID; memorandum to Mr. Edward Caffery, February 15, 1927, Subject: Mourice Roud, American Citizen who has been conducting a Supply Business for Smugglers of Liquor operating out of Habana, Cuba, p. 1, Section 811.4, Diplomatic Posts Havana, vol. 177, DOS; Henry Kime to Charles Root, July 14, 1927, box 68, USCGID.

18. *US v. William Cuevas et al.*, Case 11111, Eastern District of Louisiana, New Orleans, USDCSW.

19. Dingle, "Running the Rum Blockade," 19.

20. Report from Immigrant Inspector of New Orleans (Thomas Worden?; signature unclear) to Commissioner of Immigration, New Orleans, February 27, 1923, p. 2, Case No. 55166/31-B, INS.

21. Kime, "Uncle Sam's Booze Cops," USCGID.

22. Adams, "Right off the Boat."

23. Memorandum, "Report of Trip to Havana Cuba SAUKEE, April 17, 1925," p. 3, folder "SAUKEE," Destroyer Forces, box 82, USCGID.

24. Synopsis of rum-running vessels, June 3, 1927, folder "Cuba Smuggling Information," box 58, USCGID.

25. Report of Salvator Pena on July 2, 1926, quoted in memo dated October 28, 1926, and letter from Charles Root to Oftedal, Deputy Commissioner of Prohibition,

December 10, 1927, folder "Information File, Re: Vessels Suspected of Illicit Liquor Transportation, 1926–27" (filed alphabetically according to the name of the vessel), box 52, IRS. See also letter from Henry Kime to Charles Root, January 5, 1927, p. 2, Cuba Binder, box 68, USCGID.

26. Moray, *Diary of a Rum-Runner*.

27. Memorandum from Peter del Valle to General L. C. Andrews, Assistant Secretary of the Treasury, Subject: Secret Report on the Activities of the Cuban Government, September 6, 1925, p. 15, folder "Cuba Volume 1, 2 of 2," box 64, USCGID.

28. Memorandum, Embassy of the United States, Havana, May 27, 1926, p. 3, sec. 811.4, Diplomatic Posts Havana, vol. 191, DOS.

29. Statement of Thomas Joseph Wiseman, July 14, 1925, Diplomatic Posts Havana, vol. 177, DOS.

30. Kime, "Uncle Sam's Booze Cops," 2, USCGID; Captain Peter del Valle summarized the fraudulent clearance papers in his secret diary in 1925, pp. 13, 14, 19, folder "Cuba Volume 1, 1 of 2," box 64, USCGID.

31. Kime, "Uncle Sam's Booze Cops," 2, USCGID.

32. "The Rum Running Situation at Havana Cuba," March 12, 1926, p. 2 (this appears to be draft of Kime's report, as corrections and edits are penciled into the document), sec. 811.4, Diplomatic Posts Havana, vol. 162, DOS.

33. Memorandum, "Report of Trip to Havana Cuba SAUKEE," April 17, 1925, p. 3, folder "SAUKEE," Destroyer Forces, box 82, USCGID; reports, Agent 1001 (Kime), p. 1, folder "Cuba Report 1925, Reference d," box 64, USCGID; letter from Henry Kime to Peter (probably Peter del Valle), September 7, 1925, folder "Cuba Report 1925, Reference g," box 64, USCGID.

34. Adams, "Right off the Boat."

35. *US v. Wallace Watler, William Watler, and Lyngard Watler*, Case 301, Southern District of Florida, Key West, box 4, USDCSE. Description of *Fannie Prescott*, p. 6, and cross-examination, pp. 4–6, of hearing held September 2, 1925.

36. *Fannie Prescott*, p. 81, Record of Ship Seizures in Prohibition Cases, 1923–1927, vol. 1 of 1, DOJ. This source, probably the remaining fragment of a larger collection, listed 163 cases of ship seizures, many of which operated out of Havana.

37. Record of Ship Seizures in Prohibition Cases, 1923–1927, vol. 1 of 1, DOJ.

38. Moray, *Diary of a Rum-Runner*, 125.

39. "Booze Buccaneering along 'Rum Row'"; McNutt, "Modern Pirates Walk the Plank"; "Bootleggers abaft the Port Beam!"; Karig, "Gold from Salt Water"; Shepherd, "Biggest Rum King"; O'Donnell, "Running the Booze Blockade"; Edsall, "Whisky Below Decks."

40. Moray, *Diary of a Rum-Runner*.

41. Report, Agent 1002 (HG — Grumbert), August 18, 1925, folder "Cuba Report 1925, Reference e," box 64, USCGID; statement of crew member Curt Vock to Salvador Cancio Pena, February 9, 1927, Information File Regarding Vessels Suspected of Illicit Liquor Transportation, 1926–1927, A–C, box 52, IRS.

42. Report on ships, June 3, 1927, folder "Cuba Smuggling Information," box 58, USCGID.

43. Edsall, "Whiskey Below Decks," 149.

44. Gray, "Bootlegging from the Bahamas," 18.

45. Lythgoe, *Bahama Queen*, 81–82. Lythgoe traveled with Captain Bill McCoy on one of his voyages to Rum Row to see what it was like.

46. Splicing is the process of joining two ends of a line by interweaving their strands.

47. Moray, *Diary of a Rum-Runner*; Lythgoe, *Bahama Queen*, 83.

48. Moray, *Diary of a Rum-Runner*, 50.

49. Edsall, "Whisky Below Decks," 145; Moray, *Diary of a Rum-Runner*, 139–40; Lythgoe, *Bahama Queen*, 81.

50. Memo from F. P. Horner, Officer-in-Charge of CG-9054, April 9, 1931, folder "Florida Seizures," box 9, USCGID.

51. "British Rum Ship Fights Sea Battle," *Mobile Register*, August 10, 1926; "Rum Vessel in Fight Is in US Hands," *Mobile Register*, August 11, 1926. The *Patricia M. Behman* case was reported in *Literary Digest*. See "Hijackers — The Bane of Bootleggers."

52. Report on British Motor Yacht "Shirin" from Commanding Officer, *Vidette*, to Commander, Gulf Division, February 16, 1922, folder "Customs 1922," 64, Various Service Cooperations, box 1458, Correspondence 1910–35, GCUSCG.

53. O'Donnell, "Running the Booze Blockade," 9; interview with Raymond Dickinson, Boat K-161471; interview, Louis Dohall Alpeigh, Boat V-15723, and interview with Jessie Clarence Robinson, folder "Florida Cases and Seizures, 1928–30," box 11, USCGID.

54. Lythgoe, *Bahama Queen*, 80–82.

55. "Bootleggers abaft the Port Beam!," 39.

56. O'Donnell, "Running the Booze Blockade," 9.

57. *US v. Carl Stanton et al.*, Case 374, Southern District of Florida, Key West, USDCSE.

58. Memo from Commanding Officer, *Yamacraw*, to Commandant, January 14, 1925, Destroyer Forces, box 82, USCGID.

59. *US v. Claud Reynolds et al.*, Case 1128, Southern District of Florida, Miami, USDCSE.

60. *US v. Aloysius Fabacher et al.*, Case 11110, Eastern District of Louisiana, New Orleans, USDCSW.

61. *US v. Joe Masera*, Case 8372, Eastern District of Louisiana, New Orleans, USDCSW.

62. *US v. Albert Stander*, Case 7508, Eastern District of Louisiana, New Orleans, USDCSW.

63. *US v. John Damonte et al.*, Case 12301, Eastern District of Louisiana, New Orleans, USDCSW; *US v. Paco Enavides and Manola Rocha*, Case 372, Southern District of Florida, Key West, USDCSE.

64. *US v. Tom Madden et al.*, Case 16/326, Eastern District of New Orleans, USDCSW. The case was ultimately transferred to the District Court of the Northern District of Illinois, Eastern Division, for trial.

65. *US v. W. W. Benedict et al.*, Case 2170, Southern District of Florida, Tampa (though case record is located in files for USDC in Jacksonville, Fla.), USDCSE.

66. *Public Cooperation in Prohibition Law Enforcement*, 13–20.

67. Sanders, "Delivering Demon Rum," 95; testimony of Daniel L. Jemison, pp. 20–41 of trial transcript, *US v. Alfred Staples et al.*, Case 6180, Southern District of Alabama, Mobile, box 101, USDCSE. List of bank drafts is on pp. 173–74.

68. Dingle, "Running the Rum Blockade," 18.

Chapter Two

1. Letter from J. F. C. Griggs, Collector, to the Secretary of the Treasury, Washington, D.C., November 22, 1919, folder "Customs, 1917–1919," box 147, Community Chest—Customs General, 1910–1919, box 1457, 64, Various Service Cooperations, Correspondence 1910–1935, GCUSCG.

2. Memorandum for the Secretary from Edward Clifford, Assistant Secretary, January 25, 1923, folder "Customs 1923, January–June," box 1458, 64, Various Service Cooperations, Correspondence 1910–1935, GCUSCG.

3. Press Release, Treasury Department, May 18, 1927, p. 1, box 113, 1927, DOT.

4. Press Release, Treasury Department, May 18, 1927, p. 2, box 113, 1927, DOT.

5. Press Release, Treasury Department, May 18, 1927, pp. 3–4, box 113, 1927, DOT.

6. Press release, Treasury Department, May 18, 1927, p. 7, box 113, 1927, DOT; emphasis in the original.

7. "Prohibition, National 1923," p. 2, box 112, DOT.

8. Merz, *Dry Decade*, 206, 267–69. See also Sinclair, *Era of Excess*, 192–97.

9. See Johnson, *Guardians of the Sea*, and Bloomfield, *Compact History of the United States Coast Guard*.

10. Malcolm F. Willoughby lays out the size of the Coast Guard fleet and its 1921 report of activities in *Rum War at Sea*, 22–23.

11. It is unclear whether this document represents a report or the text of a speech. The language uses the first person, but the title page only states "Prohibition, National 1923." It is in box 112, DOT.

12. Lescarboura, "Battle of Rum Row," 955, 958.

13. Johnson, *Guardians of the Sea*, 92.

14. Letter from Commandant F. C. Billard, Coast Guard, to the Officers in Charge and Personnel of the Coast Guard Stations, April 25, 1924, folder "Customs 1924," box 1459, 64, Various Service Cooperations, Correspondence 1910–1935, GCUSCG.

15. The most in-depth discussion of the diplomatic debates surrounding Prohibition enforcement at sea is Lawrence Spinelli's *Dry Diplomacy*. Spinelli's analysis focuses on the diplomatic maneuvers between the United States and Great Britain,

which determined how the Coast Guard sought to prevent liquor smuggling along the entire U.S. coastline. For discussion of the extent to U.S. territorial waters, see *Dry Diplomacy*, 15–30. See also Sturgis, "National Prohibition and International Law"; Glasgow, "Foreign Affairs"; "Rum-Running and the Law"; Sinclair, *Era of Excess*, 144–45; and Moore, *Bootleggers and Borders*, 88.

16. Spinelli, *Dry Diplomacy*, 80–81.

17. Notes on the General Situation, Week Ending 26 August 1927, p. 2, folder August 26, 1927–November 25, 1927, box 70, USCGID.

18. Notes on the General Situation, Week Ending 13 September 1924, p. 1, folder August 30, 1924–August 29, 1925, box 68, USCGID.

19. Notes on the General Situation, Week Ending 13 September 1924, p. 2, folder August 30, 1924–August 29, 1925, box 68, USCGID.

20. Notes on the General Situation, Week Ending 22 August 1925, p. 2, folder August 30, 1924–August 29, 1925, box 68 USCGID.

21. Report of R. M. Sykes, Commanding Officer of the *Arrow*, to Commander, Gulf Division, November 4, 1921, folder "Customs-1921," box 1459, 64, Various Service Cooperations, Correspondence 1910–1935, GCUSCG.

22. Popular magazines published stories, like the one in *Popular Mechanics* called "The Battle of Rum Row," about the efforts to prevent smuggling. See also Memorandum for the Commandant, Captain, Notes on the General Situation, Week Ending 27 August 1926, pp. 2–3, folder June 11, 1926–October 22, 1926, box 68, USCGID; William Wheeler, March 21, 1927, folder "Commandant's Memoranda, 1925–1930," box 37, USCGID; Moore, "Rum Row — Finis"; Notes on the General Situation, Week Ending 16 January 1926, p. 1, folder September 11, 1925–January 23, 1926, box 69, and Week Ending 27 August 1926, pp. 2–3, folder June 11, 1926–October 22, 1926, box 68, USCGID.

23. Notes on the General Situation, Week Ending 15 April 1927, p. 2, folder February 18, 1927–March 9, 1928, box 70, USCGID.

24. Notes on the General Situation, Week Ending 3 January 1925, folder August 30, 1924-August 29, 1925, box 68, USCGID.

25. Memorandum from Commanding Officer, the *Yamacraw*, to the Commandant, October 31, 1925, Destroyer files, *Yamacraw*, box 82, USCGID.

26. Letter from the Assistant Secretary to Douglas Robinson, Assistant Secretary of the Navy, December 23, 1924, p. 2, folder "Customs 1924," box 1459, 64, Various Service Cooperations, GCUSCG.

27. Notes on the General Situation, Week Ending 14 February 1925, p. 3, folder August 30, 1924-August 29, 1925, box 68, USCGID.

28. Memorandum reporting the seizure of the *Thritie* and liquor on June 18, 1921, to Division Commander, Gulf Division, dated June 20, 1921, folder "Customs 1921," box 1458, 64, Various Division Cooperations, Correspondence 1910–1935, GCUSCG.

29. Memorandum recording the Seizure of the V-2774, from Officer in Charge,

CG-220, to Commander, Section Base 6, 3 November 1929, folder "Florida Seizures," box 9, USCGID.

30. Report of Violation, American Gas Screw V-19719, by G. H. Lybrand, 14 June 1931, folder "Florida Seizures," box 9, USCGID.

31. Notes on the General Situation, Week Ending 29 January 1926, p. 1, and Week Ending 9 April 1926, p. 3, folder January 29, 1926–May 21, 1926, box 69, USCGID; Notes on the General Situation, Week Ending 10 January 1925, p. 3, folder August 30, 1924–August 29, 1925, box 68, USCGID.

32. Notes on the General Situation, Week Ending 25 December, 1925, p. 2, folder September 11, 1925–January 23, 1926, box 69, USCGID; Willoughby, *Rum War at Sea*, 62.

33. Letter from Charles Root to Commander Jack, Ft. Lauderdale Base, November 6, 1929, box 9, USCGID; "Hide and Seek Adds Comedy to Rum Game," *Miami News*, August 6, 1925; "Coast Guard Stems Flow of Bahama Liquor," undated clippings in folder "Ft. Lauderdale Base 6," box 60, USCGID.

34. Memorandum from Commanding Officer of the Naval Yard, Boston, to Commandant, May 10, 1930, pp. 4, 5, folder "Memoranda to Commandant, 1925–1930," box 36, USCGID. The *Literary Digest* published an account of a journalist who accompanied the Coast Guard on patrol. The article's title, "Nabbing the Rum-Runner — Sometimes," gives an indication of the Coast Guard's only occasional success. On the use of radio, see Mowry, "Listening to the Rumrunners."

35. Notes on the General Situation, Week Ending 13 September 1924, p. 4, folder August 30, 1924–August 29, 1925, box 68, USCGID.

36. "Rum Chasers by a Former Officer of the Patrol," 180. See also Moore, "Fighting Rum Row." The article recounts the experiences of a journalist aboard a cruise of the Coast Guard cutter *Tampa*.

37. Memorandum from Henry Croyle, Commanding Officer, to Commandant, May 10, 1920, pp. 1, 9, folder "Commandant's Memoranda, 1925–1930," box 37, USCGID.

38. Notes on the General Situation, Week Ending 1 November 1924, folder August 30, 1924–August 29, 1925, and Week Ending 20 August 1926, p. 4, folder June 11, 1926–October 22, 1926, box 68, USCGID.

39. Shepherd, "Rum Runner's New Enemy," 5.

40. Memorandum from R. B. Adams to Commander Root, May 10, 1929, folder "Florida Seizures," box 7, USCGID; "Wet Waves and Dry Enforcers," 40; letter to Commander Root from Shaw, June 22, 1926, p. 2, folder "Ft. Lauderdale Base 6," box 60, USCGID.

41. Memorandum (to file) by Charles S. Root, June 24, 1927, p. 2, and letter to Commander Root from J. H. Smith of the Department of Justice, Washington, D.C., December 13, 1928, folder "Florida Affairs — Confidential," box 9 (pt. 2), USCGID; memorandum from Captain William Wheeler to Commandant, 3 July 1928, p. 2, folder "Memoranda to Commandant, 1924–1932," box 37, USCGID.

42. Notes on the General Situation, Week Ending 23 January 1925, p. 5, folder August 30, 1924–August 29, 1925, box 68, and Week Ending 11 September 1925, p. 2, folder September 11, 1925–January 23, 1926, box 69, USCGID; Report from "London," p. 16, undated but probably 1930, folder "Florida Cases and Seizures, 1928–30," box 11, USCGID.

43. Notes on the General Situation, Week Ending 20 June 1925, p. 2; Week Ending 27 August 1926, pp. 2–3; and Week Ending 30 May 1925, p. 4, folder August 30, 1924–August 29, 1925, box 68, USCGID.

44. Notes on the General Situation, Week Ending 3 July 1925, p. 1, folder August 30, 1924–August 29, 1925, box 68, USCGID.

45. Notes on the General Situation, Week Ending 27 December 1924, p. 4, folder August 30, 1924–August 29, 1925, box 68, USCGID.

46. Notes on the General Situation, Week Ending 23 October 1925, p. 1, folder September 11, 1925–January 23, 1926, box 69, USCGID; Confidential Memorandum for Intelligence Files, January 4, 1929, box 87, USCGID; Notes on the General Situation, Week Ending 19 March 1925, p. 3, folder August 30, 1924–August 29, 1925, box 68, and Week Ending 9 October 1925, p. 5, folder September 11, 1925–January 23, 1926, box 69, USCGID.

47. Memorandum from T. S. Klinger to Commandant, May 23, 1930, box 11, USCGID; William J. Wheeler, Memorandum to Commandant, August 27, 1932, folder "Memoranda to Commandant, 1924–1932," box 36, USCGID.

48. Notes on the General Situation, Week Ending 11 April 1925, p. 1, folder August 30, 1924–August 29, 1925, box 68, USCGID.

49. Letter from William J. Wheeler to Captain H. G. Fisher, Mobile, August 24, 1931, folder "Commander Gulf Division," box 36, USCGID.

50. Notes on the General Situation, Week Ending 13 November 1925, pp. 1–2, folder September 11, 1925–January 23, 1926, box 69, USCGID; memo from Commandant F. C. Billard to Captain Wheeler, Gulf Division, 4 May 1931, folder "Operations Memoranda, 1926–1932," box 36, USCGID.

51. Memo to Commandant from John G. Berry, Commander of the Gulf Division, November 16, 1925, p. 3, folder "Florida East Coast Patrol," box 36, USCGID.

52. Memorandum from Commandant F. C. Billard to Assistant Attorney General Mabel Walker Willebrandt, February 2, 1927, folder "Ft. Lauderdale Base 6," box 60, USCGID; Notes on the General Situation, Week Ending 6 May 1927, p. 2, folder February 18, 1927–May 27, 1927, box 70, USCGID; copy of letter without signature from the Treasury to the Attorney General, 15 June 1926, and memorandum from Intelligence Officer to Commandant, June 7, 1926, pp. 7–8, folder "Ft. Lauderdale Base 6," box 60, USCGID. See also "A Frame Up," *Hialeah Herald*, May 28, 1926, and "Praeger Held after Raid in Fashionable Hotel Room," unnamed newspaper, May 25, 1926, included in folder "Ft. Lauderdale Base 6," box 60, USCGID.

53. Memorandum from Intelligence Officer to Commandant, June 7, 1926, p. 6, and

letter from Commander Lauriat to Charles Root, November 19, 1926, p. 3, folder "Ft. Lauderdale Base 6," box 60, USCGID.

54. Letter from Citizens of Golden Beach to Commander: Coast Guard Base 6, June 4, 1929, folder "Florida Seizures," box 7, USCGID; Notes on the General Situation, Week Ending 4 February 1927, p. 2, folder November 5, 1926–February 11, 1927, box 69, USCGID.

55. "Is It Law Enforcement?," *New York Herald Tribune*, June 2, 1925, clipping in Notes on the General Situation, folder August 30, 1924–August 29, 1925, box 68, USCGID; quote from an article in the *Washington Post*, April 15, 1929; Notes on the General Situation, Week Ending 12 April 1929, p. 2, folder March 16, 1928–June 20, 1929, box 71, USCGID.

56. "Enforcement Outrages," *Miami Herald*, December 17, 1926, p. 6, included in the folder "Ft. Lauderdale Base 6," box 60, USCGID; "Retail Merchants to Have Committee Probe Coast Guard Activity," *Ft. Lauderdale News*, July 2, 1926; "Coast Guards Condemned by Club's Report," *Ft. Lauderdale News*, July 7, 1926, clippings included in file. Commander C. G. Porcher gave his report of his attempt to calm tempers in a memo titled "Criticism of conduct of men at Base 6, July 3, 1926," folder "Ft. Lauderdale Base 6," box 60, USCGID.

57. Letter from P. W. Lauriat, Commander, Florida East Coast Patrol Area, to Commandant, December 18, 1926, and memorandum from Intelligence Officer to Commandant, June 7, 1926, p. 9, folder "Ft. Lauderdale Base 6," box 60; memo to Commandant from the Commander, Section Base 6, T. S. Klinger, concerning a clipping from the *Miami Daily News* published May 23, 1930, folder "Florida Cases and Seizures, 1928–30," box 11; and letter from "an Honest Fisherman to the Commandant, April 30, 1925," box 87, USCGID.

58. In these quotes, Root was relaying information from the chief of customs for the State of Florida, referred to only as Mr. Gorman in the memo. See memorandum from Charles S. Root, Intelligence Officer, to the Commandant, April 27, 1927, included in Notes on the General Situation, Week Ending 22 April 1927, folder February 18, 1927–March 9, 1928, box 70, USCGID.

59. Letter to Commander Charles Root from W. P. Hughes, Assistant U.S. Attorney for the Southern District of Florida, October 22, 1928, folder "Miscellaneous Data," box 48, USCGID.

60. Notes on the General Situation, Week Ending 24 September 1926, p. 1, folder June 11, 1926–October 22, 1926, box 68, USCGID.

61. Notes on the General Situation, Week Ending 8 July 1927, p. 1, folder August 26, 1927–November 25, 1927, box 70, USCGID.

62. Notes on the General Situation, Week Ending 17 June 1927, p. 1, folder June 3, 1927–August 12, 1927; Week Ending 27 May 1927, p. 4, folder February 18, 1927–May 27, 1927; and Week Ending 30 September 1927, p. 3, folder August 26, 1927–November 25, 1927, box 70; Notes on the General Situation, Week Ending 13 April 1928, p. 2,

folder April 13, 1928–June 22, 1928, box 71; letter from Charles Stevenson, Supervising Customs Agent, Tampa, to Commissioner of Customs, Washington, D.C., December 31, 1929, box 11; letter to Charles S. Root from "Jack" of Coast Guard in Ft. Lauderdale, Fla., June 12, 1930, folder "Florida Cases," box 11, all in USCGID.

63. Notes on the General Situation, Week Ending 29 August 1925, p. 1, and Week Ending 22 August 1925, p. 1, folder August 30, 1924–August 29, 1925, box 68; Week Ending 9 January 1926, p. 1, folder September 11, 1925–January 23, 1926, box 69; and Week Ending 7 December 1928, p. 3, folder November 16, 1928–January 4, 1929, box 71, all in USCGID.

64. John G. Berry to Charles Root, September 1, 1926, folder "Miscellaneous Data," box 49; letter to Commandant from F. J. Gorman, Coast Guard, Ft. Lauderdale, Fla., April 29, 1932, box 10; letter to Commandant from Commanding Officer, Naval Yard, Boston, Mass., May 10, 1930, folder "Commandant Memoranda Years 1925–1930," box 37, all in USCGID.

65. Letter from Roemer to Charles Root, June 14, 1929, folder "Florida Seizures," box 7, USCGID.

66. Letter to W. P. Hughes, United States Attorney, Tampa, from Charles Root, June 11, 1929, folder "Florida Seizures," box 7, USCGID.

67. Memorandum to File, Charles Root, June 24, 1927, folder "Florida Affairs—Confidential," box 9, USCGID.

68. Notes on the General Situation, Week Ending 30 May 1925, p. 4, folder August 30, 1924–August 29, 1925, box 68, USCGID.

Chapter Three

1. Letter from G. W. H deBelleville to American Consul, Havana, Cuba (directed to no person in particular), October 7, 1926, Diplomatic Posts Havana, vols. 162–77, DOS.

2. "The Rum Smuggling Situation in Habana, Cuba," by Charles F. Payne, Vice Consul in the American Consulate-General, Habana, undated, though subsequent correspondence indicates that the report was distributed around October 25, 1926, Diplomatic Posts Havana, vol. 191, DOS.

3. Letter from (illegible) for the Secretary of State to Carleton Bailey Hurst, November 11, 1926, Diplomatic Posts Havana, vol. 191, DOS.

4. "332 Foreign Ships Found in Rum Trade," *New York Times*, February 3, 1925.

5. Sturgis, "National Prohibition and International Law"; Dickinson, "Treaties for the Prevention of Smuggling"; Dickinson, "Supreme Court Interprets the Liquor Treaties."

6. Letter from J. N. O. Sargent, Attorney General, to the Secretary of State, October 16, 1925, Diplomatic Posts Havana, vol. 172, DOS.

7. Pérez, *Cuba under the Platt Amendment*; Whitney, *State and Revolution in Cuba*.

8. While the *Literary Digest* published a short article titled "Prohibitionist Intervention in Cuba" in its January 12, 1924, issue, far more common were articles like Marcosson's "Cuba Libre" and Payne's "Case of Cuba" in the *Saturday Evening Post* in 1927 and 1929, respectively, and Frank's "Ordeal of Cuba" in *Scribner's* in July 1931. None of these articles mentioned Prohibition or smuggling.

9. *La Discusion*, quoted in "Prohibitionist Intervention in Cuba," 19.

10. Memorandum from Peter del Valle to General L. C. Andrews, Assistant Secretary of the Treasury, Subject: Secret Report on the Activities of the Cuban Government, September 6, 1925, pp. 18, 19, folder "Cuba Volume 1, 2 of 2," box 64, USCGID.

11. This information comes from a report submitted to the chief intelligence officer of the Coast Guard from Henry Kime. His conclusions are reinforced by the published memoirs of Carleton Bailey Hurst, a consular official. See Hurst, *Arms above the Door*, 284–87.

12. Telegram from State Department, January 5, 1926, and telegram, January 20, 1926, Diplomatic Posts Havana, vol. 189, DOS.

13. "America and Cuba Sign Liquor Treaty," *New York Times*, March 5, 1926, 9; "Convention between the United States and Cuba for the Prevention of Smuggling Operations."

14. Payne, "Rum-Smuggling Situation in Cuba," p. 1, Diplomatic Posts Havana, vol. 191, DOS.

15. C. Hubert Jr. (signature somewhat illegible), Collector of Customs, Tampa, to Carleton Bailey Hurst, American Consul General, Havana, August 12, 1926, Diplomatic Posts Havana, vol. 172, DOS.

16. This was a name that Henry Kime, the leader of this group, devised in a sarcastic, mock-fiction account of their efforts in 1927.

17. Henry Kime to Charles Root, December 1, 1927, box 66, USCGID.

18. Root to Kime, June 28, 1926, box 67, USCGID.

19. Letter from George P. Waller, American Consul, La Ceiba, Honduras, to the Secretary of State, January 8, 1925, folder "Cuba Report 1925, Reference c," box 64, USCGID.

20. The account of Salvado Pena's voyage on the *Varuna* appears in a report that he submitted to Kime and that was forwarded to officials in Washington, D.C., dated March 1, 1926, in box 67, USCGID. While the box label and file folder indicate the reports were submitted by William Kelly, the folder contains reports written by Henry Kime. William Kelly's reports, which describe his activities in Miami, are in box 66.

21. The seizure of the *Varuna*, along with 1,000 cases of assorted liquors, was reported in Notes on the General Situation, Week Ending 23 January 1926, folder September 11, 1925–January 23, 1926, box 69, USCGID.

22. The papers were copied from Cuban authorities in June 1926. See Kime to Root, June 4, 8, 1926, box 67, USCGID.

23. Root to Kime, March 30, 1926, box 67, USCGID.

24. Kime to Root, June 25, 1926, box 67, USCGID.

25. Kime to Root, July 30, 1926, box 67, USCGID.

26. Report of Fraudulent Health Bills and Manifests, September 16, 1926, box 67, USCGID.

27. Kime to Root, August 30, 1926, box 67, USCGID.

28. Kime to Root, August 30, 1926, box 67, USCGID.

29. Kime to Root, October 11, 1926, and January 5, 1927, box 68, USCGID.

30. Root to Kime, September 29, 1926, box 67, USCGID.

31. Kime to Root, October 22, 1926, box 68, USCGID.

32. Kime to Root, June 2, 1926, box 67; Kime to Root, January 5, 1927, box 68; Root to Kime, June 8, 1926, box 67; Kime to Root, August 30, June 30, July 18, 1927, box 68, USCGID.

33. Kime to Root, October 9, 1926, box 68, USCGID. Kime stated that Pena was "treated like a monkey in Mobile" by U.S. officials; see Kime to Root, December 13, 1926, and March 3, 1927, and Root to Kime, July 19, 1927, box 68, USCGID.

34. Kime to Root, December 15, 1927, box 66, USCGID.

35. Kime to Root, November 22, 1926, box 68, USCGID.

36. Kime to Root, February 15, 1, 1926, box 67, USCGID.

37. Kime to Root, May 21, 1926, and Root to Kime, May 25, 1926, box 67, USCGID.

38. Root to Kime, November 8, 1927, box 66, USCGID.

39. Kime to Root, April 20, May 18, 1926, box 67, USCGID.

40. Kime to Root, October 9, 1926, box 68, USCGID.

41. Kime to Root, October 9, 1926, and January 11, 1927, box 68 USCGID.

42. Root to Kime, June 21, 1927, box 68, USCGID.

43. Letter from A. B. Burns, Chief of Intelligence, U.S. Maritime Secret Police, to Kime, September 15, 1926, and Kime to Root, August 30, June 15, 1926, box 67, USCGID.

44. Root to Kime, May 25, 1926, box 67, and Root to Kime, October 5, 1926, box 68, USCGID.

45. Root to Kime, August 10, 1926, box 67, USCGID.

46. Kime to Root, August 6, 1926, box 67, and December 15, 1927, box 66, USCGID. See, for example, Kime's correspondence to Root on August 6 and 14, 1927, box 67; Kime to Root, February 7, 1927, box 68; and Kime to Root, July 6, 1926, box 67, USCGID.

47. Kime to Root, May 11, 1926, box 67, USCGID.

48. Kime to Root, August 29, 1927, and Root to Kime, August 25, 1927, box 68, USCGID.

49. Kime to Root, March 21, 1927, box 68, USCGID.

50. Kime to Root, May 18, 1927, box 68; Root to Kime, October 2, 1927, box 68, and July 22, 1927, box 67; Root to Kime September, 9, 1927, box 68, USCGID.

51. Kime to Root, February 3, August 11, May 30, 1927, and Root to Kime, July 29, 1927, box 68, USCGID.

52. Mowry, "Listening to the Rumrunners"; Root to Kime, July 29, 1927, box 68, USCGID.

53. Kime to Root, August 11, 1927, box 68, USCGID.

54. Kime to Root, December 8, 1927, box 66, USCGID.

55. Kime to Root, July 20, 1926, box 67; Root to Kime, July 19, 1927, box 68; Kime to Root, June 27, 1927, box 68; and Root to Kime, August 26, 1927, box 68, USCGID.

56. Kime to Root, November 17, October 31, 1927, box 66, USCGID.

57. Root to Kime, July 16, 1926, box 67, USCGID.

58. Root to Kime, November 26, 1927, box 66, USCGID.

59. Kime to Root, June 12, 23, August 18, September 18, 1927, box 68, USCGID.

60. Root to Kime, May 25, 1926, box 67, USCGID.

61. Root to Kime, August 31, July 20, 1926, and Kime to Root, August 3, 1926, box 67, USCGID.

62. Kime to Root, October 10, 1927, box 66; Root to Kime, October 6–14, 1927 (can't read dates), box 66; Kime to Root, September 20, 1926, box 67, USCGID.

63. Kime to Root, July 25, 1927, box 68, USCGID.

64. Kime to Root, January 5, 1926, box 67, USCGID.

65. Kime to Root, June 30, 1927, box 68, USCGID.

66. Kime to Root, July 7, 1927, box 68, USCGID.

67. Kime to Root, July 7, 1927, box 68, USCGID.

68. Kime to Root, September 5, 1927, no. 2 (Kime wrote two letters to Root on this date), box 68; Root to Kime, December 16, 1927, and Kime to Root, December 5, 1927, box 66, USCGID.

69. Pérez, *Cuba under the Platt Amendment*, 257–89. Discussion of Prohibition and the treaty with Cuba does not appear in General Enoch Crowder's papers other than in a mention of General Andrews's visit to Havana to discuss terms of the treaty in January 1925. Crowder's correspondence does show recognition of access to liquor in Cuba. An acquaintance from New York jokingly asked if there was any way he could "radio us up a daiquiri" (letter from Teressa Schultze to General Crowder, February 22, 1925, Papers of General Enoch Crowder, reel 11, University of Missouri, Columbia; I examined folders 259–425 of the Crowder papers).

70. Kime to Root, May 12, 1927, box 68, USCGID.

71. Kime to Root, November 30, 1926. box 68, USCGID. Cuba was a main source of imported grapefruit for the United States. See Deere, "Here Come the Yankees!," 757–59.

72. Kime to Root, November 24, 28, 1927, box 66, and Kime to Root, September 1, 1927, box 68, USCGID.

73. Kime to Root, August 22, 25, 1927, box 68, USCGID.

74. Kime to Root, December 19, 1927, box 66, USCGID.

75. Copies of telegrams concerning Capone's visit to Havana, April 29–May 1, 1930, folder "Correspondence Relating to individuals, Rum-Running Era, 1926–32," box 55, USCGID.

76. Root to Kim, December 12, 1927, and Kime to Root, December 19, 1927, box 66, USCGID.

77. Letter from Wilbur Carr for Secretary of State to Leo J. Keena, American Consul General, May 14, 1929, Consular Posts, Havana, Cuba, vol. 581, DOS; "Resume of Salient Points Contained in an Article in *Informacion*," March 2, 1930, vol. 611, DOS.

78. "Revised List of Foreign Vessels Suspected of Being Engaged in the Smuggling of Liquor into the United States," January 1930, Records of Foreign Service Posts, Havana, Cuba, vol. 595, DOS.

Chapter Four

1. *US v. Chester Wing*, Case 95, Northern District of Florida, Pensacola, USDCSE.

2. *Atlanta Constitution*, June 29, 1923; this followed the article "Alien Smuggling Charged to Ships in Liquor Fleet," *Atlanta Constitution*, June 18, 1923.

3. "Frustrate Attempt to Bring in Chinese," *New Smyrna (Fla.) Daily News*, August 19, 1921.

4. From Thomas J. Dublin, Customs Agent in Charge, Tampa, Florida, to the Director, Special Agency Service, U.S. Customs Service, undated but probably 1925, folder "Miscellaneous Data, 1923–1925," box 46, USCGID.

5. Oakley, "Prohibition Law and the Political Machine," 171.

6. See Okrent, *Last Call*, 236–38; Burns, *Spirits of America*, 174–76; and Pegram, *Battling Demon Rum*, 32–33, 138–39.

7. Panunzio, "Foreign Born and Prohibition." Lisa McGirr makes a persuasive case that zealous enforcement of Prohibition against immigrant groups pushed them toward the Democratic party, which represents one of the most significant legacies of Prohibition in American political culture. See McGirr, *War on Alcohol*.

8. Numerous cases appeared in federal courts, yet prosecution was never certain, nor was conviction. Most convicted smugglers received approximately a year in federal prison or lesser penalties, including fines and confiscation of watercraft, which rarely discouraged smugglers for long.

9. Daniels, *Guarding the Golden Door*; Cannato, *American Passage*; Ngai, *Impossible Subjects*.

10. "Smuggling Aliens into the U.S.A.," *Washington Post*, September 14, 1924.

11. Lee, "Enforcing the Borders"; Ngai, *Impossible Subjects*, 127–66; Ngai, "Strange Career of the Illegal Alien."

12. Sáenz Rovner, *Cuban Connection*.

13. Corbitt, "Immigration in Cuba," 304; de la Fuente, "Two Dangers, One Solution."

14. Memorandum from Peter del Valle to General L. C. Andrews, Assistant Secretary of the Treasury, Subject: Secret Report on the Activities of the Cuban Government, September 6, 1925, pp. 3–5, folder "Cuba Volume 1, 2 of 2," box 64, USCGID.

15. Kula, "Those Who Failed to Reach the United States," 19.

16. *US v. Frank Parker et al.*, Case 1526, Southern District of Florida, Tampa, USDCSE. Statements of residence appear on pp. 26, 2, 14, and 20 of the transcript.

17. Report of Inspector Feri F. Weiss and Inspector Joseph D. Mitchell in re: Cuban Smugglers, April 4, 1925, pp. 1–2, folder "Habana Counsel," box 68, USCGID.

18. Carleton Bailey Hurst to Secretary of State, December 26, 1924, vol. 519, DOS; "Alien Smuggling Adds to Profits of Rum Row Ships," *Atlanta Constitution*, July 25, 1924; "Smuggling Aliens into the U.S.A.," *Washington Post*, September 14, 1924; "Describes War on Alien Smuggling," *New York Times*, June 30, 1925; letter from William A. Whalen, Inspector in Charge, to Immigration Service, Jacksonville, Fla., July 7, 1921, Case No. 55166/31, INS; Report to Commissioner-General of Immigration, Department of Labor, Washington, D.C., from Thomas Kirk, District Director of Jacksonville, Florida, January 16, 1926, Case No. 55396/10, INS.

19. Memorandum to Division of Foreign Control, September 4, 1928, folder "John Amoros Bastre," box 63, USCGID.

20. Report by Agent 1001, pp. 3, 1, respectively, folder "Cuba Report 1925, Reference d," box 64, USCGID.

21. Letter from G. H. Hilldreth Jr., Collector, U.S. Customs Service, Tampa, Fla., to W. W. Gober, U.S. Attorney, Jacksonville, Fla., March 2, 1925, folder "Miscellaneous Data, 1923–1925," box 46, USCGID.

22. Testimony of J. W. Fredericy, in *US v. Danton Claramunt and J. W. Fredericy*, Case 1664, Southern District of Florida, Tampa, USDCSE.

23. The following description of smuggling operations is taken from the report of Feri F. Weiss and Inspector Joseph D. Mitchell to the Hon. W. W. Husband, Commissioner General of Immigration, Washington, D.C., April 4, 1925, folder "Habana Counsel," box 68, USCGID.

24. The relative success of immigrant smuggling varied over time in response to law enforcement efforts. Officials, for example, were becoming increasingly confident that they had shut down many operations in 1926, only to note in 1929 that the industry was once again thriving. They also acknowledged that ending operations in one area, either in Cuba or along Florida's coast, often merely pushed the activity to another area.

25. Memorandum from Bureau of Customs, Tampa, September 1, 1927, folder "Alien Smuggling Information," box 50, USCGID.

26. Report of Inspector Feri F. Weiss and Inspector Joseph D. Mitchell in re: Cuban Smugglers, April 4, 1925, p. 12, folder "Habana Counsel," box 68, USCGID.

27. *US v. Magil Estevez et al.*, Cases 519, 580, and 581, Southern District of Florida, Tampa, USDCSE.

28. Sworn Statement of Thomas Howard to Immigrant Inspector Isaac L. Smight at Miami, Fla., October 9, 1931, American Consular Posts, Havana, Cuba, vol. 611, DOS.

29. Henry Kime on Mariam Speiss, September 11, 1925, and Report of Agent 1002 (Grumbert), folder "Cuba Report 1925, Reference e," box 64 USCGID.

30. An international traffic in impoverished Eastern European women to the Americas for prostitution began in the 1860s. See Vincent, *Bodies and Souls*, and Guy, *Sex and Danger in Buenos Aires*.

31. Henry Kime on Mariam Speiss, September 11, 1925, and Report of Agent 1002 (Grumbert), folder "Cuba Report 1925, Reference e," box 64, USCGID.

32. Letter from Olga to her sister, June 26, 1925, folder "Cuba Report 1925, Reference e," box 64, USCGID.

33. Kime to Root, July 14, 1927, box 68, USCGID.

34. Henry Kime on Mariam Speiss, September 11, 1925, and Report of Agent 1002 (Grumbert), folder "Cuba Report 1925, Reference e," box 64, USCGID.

35. Letter to Commander from Bill (William Kelly, Prohibition agent in Miami) to Commander Root, undated (probably December 1928), folder "William Kelly's Reports," box 66, USCGID.

36. Report from Agent 1002 (who worked under Kime), box 67, USCGID.

37. Letter from Williamson S. Howell Jr., Charge d'Affaires, Havana, Cuba, to the Secretary of State, January 8, 1923, Case No. 55166/31-B, INS.

38. Report "Smuggling of Aliens and Narcotics through Cuba," Bureau File No. 39–48, p. 2, unsigned and undated, Case No. 55166/31-A, INS.

39. Affidavit of Jim Glico, November 23, 1926, taken in Attorney General's Chamber, Nassau, Bahamas, folder "Alien Smuggling Information, 1928–41," box 50, USCGID.

40. See, for example, letter to Commissioner-General of Immigration, Department of Labor, from Thomas Kirk, District Director, June 7, 1924, Case No. 55396/10, INS.

41. Report from Immigrant Inspector of New Orleans (signature unclear) to Commissioner of Immigration, New Orleans, February 27, 1923, p. 2, Case No. 55166/31-B, INS.

42. Note for Files, August 25, 1927, folder, "Alien Clean-Up — Cuba," box 60, USCGID.

43. Memorandum to Division of Foreign Control, April 30, 1927, Case No. 55166/31-I, INS.

44. Memorandum to Division of Foreign Control, August 22, 1927, folder "Alien Clean-Up — Cuba," box 60, USCGID.

45. Memorandum to Division of Foreign Control, January 9, 1928, folder "Alien Smuggling Information, 1928–41," box 50, USCGID.

46. Memorandum for Intelligence Files, August 14, 1928, folder "Alien Smuggling Information, 1928–41," box 50, USCGID.

47. Report by Agent 1001, pp. 3, 1, respectively, folder "Cuba Report 1925, Reference d," box 64, USCGID.

48. Captain Peter del Valle, Secret Diary, pp. 6, 8–9, Cuba Report 1925, folder "Cuba Volume 1, 1 of 2," box 64, USCGID.

49. Letter from Isaac Smith, Inspector in Charge, Miami, to Inspector in Charge, Jacksonville, Fla., May 11, 1922, and "Smuggling of Aliens and Narcotics through Cuba," Bureau File No. 39-48, p. 2, unsigned and undated, Case No. 55166/31-A, INS.

50. "Report," undated, probably 1924, vol. 519, DOS.

51. Unsigned, undated report, p. 2, Case No. 55166/31-A, INS.

52. Letter to Mr. I. F. Wixon, Deputy Commissioner, INS, from James E. Maker and Harry A. Ritzke, INS Ellis Island, November 30, 1936, Case No. 55607/457, INS.

53. "Appearance of Typhus at Any Point Is Feared," *Anniston Star*, February 19, 1921; Young, "Breaking into the United States," 55; Creel, "Melting Pot or Dumping Ground"; Creel, "Close the Gates!"

54. Young, "Breaking into the United States."

55. Curran, "Smuggling Aliens," 12.

56. *US v. Sotirios Targakis*, Case 1173, p. 14 of trial transcript, Southern District of Florida, Tampa, USDCSE.

57. *US v. Sotirios Targakis*, Case 1173, pp. 11, 18 of trial transcript, Southern District of Florida, Tampa, USDCSE.

58. *US v. Tom Koronas*, Case 1410, pp. 8–10 of trial transcript, Southern District of Florida, Tampa, USDCSE.

59. *US v. John Middleton*, Case 342, and *US v. Armando Alfonso*, Case 438, Southern District of Florida, Key West, USDCSE.

60. Report of Inspector Feri F. Weiss and Inspector Joseph D. Mitchell in re: Cuban Smugglers, April 4, 1925, p. 20, folder "Habana Counsel," box 68, USCGID.

61. *US v. Sotirios Targakis*, Case 1173, p. 25 of trial transcript, Southern District of Florida, Tampa, USDCSE.

62. "Big Swindles Bared in Alien Smuggling," *New York Times*, June 29, 1925; "Hoax Defrauds Aliens Seeking Entry into US," clipping dated December 15, 1926, folder "Alien Smuggling Information, 1928–41," box 50, USCGID.

63. Coast Guard files contain clippings from newspapers in both the United States and Cuba reporting the murder of illegal aliens. They also include memos reporting murders as part of their information on suspected smugglers. See *Havana Post*, October 14, 1927, and *La Prensa*, September 15, 1927, folder "Alien Clean-Up — Cuba," box 60, USCGID. See also "Report 17 Chinese Slain," *New York Times*, January 20, 1927. The murder of would-be immigrants by a smuggler also figures in the plot of Ernest Hemingway's novel *To Have and Have Not*.

64. Report of Inspector Feri F. Weiss and Inspector Joseph D. Mitchell in re: Cuban Smugglers, March 16, 1925, p. 2, folder "Habana Counsel," box 68, USCGID.

65. Letter from Assistant Commissioner Joseph H. Wallis to Commissioner of Immigration, New Orleans, March 14, 1933, Case No. 55166/31-B, INS. For discussion of Chinese individuals using the American railroad system to transit through the

country, see "Smuggling Aliens and Narcotics through Cuba, June 28, 1922," p. 5, Case No. 55166/31-B, INS.

66. Letter from Thomas Kirk, Inspector in Charge, Jacksonville, to Commissioner-General of Immigration, May 10, 1922, Case No. 55166/31, INS.

67. "Smuggling Activities in State Held Low Despite Growth of Florida Cities," undated clipping, Case No. 55396/10, INS.

68. Letter from Thomas Kirk, District Director, Immigration Service, Jacksonville, to Commissioner General of Immigration, July 30, 1925, Case No. 55396/10, INS.

69. Report from Immigrant Inspector of New Orleans (signature unclear) to Commissioner of Immigration, New Orleans, February 27, 1923, p. 1, Case No. 55166/31-B, INS.

70. Mohlman, "Anclote Keys Lighthouse," 167–69; Glover, "Lebanese, Italian, and Slavic Immigrant Women in Metropolitan Birmingham."

71. Letter from A. G. Watson Jr., Acting Collector, U.S. Customs Service, Tampa, to the Secretary of the Treasury, October 16, 1924, p. 4, folder "Miscellaneous Data 1923–1925," box 46, USCID.

72. Letter to President Warren G. Harding from B. Yorkstone Hogg, September 19, 1921, and forwarded on to the INS, Case No. 55166/31-A, INS.

73. Dr. C. E. Berkshire to INS, December 19, 1922, Case No. 55166/31-73, and H. Gross to the INS, October 8, 1923, INS.

74. US v. Sotirios Targakis, Case 1173, pp. 30, 32 of trial transcript, Southern District of Florida, Tampa, USDCSE.

75. Letter from K. Hughes (signature illegible), Commissioner of Immigration, Philadelphia, to Commissioner-General of Immigration, August 11, 1922, Case No. 55166/31, INS.

76. See memorandum from Commanding Officer TALLAPOOSA to Commander, Gulf Division, November 1, 1924, folder "TALLAPOOSA," box 82, USCGID; also letter from A. G. Watson Jr., Acting Collector, U.S. Customs Service, Tampa, to the Secretary of the Treasury, October 16, 1924, p. 3, folder "Miscellaneous Data 1923–1925," box 46, USCGID.

77. Courtwright, Forces of Habit, 171–73.

78. Acker, "Portrait of an Addicted Family"; Hickman, "Double Meaning of Addiction."

79. Vhynanek, "Illegal Drugs in New Orleans during the 1920s."

80. Schmeckebier, Bureau of Prohibition, 136–45; Kinder, "Bureaucratic Cold Warrior"; Kinder and Walker, "Stable Force in a Storm"; McWilliams, "Unsung Partner against Crime," 215–16.

81. Kime to Root, July 27, 1926, box 67, USCGID.

82. Captain Peter del Valle, Secret Diary, pp. 9–12, Cuba Report 1925, folder "Cuba Volume 1, 1 of 2," and "Secret Report on the Activities of the Cuban Government," p. 14, folder "Cuba Volume 1, 2 of 2," box 64, USCGID.

83. Kime to Root, October 6, 1927, box 66, USCGID.

84. Report of Agent 1005, July 27, 1925 (second page), folder "Cuba Report 1925, Reference g," box 64, USCGID.

85. Memorandum for Intelligence file, June 20, 1930, folder "Florida Cases and Seizures, 1928–30," box 11, USCGID.

86. Memorandum from Peter del Valle to General L. C. Andrews, Assistant Secretary of the Treasury, Subject: Secret Report on the Activities of the Cuban Government, September 6, 1925, pp. 12–15, folder "Cuba Volume 1, 2 of 2," box 64, USCGID.

87. Captain Peter del Valle, Secret Diary, p. 1, Cuba Report 1925, folder "Cuba Volume 1, 1 of 2," and Memorandum from Peter del Valle to General L. C. Andrews, Assistant Secretary of the Treasury, Subject: Secret Report on the Activities of the Cuban Government, September 6, 1925, p. 12, folder "Cuba Volume 1, 2 of 2," box 64, USCGID.

88. Memorandum from Peter del Valle to General L. C. Andrews, Assistant Secretary of the Treasury, Subject: Secret Report on the Activities of the Cuban Government, September 6, 1925, pp. 13, 14, 15, folder "Cuba Volume 1, 2 of 2," box 64, USCGID.

89. Kime to Root, August 22, 1927, box 68, USCGID.

90. Kime to Root, September 5, 1927, box 68, USCGID.

91. Kime to Root, August 18, 1927, box 68, USCGID.

92. Kime to Root, August 15, 1927, box 68, USCGID.

93. Kime to Root, July 25, 1927, box 68, USCGID.

94. Kime to Root, August 18, 1927, and Kime to Harry J. Anslinger, August 29, 1927, box 68, USCGID.

95. Kime to Root, August 29, 1927, box 68, USCGID.

96. Root to Kime, October 11, 1927, box 66, USCGID.

97. Root to Kime, responding to Kime's letter of October 6, 1927, 11 October 1927, box 66, USCGID.

Chapter Five

1. Letter, signature illegible, from Portland, Maine, November 28, 1929, folder 2, carton 58, SAF.

2. *Miami Life*, April 16, 1927, and "Coast Guardsmen to Face Prosecution in Yachtman's Death," *Miami Daily News*, April 16, 1927 (clippings in folder "Florida Affairs," box 9, USCGID); *Miami Daily News*, March 1, 1926. James A. Carter briefly covers the killing of Red Shannon in his M.A. thesis, "Florida and Rum Running during Prohibition," 22–24. See also Notes on the General Situation, Week Ending 6 May 1927, p. 2, folder February 18, 1927–May 27, 1927, box 70, USCGID.

3. "In Honor of the Bootlegger," *Miami Life*, April 16, 1927 (reprinted from February 27, 1926, as indicated by typed notation by Charles Root at top of clipping) (clipping in folder "Florida Affairs," box 9, USCGID).

4. Okrent, *Last Call*, 132–34; Kobler, *Ardent Spirits*, 274–75.

5. "The Truth about Prohibition," *Washington Post*, September 13, 1925.

6. "Haynes to Be 'Right Arm' Andrews Says," *Washington Post*, August 7, 1925; "Andrews Takes Haynes' Mop Job away from Him," *Chicago Tribute*, July 4, 1925; "Haynes Shorn of Powers by Blair's Order," *Mobile Register*, August 8, 1925. See also Sinclair, *Era of Excess*, 185–86.

7. "West Pointer Is Face of Drive on Rum," *New York Times*, April 19, 1925.

8. "Andrews Stops Dry Propaganda," *New York Times*, July 8, 1925; "Andrews Dry Drive Program Hits Snag," *Baltimore Sun*, July 9, 1925; "The Truth about Prohibition," *Washington Post*, September 13, 1925. On the veneration of business in the 1920s, see Allen, *Only Yesterday*, 146–54.

9. "The Truth about Prohibition," *New York Times*, September 13, 1925.

10. "Dry Enforcement Enters Its Fourth Phase," *New York Times*, May 8, 1927; "Politics Holds Up Naming of Dry Officials," *Mobile Register*, July 16, 1925. See also Schmeckebier, *Bureau of Prohibition*, 50–51, and "Prohibition Officials to Lose Jobs in Reorg," *Mobile Register*, July 19, 1925.

11. "Dry Enforcement Plan Indefinitely Postponed," *Mobile Register*, July 25, 1925; "Andrews Dry Quiz Plan Hit," *Mobile Register*, March 2, 1926.

12. "Dry Proposals of General Andrews Soundly Flayed," *Mobile Register*, March 3, 1926; "Andrews Concedes Charges," *Mobile Register*, April 7, 1926; "Consider Andrews Removal," *Mobile Register*, April 17, 1926; "Andrews Reply Denies Rumors of Resignation," *Christian Science Monitor*, May 17, 1927; "Wheeler out to Get Andrews," *Washington Post*, May 5, 1927.

13. "New Prohibition Chief Seeks an Honest Staff," *New York Times*, August 7, 1927; "Lowman to Become US Dry Czar Today," *Baltimore Sun*, August 1, 1927; "New Generals in the War on Rum," 10; "Dry Program to Be Sound, Says Lowman," *Anniston Star*, December 24, 1927; "New Prohibition Chief Seeks an Honest Staff," *New York Times*, August 7, 1927.

14. "Dry Enforcement Enters Fourth Phase," *New York Times*, May 8, 1927.

15. Charles Merz notes that 875 agents had been relieved of duties between 1920 and 1926. With an estimated 10,000 men serving in the role of Prohibition agent during that time, Merz argues that 1 in 12 agents were fired; see *Dry Decade*, 162–63. Schmeckebier identifies 752 agents dismissed in that same period; see *Bureau of Prohibition*, 52. See also "Graft Rampant in the Dry Forces," 10; "Gag Rule Used on Dry Chief," *Mobile Register*, September 12, 1927; "Dry Service Crooks Face Loss of Jobs," *Mobile Register*, September 10, 1927.

16. A total of 12,436 persons took the first exam; only 4,505 passed with a score of 60 or higher. Some analysts claimed that so many failed because they did not take the test seriously, considering it little more than a formality. See Schmeckebier, *Bureau of Prohibition*, 56–57; "State Prohibition Work Hit Hard by Severe Quiz," *Mobile Register*, January 13, 1928; and Turner, "Notes of a Prohibition Agent," 391–92.

17. "Dry Force Is Wrecked by New Act," *Mobile Register*, January 14, 1927.

18. "Dry Army Asks for Fighters," *Mobile Register*, January 7, 1928. According to Schmeckebier, there were no questions on spelling or arithmetic, and spelling and grammar were not considered in grading written responses; see *Bureau of Prohibition*, 56.

19. "Andrews to Divide Dry Enforcement Work with States," *Washington Post*, September 22, 1925.

20. "Radical Change Made in Dry Enforcement Plans; Small Fry in Liquor Trade Left to Police," *Mobile Register*, August 23, 1925. See also "Andrews Names Chiefs for New Prohibition Army," *Mobile Register*, August 22, 1925; "Prohibition Gains, Andrews Declares," *New York Times*, September 25, 1926; "Would Augment Prison Sentence for Bootlegger," *Mobile Register*, January 23, 1928; "Modification of Dry Law Suggested by Wickersham, if States Aid Enforcement," *Mobile Register*, July 7, 1929.

21. See Brindley, *Prohibition Survey of Alabama*, 19; Brindley, *Prohibition Survey of Mississippi*, 640; and Buckley, *Prohibition Survey of Louisiana*, 536.

22. Buckley, *Prohibition Survey of Florida*, 106.

23. Letter from W. T. Day, Deputy Prohibition Administrator, to R. E. Tuttle, Prohibition Administrator, September 20, 1927, box 55, Correspondence of the Other Offices and Division of the Bureau, IRS.

24. Memo from W. J. Harmon, Customs Agent, undated, folder "Miscellaneous Data," box 47, USCGID.

25. Letter from B. A. Crumbie to Governor Carlton, July 29, 1929, folder 10, carton 54, SAF.

26. Merz, *Dry Decade*, 35, 20–23, 211; Sinclair, *Era of Excess*, 155, 391.

27. Carmer, *Stars Fell on Alabama*, 12–17, quote on 17; Cash, *Mind of the South*, 227–28. For drinking in southern culture, see Ownby, *Subduing Satan*, and Coker, *Liquor in the Land of the Lost Cause*. See also Sinclair, *Era of Excess*, 32.

28. Lewis, *Coming of Southern Prohibition*; Willis, *Southern Prohibition*; Stewart, *Moonshiners and Prohibitionists*.

29. Rutledge, "Prohibition and the Negro," 123, 124. On Prohibition as a means of racial control, see Coker, *Liquor in the Land of the Lost Cause*, 123–74. Andrew Sinclair also makes this point in his discussion of the "psychology" of Prohibition; see Sinclair, *Era of Excess*, 29–32. Sociological studies of the South also noted white attitudes toward drinking by African Americans. See Johnson, *Shadow of the Plantation*, 5, 182, and Davis, Gardner, and Gardner, *Deep South*, 20, 522.

30. Cason, *Ninety Degrees in the Shade*, 57; Derieux, "Old Times Dar Are Not Forgotten," 9, 38.

31. Magill, "New Orleans during Prohibition," xii–xiii.

32. "Million in Booze Seized in Orleans Coast Raids," *Mobile Register*, August 12, 1925.

33. "Federal Liquor Squad Mopping Up New Orleans," *Mobile Register*, May 6, 1928.

34. "Federal Agents Clean Orleans' 'Raidproof' Clubs," *Mobile Register*, July 14, 1928.

35. See *US v. Alfred L. Staples et al.*, Case 6180, p. 86 of trial transcript, Southern District of Alabama, Mobile, box 101, folders 1, 2, 3, USDCSE.

36. "Arraign Ships' Men on Liquor Charge," *Mobile Register*, July 9, 1924.

37. "Rum Schooner Is Towed into Port by Cutter Saukee," *Mobile Register*, April 27, 1925; "Varied Cargo of Liquors Removed," *Mobile Register*, April 30, 1925; "Rum Boat Cargo May Be Brought into Port Mobile," *Mobile Register*, July 23, 1925; "Wanderer Cargo Added to Stock of Liquor Here," *Mobile Register*, August 8, 1925.

38. Reports of Michael Guillera, O. D. Beard, Correspondence and Reports regarding Prohibition, box 1, MBC.

39. Reports of W. H. Barton, Correspondence and Reports regarding Prohibition, box 1, MBC.

40. *US v. E. O. Weimer*, Case 1619, Southern District of Florida, Miami, USDCSE; "Hot Dog Changed to Bloodhound Sleuth for Prohibition Officers," *Anniston Star*, June 4, 1925.

41. Cooley, *To Live and Dine in Dixie*, 69.

42. *US v. Pauline Nunnally*, Case 2402, Southern District of Georgia, Savannah, USDCSE; *US v. Bertha Bly and Virginia Raspberry*, Case 777, and *US v. Mabel Matthews*, Case 794, Southern District of Florida, Tampa, USDCSE.

43. Entry numbers 6725 and 6726, Warden's Dockets, Ensley Prison, June 1, 1926–October 21, 1928, BPL. Both Salina and Cleveland lived at the same address. The Warden's Docket books record arrests in Birmingham, listing the date, time, name, address, arresting officer, race, charge, and disposition of the case.

44. "Women Bootleggers a Problem," 46.

45. *US v. Francisco Fleitas*, Case 316, pp. 2–3 of trial transcript, Southern District of Florida, Key West, USDCSE.

46. "Andrews Concedes Charges," *Mobile Register*, April 7, 1926; "Prohibition Director Woodcock," *Biloxi Daily Herald*, September 7, 1931; "Dry Agent Cannot Consume Whiskey to Get Evidence," *Thomasville Times-Enterprise*, September 4, 1931.

47. "Alcohol Cargo Unloaded Here after Seizure," *Mobile Register*, September 16, 1927.

48. Letter to Honorable B. E. Dyson from Andrew Lopez, Deputy U.S. Marshal, Key West, July 23, 1925, folder 1925 — Letters, Telegrams Sent to Department of Justice, USMSKW.

49. Letter to the Honorable B. E. Dyson, U.S. Marshal, Jacksonville, Fla., from Andrew Lopez, Deputy U.S. Marshal, Key West, December 9, 1925, folder 1925 — Letters, Telegrams Sent to Department of Justice, USMSKW.

50. Telegram to Dyson, U.S. Marshal, Jacksonville, from Lopez, December 12 (or 14 or 22 — date written over), folder 1925 — Letters, Telegrams Sent to Department of Justice, USMSKW.

51. Petition for Destruction of Liquor to the Honorable Lake Jones, Southern

District of Florida, from Collector of Customs, District no. 18, August 23, 1926, *US v. Roger E. Wilson et al.*, Case 696, Southern District of Florida, Miami, box 13, USDCSE.

52. "A Severe Dry Agent," *Biloxi Daily Herald*, April 15, 1925; Circular No. 1548 to United States Attorneys and Marshals, September 9, 1924, folder 1921–1924 Circulars from Dept. Of Justice, Washington, USMSKW; "Seizure of Evidence Is Ordered Ended," *Mobile Register*, January 22, 1928.

53. Cooley, *To Live and Dine in Dixie*, 43–55.

54. Preston, *Dirt Roads to Dixie*, 136–38, 150–51.

55. Letter from H. P. Campbell dated February 11, 1929, folder 1, carton 12; letter dated July 12, 1929, folder 7, carton 26; and affidavit from Mrs. Ella Chafin, November 7, 1932, folder 106, carton 35, SAF.

56. Merz, *Dry Decade*, 159–63; Turner, "Notes of a Prohibition Agent," 386–87; Mandeville, "Can a Prohibition Agent Be Honest?," 174–75; Sanders, "Delivering Demon Rum," 94. On the higher numbers of crooked local officials, see Howington, "John Barleycorn Subdued."

57. Survey of the Tenth Prohibition District, which Comprises the States of Alabama, Louisiana, Mississippi, and the Northern District of Florida, Research Material for the Report on Federal Prohibition Enforcement, Staff Committee on Prohibition, box 199, NCLOE.

58. "Net Is Woven around Cohen," *Biloxi Daily Herald*, December 27, 1925.

59. Green, "What Price Bribery?," 29.

60. Memo from C. F. Hughes, Chief of Naval Operations, to Commandant of the Coast Guard, March 28, 1929, folder "Florida Seizures," box 7, USCGID.

61. Details of Courtney's protection racket were described by Bill Kelly in a communication with Commander Root, "Special Agent William Kelly's Reports, 1925–1927," box 66, USCGID, and in *US v. Joseph E. Courtney*, Case 1436, Southern District of Florida, Miami, USDCSE. See also "Former Miami Dry Chief Arrested," *New York Times*, November 29, 1927, and "Miami Ex-Dry Agent Freed," *New York Times*, February 21, 1930.

62. Memorandum to the Commandant from Charles Root, May 31, 1929, folder "Florida Seizures," box 7, USCGID.

63. The incident apparently occurred in 1925, but the memo regarding his request for reinstatement was from 1932. See William J. Wheeler, September 10, 1932, folder "Commanders East Coast Florida Patrol Area," box 36, USCGID.

64. Letter from C. H. Hildreth, Collector of Customs, to W. M. Gober, United States Attorney, Jacksonville, box 38, USCGID.

65. Memorandum from Commander of Gulf Division to Commandant, November 16, 1924, folder "Commander, Gulf Division, 1924–32," box 36, USCGID.

66. Memorandum from Commander of Gulf Division to Commandant, November 16, 1924, folder "Commander, Gulf Division, 1924–32," box 36, USCGID.

67. C. E. Conroy Statement, June 20, 1927, box 87, USCGID.

68. This description of the operations of corrupt Coast Guard boats appeared in Green, "What Price Bribery?," 150.

69. C. E. Conroy Statement, June 20, 1927, box 87, USCGID.

70. Memorandum to Commandant from William J. Wheeler, June 16, 1927, folder "Commandant 1925-32," box 37, USCGID.

71. Memorandum from Inspector in Chief William J. Wheeler to Commandant, March 25, 1929, folder "Commandant 1925-32," box 37, and Confidential Memorandum for the Commandant from Charles Root, January 4, 1929, box 87, USCGID.

72. Commander Base Six to Commandant, January 17, 1929, p. 1, box 87, USCGID.

73. Confidential Memorandum for the Commandant from Charles Root, January 4, 1929, box 87, USCGID.

74. Commander Base Six to Commandant, January 17, 1929, p. 2, box 87, USCGID.

75. Memorandum for Personnel from P. W. Lauriat, September 20, 1932, folder "Commanders East Coast Florida Patrol Area," box 36, USCGID.

76. Report to the Division of Foreign Control, undated but likely in 1930, folder "Florida Situation," box 11, USCGID.

77. Memo from Officer in Charge, Chester Shoal Station, to Commandant, Seventh District, June 8, 1928, box 11, USCGID.

78. Letter from Walter Hawkins to Governor Doyle, March 3, 1932, folder 6, carton 24, SAF.

79. Memo from Intelligence Officer to Commandant, December 12, 1927, box 10, USCGID.

80. Root to Kime, December 9, 1927, box 66, USCGID.

81. Affidavit of C. A. McCrary, July 22, 1929; affidavit of N. F. Chase, July 6, 1929; affidavit of P. J. Whaling of Detroit, July 2, 1929; letter from M. R. Cartwright, June 5, 1929; affidavit of Vaughn Salette, June 25, 1929; and affidavit of M. J. Hutson, August 20, 1929, folder 12, carton 55, SAF. Quotes from Chase's affidavit.

82. Letter from Lollie J. Williams, folder 8, carton 14; anonymous letter dated August 12, 1931, folder 7, carton 26; and affidavit from Arthur Thompson, folder 9, carton 60, SAF.

83. Affidavit by B. Fropan (illegible), October 29, 1929, folder 2, carton 28, SAF.

84. Mundt, "'Justice Is Only a Name in This City.'"

85. Letter from J. Henry Hidalgo to Governor, March 25, 1931, folder 8, carton 39, SAF. There were numerous affidavits in this file attesting to Hidalgo's corruption.

86. Many residents wrote to the governor expressing their displeasure with the liquor situation in Ocala. The description of alcohol sold at the Dixie Filling Station appears in an undated newspaper clipping from an unknown newspaper included in the complaint from G. C. Hoffman dated December 20, 1929. The letters are in the papers of Governor Doyle Carlton, which are organized by county. Complaints about Ocala, in Marion County, are located in folders 1, 3, and 6, carton 55, SAF.

87. Letter from R. N. Dosh to Governor, August 3, 1929, folder 1, and affidavit of E. W. Henderly, October 16, 1929, folder 3, carton 55, SAF.

88. Letter from R. N. Dosh to Governor, August 3, 1929, folder 1, carton 55; affidavits of T. Perkins, October 16, 1929; E. W. Henderly, October 16, 1929; and L. J. Johnson, October 16, 1929; letter from Dosh, August 3, 1929; and affidavit from Walter Farris, October 16, 1929, folder 3, carton 55, SAF.

89. Letter from G. C. Hoffman, August 20, 1929, folder 6, carton 55, SAF.

90. Letter from G. C. Hoffman to Governor, April 3, 1930, folder 3, carton 55, SAF.

91. Letter from G. C. Hoffman to Governor July 24, 1929, folder 6, carton 55, SAF.

92. *Public Cooperation in Prohibition Law Enforcement*, 44–45.

93. Letter from G. C. Hoffman to Governor, April 20, 1929, folder 6, carton 55, SAF.

94. Affidavit of T. Perkins, October 16, 1929, folder 3, carton 55, SAF.

95. Affidavit of S. F. Strickland, October 16, 1929, folder 3, carton 55, SAF.

96. Both Lisa McGirr and John J. Guthrie discuss the selective enforcement of Prohibition, arguing that enforcement officials frequently targeted the most marginalized in any community. McGirr argues that this selective enforcement engendered widespread dislike for the law and for the political officials who promoted it, contributing to a political realignment that shifted many immigrants and the poor from Republicans to Democrats. See McGirr, *War on Alcohol*, 71–72, 157–89, and Guthrie, "Hard Times, Hard Liquor, and Hard Luck."

97. Letter from Joe Borden to Governor, October 10, 1929, folder 3, carton 55, SAF.

98. Letter from W. W. Callahan to Governor Thomas Kilby, July 6, 1922, Kilby Administrative Files, folder 12, SG 22128, ADAH.

99. Letter from James W. Connell to Governor, April 19, 1929, folder 15, carton 68, SAF.

100. "Officers Seize Three Cars, 140 Gallons Liquor," *Mobile Register*, January 1, 1928.

101. "State Officers Capture Stills and Wet Goods," *Mobile Register*, January 24, 1928.

102. Davis, "Race Menace in Bootlegging," 337; Ethridge, "Georgia Drinks with Decorum," 317. Ethridge estimated that in Macon, Georgia, 90 percent of bootleggers were African American. See H. A. Pierce to Board of Pardons, May 13, 1930, folder "Letters Written Regarding Indeterminates," box 8567, Alabama Board of Pardons and Paroles, ADAH.

103. Davis, Gardner, and Gardner, *Deep South*, 510–11; Bruère, *Does Prohibition Work?*, 109–10.

104. S. W. Ragsdale, Solicitor General, Dallas, Georgia, October 29, 1929, folder P–R, box 66, NCLOE; Crawford, "Citadel of Enforcement," 488; Ethridge, "Georgia Drinks with Decorum," 286; Derieux, "Old Times Dar Are Not Forgotten," 8. See also Sinclair, *Era of Excess*, 346–47; McGirr, *War on Alcohol*, 71–72; and Merz, *Dry Decade*.

105. Rutledge, "Prohibition and the Negro," 122–25, 157, 158.

106. Affidavit of H. S. Frear, undated, and affidavit of H. P. Latsbaugh, February 1, 1928, folder 5, carton 39; affidavit signed Legal Voters and Taxpayers, undated;

affidavit of Alberto Martinez, December 27, 1930; affidavit of Rafael Gonzales, December 27, 1930; affidavit of Arturo Peres and Aurelio Pages, December 27, 1930; letter from A. Q. Ray to Governor, May 26, 1930; and letter from J. Robert Einbinder to Governor, January 17, 1931, folder 8, carton 39, SAF.

107. There are numerous affidavits recounting L. M. Hatton's misdeeds. See folder 9, carton 40, SAF.

108. Letter from L. M. Hatton to Governor, August 28, 1930, folder 9, carton 40, SAF.

109. Bliven, "Away Down South," 297; Derieux, "Old Times Dar Are Not Forgotten," 38; Davis, "Race Menace in Bootlegging," 337-44.

Chapter Six

1. Sellers, *Prohibition Movement in Alabama*, 191-92.

2. Anonymous letter to Governor Kilby, March 9, 1922, Kilby Administrative Files, folder 11, SG 22128; anonymous letter to Governor Kilby, September 19, 1922, Kilby Administrative Files, folder 12, SG 22128; letter to Governor Bibb Graves from Horace Baggett, November 18, 1929, Special Files, Graves Papers, folder 10, SG 21177; anonymous letter to Governor Kilby, October 30, 1921, Kilby Administrative Files, folder 10, SG 22128, ADAH.

3. Kuhn, Joye, and West, *Living Atlanta*, 179.

4. Hardin, "Volstead English," 81-88. Hardin compiled his extensive list of terms from the popular press.

5. Merz, *Dry Decade*, 167-80. Two economists attempted a less biased analysis and concluded that alcohol consumption declined initially to 30 percent of previous levels at the beginning of Prohibition and then increased to about 60 to 70 percent of pre-Prohibition levels. There it remained until well after repeal. See Miron and Zwiebel, "Alcohol Consumption during Prohibition."

6. "Municipal Court," *New Smyrna Daily News*, February 20, 1925; "Municipal Court Docket," *Tampa Tribune*, October 22, 1929.

7. "If Drunk, 6 to 1 You'll Be Found Guilty by Court," *Mobile Register*, November 1, 1925. While several other municipalities included some statistics in letters to the national commission, those from Rome, Georgia, were the only ones categorized by specific offense. See letter from John W. Bale, Judge, Circuit Court of Floyd County, November 12, 1929, folder "Judges A-C," box 69, NCLOE.

8. *Rosalind Green v. James Roy Green*, Tuscaloosa County Court in Equity, Case 621; *A. A. Woods v. Inez Woods*, Tuscaloosa County Court in Equity, Case 516. I located these records in the files of the Tuscaloosa County Courthouse, but they have since been relocated to the Alabama Department of Archives and History.

9. "Two Divorces a Day Granted Here Laid Mostly to Liquor," *Tampa Tribune*, October 20, 1929.

10. Letter from Mrs. Ira Champion to Mr. A. Eustress, Secretary to the Governor, July 1, 1929, folder 41 "State Training School for Girls," Graves Papers, 1927–31, SG 21170, and memo from C. W. Austin to Governor Kilby, undated, Kilby Administrative Files, folder 12, box 22128, ADAH.

11. Bruère, *Does Prohibition Work?*, 97, 111, 93, 87.

12. Survey of the Tenth Prohibition District which Comprises the States of Alabama, Louisiana, Mississippi, and the Northern District of Florida, Research Material for the Report on Federal Prohibition Enforcement, Staff Committee on Prohibition, box 199, NCLOE.

13. There are many boxes of these letters in the collection related to the National Commission on Law Observance and Enforcement. I sampled every other folder and focused on letters from southerners, which admittedly were a minority. Letters were grouped by office and arranged alphabetically by the name of the author.

14. Letter from Charles G. Dibrell, November 8, 1929, folder "Judges G–K," box 69; letter from Gaston Dutel, August 29, 1929, folder "Police," box 70; letter from R. Don McLeod Jr., November 7, 1929, folder "M–R," box 66; letter from W. A. White, October 30, 1929, folder "Judges (St. Courts)," box 67, NCLOE.

15. S. W. Ragsdale, October 29, 1929, folder "Attorneys P–R," box 66; E. D. Thomas, October 25, 1929, p. 2, folder "Judges — to be digested," box 70; and William Seibels, October 1929, p. 2, folder "Attorneys S–Z," box 66, NCLOE.

16. Ethridge, "Georgia Drinks with Decorum," 286, 319.

17. Frank B. Willingham, October 21, 1929, folder "Attorneys S–Z," box 66, NCLOE.

18. Letter from J. A. Brown to Governor Bibb Graves, June 5, 1929, folder 10 "Special Files," SG 21177, Graves Papers, ADAH.

19. Letter to Judge L. H. Reynolds from Kittye Clyde Austin, April 17, 1933, folder "Miscellaneous Convict Mail K–L, Administrative Files relating to Parole," box SG8567, 1926–41, Alabama Board of Pardons and Paroles, ADAH; letter from Joseph H. James, solicitor, Fourth Judicial Circuit, Greensboro, Alabama, undated, Governor Miller, Administrative Files Law Enforcement, SG 19935, ADAH; Derieux, "Old Times Dar Are Not Forgotten," 8.

20. G. C. Bidgood, Judge, Circuit Court of Dublin, Georgia, October 21, 1929, folder "Judges A–C," box 69, NCLOE. The desire to permit the sale of light beer and wine was shared by others.

21. Allen, *Only Yesterday*, 215; Lusk, "Drinking Habit"; Sinclair, *Era of Excess*, 247.

22. J. A. Morton, August 20, 1929, folder "Police," box 70, NCLOE.

23. Letter from Gaston Dutel, August 29, 1929, folder "Police," box 70, and letter from John N. Story, November 11, 1929, folder "Attorneys S–Z," box 66, RG 10, NCLOE.

24. Derieux, "Old Times Dar Are Not Forgotten"; Ethridge, "Georgia Drinks with Decorum"; Kennedy, "Sisters of the Hollow Leg"; Crawford, "Citadel of Enforcement"; Barnett, "College Seniors and the Liquor Problem."

25. Letter to Governor Bibb Graves from Mrs. Alexander Greet, February 15, 1929, Graves Papers, folder 11, Special Files, SG 21177, ADAH; anonymous letter to Governor Brandon, April 14, 1923, copy in folder "March–April 1923," Denny Correspondence, box 4, WSHUA.

26. Sinclair, *Era of Excess*, 233–36.

27. Kennedy, "Sisters of the Hollow Leg," 92, 119; Ethridge, "Georgia Drinks with Decorum," 286; letter to Sara Mayfield from a boyfriend who signed his name "Day," April 8, 1924, Incoming Correspondence, Mayfield Papers, WSHUA.

28. Pegram, *Battling Demon Rum*, 175; Murdock, *Domesticating Drink*, 110–13; Barnett, "College Seniors and the Liquor Problem" 139.

29. *Rammer Jammer* 1, no. 1 (1924): 36, WSHUA. For more on the nexus of college life, drinking, and dating, see Dorr, "Fifty Percent Moonshine and Fifty Percent Moonshine." Students in Alabama consciously aligned themselves with national college culture so well described in Fass, *Damned and the Beautiful*.

30. See Fass, *Damned and the Beautiful*, 310–24. See also contemporary sociological studies of college students, all of which addressed the problem of drinking on campuses. Certainly not all students drank, but one study estimated that approximately 64 percent of male students and as many as 56 percent of female students occasionally imbibed. See Blanchard and Manasses, *New Girls for Old*, 67. Barnett reported that of 3,250 students, 2,178 drank at least occasionally; see Barnett, "College Seniors and the Liquor Problem," 139. Concerns about college student life almost invariably included efforts to control student drinking and to make sure that inebriated students did not attend college functions. See Bromley and Britton, *Youth and Sex*, 161–65, and Edwards, Artman, and Fisher, *Undergraduates*, 182–85.

31. A. A. Kirk to President Denny, January 27, 1923, and Mrs. E. H. Jewell-Loudermilk to President Denny, February 6, 1923, folder "To Dr. Denny, February 1923," Denny Correspondence, box 4, WSHUA.

32. McCandless, *Past in the Present*, 131–32.

33. After several letters, Auburn University officials reassured the governor that the report was merely vicious rumor. See Kilby Administrative Files, folder 12, SG 22128, ADAH.

34. See, for example, President Denny to T. V. Ballard, August 6, 1921, folder "July, August, September, 1921," Denny Correspondence, box 3, WSHUA. Also see report to the Board of Trustees, February 12, 1926, p. 16, and report of the Dean of Women, 1925–1926, p. 3, box 1, and Social Activities Report of the Directory, May 18, 1927, box 2, RG 533, Dowell Papers, AUA; *Rammer Jammer* 6 (no. 2): 27, WSHUA.

35. "Ten Commandments," *Crimson-White*, June 22, 1922, 1; *Rammer Jammer* 2 (no. 5): 117 and *Rammer Jammer* 3 (no. 2): 132, WSHUA. The successive stages of inebriation included "high, tight, looping, stinking, plastered, [and] out." See Bromley and Britton, *Youth and Sex*, 165; *Rammer Jammer* 5 (no. 1): 23, WSHUA; *Glomerata* (1926), 188, AUA; and "An Alumnus's Recollection of a Few Classy Myths," *Rammer Jammer* 2 (no. 3): 54, WSHUA.

36. Mattie Ellis, p. 88, and Laura Champion, p. 315, Warden's Docket, May 17–November 12, 1912, BPL. Arrests were not identified by number in the 1912 docket book.

37. Entry number 1469, entry numbers 1824 and 1825, and entry number 5778, Warden's Docket, Ensley Prison, June 1, 1926–October 21, 1928, BPL.

38. For a more complete discussion of women and alcohol during Prohibition, see Dorr, "Fifty Percent Moonshine and Fifty Percent Moonshine," and Dorr, "Place for Themselves in the Modern World."

39. Moore, *Bootleggers and Borders*, 46–52; Karibo, *Sin City North*, 15–43.

40. Anthony Stanonis's work provides some of the most evocative analyses of tourism in the South. He also taught me much about using commas. See Stanonis, *Creating the Big Easy* and *Faith in Bikinis*; Preston, *Dirt Roads to Dixie*; and Belasco, *Americans on the Road*.

41. Revels, *Sunshine Paradise*, 63–78; Mormino, *Land of Sunshine*, 11–43.

42. Stockbridge, "Shall We Go to Florida?," 489; Cooper, "Uncle Sam's Great Winter Playground"; Roberts, "Florida Loafing."

43. Mary Goodleare to Timmie Ritchie, Battle Creek, Michigan, postmarked West Palm Beach, Florida, December 31, 1928; Dorothy to Mrs. Louise de Prosse, Detroit, Michigan, postmarked Deland, Florida, January 17, 1928; Emma B. to Miss Florence Hathaway, Detroit, postmarked St. Petersburg, Florida, February 13, 1925; Carolyn to Mrs. Albert Bauman, Milwaukee, Wisconsin, postmarked Miami, Florida, March 30, 1928; Adela to Mrs. Walter Brown, Glen Ridge, New Jersey, postmarked Miami, Florida, March 6, 1925; Bird W. to James Ferry, Perry, Michigan, postmarked Lake Worth, Florida, October 7, 1925; Mrs. E. M. Stanard to Miss Eva Howard, Chior, Illinois, postmarked St. Petersburg, Florida, January 26, 1925. All images in author's possession, located as vintage postcards for sale on eBay, November 2015.

44. Name illegible to Mrs. Earl Hatch, Framingham, Massachusetts, postmarked Ft. Myers, Florida, February 14, 1925; Hap to Mr. Lingood Roberts, Sag Harbor, New York, postmarked January 2, 1925. All images in author's possession, located as vintage postcards for sale on eBay, November 2015.

45. Buckley, *Prohibition Survey of Florida*, 105, 107, 106; "Coast Guards Stem Flow of Bahama Liquor," undated, from an unknown newspaper, folder "Ft. Lauderdale Base 6," box 60, USCGID.

46. Report from Bill Kelly, undated but likely the winter of 1929, box 66, USCGID.

47. Unsigned letter, November 26, 1925, and Office Memorandum, Bureau of Customs, Tampa, Florida, June 15, 1927, folder "Correspondence Relating to Individuals, Rum-Running Era, 1926–31," box 55, USCGID; A. G. Watson Jr., Acting Collector of Customs, Tampa, Florida, to Secretary of the Treasury, October 16, 1924, p. 5, folder "Miscellaneous Data, 1923–25," box 46, USCGID; survey of liquor smuggling from Bahamas written by "London" to the Division of Foreign Control, 1930, p. 8, folder "Florida Cases," box 11, USCGID; *Public Cooperation in Prohibition Law Enforcement*, 61–62.

48. "Found Too Many Drunks in Miami," *New York Evening Sun*, March 22, 1929, folder 1, carton 6, SAF.

49. Buckley, *Prohibition Survey of Florida*, 124, 125; letter from Edward Wilson to General Andrews, August 26, 1925, folder "Miscellaneous Data," box 47, USCGID; *Public Cooperation in Prohibition Law Enforcement*, 12.

50. Letter from Jordan of Base Six to Commander Root, April 22, 1928, folder "Florida Cases and Seizures, 1928–30," box 11; memorandum for the Commandant from H. G. Hamlet of Coast Guard Cutter the *Tampa*, February 20, 1928, box 10; excerpt of personal letter sent to William J. Wheeler, who forwarded it on to the Commandant, March 23, 1929, and memo from William J. Wheeler to Commandant, July 3, 1928, p. 4, folder "Commandant's Memoranda, 1925–1930," box 37; report of Weiss and Mitchell in re: Smugglers, to Mr. W. W. Husband, Washington, D.C., March 1, 1925, pp. 4–5, folder "Cuba Information General, 1925–30," box 65, all in USCGID.

51. Rosalie Schwartz describes the creation of Cuba's tourist economy and notes that the "fat time" for tourism in Cuba was 1924 to 1931; see Schwartz, *Pleasure Island*, 80. See also Skwiot, *Purposes of Paradise*, 7.

52. Bacardi ad in Moruzzi, *Havana before Castro*, 28; advertisement in Garcia, *Official Illustrated Tourist's and Traveller's Guide to Cuba*, XVII.

53. Schwartz, *Pleasure Island*, 42, 46; *Terry's Guide to Cuba*, iii.

54. USS *Franconia* Travel Diary, 1925, Collection 256, Vol. 1, Blunt Library, Mystic, Conn.; card to Betty Jane Moats postmarked 1931; card to Mrs. Roy Danks postmarked 1923; card to Paul O'Neal postmarked 1927; and card to Miss Francis Goylewicz postmarked 1934, all in possession of author.

55. Brown, "Cuba's Vivacious Metropolis"; Thompson, "Paris of the Caribbean"; Williams, "Emerald Isle of Cuba"; Canova, "Cuba"; Bliven, "And Cuba for the Winter"; "December Vacations at Home and Abroad."

56. Ybarra, "Cuban Cocktail"; Bliven, "And Cuba for the Winter," 61; *Terry's Guide to Cuba*, 27. The recipe for the George Washington does not appear in the 1933 guide to mixing drinks at Sloppy Joe's. I am not sure what it is.

57. Woon, *When It's Cocktail Time in Cuba*, 4.

58. Letter from R. Don McLeod Jr., November 7, 1929, folder "Attorneys M–O," box 66, NCLOE.

59. Woon, *When It's Cocktail Time in Cuba*, 6–7.

60. Woon, *When It's Cocktail Time in Cuba*, 33–46

61. Hurst, *Arms above the Door*, 276.

62. Woon, *When It's Cocktail Time in Cuba*, 53, 45.

63. Postcard to Dot from Sallie, mailed in 1931, Cuban Postcard Collection, Cuban Heritage Digital Collection, University of Miami; card to Charles Boltz postmarked 1928, in possession of author.

64. Letter from Helmholz Shoe Manufacturing in Milwaukee to American Consular Service, June 20, 1927, Consular Posts Havana, vol. 552, DOS.

65. Memorandum in the E. E. Lomax Whereabouts Case, May 4, 1923, and letter from American Consulate-General, Havana, Cuba, to the Secretary of State,

November 14, 1922, both in Consular Posts Havana, vol. 501, DOS; Woon, *When It's Cocktail Time in Cuba*, 161–62; Carleton Bailey Hurst to the Secretary of State, June 18, 1925, vol. 528; memorandum, February 25, 1932, vol. 581; letter to Miss Helen Pratt from Edward Caffery, American Consul in Charge, March 10, 1927, vol. 552; and letter from Francis Steward Consul to the American Ambassador, February 12, 1924, vol. 515, all in Consular Posts Havana, DOS.

66. Memorandum to file, March 13, 1926, vol. 538, and telegram from Schuyler Merritt to American Consul, Havana, May 10, 1927, vol. 552, Consular Posts Havana, DOS; Garcia, *Official Illustrated Tourist's and Traveler's Guide to Cuba*, VII.

67. Memorandum on case of Helen Cautin, Babe Darling, Danny Albasio, and Thomas Frungillo, undated, vol. 563, and James V. Whitfield to Dr. Diego Vicente Tejera, September 18, 1924, vol. 515, Consular Posts Havana, DOS.

68. Note from Root to Kime, May 3, 1929, with Kime's typewritten response at bottom, folder "Florida Seizures," box 7, USCGID.

69. Mark F. Williams to Consulate, November 30, 1928, vol. 562, sec. 310, and letter from C. W. Winstedt to the American Consulate, March 30, 1926, vol. 538, Consular Posts Havana, DOS; *Terry's Guide to Cuba*, 43.

70. Letter from George Irwin to Charles Page, American Vice Consul, October 22, 1928, Consular Posts Havana, vol. 562, DOS.

71. Letter from Carleton Bailey Hurst to Enoch Crowder concerning the Dement situation, November 20, 1924, Diplomatic Posts Havana, vol. 176, DOS. The Sevilla-Biltmore was considered a fashionable spot not only for American tourists but also for wealthy or elite Cubans and diplomats, which explains the table of Cuban men tied to Congress at the rooftop patio. See *Terry's Guide to Cuba*, 43.

72. *US v. Carmela Perez*, Case 241, and affidavit of L. T. Bragossa, Deputy Collector in Charge, February 24, 1921, *US v. Lucy A. Thistlewaite*, Case 191, Southern District of Florida, Key West, USDCSE.

73. *US v. M. A. Michaelson*, Case 353, telegram signed D.O.W. to Customs Officials, Key West, in Washington, December 30, 1928, Southern District of Florida, Key West, USDCSE.

74. "200 Aboard Ship Taxed $800 for Bringing in Rum," *Mobile Register*, March 9, 1929; letter from Charles D. Clarke, July 30, 1927, folder Savannah, Georgia, box 56, IRS.

75. Merz, *Dry Decade*, 213.

Conclusion

1. U.S. Congress, *Investigation of Prohibition Enforcement*, 1.

2. Frankfurter, "National Policy for Prohibition Enforcement"; "Open Letter to the Alabama Dry."

3. McGirr, *War on Alcohol*, 246.

4. Sinclair, *Era of Excess*, 196, 358.

5. Howington, "John Barley Corn Subdued," 220.

6. McGirr, *War on Alcohol*; Murdock, *Domesticating Drink*, 114–33.

7. *Crimson-White*, June 24, 1921. An internet search located its publication at these other schools over the 1920s.

Bibliography

Archival Sources

Alabama Department of Archives and History, Montgomery
    Alabama Board of Pardons and Paroles
    Bibb Graves Papers
    Thomas E. Kilby Administrative Files
    Tuscaloosa County Court in Equity
Auburn University Archives, Auburn, Alabama
    Dowell Papers
    Glomerata
Birmingham Public Library Archives, Birmingham Municipal Court Dockets,
        Birmingham, Alabama
    Warden's Dockets
Blunt Library, Mystic Seaport, Mystic, Connecticut
    USS *Franconia* Travel Diary
Georgia State Archives, Morrow
    Clemency Files
W. S. Hoole Special Collections, University of Alabama, Tuscaloosa
    The Corolla
    George Denny Correspondence
    Sara Mayfield Papers
    Rammer Jammer
Library of Congress, Washington, D.C.
    Charles Evans Hughes Papers
    Mabel Walker Willebrandt Papers
National Archives and Records Administration, College Park, Maryland
    Internal Revenue Service, RG 58
    National Commission on Law Observance and Enforcement, RG 10
    Prints of Suspected Rum Runners, ca. 1918–1941, Records of the U.S. Coast
        Guard, RG-RR
    U.S. Department of Justice, RG 60
    U.S. Department of State, RG 84
    U.S. Department of the Treasury, RG 56

National Archives and Records Administration, Southwest Region, Ft. Worth,
     Texas
   United States District Court Records, RG 21
      Louisiana
         New Orleans
National Archives and Records Administration, Southeast Region, Morrow,
     Georgia
   U.S. Bureau of Customs, Mobile, RG 36
   U.S. Marshall's Service, Key West, RG 527
   United States District Court Records, RG 21
      Alabama
         Mobile
      Florida
         Jacksonville
         Key West
         Miami
         Pensacola
         Tampa
      Georgia
         Macon
      Mississippi
         Biloxi
National Archives and Records Administration, Washington, D.C.
   U.S. Coast Guard, RG 26
   U.S. Coast Guard Intelligence Division, RG 26
   U.S. Immigration and Naturalization Services, RG 85
State Archives of Florida, Tallahassee
   Doyle Elam Carlton Papers, 1929–1933, Series 204
University of Missouri, Columbia
   Papers of General Enoch Crowder

Newspapers

Anniston (Ala.) Star
Atlanta Constitution
Baltimore Sun
Biloxi Daily Herald
Chicago Tribune
Christian Science Monitor
Crimson-White (University of Alabama)
Dothan (Ala.) Eagle
Hattiesburg (Miss.) American

Laurel (Miss.) Daily Leader
Miami News
Mobile (Ala.) Register
Monroe (La.) News-Star
New Smyrna (Fla.) Daily News
New York Evening Sun
New York Herald Tribune
New York Times
Tampa Tribune
Thomasville (Ga.) Times-Enterprise
Washington Post

Published Primary Sources

Abbott, M. Edwin. "Laws Men Break and Why." *Annals of the American Academy of Political and Social Science* 125 (May 1926): 35–39.

Adams, Phelps Haviland. "Right off the Boat." *North American Review* 230 (September 1930): 284.

"Alcohol: Its Use and Abuse." *Outlook*, October 24, 1917, 285–86.

Allen, Frederick Lewis. *Only Yesterday: An Informal History of the 1920s.* New York: Harper and Row, 1931.

"Bad News for Bootleggers." *Literary Digest*, November 20, 1926, 18.

Baillard, Maude Littlefield. "Creating the New Florida." *Travel*, January 1922, 5–9.

Barnett, J. H. "College Seniors and the Liquor Problem." In *Prohibition: A National Experiment*, 130–46. Philadelphia: Annals of the American Academy of Political and Social Science, 1932.

Blanchard, Phyllis, and Carlyn Manasses. *New Girls for Old.* New York: Macauley, 1930.

Bliven, Bruce. "And Cuba for the Winter." *New Republic*, February 29, 1928, 61–64.

———. "Away Down South: Casual Notes of a Traveler in the Land of the New Frontier." *New Yorker*, May 4, 1927, 296–98.

"Bootleggers abaft the Port Beam!" *Literary Digest*, May 31, 1924, 39.

"Booze Buccaneering along 'Rum Row.'" *Literary Digest*, May 26, 1923, 52.

Brindley, A. R. *Prohibition Survey of Alabama: Enforcement of the Prohibition Laws.* Official Records of the National Commission on Law Observance and Enforcement. Washington, D.C.: Government Printing Office, 1931.

———. *Prohibition Survey of Mississippi: Enforcement of the Prohibition Laws.* Official Records of the National Commission on Law Observance and Enforcement. Washington, D.C.: Government Printing Office, 1931.

Bromley, Dorothy Dunbar, and Florence Haxton Britton. *Youth and Sex: A Study of 1300 College Students.* New York: Harper and Brothers, 1938.

Brown, Irving. "Cuba's Vivacious Metropolis." *Travel*, December 1922, 11–14.

Bruère, Martha Bensley. *Does Prohibition Work? A Study of the Operation of the Eighteenth Amendment Made by the National Association of Settlements*. New York: Harper and Brothers, 1927.

Buckley, Frank. *Prohibition Survey of Florida: Enforcement of the Prohibition Laws*. Official Records of the National Commission on Law Observance and Enforcement. Washington, D.C.: Government Printing Office, 1931.

———. *Prohibition Survey of Louisiana: Enforcement of the Prohibition Laws*. Official Records of the National Commission on Law Observance and Enforcement. Washington, D.C.: Government Printing Office, 1931.

Canova, Enrique C. "Cuba—The Isle of Romance." *National Geographic*, September 1933, 344–80.

Carmer, Carl. *Stars Fell on Alabama*. 1934. Reprint, Tuscaloosa: University of Alabama Press, 1990.

Cash, W. J. *The Mind of the South*. 1941. Reprint, New York: Vintage, 1991.

Cason, Clarence. *Ninety Degrees in the Shade*. 1935. Reprint, Tuscaloosa: University of Alabama Press, 2001.

"Convention between the United States and Cuba for the Prevention of Smuggling Operations." *American Journal of International Law* 20 (October 1926): 136–41.

Cooper, Clayton Sedwick. "Uncle Sam's Great Winter Playground." *Travel*, November 1925, 35–37.

Crabites, Pierre. "Rum Runners and Blockade Runners." *North American Review* 225 (May 1928): 545–47.

Crawford, Bruce. "Citadel of Enforcement." *Outlook and Independent* 154 (March 26, 1930): 488–89+.

Creel, George. "Close the Gates!" *Collier's*, May 6, 1922, 9–10.

———. "Melting Pot or Dumping Ground." *Collier's*, September 3, 1921, 9–10.

"Crime and the Bootlegger." *Literary Digest*, August 25, 1928.

"Cuba's Sugar Coated Pill." *Literary Digest*, May 8, 1926, 12.

Curran, Henry H. "Smuggling Aliens." *Saturday Evening Post*, January 31, 1925, 12.

Davis, Allison, Burleigh B. Gardner, and Mary R. Gardner. *Deep South: A Social Anthropological Study of Caste and Class*. Chicago: University of Chicago Press, 1941.

Davis, Charles Hall. "The Race Menace in Bootlegging." *Virginia Law Register* (1921): 337–44.

"December Vacations at Home and Abroad." *Woman's Home Companion*, November 1929, 20.

Derieux, James C. "Old Times Dar Are Not Forgotten." *Collier's*, June 1, 1929, 8–9, 38.

Dickinson, Edwin D. "The Supreme Court Interprets the Liquor Treaties." *American Journal of International Law* 27 (April 1933): 305–10.

———. "Treaties for the Prevention of Smuggling." *American Journal of International Law* 20 (April 1926): 340–46.

Dingle, Captain. "Running the Rum Blockade." *Collier's*, July 25, 1925, 18–19+.

"Does the Eighteenth Amendment Violate International Law?" *Yale Law Journal* 33 (November 1923): 72–78.

Dunne, F. P. "Dark Days for Bootleggers." *Outlook and Independent* 153 (December 25, 1929): 652–53.

Edsall, Howard Linn. "Whiskey Below Decks: The Adventures of a Rum Runner's Mate." *Harper's Monthly Magazine*, July 1929, 143–55.

Edwards, R. H., J. M. Artman, and Galen M. Fisher. *Undergraduates: A Study of Morale in Twenty-Three Colleges and Universities*. New York: Doubleday, 1928.

Ethridge, Willie Snow. "Georgia Drinks with Decorum." *Outlook and Independent*, June 25, 1930, 286–88+.

"Firing All the Volstead Agents." *Literary Digest*, August 1, 1925, 12.

"Firing Lax Dry Enforcers." *Literary Digest*, November 15, 1924, 14.

"Florida the Irresistible." *Literary Digest*, December 18, 1926, 42–72.

Frank, Waldo. "The Ordeal of Cuba." *Scribner's* 90 (July 1931): 15–23.

Frankfurter, Felix. "A National Policy for Prohibition Enforcement." *Annals of the American Academy of Political and Social Science* 109 (September 1923): 193–95.

Garcia, Frank Rojo. *Official Illustrated Tourist's and Traveller's Guide to Cuba*. 1928.

"Gearing Up Prohibition Enforcement." *Outlook*, February 17, 1926, 236–38.

Gebhart, John. "Movement against Prohibition." *Annals of the American Academy of Political and Social Science* 163 (September 1932): 172–80.

Glasgow, G. "Foreign Affairs: Rum and the Bahamas." *Contemporary Review* 130 (September 1926): 373–77.

"Graft Rampant in the Dry Forces." *Literary Digest*, September 24, 1927, 10.

Gray, David. "Bootlegging from the Bahamas." *Collier's*, June 24, 1922, 18.

Green, Walter. "Name Your Poison, Gents." *Saturday Evening Post*, March 13, 1926, 22–23+.

———. "What Price Bribery?" *Saturday Evening Post*, August 14, 1926, 29, 148–50.

———. "Who's Who in Hooch." *Saturday Evening Post*, June 12, 1926, 22–23.

Hardin, Achsah. "Volstead English." *American Speech* 7 (December 1931): 81–88.

"Hijackers—The Bane of Bootleggers." *Literary Digest*, August 4, 1923, 55.

Hurst, Carleton Bailey. *Arms above the Door*. New York: Dodd, Meade, 1932.

Johnson, Charles S. *Shadow of the Plantation*. Chicago: University of Chicago Press, 1934.

Jordon, Louis F. "Impressions of a Country Lawyer." *Virginia Law Register* 11 (October 1925): 323–29.

Karig, Walter. "Gold from Salt Water: Episodes in the Career of the King of Rum Row." *Scribner's*, February 1927, 203–6.

Kennedy, John B. "And Mix with Fresh Water." *Collier's*, October 27, 1928, 8–9+.

Kennedy, Kay. "Sisters of the Hollow Leg." *Outlook*, May 21, 1930, 92–93+.

Lescarboura, Austin. "Battle of Rum Row." *Popular Mechanics* 45 (June 1926): 955–59.

Lingle, Thomas W. "The South and Prohibition." *New Republic*, September 19, 1928, 127–28.

Littell, Robert. "The Higher Alcohol." *New Republic*, October 7, 1925, 178–79.

Lusk, Rufus S. "The Drinking Habit." In *Prohibition: A National Experiment*, 46–52. Philadelphia: Annals of the American Academy of Political and Social Science, 1932.

Lythgoe, Gertrude. *The Bahama Queen, Prohibition's Daring Beauty: The Autobiography of Gertrude "Cleo" Lythgoe*. 1964. Reprint, Mystic, Conn.: Flat Hammock Press, 2007.

"Making Bootleggers Felons." *Literary Digest*, March 23, 1929, 11.

Mandeville, Ernest W. "Can a Prohibition Agent Be Honest?" *Outlook*, June 2, 1926, 174–75.

———. "More Sin and Gin." *Outlook*, February 25, 1925, 299–302.

———. "A Most Amazing Story of Corruption." *Outlook*, January 19, 1927, 81–82.

———. "The Sources of the Booze Supply." *Outlook*, July 15, 1925, 400–403.

"A Man's Home Is Still His Castle." *Literary Digest*, October 31, 1925, 13.

Marcosson, Isaac F. "Cuba Libre: New Edition." *Saturday Evening Post*, April 25, 1927, 14+.

McNutt, William Slavens. "Modern Pirates Walk the Plank." *Collier's*, January 25, 1925, 12–13, 42.

Merz, Charles. *The Dry Decade*. New York: Doubleday, Doran, 1931.

Moore, Samuel Taylor. "Fighting Rum Row: A Cruise on the 'White Terror.'" *Independent*, January 1925, 34–36.

———. "Rum Row—Finis: The Coast Guard Wields the Mop." *Independent*, January 24, 1925, 93.

Moray, Alastair. *The Diary of a Rum-Runner*. 1929. Reprint, Mystic, Conn.: Flat Hammock Press, 2007.

Mullen, Kate. "The Bootlegging Woman." *Forum*, October 1926, 577–85.

"Nabbing the Rum Runner—Sometimes." *Literary Digest*, January 26, 1924, 46.

"New Generals in the War on Rum." *Literary Digest*, June 4, 1927, 10–11.

Oakley, Imogen B. "The Prohibition Law and the Political Machine." *Annals of the American Academy of Political and Social Sciences* 109 (November 1923): 165–74.

O'Donnell, Jack. "Running the Booze Blockade." *Collier's*, June 2, 1923, 9, 27.

O'Malley, Frank Ward. "The Street of Dreadful Drought." *Saturday Evening Post*, April 17, 1920, 3–4.

"An Open Letter to the Alabama Dry." *World's Work*, May 1926, 13–14.

Panunzio, Constantine. "The Foreign Born and Prohibition." In *Prohibition: The National Experiment*, 147–54. Philadelphia: Annals of the American Academy of Political and Social Science, 1932.

Park, Bart. "The Bootlegger and His Forerunners." *American Mercury*, July 1926, 319–21.

Payne, Will. "The Case of Cuba." *Saturday Evening Post*, March 30, 1929, 27+.

Phillips, H. I. "The Book of Bootlegging Etiquette." *Collier's*, March 20, 1926, 9–10+.

"Porosity of Prohibition." *Literary Digest*, October 15, 1921, 12.

"Problems in the Prevention of 'Rum-Running.'" *Yale Law Journal* 35 (June 1926): 979–89.

Prohibition: The National Experiment. Philadelphia: Annals of the American Academy of Political and Social Science, 1932.

"Prohibitionist Intervention in Cuba." *Literary Digest*, January 12, 1924, 19.

Public Cooperation in Prohibition Law Enforcement: Business, Civic, and Industrial Groups Aid in Promoting Better Observance and Enforcement of the Law. Bureau of Prohibition. Washington, D.C.: Government Printing Office, 1930.

Railey, Hilton Howell. "The Bootleggers." *Saturday Evening Post*, August 28, 1920, 14–15+.

Reid, William A. *Seeing the Latin Republics of North America.* N.p.: Foreign Trade Advisor of the Pan American Union, 1931.

"The Repulse of the Rum-Runners." *Outlook*, May 20, 1925, 85.

"The Road from Rum and Ruin." *Collier's*, October 17, 1925, 22–23.

Roberts, Kenneth L. "Florida Loafing." *Saturday Evening Post*, May 17, 1924, 20.

"The Rum Chasers by a Former Officer of the Patrol." *Saturday Evening Post*, June 14, 1924, 6–7, 180.

"Rum-Running and the Law." *Outlook*, August 29, 1923, 652.

"Rum Ships That Pass in the Night." *Literary Digest*, August 20, 1921, 10–11.

Rutledge, Archibald. "Prohibition and the Negro." *Outlook and Independent*, May 28, 1930, 123–25+.

Schmeckebier, Laurence F. *The Bureau of Prohibition: Its History, Activities, and Organization.* Service Monographs of the United States Government No. 57. Washington, D.C: Brookings Institution, 1929.

Shepherd, William G. "After the Bootlegger—What?" *Collier's*, March 21, 1925, 5–6+.

———. "A Big Catch on Rum Row." *Collier's*, June 6, 1925, 13–14+.

———. "The Biggest Rum King." *Collier's*, March 13, 1926, 10–11.

———. "The Rum Runner's New Enemy." *Collier's*, May 23, 1925, 5.

Shepherd, William G., and W. O. Saunders. "Who's Drinking Now." *Collier's*, May 2, 1925, 5–6+.

Stayton, William H. "Have We Prohibition or Only Prohibition Laws?" *North American Review* 220 (June 1, 1925): 591–96.

Stockbridge, Frank. "Shall We Go to Florida?" *American Review of Reviews*, November 1925, 489–508.

Sturgis, Wesley A. "National Prohibition and International Law." *Yale Law Journal* 32 (January 1923): 259–66.

Terry's Guide to Cuba. 1926. Reprint, Cambridge, Mass.: Riverside Press, 1929.

Thompson, Basil. "The Paris of the Caribbean." *Travel*, December 1923, 5–9.

Turner, Homer. "Notes of a Prohibition Agent." *American Mercury*, April 1928, 385–92.

"Ups and Downs of the Flying Bootleggers." *Literary Digest*, April 4, 1925, 76–79.

U.S. Congress. Senate. Committee on the Judiciary. *Investigation of Prohibition Enforcement: Hearing before the United States Senate.* 71st Cong., 2nd Sess., 1930. Washington, D.C.: Government Printing Office, 1930.

Van Buren, J. M. *Gospel Temperance, A New Principle.* National Temperance Society and Publication House, 1883. In *Pamphlets: Temperance Volume 2.* Google Books, accessed December 2010.

"The War on Rum Row." *Outlook,* August 27, 1924, 620.

Washington, Booker T. "Negro Crime and Strong Drink." *Journal of the American Institute of Criminal Law and Criminology* 3 (September 1912): 384–392.

Wellever, Judson C. "The Rum Smugglers: Piracy, Maritime Bootlegging, and 'Hyjacking.'" *American Review of Reviews* 67 (June 1923): 605–14.

"Wet Waves and Dry Enforcers." *Literary Digest*, March 14, 1925, 40–46.

White, Owen P. "Lips That Touch Liquor." *Collier's*, March 6, 1926, 9–10+.

———. "Meet and Drink." *Collier's*, August 17, 1929, 8–9+.

Williams, Hershel. "The Emerald Isle of Cuba." *Travel*, November 1925, 7–9.

Winston, Sanford, and Mosette Butler. "Negro Bootleggers in Eastern North Carolina." *American Sociological Review* 8 (December 1943): 692–97.

"Winter Playgrounds the World Over." *Literary Digest*, December 17, 1927, 45–77.

"Women Bootleggers a Problem." *Literary Digest*, February 5, 1927, 46.

Woon, Basil. *When It's Cocktail Time in Cuba.* New York: Horace Liveright, 1928.

Ybarra, T. R. "The Cuban Cocktail." *Outlook and Independent*, February 5, 1930, 207.

Young, James C. "Breaking into the United States." *World's Work*, November 1924, 53–58.

Secondary Sources

Acker, Caroline Jean. "Portrait of an Addicted Family: Dynamics of Opiate Addiction in the Early Twentieth Century." In *Altering American Consciousness: The History of Alcohol and Drug Use in the United States, 1800–2000*, edited by Sarah W. Tracy and Caroline Jean Acker, 165–81. Amherst: University of Massachusetts Press, 2004.

Alduino, Frank. "Prohibition in Tampa." *Tampa Bay History* 9 (Spring–Summer 1987): 17–28.

Allen, Everett S. *The Black Ships: Rumrunners of Prohibition.* Boston: Little, Brown, 1965.

Andreas, Peter. *Smuggler Nation: How Illicit Trade Made America*. New York: Oxford University Press, 2013.

Ashmore, Susan Youngblood, and Lisa Lindquist Dorr, eds. *Alabama Women: Their Lives and Times*. Athens: University of Georgia Press, 2017.

Belasco, Warren James. *Americans on the Road: From Autocamp to Motel, 1910–1945*. Cambridge, Mass.: MIT Press, 1979.

Bloomfield, Howard V. L. *The Compact History of the United States Coast Guard*. New York: Hawthorn Books, 1966.

Bousquet, Stephen C. "The Gangster in Our Midst: Al Capone in South Florida, 1930–1947." *Florida Historical Quarterly* 76 (Winter 1998): 297–309.

Burns, Eric. *The Spirits of America: A Social History of Alcohol*. Philadelphia: Temple University Press, 2004.

Cannato, Vincent. *American Passage: The History of Ellis Island*. New York: Harper, 2009.

Carse, Robert. *Rum Row*. London: Jarrolds, 1961.

Carter, James A. "Florida and Rum Running during Prohibition." M.A. thesis, Florida State University, 1965.

Cirules, Enrique. *The Mafia in Havana: A Caribbean Mob Story*. Melbourne: Ocean Press, 2004.

Cluster, Dick, and Rafael Hernandez. *The History of Havana*. New York: Palgrave, 2006.

Coffey, Thomas M. *The Long Thirst: Prohibition in America, 1920–1933*. New York: Norton, 1975.

Coker, Joe L. *Liquor in the Land of the Lost Cause: Southern White Evangelicals and the Prohibition Movement* Lexington: University of Kentucky Press, 2007.

Cooley, Angela Jill. *To Live and Dine in Dixie: The Evolution of Urban Food Culture in the Jim Crow South*. Athens: University of Georgia Press, 2015.

Corbitt, Duvon C. "Immigration in Cuba." *Hispanic American Historical Review* 22 (May 1942): 304.

Courtwright, David T., ed. *Forces of Habit: Drugs and the Making of the Modern World*. Cambridge, Mass.: Harvard University Press, 2001.

Daniels, Roger. *Guarding the Golden Door: American Immigration Policy and Immigrants since 1882*. New York: Hill and Wang, 2004.

Deere, Carmen Diana. "Here Come the Yankees! The Rise and Decline of United States Colonies in Cuba, 1898–1930." *Hispanic American Historical Review* 78 (November 1998): 729–65.

de la Fuente, Alejandro. "Two Dangers, One Solution: Immigration, Race, and Labor in Cuba, 1900–1930." *International Labor and Working Class History* 51 (Spring 1997): 30–49.

Denmark, Lisa L. "Worshipping Bacchus: Prohibition in Savannah, 1899–1922." *Law, Crime and History* (2011): 109–40.

Dorr, Lisa Lindquist. "Fifty Percent Moonshine and Fifty Percent Moonshine: Social Life and College Youth Culture in Alabama, 1913–1933." In *Manners and Southern History*, edited by Ted Ownby, 45–75. Jackson: University Press of Mississippi, 2007.

———. "A Place for Themselves in the Modern World: Southern Women and Alcohol in the Age of Prohibition, 1912–1933." In *Signposts: New Directions in Southern Legal History*, edited by Sally E. Hadden and Patricia Hagler Minter, 317–44. Athens: University of Georgia Press, 2013.

Dumenil, Lynn. *The Modern Temper: American Culture and Society in the 1920s.* New York: Hill and Wang, 1995.

English, T. J. *Havana Nocturne: How the Mob Owned Cuba . . . and Then Lost It to the Revolution.* New York: HarperCollins, 2007.

Fass, Paula. *The Damned and the Beautiful: American Youth in the 1920s.* New York: Oxford University Press, 1978.

Gentry, Cynthia. "A Place of Gathering: Carolina Drink Houses." *Journal of Black Studies* 34 (March 2004): 449–61.

George, Paul S. "Passage to a New Eden: Tourism in Miami from Flagler through Everest G. Sewell." *Florida Historical Quarterly* 59 (April 1981): 440–63.

Glover, Staci. "Lebanese, Italian, and Slavic Immigrant Women in Metropolitan Birmingham: Just Mud Roads." In *Alabama Women: Their Lives and Times*, edited by Susan Youngblood Ashmore and Lisa Lindquist Dorr, 239–54. Athens: University of Georgia Press, 2017.

Guthrie, John J., Jr. "Hard Times, Hard Liquor, and Hard Luck: Selective Enforcement of Prohibition in North Florida, 1928–1933." *Florida Historical Quarterly* 72 (April 1994): 435–52.

———. *Keepers of the Spirits: The Judicial Response to Prohibition Enforcement in Florida, 1885–1935.* Westport, Conn.: Greenwood, 1998.

———. "Rekindling the Spirits: From National Prohibition to Local Option in Florida, 1928–1935." *Florida Historical Quarterly* 74 (Summer 1995): 23–39.

Guy, Donna J. *Sex and Danger in Buenos Aires: Prostitution, Family, and Nation in Argentina.* Lincoln: University of Nebraska Press, 1990.

Hickman, Timothy. "The Double Meaning of Addiction: Habitual Narcotic Use and the Logic of Professionalizing Medical Authority in the United States, 1900–1920." In *Altering American Consciousness: The History of Alcohol and Drug Use in the United States, 1800–2000*, edited by Sarah W. Tracy and Caroline Jean Acker, 165–81. Amherst: University of Massachusetts Press, 2004.

Howington, Arthur F. "John Barleycorn Subdued: The Enforcement of Prohibition in Alabama." *Alabama Review* (July 1970): 212–25.

Jackson, Joy. "Prohibition in New Orleans: The Unlikeliest Crusade." *Louisiana History* 19 (Summer 1978): 261–84.

Jarmon, Charles. "The Sploe House: A Drinking Place of Lower Socio-Economic

Status Negroes in a Southern City." *Black Experience: A Southern University Journal* (1969): 55–61.

Johnson, Robert Erwin. *Guardians of the Sea: The History of the United States Coast Guard, 1915–Present*. Annapolis, Md.: Naval Institute Press, 1987.

Karibo, Holly. *Sin City North: Sex, Drugs, and Citizenship in the Detroit-Windsor Borderland*. Chapel Hill: University of North Carolina Press, 2015.

Kinder, Douglas Clark. "Bureaucratic Cold Warrior: Harry J. Anslinger and Illicit Narcotics Traffic." *Pacific Historical Review* 50 (May 1981): 169–91.

Kinder, Douglas Clark, and William O. Walker, III. "Stable Force in a Storm: Harry J. Anslinger and United States Narcotic Foreign Policy." *Journal of American History* 72 (March 1986): 908–27.

Kobler, John. *Ardent Spirits: The Rise and Fall of Prohibition*. 1973. Reprint, New York: Da Capo Press, 1993.

Kuhn, Clifford M., Harlon E. Joye, and E. Bernard West. *Living Atlanta: An Oral History of the City, 1914–1948*. Athens: University of Georgia Press, 2005.

Kula, Marcin. "Those Who Failed to Reach the United States: Polish Proletarians in Cuba during the Interwar Period." *Polish American Studies* 46 (Spring 1989): 19–41.

Kurtz, Michael L. "Organized Crime in Louisiana History: Myth and Reality." *Louisiana History* 24 (Autumn 1983): 355–76.

Kyvig, David E. Law. *Alcohol and Order: Perspectives on National Prohibition*. Westport, Conn.: Greenwood, 1985.

———. *Repealing National Prohibition*. Chicago: University of Chicago Press, 1979.

Lee, Erica. "Enforcing the Borders: Chinese Exclusion along the U.S. Borders with Canada and Mexico, 1882–1924." *Journal of American History* 89 (June 2002): 54–86.

Leonhardt, Olive, and Hilda Phelps Hammond. *Shaking Up Prohibition in New Orleans: Authentic Vintage Cocktails from A to Z*. Baton Rouge: Louisiana State University Press, 2015.

Lerner, Michael A. *Dry Manhattan: Prohibition in New York City*. Cambridge, Mass.: Harvard University Press, 2007.

Levine, Harry G., and Craig Reinarman. "From Prohibition to Regulation: Lessons from Alcohol Policy for Drug Policy." *Milbank Quarterly* 69 (1991): 461–94.

Lewis, Michael. *The Coming of Southern Prohibition: The Dispensary System and the Battle over Liquor in South Carolina, 1907–1915*. Baton Rouge: Louisiana State University Press, 2016.

Ling, Sally J. *Run the Rum In: Rumrunners, Bootleggers, and Stills*. Charleston, S.C.: History Press, 2007.

López, Kathleen M. *Chinese Cubans: A Transnational History*. Chapel Hill: University of North Carolina Press, 2013.

Lowe, John Wharton. *Calypso Magnolia: The Crosscurrents of Caribbean and Southern Literature*. Chapel Hill: University of North Carolina Press, 2016.

Magill, John. "New Orleans during Prohibition: Belligerently Wet." In *Shaking Up Prohibition in New Orleans: Authentic Vintage Cocktails from A to Z*, edited by Gay Leonhardt, ix–xv. Baton Rouge: Louisiana State University Press, 2015.

McCandless, Amy. *The Past in the Present: Women's Higher Education in the Twentieth-Century American South*. Tuscaloosa: University of Alabama Press, 1999.

McGirr, Lisa. *The War on Alcohol: Prohibition and the Rise of the American State*. New York: Norton, 2016.

McWilliams, John C. "Unsung Partner against Crime: Henry J. Anslinger and the Federal Bureau of Narcotics, 1930–1962." *Pennsylvania Magazine of History and Biography* 113 (April 1989): 207–36.

Miron, Jeffrey, and Jeffrey Zwiebel. "Alcohol Consumption during Prohibition." *American Economic Review* 81 (May 1991): 242–47.

Mohlman, Geoffrey. "Anclote Keys Lighthouse: Guiding Light to Safe Anchorage." *Florida Historical Quarterly* 78 (Fall 1999): 159–88.

Moore, Stephen T. *Bootleggers and Borders: The Paradox of Prohibition on a Canada-U.S. Border*. Lincoln: University of Nebraska Press, 2014.

Mormino, Gary R. *Land of Sunshine, State of Dreams: A Social History of Modern Florida*. Gainesville: University Press of Florida, 2005.

Moruzzi, Peter. *Havana before Castro: When Cuba Was a Tropical Playground*. Layton, Utah: Gibbs Smith, 2008.

Mowry, David P. "Listening to the Rumrunners." NSA.gov Publication. Accessed September 30, 2017.

Mundt, Michael H. "'Justice Is Only a Name in This City': Tampa Confronts the Roaring Twenties." *Gulf Coast Historical Review* 12 (Fall 1996): 29–41.

Murchison, Kenneth. *Federal Criminal Law Doctrines: The Forgotten Influence of National Prohibition*. Durham, N.C.: Duke University Press.

Murdock, Catherine Gilbert. *Domesticating Drink: Women, Men, and Alcohol in America, 1870–1940*. Baltimore: Johns Hopkins University Press, 1998.

Ngai, Mai M. *Impossible Subjects: Illegal Aliens and the Making of Modern America*. New Brunswick, N.J.: Princeton University Press, 2004.

———. "The Strange Career of the Illegal Alien: Immigration Restriction and Deportation Policy in the U.S, 1921–1945." *Law and History Review* 21 (Spring 2003): 69–107.

Okrent, Daniel. *Last Call: The Rise and Fall of Prohibition*. New York: Scribner, 2010.

Ownby, Ted. *Subduing Satan: Religion, Recreation, and Manhood in the Rural South, 1865–1920*. Chapel Hill: University of North Carolina Press, 1990.

Pegram, Thomas. "The Anti-Saloon League and the Ku Klux Klan in 1920s

Prohibition Enforcement." *Journal of the Gilded Age and Progressive Era* 7 (January 2008): 89–119.

———. *Battling Demon Rum: The Struggle for a Dry America, 1800–1933*. Chicago: Ivan R. Dee, 1998.

———. "Brewing Trouble: Federal, State, and Private Authority in Pennsylvania Prohibition Enforcement under Gifford Pinchot, 1923–1927." *Pennsylvania Magazine of History and Biography* 138 (April 2014): 163–91.

Pérez, Louis A., Jr. *Cuba under the Platt Amendment*. Pittsburgh: University of Pittsburgh Press, 1986.

———. *On Becoming Cuban: Identity, Nationality, and Culture*. New York: Harper Collins, 1999.

Preston, Howard Lawrence. *Dirt Roads to Dixie: Accessibility and Modernization in the South, 1885–1935*. Knoxville: University of Tennessee Press, 1991.

Revels, Tracy J. *Sunshine Paradise: A History of Florida Tourism*. Gainesville: University Press of Florida, 2011.

Ring, Natalie. *The Problem South: Region, Empire, and the New Liberal State, 1880–1930*. Athens: University of Georgia Press, 2012.

Sáenz Rovner, Eduardo. *The Cuban Connection: Drug Trafficking, Smuggling, and Gambling in Cuba from the 1920s to the Revolution*. Chapel Hill: University of North Carolina Press, 2009.

Sanders, Randy. "Delivering Demon Rum: Prohibition Era Rum Running in the Gulf of Mexico." *Gulf Coast Historical Review* 12 (Fall 1996): 92–113.

Schwartz, Rosalie. *Pleasure Island: Tourism and Temptation in Cuba*. Lincoln: University of Nebraska Press, 1997.

Sellers, James Benson. *The Prohibition Movement in Alabama, 1702–1943*. Chapel Hill: University of North Carolina Press, 1943.

Sims, Anastatia. *The Power of Femininity in the New South: Women's Organizations and Politics in North Carolina, 1880–1930*. Columbia: University of South Carolina Press, 1997.

Sinclair, Andrew. *Era of Excess: A Social History of the Prohibition Movement*. New York: Harper Colophon, 1962.

Skwiot, Christine. *The Purposes of Paradise: U.S. Tourism and Empire in Cuba and Hawaii*. Philadelphia: University of Pennsylvania Press, 2010.

Speaker, Susan L. "Demons for the Twentieth Century: The Rhetoric of Drug Reform, 1920–1940." In *Altering American Consciousness: The History of Alcohol and Drug Use in the United States, 1800–2000*, edited by Sarah W. Tracy and Caroline Jean Acker, 203–24. Amherst: University of Massachusetts Press, 2004.

Spinelli, Lawrence. *Dry Diplomacy: The United States, Great Britain, and Prohibition*. Wilmington, Del.: Scholarly Resources, 1989.

Stanonis, Anthony J. *Creating the Big Easy: New Orleans and the Emergence of Modern Tourism*. Athens: University of Georgia Press, 2006.

————. *Faith in Bikinis: Politics and Leisure in the Coastal South since the Civil War.* Athens: University of Georgia Press, 2014.

Stewart, Bruce E. *Moonshiners and Prohibitionists: The Battle over Alcohol in Southern Appalachia.* Lexington: University Press of Kentucky, 2011.

Thomas, Mary Martha. *The New Woman in Alabama: Social Reforms and Suffrage, 1890–1920.* Tuscaloosa: University of Alabama Press, 1992.

Thompson, H. Paul, Jr. *A Most Stirring and Significant Episode: Religion and the Rise and Fall of Prohibition in Black Atlanta, 1865–1887.* DeKalb: Northern Illinois University Press, 2012.

Tracy, Sarah W., and Caroline Jean Acker. *Altering American Consciousness: The History of Alcohol and Drug Use in the United States, 1800–2000.* Amherst: University of Massachusetts Press, 2004.

Triana, Mauro Garcia, and Pedro Eng Herrera. *The Chinese in Cuba, 1847–Now.* Lanham, Md.: Lexington Books, 2009.

Van de Water, Frederic. *The Real McCoy.* Mystic, Conn.: Flat Hammock Press, 2007.

Vhynanek, Louis. "'Muggles,' 'Inchy,' and 'Mud': Illegal Drugs in New Orleans during the 1920s." *Louisiana History* 22 (Summer 1981): 253–79.

Vincent, Isabel. *Bodies and Souls: The Tragic Plight of Three Jewish Women Forced into Prostitution in the Americas.* New York: William Morrow, 2005.

Waters, Harold. *Smugglers of Spirits: Prohibition and the Coast Guard Patrol.* New York: Hastings House, 1971.

Webb, Samuel. "The Great Mobile Whiskey War." *Alabama Heritage* 76 (Spring 2005): 30–44.

Whitney, Robert. *State and Revolution in Cuba: Mass Mobilization and Political Change, 1920–1940.* Chapel Hill: University of North Carolina Press, 2001.

Willis, Lee L. *Southern Prohibition: Race, Reform, and Public Life in Middle Florida, 1821–1920.* Athens: University of Georgia Press, 2011.

Willoughby, Malcolm F. *Rum War at Sea.* Washington, D.C.: U.S. Government Printing Office, 1964.

Index

CPSIA information can be obtained
at www.ICGtesting.com
Printed in the USA
LVHW031622100821
694913LV00014B/2010